Praise for *Eating at God'*

"Food matters, always and everywhere. But sometimes ... .
Myers's excavation of the food lives of the Orthodox Jews who live in Los Angeles's
Pico-Robertson neighborhood provides a stunning example of the inextricable
bonds between life, food, religion, and community."

—Hasia Diner, professor emerita, New York University

"*Eating at God's Table* employs the Pico-Robertson neighborhood of Los Ange-
les as an 'ethnographic laboratory' for studying the wide range of Orthodox
Jewish approaches to eating and sharing food. Focusing on women, 'lived reli-
gion,' and the rules and customs associated with keeping kosher, it shows how
Orthodox communities use food as a marker of identity and tool for survival.
A major contribution to Jewish studies and the study of religion."

—Jonathan D. Sarna, university professor and Joseph H. and
Belle R. Braun Professor of American Jewish History, Brandeis
University, and author of *American Judaism: A History*

"In *Eating at God's Table*, Jody Myers takes us inside the kitchens of Orthodox
communities in Pico-Robertson. When we open the pages of this book, we sit
at their tables and enter her wonderfully curated conversation about the vibrant
dynamics and lived religion of these communities."

—Jordan Rosenblum, Belzer Professor of Classical
Judaism, University of Wisconsin–Madison

"With a remarkable combination of scholarly rigor, empathy, exacting analysis,
and love, *Eating at God's Table* uses an exploration of foodways to make vividly present the lived religious world of contemporary Orthodox Judaism. Its
seemingly narrow focus on the foodways of one Los Angeles neighborhood
becomes a kind of keyhole through which one can view an entire religious
universe. Dr. Myers shows that to understand religious foodways requires us
to delve into history, the interpretation of scripture, gendered and racialized
social dynamics, ethical worldviews, and much else. This is the most meticulously researched and fertile study of any Jewish community's foodways I've
ever encountered, and a model of how a religious studies approach to food can
cut to the heart of the complexities through which humans make meaning,
revealing things both beautiful and disturbing and a great deal in between."

—Aaron Gross, author of *The Question of the Animal and Religion:
Theoretical Stakes, Practical Implications* and coeditor of *Feasting
and Fasting: The History and Ethics of Jewish Food*

EATING AT GOD'S TABLE

**Raphael Patai Series in Jewish Folklore
and Anthropology**

A complete listing of the books in this series can be found online
at wsupress.wayne.edu.

EATING AT GOD'S TABLE

How Foodways Create and Sustain
Orthodox Jewish Communities

JODY MYERS

with Jane Myers
Foreword by Matt Goldish

Wayne State University Press
Detroit

ISBN 9780814349540 (paperback)
ISBN 9780814349557 (hardcover)
ISBN 9780814349564 (e-book)

Library of Congress Control Number: 2023931113

Cover photo by David Ackerman. Cover design by Tracy Cox.

Published with support from the fund for the Raphael Patai Series in Jewish Folklore and Anthropology.

Wayne State University Press rests on Waawiyaataanong, also referred to as Detroit, the ancestral and contemporary homeland of the Three Fires Confederacy. These sovereign lands were granted by the Ojibwe, Odawa, Potawatomi, and Wyandot Nations, in 1807, through the Treaty of Detroit. Wayne State University Press affirms Indigenous sovereignty and honors all tribes with a connection to Detroit. With our Native neighbors, the press works to advance educational equity and promote a better future for the earth and all people.

Wayne State University Press
Leonard N. Simons Building
4809 Woodward Avenue
Detroit, Michigan 48201-1309

Visit us online at wsupress.wayne.edu.

For my children, Adina, Aaron, and Benja

Whenever three have eaten at one table and have spoken over it words of the Torah, it is as if they had eaten at the table of God.

MISHNAH *AVOT* 3:3

Contents

Foreword

I met Jody Myers around 1983, when I was an undergraduate student at UCLA and she was a graduate teaching assistant in my Western Civilization course. She was working under the enigmatic genius Amos Funkenstein, *a"h*. I did not particularly connect with Jody at that time. It was years later, when I had finished graduate school myself and we were both working academics, that we became friends. I was interested in her research on Rabbi Zvi Hirsch Kalischer. Jody and I ended up speaking often. At the annual Association for Jewish Studies conferences, we used to plop down on random lobby chairs for hours during the evening as various colleagues drifted in and out of our conversations.

Among Jody's qualities that I enjoyed were her honesty, her modesty, and her curiosity. I believe one of the reasons that she became so successful in eliciting candid thoughts from persons who might have reasons not to be quite so frank was her guileless persona. Jody was absolutely straight with everyone, but her unaffected manner led people to open up with her in astonishing ways. These qualities complemented her deep curiosity about all aspects of Judaism and of Jewish culture and her keen intellect. She was always fun to talk to. I looked forward to her calls, which usually started with something like, "Listen to this!" or "You won't believe what Rabbi X just said to me!" or "Listen to what I just found in this book!"

I had expected that the follow-up to Jody's first monograph on the early ("proto-") Zionist thinker Rabbi Zvi Hirsch Kalischer would be a book on another famous early "proto-" Zionist thinker, Rabbi Yehudah Alkalai. Instead, Jody went in a completely different direction and wrote the only scholarly monograph about Los Angeles's Kabbalah Centre. I was mesmerized by this research and its accompanying local insights. Jody used to take me on cultural walking tours around the Pico-Robertson neighborhood, where she lived and where I had spent many years myself. She would show me weird little Jewish curiosities—the "frame shop" that housed a kabbalist Sephardic kollel; the car wash that turned into a kosher street-food venue late on Saturday nights; the Xeroxed rabbinical notices about a cheating husband that were not what they seemed.

I had always loved the Pico-Robertson neighborhood, but I became a little obsessed as Jody peeled off the layers of culture and religion to which I had never been privy. Inspired by Jody, I hatched the idea of writing a book about the neighborhood and the multiple ethnic, religious, and cultural strands of Jewish life that coexisted there. I was teaching at The Ohio State University, however, and I rapidly realized that I could not pull off this project. So, I pitched the idea to Jody, though in retrospect I realize that she was already thinking about a study of the neighborhood. She indulged me, however, and we discussed the topic extensively. I was thrilled when she indeed decided to write about the Pico-Robertson neighborhood, but it took me some time to appreciate why she chose to focus on food topics. The current volume illuminates the breadth and depth of her thinking and her research about Pico-Robertson and food. I now understand.

This book is creative and innovative in numerous ways, which I watched forming during the years of its composition. It fits loosely into a new genre, the study of lived religion. Jody interrogates the very concepts underlying the laws of *kashrut*. She questions how *kashrut* is taught in the Pico-Robertson neighborhood and what lessons its teachers seek to promote. (Her conclusions can be disturbing.) She examines who eats with whom, who does not eat with whom, and why. She considers the ethics and economics of the kosher food business in the neighborhood. She investigates the restaurants, the cuisines, the markets, the ingredients, and the people.

I was especially delighted with the opening section of the book, in which Jody presents a number of "itineraries" of Pico-Robertson neighborhood locals dealing with food. These vignettes brilliantly highlight the various communities, the food issues, the religious commitments, the tensions, and the rhythms of life of the Pico-Robertson Jews. Nothing else short of a documentary film could come close to this approach as a technique for pulling the reader into the soul of the neighborhood, the cadences of observant Jewish life, which are such necessary background for the ensuing chapters.

Anyone accustomed to reading books that are easily pigeonholed or that fit conveniently into a disciplinary box may find this study incommodious or problematic. The combination of approaches and methods, however, gives it both depth and charm. It is stamped with the modesty, curiosity, insight, learning, and wit that characterized its author and for which she will be sorely missed.

Matt Goldish
Samuel M. and Esther Melton Chair in
History at The Ohio State University

Author's Preface

When I arrived in Los Angeles in 1975 for graduate study in Jewish thought and history, I settled in the West Los Angeles Pico-Robertson neighborhood because of its cheap housing and easy commute to UCLA. I was astonished by the rich variety of low-cost fresh fruits and vegetables that could be purchased there. The Israeli-owned mom-and-pop grocery stores on Pico Boulevard sold produce I had rarely seen growing up in Minnesota (certainly not during the winter): avocadoes, red and orange and green peppers, plump artichokes, lemons and limes, summer squashes, a wide variety of tomatoes, fresh, moist bunches of basil, cilantro, dill, and parsley, and glossy globular and elongated purple eggplants. In Los Angeles these items sat on the produce shelves in abundance.

From my vantage point as a newcomer to the area, I watched as the neighborhood was transformed by the Jewish immigrants from Iran who had fled their homeland after the 1979 Iranian Islamic revolution. They bought the food businesses from the Israelis and added a different array of produce and prepared foods to the shelves: Persian cucumbers, dried and pickled limes and lemons, fresh herbs I did not recognize and could not identify by their Farsi shelf tags, and multiple flavors of halvah studded with pistachio nuts. I knew the herbs were crucial ingredients for a beloved Persian dish called sabzi polo. Persian men would place armloads of the herbs into their grocery carts, and at home, the women of the household would chop the stems and leaves into hundreds of tiny bits. They would push the greens into the bottom of an oiled heavy pot and then top them with a layer of fragrant jasmine rice. The whole combination would be baked and steamed, and a delicious crusty bottom layer of savory rice (tahdig) would form and could be broken off and nibbled.

During the 1980s, when an influx of American-born Orthodox Jews moved into the neighborhood, the foods did not change, but the kosher signs increased. It seemed as if new kosher bakeries, cafés, and restaurants opened weekly. The central retail area became a destination for getting together over coffee and meals and for purchasing baked and prepared foods for dinners, parties, and events. Pico-Robertson's older Orthodox synagogues gained members and became more religiously stringent, and smaller storefront synagogues appeared. The Orthodox day schools increased their square footage and number of students, many of them of Iranian heritage. They walked together to and from the schools and hung out in groups in front of the candy and frozen yogurt stores. More Orthodox study centers and synagogues materialized, each labeled to appeal to a particular cohort within the Orthodox population: Modern Orthodox, Hasidic (mostly Chabad Hasidic), the newly religious, devotees of a Moroccan kabbalistic sage, Jews of Yemenite heritage, and people who wanted to pray with the ecstatic spiritual melodies of Rabbi Shlomo Carlebach.

I continued to live near this neighborhood, and, eventually, after I became a professor of religious studies at California State University in Northridge, I settled a short walk away. I was not Orthodox myself but rather a long-standing member of a nearby congregation affiliated with the Conservative movement. This denomination is more liberal and flexible in its interpretation and application of Jewish religious law and (unlike Orthodox Judaism) permits women equal access to leadership in synagogue prayer services. I frequented the Orthodox synagogues not for worship or for religious guidance but for their public lectures and classes on classical Jewish texts and rabbinic law that I, as an academic professionally engaged with Jewish thought and practice, found to be of value.

Conservative synagogues such as mine were generally dwindling in number and size across the country, despite their greater compatibility with modern values.[1] The retention rate of the younger generation—that is, the rate at which the young affirmed their commitment to the practices and beliefs of their parents and retained their institutional loyalty—lagged behind the Orthodox. In the Orthodox enclave in Pico-Robertson, at the onset of the Sabbath on Friday nights and before and after Sabbath prayers on Saturday mornings, the sidewalks were filled with adults and children, walking together in small clusters. They were wearing Orthodox dress: for women, an ankle-length skirt, high-neck top with sleeves from shoulder to wrist, stocking-covered legs, and a wig or hair covering; for men, a yarmulke or hat. I imagined them in their homes and synagogue social halls eating sumptuous meals together in happy harmony, confident and content with their religious choices.

I reflected upon the remarkable phenomenon of the growth of the Orthodox population, both nationally and locally, relative to other types of Jews—this within a broader culture that often ridicules religious rituals, especially those that appear impervious to reason and to self-interest. Given the very visible importance of food I observed in the lives of the local Orthodox community, I wondered whether there might be a connection between Orthodox foodways and the revival and vibrancy of the American Orthodox community. What role did Orthodox foodways play in the growth of this diverse Orthodox community? What drew so many Jews to the Pico-Robertson area in particular?

These questions remained in my mind as I conducted research on the teachings and followers of the Kabbalah Centre, an international nonprofit organization headquartered in the Pico-Robertson neighborhood, with many of its hundreds of followers and all of its teachers living nearby. I realized that a historical methodology was not enough for a full understanding of why Kabbalah Centre members were devoted to the center's teachings or how they incorporated its teachings into their lives. Ethnography and participant observer research were essential, too. Once I decided to write a book on the center, I attended the center for six years as an outside, fly-on-the-wall observer before becoming a participant observer. My research did not depend on any single information resource; it was multidimensional. I enrolled in classes, where I sat attentively, took notes, and asked questions. I occasionally attended

Sabbath prayers and communal meals, listened to old audiotaped lectures, collected and examined ephemera, and had a private session with the Kabbalah Centre kabbalistic palm reader, who told me of my past lives and present-life kabbalistic challenges. As a participant observer I strived to maintain a stance of disciplined empathy, a method used in the field of religious studies that incorporates both an objective perspective and an insider's view of the religious phenomena being examined. My research led to a book, *Kabbalah and the Spiritual Quest: The Kabbalah Centre in America.*[2] Subsequently, becoming increasingly interested in Jewish foodways, I coedited and contributed to a book titled *Feasting and Fasting: The History and Ethics of Jewish Food.*[3]

While conducting research on the Kabbalah Centre, I continued to be intrigued by the Pico-Robertson neighborhood as a burgeoning Orthodox community within the food mecca of Los Angeles. For my next book I wanted to study Orthodox Jewish life in the Pico-Robertson neighborhood. I decided to explore the effect of Orthodox foodways on the rise of the American Orthodox population and higher retention of the younger generation relative to other types of American Jews. I wondered: How are Orthodox foodways connected to the community's ability to perpetuate its culture to the younger generation? Focusing on foodways, I thought, would enable me to examine the great variety of beliefs and practices within the Orthodox population and to test whether my assumptions regarding a connection between their foodways and their thriving community—and my imagined vision of the members of the community eating together in harmony—were accurate.

I was already aware that Orthodox foodways are designed to build Orthodox separateness and strong boundaries. Orthodox Jews recognize that "for thousands of years of exile, the biblical and rabbinic kosher laws have formed a natural fortress that prevented the assimilation of the Jewish people into many different cultures of the world."[4] The laws of *kashrut* (proper food) do not merely dictate which animal species may not be eaten; these laws also mandate that only Orthodox slaughterers produce the meat and prevent its mixture with certain foods, and they require that much of the food preparation is in Orthodox hands. The participation of non-Orthodox Jews and non-Jews in the kosher food realm is socially managed so that their visibility is reduced and their dominion is secondary to that of the Jews in charge.

Furthermore, although there is no religious law explicitly forbidding sharing meals with non-Jews, Orthodox Jews have adopted social norms strongly discouraging such activities and social closeness. This is not what the law says, but their practice avoids the many halakhic (rabbinic legal) complications that eating with non-Jews would create. Consequently, Orthodox Jews who obey these laws and have non-Jewish friends, neighbors, and relatives will not sit together with them in a social exchange over food or drink. These restrictions are designed to prevent the level of intimacy and familiarity that could easily lead to Jews imitating the ways of the "others" or intermarrying with them.

I also knew that Orthodox foodways are not uniform; indeed, the kosher laws easily lend themselves to creating multiple styles of Orthodox religiosity, ranging from those who wish to be very strict to those who aim for "the golden mean" between highly exact and very permissive to groups defined by ethnic or regional loyalties. In the Pico-Robertson neighborhood, the largest groups among the approximately ten thousand Orthodox Jews and their thirty synagogues are Ashkenazic Modern and Centrist Orthodox, Sephardic, Persian, and Chabad Hasidic. Each group practices and teaches its foodways in a manner slightly different from that of the others.

I began this research in 2013, using the residents of the Pico-Robertson Orthodox enclave as a case study. While conducting research on the Kabbalah Centre, I had already chosen a research methodology appropriate for a community-wide study. In that research and for this book, I employed the multidimensional approach used for studying topics in the field of lived religion. This area of study was first pursued by sociologists in France and termed *la religion vécue*. David Hall and Robert Orsi introduced this area of study to America in a series of papers presented at a conference held at Harvard University and published in 1997. Calling this area of study *lived religion*, they focused mostly on historical examples of religion in America.[5]

Hall's historical approach to studying the lived religion of Christianity rejects the distinction between "high" and "low" religion often made by scholars describing popular religious practice. In examining the interactions between Christian clergy and congregations in the cases he studied, he describes the way religious beliefs and practices can evolve as the religion is practiced over time by its followers. According to Hall, even though the clergy were sometimes angered by their congregants' adoption of new thinking and behaviors, the clergy accepted these new beliefs and practices "because they realized that the looser meanings of baptism and saint that came to prevail were advantageous in allowing their congregations to grow."

> Because of this dynamic relationship between institutional authorities and regular lay people, the religion [of the groups studied] encompassed a range of possibilities, some with the sanction of official religion and others not, or perhaps ambiguously so. The concept of lived religion has thus made it possible for historians to expand their understanding of the scope of belief and practice that go beyond what is authorized by the institutional church.[6]

Hall's findings regarding the interactions between Christian clergy and congregations that led to the variations in beliefs and practices also apply to what has occurred in Judaism and to what I noticed in the Pico-Robertson community. In chapter 4, which deals with practices and beliefs related to meat in *kashrut*, for example, I show this clearly: While the basic rules and framework were established in the rabbinic law code called the Mishnah and its Talmudic commentary, additions and emendations were made by Jews who sought to make food choices reflect local customs. How one performed the dietary laws became a signal that one was loyal to the Ashkenazic heritage or that one was part of an intellectual or spiritual elite.

Nancy Tatom Ammerman's 2021 book, *Studying Lived Religion: Contexts and Practices*, builds on the past three decades of work in the field of lived religion and explores in depth the multidimensionality of its methodology. Ammerman describes lived religion as "how religion happens in everyday life." The researcher draws on a wide variety of sources: observations, interviews, conversations, ephemera, the books studied by the subjects, and the websites they design—websites that guide them in how to behave, how to think, and how to teach their children. Tools used to study these dimensions include history, geography, participant observation research, and interviews. Among these, she states that participant observation is the most common method chosen by students of lived religion. To learn about the Orthodox Pico-Robertson neighborhood and to answer the questions that brought me to study it, I employed all of these tools.[7]

Unlike other social practices, Ammerman notes, lived religion has a spiritual dimension. It incorporates—either directly or indirectly—the presence of a reality beyond the ordinary. In addition, religious and secular urban spaces are often interwoven: "Lived religious practice is likely to happen on the streets and in the shops, as well as in the churches and synagogues." Most importantly, she states: "No bodily practices are perhaps more signifying than food practices." As the title of this book, *Eating at God's Table*, suggests, for Orthodox Jews, practicing their foodways "involves," in Ammerman's words, "consciousness of and acting within multiple layers of reality at once, recognizing the 'more than' while not necessarily losing touch with the ordinary."[8]

The imagined scenarios that begin this book, based on my actual observations and experiences, are meant to capture the way the Orthodox residents of Pico-Robertson live their religion in terms of their foodways. The scenarios show some of the ways in which their religious beliefs and practices are integrated into, even inseparable from, their daily activities.

From the fall of 2013 until the March 2020 COVID-19 shutdown, I approached school principals, schoolteachers, owners of food eateries, kosher food inspectors, high school students, parents, and laypersons from the array of Orthodox congregations in the neighborhood to discover their thoughts and practices around food. As I had done while studying the Kabbalah Centre, I explained to those who asked that I aspired to disciplined empathy. That is, in my self-presentation, I was both an insider and an outsider. There were aspects of my persona that led me to be regarded as exceptional and that I did not hide: I was an academic (a professor of Jewish studies), a published author, a lifelong vegetarian, a divorced mother who was not seeking to find a marriage partner, and a member of a Conservative synagogue. Nevertheless, my knowledge of and respect for Orthodox Jews was obvious, as was my enthusiasm for Torah learning, and I was treated as a trusted ally.

My habit of attending synagogue lectures and Torah study sessions over the previous several years made me a familiar person to Orthodox rabbis and teachers. As a professor, I had formed respectful and supportive relationships with students who were Orthodox. My respect for these students, one rabbi told me, was a factor in their Orthodox rabbis' willingness to meet with me and discuss their community and practices. The rabbis professed enthusiasm for my research and helped me find a diversity of interview subjects, who in turn suggested others to interview. I continued to frequent synagogue lectures and added several small Torah study groups to my weekly schedule; I attended at least one Sabbath morning prayer service in each synagogue and examined the websites of local institutions and the denominational organizations with which they were affiliated—Chabad, Orthodox Union, the Rabbinical Council of California—several popular websites providing information about and resources for the Orthodox kosher diet, and an online Los Angeles newsletter written by and for local Orthodox Jews; and I accepted Sabbath meal invitations from various families.

To help answer my overall research questions regarding whether there was a connection between Orthodox foodways and the revival, vibrancy, and growth of the diverse American Orthodox community and what that role was, I would ask the following questions:

"What do the kosher laws mean to you?"
"Do ethics and morality figure in your understanding of why the dietary laws look the way they do? For example, do you believe that the prohibited and permitted ingredients,

or prohibited food combinations, are due to ethical
considerations or that they were designed to foster moral
traits?"

"How do you explain to people close to you (say, to your
children) why you keep kosher?"

"How do you determine what is kosher and what is not—that
is, do you have a particular rabbi whose guidance you
trust or a family or community tradition?"

"Where do you shop for groceries, which restaurants and
bakeries do you patronize, and how do you determine that
the food items meet your kosher standards?"

"What considerations do you make when deciding whether to
eat at another person's home and when deciding to use the
food gifts from others in your own home?"

"Do you invite strangers, that is, people other than friends
and relatives, to your home to eat?"

"Why and when do you offer this home hospitality?"

"How do you determine whom to invite?"

"How do you respond when beggars ask you for money
for food, or do you fulfill the mitzvah to feed the poor in
another way?"

In the following pages I share the insights I gained into why the foodways were so compelling and just how they were performed within the diverse population.

In my desire to capture, in all their dimensions and immediacy, how Orthodox residents of Pico-Robertson live their religion in relation to their foodways, I created out of my interviews and participant observation research the four fictional tours through the neighborhood that open chapter 1. These illustrate the way religion and culture, including Jewish law, express themselves in their familial, communal, and spatial contexts. These scenarios are meant to present my subjects' emotional worlds and the caring, compassion, thoughtfulness, and serious decision-making processes that I found to be typical among the local Orthodox Jews.

Following the scenarios, the chapters describe the Pico-Robertson neighborhood and examine the practices of the Orthodox groups within it in relation to food. Chapter 1 continues by providing the geographic, historical, and demographic information necessary for understanding the growth of the neighborhood in relation to its foodways. Chapters 2 through 5 provide detailed explanations of the *kashrut* practices and standards among the various Orthodox groups; the spiritual aspects of the kosher diet and the way they are taught; attitudes toward eating meat and its primacy in the Orthodox diet; and the mandates, which vary across the community, to provide hospitality and food support to those in need.

My research confirmed my initial surmise that there was a connection between the vibrant Orthodox food culture and the vibrancy of the local Orthodox community. The Orthodox themselves believed this to be true. In the following pages, I share the insights I gained into why the Orthodox foodways were so compelling and how they were practiced within the diverse population.

Acknowledgments

Once Jody learned she was seriously ill, she asked me to shepherd *Eating at God's Table* through to publication. While she was still able, I worked with her on revisions to the completed manuscript. Dates for interview materials were added posthumously based on Jody's available notes and records.

When it came time for Jody to write the acknowledgments, she was able only to begin the list. What follows are her words and then my additions.

I want to express gratitude to my doctors and all who took care of me.

I am grateful to my friend Professor Matt Goldish, because if not for him, my book would not have happened. He is the one who wanted me to write the book about the Pico-Robertson neighborhood and who discussed it with me along the way.

I want to thank Adam Morgenstern, my research assistant and really good friend. He also helped me when my visual ability had lessened.

Professor Arnold Band was the one who first encouraged me to write about food because it reaches all groups: everyone eats.

I am grateful to my Orthodox friend Rabbi Yitzchak (Kenny) Kaufman, from whom I learned and with whom I enjoyed conversations.

I want to thank Professor Bruce Phillips for his valuable help in providing the demographic data on the Pico-Robertson neighborhood.

Conversations I shared with my friend Professor Aaron Gross about my ethical concerns about animals led me to include these concerns in my research even more than I expected.

I thank Shifra Revah, Torah teacher extraordinaire (who could speak a mile a minute), who held a stimulating weekly women's study group in which I participated.

JODY MYERS

I know there are others Jody would have thanked if she had been able to do so. Please know your contribution is valued as an act of *gemilut ḥasadim*—kindness that could not be acknowledged.

For their invaluable help to me in bringing Jody's book to publication as she had asked me to do, I want to thank Professor Matt Goldish, who provided scholarly expertise, editing, and support throughout the publication process; John Sears, my husband, for his invaluable editing and ongoing support; and my sister Kathryn de Boer for her wise suggestions.

I am grateful for those at Wayne State University Press who enabled this book to be published posthumously. I thank Marie Sweetman, acquisitions editor, for her support, patience, and trust during the early months of preparing the manuscript for publication. Thanks also to all on the excellent editorial and design team involved in the production process: Emily Gauronskas, production editor; Carrie Teefey, design and production manager; Kelsey Giffin, publicist; and, last but not least, Anne Taylor, for her expert and thoughtful copyediting of the manuscript.

Finally, and as I believe Jody would have done, I want to thank all the people of the Pico-Robertson neighborhood—rabbis, teachers, workers, and all other women and men, young and old—who agreed to be interviewed and observed for Jody's research. Without the diverse perspectives and information they provided through their discussions with her, this book about their community could not have existed.

Jane Myers

1

Streets Paved
with Food

"Spirituality is the heart of the Pico-Robertson," declared a local journalist surveying the many synagogues lining the neighborhood's main streets.[1] If spirituality is the heart, kosher food is the blood circulating through it. This point was made explicit by the rabbi and director of Aish HaTorah Los Angeles, the city's largest religious outreach center, who declared, "Every new shul [synagogue] and restaurant solidifies Pico-Robertson as a world-class Torah destination."[2]

At the start of 2020, I counted fifty-three separate kosher food businesses on the two main commercial streets in the neighborhood. With obvious pride, a local rabbi told me that the one-mile stretch of Pico Boulevard bisecting the neighborhood contains more kosher groceries, restaurants, and fast-food eateries than any other similarly sized real estate in the world. These businesses cater to the palates of Jewish people from many different geographic origins and offer foods and dishes from regional, national, and international cuisines. Diversity reigns not only in the cuisines but also in the types of Orthodox Jews: Modern and Centrist Orthodox, Chabad Hasidic, Persian, Sephardic, and Middle Eastern. Each group practices and promotes slightly varying foodways and kosher laws. These varied practices distinguish the groups from each other, guard them from secular influences, enable them to perpetuate their communities, and exhibit their devotion to God.

• • •

The following four fictional accounts of representative individuals as they walk, ride, or bike through the Pico-Robertson neighborhood exemplify some of the daily experiences and concerns of the Orthodox Jews living there. These scenarios include a midday walk of three Ashkenazic Modern and Centrist Orthodox Jews, an evening drive of an Iranian Jewish man, an afternoon drive of a busy Chabad mother doing her errands and picking up her children at school, and a bicycle ride of three teenagers through the alleyways behind Pico Boulevard. We follow them as they purchase food, eat in the restaurants, socialize, observe, visit, and comment on the religious and food resources in the area. Based on actual people with whom I spent time as they went about their daily life, these scenarios illustrate the centrality of foodways within Orthodox Judaism today and provide an animated picture of the reasoning, emotions, compassion, and actions that are integral to their life and their Orthodox foodways.

FOUR EXPERIENCES OF DAILY LIFE IN THE PICO-ROBERTSON NEIGHBORHOOD

Ashkenazic Modern and Centrist Orthodox Jews on a Midday Walk

For a Thursday late morning, fifty-two-year-old Deborah has planned a midday stroll and lunch along Pico Boulevard with her cousin Jonathan, younger by eight years, and her seventy-five-year-old mother, Ruth. Deborah, an accounts manager at a medical supply company, requested a personal day off for the occasion. The three of them meet at the home of Deborah's mother and father and chat before they set off. It is a beautiful November day, cool, breezy, and sunny. Their clothing barely hints at their religious identities. Deborah, more dedicated to prevailing Orthodox standards of women's modesty than her mother, wears

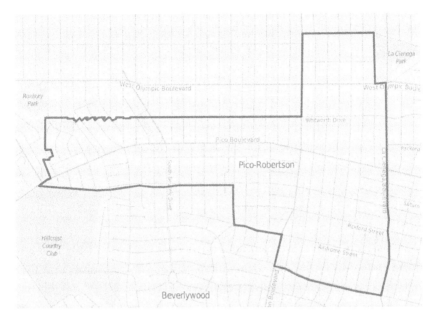

FIGURE 1. Pico-Robertson neighborhood, *Los Angeles Times*, "Mapping L.A." project, http://maps.latimes.com/neighborhoods/neighborhood/pico-robertson/ (© OpenStreetMap, openstreetmap.org/copyright. Available under the Open Data Commons Open Database License)

a mid-calf-length skirt, a cotton long-sleeved sweater over a blouse, and a scarf and straw hat covering her hair; her mother wears loose pants and an elbow-sleeved tunic and is bareheaded. Jonathan has a short, trim beard and wears a plaid shirt, jeans, and a baseball cap—underneath, out of view, is a black leather yarmulke.[3] Jonathan is visiting Los Angeles for a job interview. He has lived and worked in New York for decades, and he and his wife think a move to a different city will breathe new life into their marriage and family. Deborah has been doing her best to persuade Jonathan that Los Angeles, and specifically her neighborhood, would provide the emotional support, vibrancy, and *Torah* culture that they need.

With Ruth alongside her, Deborah describes why she thinks Jonathan and his wife would fit perfectly into her Centrist Orthodox synagogue: it's neither liberal, where they adjust *halakhah* (religious law) to fit secular values, nor a place where people add stringencies to the law; and its rabbi focuses on Torah and does not get embroiled in American political issues. "Why so many 'nots'?" her mother responds. "All the synagogues have decent people. You want a friendly and caring community that keeps your children happy and on the right path." Ruth raised Deborah and her brothers in a Modern Orthodox synagogue, and Ruth does not want such synagogues, or any others, disparaged. The three get into the car. Deborah's plan is to pick up the last groceries she needs for Shabbat and then take Jonathan on a short walking tour before the two of them eat lunch on Pico Boulevard. Her mother will accompany them only partway until they reach the kosher Pico Café, where she'll sit and have coffee, so Deborah and Jonathan can be by themselves and then pick her up on their way back to the car.

Their first stop is the grocery errand. There are four main Jewish markets in Pico-Robertson, each with a different personality and patronage. Deborah steers them toward Elat Market, the large Persian store. Like most of her Ashkenazic friends, she usually avoids this place, especially on Thursdays and Fridays when there are so many shoppers.[4] However, Deborah knows that no other store carries the exotic greens and fresh herbs for the big salad she wants to make for Shabbat dinner, and she is certain to find pomegranate molasses there. Deborah's Israeli Moroccan friend gave her a recipe for a delicious hybrid Middle Eastern–American side dish of roasted sweet potatoes and walnuts coated with the tangy pomegranate syrup. She wants to impress Jonathan with the variety of fresh foods available here year-round. It takes Deborah ten minutes of waiting to secure a spot in the public metered lot off the adjacent side street. Their way across the road is blocked by a line of cars waiting to enter the store's free parking lot. Drivers pay no attention to the message on the huge banner hanging on the wall separating the area from the nearby residences: "Please do not honk." Deborah locks her arm into her mother's, and they weave through the cars to the sidewalk. Part of the sidewalk is blocked by a truck and Latino workers unloading pallets of Persian cucumbers onto a dolly. Deborah warns Jonathan, "This store is a bit of a madhouse. We'll go inside, get a shopping cart, and find an open place next to the condiments. Your job is to find a jar of the syrup and stay in one spot with Mom and the cart while I get the salad greens." At Elat Market customers do not walk through the aisles with their shopping carts. Instead, they "park" their carts in a grocery aisle, walk around the store gathering up food items, and bring their load back to the cart before venturing off again for more.

The produce section is especially crowded. Older Persian men and women of all ages crowd in front of the produce, angling their bodies and reaching their arms to get to the foods, talking with each other in Farsi. An Ashkenazic Jew like Deborah holds back, waiting for an opening to dart in and get what she needs. She has had a lot of practice at this, and it takes her only two trips between the produce section and her cart. Jonathan has been combing through the condiment jars, but none of the pomegranate syrup brands bear a label with a symbol of kosher certification, *hashgahah*. There are probably no *treif* (nonkosher) ingredients in these jars of pomegranate molasses, but Deborah and her family insist on kosher-certified processed foods only. Ruth tells Jonathan that the owners claim their store is kosher, but everyone knows they also stock nonkosher items. Elat Market owners want customers who seek uniquely Middle Eastern products, whether or not the foods are kosher certified. Ruth says, "I'm sure they have some next door."

Next door is Glatt Mart, and it fits their style better. In this store customers wheel their shopping carts through the aisles and give each other more space. They speak English and Hebrew rather than Farsi. As in all the local grocery stores, the lower-level workers are non-Jewish Latinos who speak English and Spanish. This store, too, is owned by Persian Jews, but they cater to the Orthodox Jewish community at large and carry the favorites of the Ashkenazi cuisines. The store is certified kosher by rabbinic authorities from the Rabbinical Council of California (RCC), a group of Modern and Centrist Orthodox rabbis. Store certification means that the owners have agreed to only stock products with *hashgahah* from kosher food agencies approved by the RCC. Ruth tells Jonathan, "No need to hunt for a label or decide if it's a reliable *hashgahah*—it will all be good." The RCC exerts its authority even in the produce section. According to Jewish law, fruits and vegetables are kosher and need no certification, but insects and worms are prohibited. The RCC had posted a sign on the produce section wall warning customers to carefully wash and inspect produce at home to ensure there are no hidden bugs. When Deborah and Jonathan cannot find pomegranate molasses, Ruth seeks out the help of the manager, whom she has known for years, and he tells her the store does not regularly stock the item. They depart. Deborah brings the groceries back to her car, while Jonathan and her mother wait outside the store.

Left on her own with her nephew, Ruth confides her worries about her granddaughter Rina, Deborah's middle child. Deborah would not like to hear this; she gets angry when her mother "mixes in." Ruth is upset that Rina is still single at the age of twenty-nine. She is pretty, thin, and kind, and Ruth doesn't understand why her granddaughter is having problems finding a mate. All her friends are married and having babies. Rina has tried out different *shuls* (synagogues) in the neighborhood for a fresh group of friends, but she says she doesn't fit in anywhere: this one is too cliquey, that one is full of BTs (*ba'alei teshuvah*, newly religious), another one has too much singing, and so on. So she has stopped attending *shul*, Ruth laments, and how will she meet anyone or have anyone keep her in mind for a match if she is not there? Maybe Rina should move to New York, where there are more available men, Ruth says, and asks Jonathan if he would encourage her.

Seeing Deborah approach, Ruth abruptly switches the topic. She describes the menu of the kosher Israeli restaurant (Haifa Restaurant) across the street. The restaurant abuts a nail salon, a kosher pizza joint (Shalom Pizza), a kosher caterer (Lieder's), and a shabby, lavender, boxy building labeled "Young Israel of Beverly Hills." Ruth says, "That synagogue is not for you. It was privately owned by a fine rabbi, an educator, and after he died there were years of court fights among the congregants over ownership."[5] Deborah adds, "There is another Young Israel in Pico-Robertson, called Young Israel of Century City." Jonathan has heard of it. The rabbi is nationally known and was president of the Orthodox

Rabbinical Council of America. He invites his colleagues from across the country to his *shul* to deliver community lectures for a wide audience.

Jonathan, however, wants a place that fosters more intensive, text-based Torah learning. After attending a religious high school in New York, he spent two years in an Israeli yeshiva, a school for men focusing on the study of the Talmud, Jewish law, and Torah commentaries. He returned to New York for graduate training and a job in bioengineering. He has always managed to study Talmud on the side, and Deborah wants to show him the places where he may do that. They walk east past a dentist, some closed-down stores, and a pharmacy. Ahead of them is a kabob restaurant and meat market, its outside wall mural proclaiming that it has the best kosher meat in town. But when Deborah sees Jonathan examining its front window, she says, "No certification. Not kosher. The genuine kosher Persian kabob place, with Chinese food, too, is five blocks up the street." They pass a certified kosher bakery and stop in front of two old commercial buildings in the midst of being rebuilt as one large two-story building. A big sign on top reads, "Future Home of Kollel."[6]

A kollel is a small group of male scholars who have completed yeshiva, are married, and have the temperament and intellectual capacity to engage in Torah study for more than ten hours per day and nearly twelve months per year, for at least a year, probably more. One or two senior rabbinic scholars serve as intellectual and spiritual guides and raise funds for the kollel. The young men, typically in their twenties, receive a stipend to cover their basic food, clothing, and shelter—not enough to support a family, however, so their wives must be wage earners. A kollel may occupy a single room in a yeshiva or synagogue, sharing with its host a library–study hall containing rabbinic books, a place for prayer, and a place for dining; or it may be a separate structure with its own facilities. On Shabbat, on holidays, and at daily prayer times, the kollel may be a gathering place for men from the community to pray with the scholars and to hear them share bits of their Torah learning.

The first kollel in Los Angeles, a "community kollel" founded in 1975, combined Torah study and direct community service. In this kind of kollel, the young scholars fulfill their hours of study and also must teach a few hours weekly in the nearby religious high schools, or they are assigned to give talks and lead classes for adults. Such a kollel raises the level of Torah knowledge within the community not only through the scholars' community service but also by the decision of the kollel's alumni to settle and raise their families within the host community.[7] The LINK Kollel is a community kollel with a strong mission of outreach—*kiruv*—that is, bringing nonreligious Jews into Orthodox Judaism. It also offers study opportunities for advanced learners.

Decades ago, a community kollel rabbi had changed the course of Ruth's life. She and her husband grew up in Los Angeles and were not religious, and they were expecting their first child. They read about the high rate of intermarriage among Jews and were determined to prevent such a dire outcome for their future children. They attended a kollel rabbi's lecture on the topic and then took private lessons with him. They moved to Pico-Robertson, joined the Modern Orthodox synagogue in nearby Beverly Hills, and sent their children to Orthodox schools. Theirs is a history shared with many from their own and the following generation in the Los Angeles Orthodox community. Ruth likes to say, "I am so proud that none of my children have gone 'off the *derekh*,'" that is, off the path of Orthodoxy. She cannot yet say that about her grandchildren because they are not all married. It is an accepted truth that once an Orthodox couple marries and has children, the parents are going to stay in the Orthodox community.

The three walkers backtrack and walk west to the intersection that gives the neighborhood its name: the junction of Pico and Robertson Boulevards. It looks like many other unattractive corners in urban Los Angeles where well-being and adversity commingle. Two men wrapped in torn blankets and surrounded by trash and big plastic bags lie on the sidewalk alongside Walgreens, seemingly oblivious to the foot traffic, cars, and noise. A Starbucks occupies the opposite street corner, and another corner holds an old stucco and brick two-story building whose ground-level commercial space is being either disassembled or refurbished. At the fourth corner is the McNoon Lighting and Crystal Store, its open door revealing gaudy chandeliers inside. On the storefront window is a banner declaring "Liquidation Sale." The banner has been there for months.

Continuing west on Pico, they pass a well-equipped storefront gym, a computer store, Pico Kosher Deli with a large *hashgaḥah* certificate in its window, and a nonkosher café. The Jewish Family Service of the Los Angeles Jewish Federation fills the next three commercial units, followed by the Chabad Bais Bezalel synagogue and a small kosher grocery (Schwartz's Marketplace) offering meat and ready-made foods. Next is a government-supported low-income seniors and veterans apartment building under construction. By far the most unusual structure on the block is a huge, long, regal-looking stucco building. Erected in the 1930s as the Fox Stadium Movie Theater, it was abandoned in the 1960s and refurbished as the Modern Orthodox B'nai David (later B'nai David-Judea) Congregation. At the top of the narrow tower on its roof there was once a beacon lighting up the night sky when films premiered. Now the tower is topped by a menorah, the Jewish seven-branched candelabra. In the early 1990s, Deborah and her new husband, an attorney, joined the synagogue when its board hired a charismatic young rabbi. Her parents soon followed suit. After the rabbi moved to Israel, the board hired another promising young rabbi. Eventually, he led the congregation toward policies that Deborah and her husband felt were "too feminist." It is the most liberal of the Modern Orthodox synagogues in Los Angeles, and its decision to hire an Orthodox female rabbi widened the gap between it and all the other synagogues in the neighborhood. Deborah and her husband left it for a more conservative one; her mother and father are content to remain.

The next stretch has the components seen on nearly every block of this one-mile stretch of Pico Boulevard: kosher and nonkosher eateries, synagogues, retail shops, auto repair garages, and empty commercial units being refurbished or littered inside with the remnants of a failed business. Also seen here is one of the several shabby-looking retail stores selling rugs or Judaica gift items. Residents surmise that these stores must launder money since there never seem to be any customers or workers inside. Ruth and Jonathan wait outside a corner kosher grocery store, Livonia Glatt, while Deborah enters to look for the pomegranate molasses. This, too, is an RCC-approved store but smaller, more compact, and with fewer choices than the larger RCC-approved markets, yet it has everything a household requires—almost everything. Deborah again comes out empty-handed, saying, "I texted Rina. Maybe she can get her hands on some." Ruth has meanwhile run into a friend, and the two women go ahead to Pico Café. Jonathan and Deborah tarry in front of the kosher eateries and look at the posted menus: Bibi's Warmstone with its pizza, bagels, and bourekas (stuffed Middle Eastern pastries); Jeff's Gourmet Sausage with its seasoned meat and salads; and Meshuga 4 Sushi (*meshugah* is Hebrew and Yiddish, meaning crazy). They continue past Pico Café, where Ruth is sitting with her friend.

Walking further, Deborah stops Jonathan in front of her synagogue, Adas Torah. Deborah recounts a bit of its history. The rabbi was brought to Los Angeles in the 1990s to be part of a kollel, and his wife taught in a religious high school. The board of the synagogue hired them both, he to be pulpit rabbi and teacher and she to counsel and teach classes for the women and brides. The congregation's first home was a rented community room in a hotel just off Pico. Now it is housed in this huge new building occupying a large part of the block. It is a serious-minded congregation: many members engage regularly in Torah learning, and no one chats during the Shabbat prayers. The *rebbetzin* (rabbi's wife) offers a text-study class for women that meets one night a week in a congregant's home. Deborah attends, and her husband is an avid student in the rabbi's Sunday morning lesson on the *Shulḥan arukh*, a major code of Jewish law. The synagogue even has its own semiannual journal of Torah essays written by the members, and it is available in a digitized version on the synagogue website.

They walk on, passing a tailor, an empty store, a Persian synagogue, and another kosher bakery, until Deborah points across the street to a small, boxy building with gold trim all around the roof line. She explains, "It looks like a bank because it used to be one. I used to go there before it closed. Now it's being rebuilt for the Merkaz HaTorah [Center of Torah]

Community Kollel. Its leader is the rabbi who made my parents religious." Deborah's phone pings; she looks at it, smiles, and says, "Rina has a Sephardic friend who'll give her a half jar of pomegranate syrup for us. Let's go eat."

An Iranian Jewish Man on an Evening Drive

On Wednesday evening Aziz sets out for the supermarket to pick up the salt Hana forgot to buy during her weekly Wednesday "beat the rush" shopping trip. Twenty guests, most of them family, will be at their Shabbat Friday night meal, and Hana likes to start on Wednesdays to prepare the savory and sweet Persian dishes everyone loves. This week's menu includes ghondi (ground turkey and chickpea dumplings in chicken soup), ghormeh sabzi (herbed beef and bean stew), and a lima bean and dill rice tahdig. Aziz knows that at 9:00 p.m. there will be no traffic and few pedestrians along Pico Boulevard, and he enjoys driving through the peaceful though not-yet-asleep neighborhood that is now his home. Almost fifty years ago, before the 1979 Iranian revolution, he and his older brother left Shiraz for Los Angeles. Aziz spent years building his import business. Not until he was thirty-five did he marry Hana, a much younger woman newly arrived in LA from Shiraz. She worked part-time as a bookkeeper while raising their three sons.

Aziz and Hana feel very fortunate and blessed by God. Their youngest child, Michael, fifteen years old, attends Yeshiva University of Los Angeles (YULA) High School and is committed to a life of Torah; perhaps he will be a rabbi, or perhaps he will enter business and study on the side. The middle child, Eli, is in medical school at UCLA and engaged to a lovely, Orthodox pharmacy student at the University of Southern California. Samuel, their oldest, is Aziz's business partner. His wife was born to a family from the Tehran Jewish community, and they have a little boy and another baby on the way. Her parents live in Beverly Hills, and the entire family often gathers together at Aziz and Hana's home to enjoy Shabbat and holiday dinners. Every Tuesday morning Aziz takes off from work so he can enjoy a Torah class offered by a Persian rabbi who, like his family, calls this part of Los Angeles his home.

Aziz slips on a lightweight zip-front collared jacket, sets a fedora over his black cloth yarmulke,[8] exits from the back of the duplex—they rent the second floor to another Persian couple—and drives his car out of the garage through the alley to Wetherly Drive and Pico. There at the corner is the Chabad girls' school, a replica of the Chabad-Lubavitch headquarters in Brooklyn with its red brick exterior and a sharply pitched roof so unlike all nearby structures. At this hour there are no strolling girls in pleated skirts and mothers driving carpools to impede his turn westward onto Pico Boulevard. Up ahead, across Doheny Boulevard on the right, are two densely tree-lined blocks, now unlit and sunk in darkness. These comprise one of the several drilling stations for the Beverly Hills Oil Field. The drills from the derricks descend more than two thousand feet into a long and narrow layer of oil underneath Beverly Hills and neighboring Los Angeles. Nearly the entirety of the Pico-Robertson neighborhood sits over the oil field. Hidden in plain sight by encompassing ivy-covered walls, this drilling island contains storage tanks and several windowless, soundproofed buildings, including a beige brick-covered tower encompassing the four-story-high oil derrick.

The oil field has been productive since 1900, and residents with mineral rights receive small royalty payments. Aziz tried but failed to convince the duplex owner to sell them along with the building, but the loss no longer bothers him. The oil field evokes other feelings now. When he passes by, he remembers the tense period decades ago in 1974 when the Shah refused to lower the price of oil and earned the anger of the US government. Demonstrators filled the streets. The family decided it was best for their two sons to leave Iran. Their plan was to establish a foothold in the United States before the fundamentalist Muslims blamed the Jews for the regime's failures. Aziz and his brother left that summer, and the rest of the family followed a few years later. Aziz finds it ironic that here in this neighborhood the oil machinery is surrounded by so many Iranian Jews.

On the next block he passes an auto repair shop, some retail stores, and a kosher butcher shop with such a bad history of scandal that he and Hana refuse to enter it.[9] At the end of the block is Pat's, a fancy kosher restaurant, its pale exterior brightened by the stoplight. The next three blocks are tightly packed with two Ashkenazic synagogues (the little Beth Menahem and the big Young Israel of Century City), a kosher fast-food place (Chick 'n Chow), a dry cleaner, and a coin-operated laundry. On the next block, crowded together, are three more kosher places (Shanghai Diamond, Psy Café, and Nagila Pizza), a tailor, and then the kosher grocery store (Pico Glatt Mart) that Hana will go to only in a pinch. She says the customers are unfriendly *Ashkenazim* and the store doesn't stock the products she prefers. Her regular place is Elat Market, a favorite of Persian customers, or she'll go to Glatt Mart one door from there. Aziz turns his car into the underground parking garage of Ralphs supermarket, a branch of a national chain.[10] This Ralphs is topped by two stories of retail shops, a bank, and some food venues. Among them is the kosher Fish Grill, whose spiced dishes Aziz and Hana enjoy and where they go on weeknights when Hana is too busy to cook. The supermarket, responding to local consumers, employs a full-time *mashgiaḥ* (inspector of kosher food) to oversee its separate kosher meat department and bakery. Ralphs is the best place to go at night to quickly purchase staples. At the self-checkout line, Aziz greets a Chabad man, a computer expert who installed the new computer system in his office.

Driving out of the supermarket garage, Aziz notes with great satisfaction the small crowd of men wearing black coats and hats across the street on the sidewalk beside the three-story building housing the Yachad Kollel. They must be socializing after the evening prayers. Yachad is a Persian kollel of almost ten Persian rabbis, all of them Talmud scholars. From Aziz's perspective, the kollel's very existence shows the great religious progress made by Iranian Jews. When the media describes the exodus of the tens of thousands of Persian Jews from their home of more than two thousand years, it rarely mentions those who, like Aziz, now count themselves part of the Orthodox community. The focus is on the Persians who are wealthy, stylish, and cosmopolitan and attend Conservative or Reform Jewish synagogues. Although many of them attend Shabbat services, they drive there. They violate other religious laws: they ignore the obligations of daily prayer, and the women dress immodestly and do not attend the *mikvah* (ritual pool). The more strictly religious Iranians like Aziz who call themselves Persian Orthodox call these others "traditional." In Iran there was no kosher certification—there was no need because there was barely any ready-made food; people would buy the raw foods and prepare the dishes at home. So, here in America they act like they did in Iran and do not look for kosher certification. They buy prepared foods that seem free of nonkosher ingredients, and they trust the word of store owners who say their meat is kosher. Their ways are traditionally Iranian but not, in Aziz's opinion, authentically Jewish.[11] In contrast, the smaller circle of Persian Jews that Aziz belongs to has adopted the religious practices of the Ashkenazic Orthodox, which in many cases they had not even known about or could not perform in Iran. Aziz is proud to support the Persian kollel. It shows that Iranian Jews are reaching the high level of Torah learning common among the Ashkenazic Jews.

The transformation in religious life for Iranian Jews actually began to occur in Iran at about the time Aziz and his brother departed in 1974. Contacts between Iranian Jews and relatives in Europe, Israel, and the United States increased in the mid-1970s. The dire situation for Jews in Iran came to the attention of Rabbi Herman Neuberger, the Ashkenazic Orthodox leader of the Ner Yisrael Yeshiva of Baltimore, who initially brought just a few college-age Jewish men from Shiraz to study at his yeshiva. The plan was to train them and then send them back to Iran to improve Jewish education there. The political turmoil made this impossible. After the revolution and then the war with Iraq, Iranian Jews were desperate to leave. Nearly 90 percent did so during the 1980s, and about half came as refugees to the United States, with about thirty thousand settling in Los Angeles.[12] Thanks to the generosity of Ashkenazic and Sephardic Orthodox Jewish benefactors, more than a thousand young Persian men were brought to Ner Yisrael Yeshiva for rabbinic studies. Due to the dangerous situation in Iran, most of them remained in the United States. Although Jewish religious culture is currently thriving in Iran, the immigrants have no desire to return.

Another Ashkenazic group, Chabad-Lubavitcher Hasidim, focused its rescue efforts on Persian children. Many of the children, brought out without their parents, were placed into Brooklyn Chabad families and educated in the Chabad schools.[13] In addition, Chabad rabbis were dispatched to Los Angeles to keep the thousands of Persian Jewish immigrants and their offspring from assimilating. The more religious among them—and the ones with fewer financial resources for Orthodox day school tuition—sent their children to the Chabad preschools and to the Chabad-organized activities for Persian teenagers, including programs at the Chabad Persian Youth Center on Pico Boulevard.

By the 1990s, Farsi-speaking Persian rabbis trained at Ner Yisrael and Israeli yeshivas began to arrive in Los Angeles. They, too, had a mission of religious outreach. Aziz was deeply impressed by the Persian rabbis who visited his downtown office to chat. They offered Torah classes over lunch for Persian businessmen. They were warm and friendly, they were "his people," and, like him, they were from Shiraz. Aziz began going to Shabbat and daily morning services at the Ahavat Shalom Persian synagogue led by one of these rabbis. He and Hana attended—and still attend—the lectures held in the Persian Jewish center on Robertson (Torat Hayim) or in private homes. Now, many classes are held in the Pico Boulevard Yachad Kollel building. His daughter-in-law used to go to the Yachad Kollel programs for young women when she was a teenager and became more religious than her parents. For that reason, the extended family meals take place at Aziz and Hana's home, where the *kashrut* laws, which specify proper food, are strictly practiced. Aziz's son Michael goes to the teen group at the Yachad Kollel. Michael recently reported that a new teacher was added to the kollel faculty, a Persian man who was born in Los Angeles, graduated from the Orthodox schools, and then attended yeshivas in Philadelphia and in Israel. Now he has returned to Los Angeles with his wife and children—the first Persian Jew born and raised in Los Angeles to join the kollel faculty!

As Aziz proceeds home to his own wife and child, he thinks about his son's new enthusiasm for religious outreach. Michael has a part-time job, one afternoon a week and Shabbat mornings, at Mogen David, a

Sephardic synagogue on Pico a few blocks west of Ralphs. Michael's main responsibility is the prayer group and social activities for teenagers his age and a bit younger. Michael explains that the prayers and discussions strengthen the teens' bonds with God and that they are bonded to each other by fun activities, like a weekly raffle of brand-name clothing; the money goes to charity. The big draw is the Shabbat afternoon *kiddush* (after-worship repast). Every week, Michael orders from the local kosher businesses and posts the menu on Instagram and the synagogue website. At dinner he showed his parents his post of the coming offerings: trays of wings from Jeff's Gourmet Sausage and "poppers" (sweet and spicy chicken) and cholent (beef and bean stew) from Lieder's.

Up ahead is Factor's Famous Deli, which, Aziz likes to say, is more infamous than famous to him. A few years ago, the owners hung a banner celebrating the deli's seventy years of serving Jewish food, but the food is not kosher, and they even serve meat and milk together. The next block puts him in a better frame of mind. It holds two kosher restaurants, a flower shop, and a catering hall called The Mark. Orthodox Jews rent the hall—anyone can—and use their own caterers. Because it is right in the midst of the neighborhood, The Mark is used for Bar Mitzvah luncheons when the synagogue is too small for all the guests. It is not a fancy place, and the very wealthy people in the community prefer to hold their events in the hotels outside the immediate neighborhood that are outfitted to serve kosher food.

Aziz slows down and stops his car in front of the little building on the next corner—his synagogue, Ahavat Shalom. Aziz thinks it has the most beautiful facade of all the synagogues in the neighborhood. It is white with beige stones, topped by a white sculptured relief of graceful vines and buds flowing from vases and bracketed by scrollwork. The synagogue's name in Hebrew and English gold-colored letters is displayed above the wooden front door. The synagogue was originally built in 1928, the corner unit of a two-story commercial building; the decorative exterior topping and plate-glass windows of the building's front facade would draw the eye to it and to the pianos for sale within. When, like many other storefronts in Pico-Robertson, it was refurbished as a synagogue, the plate-glass windows were closed up by stucco and the front door was made solid. The synagogue has done its best to "stay under the radar." It does not have a website, and the announcement flyer in the glass-covered cabinet next to the front door is written mostly in Farsi. Despite this, a few months ago, the outside front was defaced with antisemitic graffiti. All the rightful authorities were notified and an investigation was launched, but the perpetrator has not been found. Of course, the graffiti was painted over. Still, it is unsettling. Aziz checks to see that the building front is unsullied, and then he drives down the street and turns into the alley to check the building's back side. Everything is in order. He turns back onto Pico Boulevard and heads home. He will return in a few hours just after dawn for the morning prayers.

A Chabad Mother and Her Afternoon Errands and Carpool

Rivka is still exhausted when she gets up from the living room couch. She looks into the full-length mirror next to the front door and, checking to see that her appearance conforms to that of a proper Chabad married woman, tucks the loose strands of her hair under her wig and straightens her long-sleeved blouse and long skirt over her dark-stockinged legs. She grabs her purse and keys and heads outside to her car. Rivka is thirty-three years old and healthy, but she is almost four months pregnant, and the nap was not enough. She and her husband, Moishe, have five children, and even with her husband's help she is exhausted nearly all the time. Mornings are particularly draining, what with getting out the breakfast, preparing the kids' lunches and snacks, checking to see that they have the right books in their backpacks, and sending the four youngest with Moishe. Today, Tuesday, is her busiest morning. After driving their oldest daughter, Sarah, and two other girls to their high school, she visits four different homes and offices to work with her speech therapy clients. Like many working Los Angeles Chabad Hasidic mothers of school-age children, Rivka spends hours every day, except Shabbat, on the road.

Sitting in the driveway behind the steering wheel of her minivan, Rivka reminds herself to be grateful. She turns up the car's air-conditioning and asks God for the strength to manage the next several hours until she can get into bed for the night. She looks outside and counts her blessings. She knows she would be spending even more time in her car if not for her parents. They paid for this five-bedroom house behind Robertson Boulevard near the kids' schools. Her parents grew up in Minneapolis and became *frum* (religious) in their college years at the St. Paul Chabad Center. Their devotion to God and the Rebbe grew stronger when they moved to Los Angeles, had their first child—Rivka is the third of five—and Rivka's father became enormously successful in the film business. He has never stinted in his support for Chabad and for his children's Torah education. When Rivka became engaged to Moishe, Rivka's father told them he would consider it a great *zekhus* (merit; Ashkenazic pronunciation of *zekhut*) to support them in raising their Torah-observant children. He has been unfailingly generous. Moishe's work as a designer and installer of computer systems and phones for businesses and Rivka's income from speech therapy would never cover their family expenses.

Rivka wants to make this coming Shabbat dinner extra special when they tell her parents about the coming baby. Another couple—younger friends—and their toddler will be joining them along with their "regulars": two single women, an elderly widower, and a young man with an intellectual disability whose family is not religious and who loves to sing at their Shabbos table. Moishe will likely come home from the synagogue with one or two guests. That makes an auspicious *ḥai* (eighteen). She is preparing food for twenty, though. Hosting guests is such a great mitzvah (divine commandment; good deed) that neither she nor Moishe would hold back if they happen upon two more people who need to join them.

The first stop on Rivka's afternoon route is the grocery store. Leaving her home, she turns east on Pickford and then north onto Robertson Boulevard. Stalled by the fire engine backing into the station garage on the corner, she looks to the right past the new Chofetz Chaim yeshiva and the Chabad Israel Center (her synagogue) toward the Gan Chabad preschool, where her youngest son, Dovid, she hopes, is playing happily. At the end of the next block she turns into the residential street for a shortcut to the Glatt Mart parking lot. This should not take long, since it is midday and three days before Shabbat. She fills up her grocery cart with everything but the two chickens and the beef for a shoulder roast—her father's favorite. Rivka frowns as she stands in front of the meat counter: despite the ample supply of different meat cuts and kosher brands, there are no shoulder cuts with Crown Heights or Shor HaBor labels. These are Chabad-approved kosher meat brands, and she will not purchase any other brand. A new wave of exhaustion passes over Rivka as she realizes she will need to go tonight or tomorrow to the kosher store in Mid-City LA that stocks the most Chabad-approved meat.

After paying, loading up her car, and packing the frozen foods into the large picnic cooler she keeps in the rear of the minivan, Rivka maneuvers out of the lot and again winds through residential streets. She passes many original 1930s duplexes, one-story houses, and two-story apartment buildings. Over the past few decades, well-to-do residents and developers have altered the uniform look of the neighborhood. Nearly every block now includes new or renovated houses with first- and second-story additions and new three- and four-story apartment buildings. The increased number of native-born Angelenos or relocated East Coast religious families who wish to live in Pico-Robertson has pushed rents and prices to new heights. Rivka cannot count the times she has heard other Chabad parents confess (during the all-too-frequent discussions about local real estate) that they are considering moving to Denver or Phoenix. Lots of school families live in the San Fernando Valley and drive their children ten to fifteen miles to and from school.

Rivka reaches the boulevard, crosses at the stoplight, and stops at the back of the line of cars leading up to Cheder Menachem, the Chabad elementary boys' school. She inches forward in the carpool lane. A few dozen clusters of boys, each wearing the requisite dark pants, black or blue velvet yarmulke, and *tzitzit* (ritual fringes) hanging down below their white or blue shirts, are arranged in rows behind the teacher on duty. Eventually Rivka advances enough so that the teacher sees her and signals to her sons, five-year-old Leib and eight-year-old Shauly, standing together with the fifth-grade neighbor who is part of the carpool.

Meanwhile, Rivka sees a friend walking alongside the lane with her three children. The friend stops, and the two women chat through the car window as the boys get in the car and buckle up. Rivka is delighted to learn that her friend is going this afternoon to the Mid-City kosher market and will buy the meat Rivka needs and drop it off at her house on her way home. Further back in the carpool line someone honks the car horn, and the teacher steps forward to tell the women that they are holding up the line. Ashamed but greatly relieved about one less errand, Rivka waves apologetically and accelerates out to the street.

Rivka greets her young passengers and tells them of the two stops they will be making on their way home. The first, she says, is "a real treat and an important mitzvah: going to the Keylim Mikvah!" This is a small ritual immersion pool for ritually cleansing new metal and glass utensils and dishware (*kelim*). As Rivka turns onto Pico Boulevard and slowly drives through the traffic to Robertson Boulevard, Shauly and his little brother argue about who will get to dip the items into the water. "Don't argue. There is something for each of you," Rivka tells them. She parks in the Walgreens lot and shows them the bag of metal measuring cups and a silver platter she had placed this morning into the back of the minivan. "Now stay close," she warns as each boy exits the minivan. A car approaches and veers into a nearby parking spot, and an unkempt, ragged man weaves in front of them at the sidewalk's edge.

The fifth grader's eyes widen when they walk past the Hookah and Cigar Lounge, and he remembers the forbidden businesses on this block. He calls out excitedly, "Up ahead is the magic store and the tattoo place!" Rivka, alarmed, responds, "Magic is *goyishe* [non-Jewish] nonsense and tattooing is a *ḥillul Hashem* [desecration of God]!" Ahead she sees the Mezuzah Store, a Chabad-owned shop that sells the protective cases and the parchments of Torah passages Jews are commanded to post on their doorposts, and she is relieved: the mezuzah store is like an antidote to the street's poison. She encourages the children to peer into the store's window and notice the decorated colorful, shiny little cases and the Hebrew-inscribed parchments. Making a guessing game for them, she asks, "Who can see the case with the twelve stones for the twelve *shevatim* [tribes of

Israel]? Who can see the one with the *etz heḥayyim* [tree of life]?" She looks at her watch, and they move on, passing a *treif* (nonkosher) restaurant, a dentist's office, an antiques store, and a large nursing home. The next building is the Orthodox synagogue Anshe Emes. Members of the synagogue built and operate the Keylim Mikvah for the community and serve as volunteer guards during the mikvah's open hours. A religious man is posted outside, and Rivka stops to speak to him. She thanks him for his service, signs the guest book, and leads the boys through the narrow passageway on the side of the synagogue to the back lot.

The ritual immersion of new food utensils and dishware, *toveling*, is practiced today almost exclusively by Orthodox Jews, but it is unknown how widely even they practice it. Los Angeles Chabad Jews take the commandment seriously, as do the members of the non-Chabad Anshe Emes congregation. The rule is based on the Numbers 31:23 law commanding the Israelites to ritually purify, through fire or water, items taken from the Midianites as spoils of war. The Talmudic rabbis defined the obligation as pertaining to food vessels formerly owned or constructed by "idol worshipers" generally, that is, non-Jews no matter their religious practices. Subsequent rabbinic authorities ruled according to this precedent. In the modern era, Orthodox rabbis have differed on whether it applies to machine-produced dishes and utensils; those who affirm the practice apply it to any new metal or glass dish or utensil, including those mass-produced by manufacturers and corporations not identifiably Jewish.[14] Immersion requires "living water," that is, water collected from melted snow, rainfall, or a spring, or one may immerse the items directly into the ocean. This is the same quality of water in a mikvah designed for women's monthly immersions, and dishes theoretically could be immersed in such a pool.[15]

The synagogue's back lot is paved with cement and surrounded by a stucco wall, cement bricks, and a wire fence. In the middle is the Keylim Mikvah. It is a white poured concrete cube, lined inside with white ceramic tiles, filled with water, and topped by a hinged wooden lid. Rivka takes out a metal measuring cup and places it into the white plastic basket sitting on the nearby table, hands the basket to Shauly, and reminds him of the *berakhah* (blessing) to recite before he dips the basket in the water. She places another metal cup into the basket for Leib, and Shauly boosts his little brother to the top of the four-foot-high cube to repeat the ritual. The fifth-grade neighbor is next, and Rivka herself finishes the dipping. She extracts a five-dollar bill from her purse and hands it to Leib to slip through the slot near the synagogue back door. She smiles at the boys and says, "You've done a mitzvah, and now you've earned a snack."

The boys race through the passageway and wait for her on the sidewalk. They discuss the local snack possibilities and agree on Milky's, the kosher frozen yogurt shop a block down and across the boulevard. Shauly tells his mother, "Can we go to Milky's? They now have some *ḥalav yisraʾel* yogurt flavors." This term indicates that the milk was taken from the cow (or other permitted mammal) by a Jew or by a person under the watch of a Jew. Most Orthodox Jews consider cow's milk kosher without this level of supervision, but Chabad rabbis regard the *ḥalav yisraʾel* standard as supremely important. "Not today," she tells them. "We have to pick up Esty and her friend at the dentist. I packed you all a special nosh in the car." They walk back to the car, and Rivka pulls out three small packages of Bamba, an Israeli snack of peanut butter–flavored puffed corn. "Say the *berakhah*," she tells the boys, waiting for them to recite the prayer before handing each one a little bag. She finds a package of peanuts and a bottle of water for herself and recites her own blessing, and they all get into the car again.

Back on Pico Boulevard, Rivka heads east toward the dentist office to pick up her ten-year-old daughter, Esty, and her schoolmate Hindy, age thirteen. Both are students at Chaya Mushka School, the Chabad girls' elementary and junior high school. Rivka and Hindy's mother always schedule back-to-back teeth-cleaning appointments for the girls so they can walk together from school and get picked up afterward by one mother. The three-fourths-mile walk is safe, especially with sensible Hindy in charge. By this time of day, students from the local religious schools are walking home from school, Jewish Persian teenage boys are congregating in front of the youth centers, and adults are shopping for food or doing errands. Rivka turns into the Bank of America parking lot, she chooses a space in the empty back corner where she hopes no one will object, and they all exit and walk a few doors down to the dentist. The girls are waiting in the lobby. Rivka schedules their next visit and pays, and they all leave.

Esty has been chattering nonstop to her mother since they walked out the dentist office's door. Wearing a light-blue long-sleeved shirt, the school's required plaid pleated skirt, and white tights, she is nearly jumping out of her pink sneakers while reciting her day's achievements: the good grade she received on a math quiz, her correct answer to a question in Bible class when no one else knew it, her discovery that she was in second place for the number of points earned in her weekly tally of mitzvahs performed, and so on. This is typical of how Esty greets her mother after school, but Rivka is of two minds about it. She knows it is important to encourage a child's good deeds, but Esty can be self-righteous and a bit of a show-off. She must learn greater self-restraint and modesty.

As they drive west on Pico Boulevard, Rivka asks Hindy whether there were any problems during the walk to the dentist. Esty, however, jumps in and responds animatedly with the tale of how they were stopped by two grown-ups who asked them for directions to a restaurant. The people were nice, and they said they could tell the girls were Jewish and they were, too. Esty says, "So I told them they should go to a *kosher* restaurant, not the one they asked about, and I pointed to the one right there, the Holy Grill." Hindy intervenes, "They just laughed. She shouldn't have said that to them. Now they will think religious people are rude." "But Mommy," Esty retorts, "Mrs. Spector says the Rebbe says we are soldiers for Hashem full-time!" Rivka doesn't have the energy or capability to deal with this now—best to hand it back to her daughter's teacher. "I know your heart is in the right place," Rivka says, "and I don't think what you said is so wrong. But how about tomorrow asking Mrs. Spector what she thinks is the best way to respond?" Esty promises to do just that.

Rivka turns off the boulevard with a sigh of relief: the afternoon's circuit is nearing its end. She first stops at Hindy's apartment, and then a few streets later she drops off the fifth-grade boy. Up ahead she sees her own house. Home, finally! But why is Moishe backing his car out of the driveway? Moishe parks his car at the curb and walks out to greet Rivka. He looks at his wife, who appears exhausted and dismayed by his imminent departure. "I won't be too long," he assures her. "I'll bring in the groceries, and Dovid is already home. I have to just put the finishing touches on an installation job. Sarah can take charge. Let me help you inside and you can lie down."

Three Teenagers Biking through the Alleyways behind Pico Boulevard

It is a Sunday afternoon in mid-September 2020, six months into the COVID-19 shutdown. Fifteen-year-old Asher cannot bear to spend another minute in the same house as his older sister. He stuffs his wallet and phone in his back pocket, dons a face mask (as a precaution against the virus), sets his helmet over his colorful crocheted yarmulke, and gets on his bike. He and his friend Daniel, a fellow tenth grader at YULA Boys High School, have arranged to bike around Pico and buy some snacks. Daniel is easy to be with and has a fun sense of humor. Like Asher's, his family is Modern Orthodox, but unlike Asher, Daniel is "100 percent Ashkenazic," with Holocaust survivor great-grandparents and family connections in Australia, Argentina, and Europe. An avid fan of the Tour de France bicycle competition, he texted Asher earlier, "Wanna do a tour de alleys?" Because dining in is no longer permitted, restaurant owners have been erecting eating places in their back lots, and, with Rosh Hashana coming soon, synagogues are constructing bigger outdoor spaces for socially distant worship services in their back lots. When Asher arrives at Daniel's apartment on Shenandoah, he finds his friend biking in circles on the street with another boy. Like Asher, they are wearing face masks and helmets and are dressed in T-shirts and shorts. Daniel tells Asher, "This is Josh. He lives next door, and he went with me to Hillel Academy. I told him he could come with us." The three head south to Cashio, cross Robertson Boulevard at the light, and bike up to the alley behind the south side of Pico.

Josh is not quite part of Asher and Daniel's social world. Although he is Orthodox and a tenth grader, he attends public school. After Josh graduated eighth grade at the religious day school, his parents decided they would no longer go through the humiliating process of requesting school financial aid. Daniel's parents cannot afford full tuition, either, but they are not as bad off, and they requested and received funds to help pay his tuition. Unlike Daniel, Josh is a bit ashamed about his situation, and he hopes Asher will not ask him where he goes to school. Josh's father tells the family to hold their heads high. He and his wife are Ashkenazic Orthodox and were born in Los Angeles to Orthodox parents, who were also born in Los Angeles. He is proud and self-assured and acts like a full-fledged member of every gathering and synagogue they attend. "You are unique and irreplaceable," he tells Josh and his younger brothers. Josh has a good voice, loves to pray, and is an ace Torah chanter. Parents hire him to tutor their boys to prepare them for their Bar Mitzvahs. The past year before the pandemic, his family attended a variety of Ashkenazic Orthodox and Chabad synagogues to become expert in their prayer melodies and *zemirot*, Shabbat and holiday table songs. The prohibition on communal gatherings during the pandemic put an end to both the music and the free food. The Orthodox communities in Pico-Robertson have taken seriously the precautions against COVID-19. At first the synagogues were entirely shut down, but they eventually learned how to hold communal prayer services outside with a smaller number of spaced seats—typically these go to paying members. Josh, his brother, mother, and father pray together at home, and then they take a long walk through the neighborhood.

The boys stop in front of the two high, long, white canopies that fill the entire back lot of the Jewish Family Service building. The covered area is empty except for a dumpster. They gaze at the open space, puzzled. Josh suggests, "They closed this branch in March, so I'm betting they rented it to Bais Bezalel Chabad for Rosh Hashana and Yom Kippur services." Bais Bezalel, further up the alley, is a relatively new, narrow, three-story building. During the pandemic the synagogue erected in the back lot a metal pole framework with brown shade-cloth walls and roof. It might hold a few dozen socially distanced people but hardly enough for a holiday crowd. Everyone is familiar with Chabad's boast that no one needs to buy an annual membership—the standard synagogue practice—to attend its High Holiday services. "You get what you pay for," Asher quips; he can joke about such things because his family is well-off. Josh blushes. His family has attended the free Chabad services on High Holidays. Daniel, who knows this, draws their attention to the new fenced-in area abutting the outside wall of Pico Kosher Deli. Founded in 1968, it is likely the oldest kosher restaurant in all of Los Angeles. For decades it has served traditional Ashkenazic deli food like pastrami sandwiches on rye bread, chicken soup with matza balls, and chopped liver. Recently the proprietors bowed to regional tastes and added some Mexican dishes, such as tacos, tostadas, and nachos—albeit with nondairy sour cream because of the kosher laws. Asher grimaces at the back lot dining room. Visible through the green polyethylene shade-cloth walls is a lone man sitting at one of two round umbrella-covered tables. The "floor" is stained, cracked asphalt marked by parking space lines. "Better to order takeout," Asher says. They mount their bikes and ride on.

Asher has been doing a lot of cooking during the pandemic—grilling, in particular—and on the next block he stops the boys at his favorite meat place, Jeff's Gourmet Sausage Factory, which is kosher. Perhaps one day he will be a master chef like the ones on TV. Asher would like to get a job here when he turns sixteen, but not as a lowly busboy or order taker. He would ask the owner, who is a friend of his uncle, to be a paid intern and advise him about menu items attractive for the younger generation. Asher's mother is encouraging his interest. As a Moroccan Israeli who develops her own recipes, she suggested he master traditional international regional seasonings—Korean, Chinese, Moroccan, Mexican—and then develop his own distinctive spice mixes for grilled meat and vegetables. His father, who is American Ashkenazic, loves everything Asher has made, and Asher has served his best dishes in the backyard to appreciative friends and relatives. Daniel says, "Let me know when you make ribs again. That was awesome. Everyone liked that one, except of course your sister—but she doesn't count." He explains to Josh, "She won't eat meat, not even on Shabbos. She's a vegetarian." Josh asks, "Why is she vegetarian?" Asher is silent, so Daniel says, "She doesn't think it is ethical for people to kill animals for food." Asher doesn't want to talk about his older sister. His friends don't know—and he doesn't think his parents or other siblings suspect—that Aliza is going "off the *derekh*." Last month he walked into her room on Shabbat and caught her drawing, a violation of the Sabbath work prohibition. She was unapologetic. She told him that she thinks the leaders are hypocritical and don't care about ethics and the rules are oppressive. Asher was outraged and ashamed. Before this he was not getting along with her, and now it is worse. "Let's go," he says.

The boys bike through the alley and stop behind Adas Torah, a Centrist Orthodox synagogue that only Josh has entered. Its new addition is a heavy-duty metal sliding wall, within which sits a white event tent. They step inside the open tent and see portable tables, chairs, and a podium. Two men sit opposite each other, studying together from books on the table. They look up, and the boys withdraw. Asher is reminded of the Talmud assignment due tomorrow. He asks Daniel, "Did you write your summary for Rabbi Malowitz? I couldn't figure it out." They complain about their homework, and Daniel volunteers to help Asher later. Josh, meanwhile, walks over to the green metal mesh structure behind the next building, the Chabad Persian Youth Center. He squints through tiny holes and calls out, "Tables, chairs, a cabinet. This has been around for a while. I knew a Persian guy who used to come here for afternoon classes and food. He said there was a *lot* of food." Josh's comment starts the three of them speculating about the kind of food that would be served. This talk of food makes them hungry, and they decide to take a break from exploring to get a snack.

They bike through a narrow passageway connecting the alley to Pico. The stoplight on Doheny takes too long, so they bike alongside the parked cars until they see an opening in the flow of cars and then speed across the street to the north side of Pico Boulevard. They stop in the front parking lot facing kosher Chick 'n Chow, a coin-operated laundry, a dry cleaner, and the Beth Menahem synagogue. Asher contends that the Chinese orange chicken made by Chick 'n Chow is far superior to the one from Shanghai Diamond Garden, also kosher, located two blocks further up Pico.[16] Daniel agrees but prefers Shanghai because it is a better deal. He tells Josh, "For the same price you also get a side, soup, and egg roll. They call it 'the YULA special.'" YULA Boys High School (when it meets in person) permits students to order lunch from the local kosher restaurants. The previous year, a senior whose father owns Shanghai ran for school president with the platform that, if he won, he'd get the cost of the special down to eight dollars. Asher sniffed in disdain, "He won but the price stayed the same; they just waived the delivery fee if there were enough school orders." Daniel looks over at Josh. He is pretty sure Josh cannot afford to eat here. "Tell you what," he tells Asher, "you order your chicken. All I want are some chocolate buns from Pico Glatt. Josh and I will get some stuff at the market, and we'll meet you in front of the bank on Beverly. We can sit there and eat."

Daniel and Josh hop on their bikes and head into the alley. After a few yards, they stop to investigate a wall behind the synagogue. Barely visible underneath the top layer of brown paint are two large faces and the words "We are watching you!" Daniel quips, "That was the old security system. Look at the new one." He points at the synagogue's back door, upon which is a sign that reads, "Protected by RIBONO SHEL OLAM security system." (*Ribono shel olam* is a Hebrew term for God, literally, "Master of the universe.") If that does not dissuade an intruder, the door is heavy and metal clad, and the entrance is secured by an electronic number-pad doorknob lock. Josh tells Daniel about a different sign he saw on this door when he attended last year. "It was during that measles outbreak. It told people not to come in if they were not vaccinated, because of all the pregnant women and children in the shul. It said that God will protect people from disease only if people do their part." Further down the alley they pass behind the long iron walls and gates of Young Israel of Century City. "This place is like a fortress, and they have real guards," Daniel says. "I don't worry when I come here." After the deadly shootings at synagogues in Pittsburgh and Poway in 2018 and 2019, all Los Angeles synagogues upgraded their security. Those with front doors on Pico hired guards and placed congregational volunteers at the street-facing door on Shabbat. Many synagogues simply moved the Sabbath entrance to the alleyway door, where guards and volunteers have greater control and attendees are out of public view. On the front door there may be a note posted directing attendees to the rear. Daniel says, "At my shul we don't even bother with a sign on the front door. We figure if someone doesn't know to enter from the back they probably don't belong."

They park and lock their bikes and enter Pico Glatt Mart. A cashier looks up and notes approvingly that they are wearing masks. Daniel leads Josh to the packaged desserts. "I love these chocolate things. There are eight, each separately wrapped. Just right for keeping in my backpack and eating between classes. I'll get a pack and give you some." Josh responds, "I'm getting lollipops for me and my brothers, and one for you if you want." They pay, exit, wheel their bikes across the street, and sit on the artificial grass bordering the sloping, polished stone of the Chase Bank plaza. Two younger boys are doing tricks with their skateboards. A woman, looking old and poor, approaches. She is a fixture in this part of the neighborhood, and despite the September heat she is swathed in fringed scarves. She mumbles something. Josh looks up at Daniel and says, "I don't have any more money." He offers the woman one of the wrapped chocolate buns Daniel gave him, and Daniel then offers her another. She accepts the buns just as Asher pulls up on his bike, and she turns to him with her hand out. Setting down the plastic bag from Chick 'n Chow, Asher takes a dollar bill from his wallet and gives it to her.

The boys walk their bikes to the rear of the bank to the table overlooking the parking lot. Asher sets down the takeout trays and announces, "Instead of orange chicken I got two orders of the spicy wings for us to split." The three eat contentedly and talk about the Los Angeles Lakers and the playoffs. Once finished, they resume their alley tour. Crossing to the south side of Pico at the light on Beverly, they turn into the alley behind the gas station and bike behind food businesses (Factor's Deli, Shalom Grill, Sushiko) and stop at the rear of the space between the flower store (Sonny Alexander's Flowers) and The Mark catering hall. What used to be a parking lot is now fenced, and workers cluster around the delivery vans at the back gate. Asher explains that this is the new evening dining spot for Pat's, the fancy kosher meat restaurant across the street. "My family ate here last week. 'Dine under the Stars,' they call it. Same food, same waiters. They put a lot into making this look good." The boys peek around the back opening where busboys are wheeling in carts in preparation for the evening meal. Two parallel back fences, each covered in cloth, protect the diners from seeing the workers or the alley. All the walls are covered with green Astroturf, as is the ground. Umbrellas and strings of light hang over round, white tablecloth-covered tables. Daniel jokes, "How about that—we have the same carpeting on my synagogue's back lot."

They bike down the alley to Rokah Karate. This is the meeting place of Daniel's Hassidic *shul*, the Happy Minyan, so-called because its congregants are devoted to prolonged, joyous singing, particularly the melodies of Rabbi Shlomo Carlebach. Daniel reminisces about incidents that happened here pre-COVID. On Friday afternoons, congregants would fill the karate studio with about a hundred chairs, a Torah cabinet, a podium, and a curtained divider separating the room into the front men's section and the rear women's section. Men would enter from Pico and women from the back alley door. The enhanced 2019 security then required both men and women to enter only from the back after getting the approval of a guard. Once a month, on the Sabbath of the new moon, the congregation provided a free lunch in the event tents and back patios a few doors down the alley behind two nearby congregations, Pico Shul and Aish HaTorah. On regular Shabbat mornings, nicely dressed Orthodox Jews would walk to and from these three synagogues through the dumpster-lined potholed alley and offer greetings to their friends. Now it is empty on Shabbat. The Happy Minyan meets elsewhere during the pandemic, and perhaps the other two synagogues have alternative sites. The karate studio, however, is still training students. Its owner carpeted the entire back lot with Astroturf and shaded it with sun cloth stretched above.

For the next hour the boys make their way through the south side alley. They manage to draw out their exploration—poking through discarded building material, balancing on a wall, tossing stones at targets—in order to prolong their time away from the homes they have been stuck in for months. Asher discovers his back tire is flat, and Josh finds a sharp piece of metal protruding from the bottom. He says, "I'm really good at patching if you have one of those kits." Asher says, "I do at home. That would be terrific. Let's all walk over to my house. While Daniel and I go over the Talmud, you fix my tire and maybe keep my sister at bay. Then I'll make us dinner in the backyard."

THE GEOGRAPHY, HISTORY, AND DEMOGRAPHY OF THE ORTHODOX COMMUNITY IN THE PICO-ROBERTSON AREA

What drew people like the representative individuals portrayed here and other Orthodox Jews to the Pico-Robertson area, making it a burgeoning center of Orthodoxy within the city? Examining the geography, history, and demography of Los Angeles and the local Pico-Robertson area will help answer this question.

Certainly, the moderate, dry, sunny climate is appealing and played a major role in drawing people and businesses, including those in the film industry, to Los Angeles, particularly to the western side of the city. Year-round the temperature ranges from fifty to eighty degrees Fahrenheit, humidity is low, and rain falls in short bursts only three months a year. Although in recent years the weather has become warmer and the hot late summer period extends longer, indoor air-conditioning ameliorates the discomfort. No matter the daytime heat, in the late afternoons and evenings a cool wind from the Pacific Ocean seven miles to the west blows across western Los Angeles. Today, open-air playgrounds and patios, fenced and covered by a light sun-protecting material, are set on the flat rooftops of the area schools and synagogues for year-round use. The ease and comfort when utilizing outdoor spaces make Pico-Robertson particularly attractive to Orthodox Jews. Temperate weather makes heating less expensive for families who must utilize their incomes for so many religious concerns, such as sending their children to religious schools. In her book *To the Golden Cities*, Deborah Dash Moore mentions climate as a reason why Jews moved to Los Angeles, as well as to Miami, but she does not connect these climate features to the growth of Orthodoxy.[17]

Southern California's economy expanded significantly during the last two decades of the twentieth century. Opportunities in the film industry, universities, retail and wholesale trades, research, and law attracted new settlers. Los Angeles County's population grew from approximately seven million in 1970 to ten million in 2019.[18] Census data from 2000 indicated that Pico-Robertson's population was nineteen thousand. Sociologist Bruce Phillips estimates that in that year, the Jewish household density in the area reached 48 percent, meaning that its Jewish population was approximately ten thousand.[19]

The location of Los Angeles and its close ties to the farms where much of its food is grown make it easy for people to obtain the food they want. The abundance of food is due to the fact that California is so fertile. The Central Valley is responsible for growing over one-third of America's vegetables and three-quarters of its fruits and nuts.[20] There is ready access to a wide variety of produce and to prepared and packaged foods as well. Immigrants can start successful small businesses that provide food from the homeland to other immigrants. From the beginning of the twentieth century, farmers and merchants built an infrastructure for getting agricultural and prepared foods to store owners and to grocery stores. They set up a food mart downtown, which has huge warehouses at the end of rail lines and truck routes and offices with clerks who facilitated matchmaking between farmers and grocery stores and distributors. An enterprising businessman can also bypass that and go straight to the farmer and say, "This is the kind of cucumber or cilantro I want you to grow. I will buy what you produce. If I bring my truck, you can fill it up."

Los Angeles as a whole was founded in 1781 when the region was under Mexican rule. The United States acquired it in 1848 during the Mexican-American War, and with the 1885 completion of the Santa Fe railroad line from Chicago to Los Angeles, mostly Protestant white Americans from the Lower Midwest and South flooded in. The city was developed in a multinucleated urban pattern; that is, it was composed of multiple core areas for markets and shopping, industry, and governance, and these were surrounded by blocks of housing somewhat homogeneous in terms of price and size.

Until the 1920s, much of western Los Angeles was flat farmland. Pico stretched fourteen miles from downtown in the east to the Pacific Ocean in the west; today's Pico-Robertson is at the midpoint. To the north and northwest was the separate city of Beverly Hills, incorporated in 1914; and eventually to its northeast, the Fairfax retail center grew, bounded by residential neighborhoods at the south end of Hollywood. In the 1920s and 1930s, Pico-Robertson was developed for residential use. The housing was designed for a middle-class and lower-middle-class population who could easily commute on Pico Boulevard or, to the north, on Olympic Boulevard to jobs downtown, or they could quickly reach Hollywood on other city streets. Pico-Robertson was not distinctive in appearance, nor did it have a name. People only began to call it "Pico-Robertson" in the late twentieth century. Its borders on the maps (see figs. 1 and 2) are unofficial and the product of the Los Angeles Times's "Mapping L.A." project in 2009.[21]

From the start, the Los Angeles City Council's lack of concern for the area was obvious in its zoning regulations permitting dozens of auto body and auto engine repair shops on the main streets. Many such businesses are still there. Some of the original structures, refurbished for other purposes, betray their origins in their simple, boxy, and flimsy edifices. The zoning regulations that allowed for a wide range of businesses in one area made it a convenient place for the Orthodox Jews who eventually settled there to get their many needs met within a short distance. During those early days, a few substantial two-story brick and stucco buildings—the bottom floor created for business space and the second floor consisting of apartment units—were erected on Pico Boulevard, and some of these remain today. The largest and most glamorous structure was the Fox Stadium Theatre, opened in 1931 with a seating capacity of one thousand.[22] Religious Jews who moved to this part of town prayed together in homes or storefronts. By the late 1930s

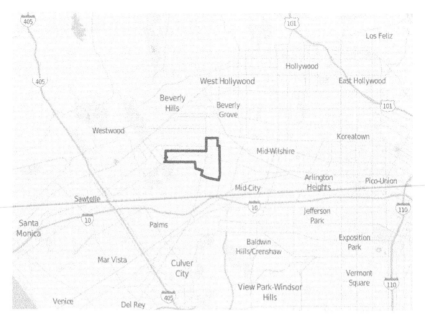

FIGURE 2. Pico-Robertson neighborhood within western Los Angeles, *Los Angeles Times*, "Mapping L.A." project, http://maps.latimes.com/neighborhoods/neighborhood/pico-robertson/ (© OpenStreetMap, openstreetmap.org/copyright. Available under the Open Data Commons Open Database License)

a Conservative synagogue was built that remains to this day.[23] South of the Pico-Robertson residential streets, a developer in the 1940s built a wealthier neighborhood he named Beverlywood. It was legally designated as a home association with rules mandating housing size, style, landscaping, and features that would ensure its more luxurious character.

The Orthodox enclave in Pico-Robertson is a recent addition to Los Angeles social life. A noticeable influx of Jews settled in Pico-Robertson and Beverlywood in the immediate post–World War II era. One cohort consisted of Jews moving from the downtown-adjacent West Adams neighborhood, where they had established several synagogues and Jewish community buildings.[24] In the 1940s and 1950s, the Jews of West Adams moved westward. They established at least two Orthodox synagogues near the intersection of Pico and Robertson Boulevards, another one about a mile and a half farther west on Pico Boulevard, and religious schools. Beth Jacob, a West Adams Orthodox synagogue, relocated in 1954 to nearby Beverly Hills, where it soon became—and remains to this day—the largest Orthodox congregation on the West Coast.[25] Most of the new Jewish residents in western Los Angeles, however, were part of the Jewish population boom made up of the thousands of American Jews who relocated to Southern California every decade from the American Midwest. These settlers did not make homes in the declining urban core but preferred the newer areas in western Los Angeles and in the sub-urbs of the San Fernando Valley on the northern side of the hills (the Santa Monica Mountains) that bisect Los Angeles. Like most American Jews, these Jews predominantly identified as Reform or Conservative or were unaffiliated. Yet the Orthodox community grew also, and during the 1960s, Orthodox children and teenagers in western Los Angeles and Beverly Hills could attend all-day religious schools, socialize with friends in Orthodox youth groups, and attend Orthodox day and sleep-away camps in the summer.

By the mid-1960s, many Jews and non-Jewish whites from the Fair-fax and Pico-Robertson neighborhoods, responding to the in-migration of African Americans from the urban core, moved again. Many bought houses farther west or in the San Fernando Valley suburbs. Orthodox Jews, however, determined to stay near their neighborhood's religious institutions and communal life, were slower to join in the white flight. Research conducted by the planning committee of the Jewish Federation in 1968 forecasted a dismal future for Jewish life in the Pico-Robertson area.[26] However, within a few years, younger newcomers and Los Angeles Jews, including those raised in Los Angeles suburbs, moved into the neighborhood because of its cheaper housing, convenience, and proximity to the universities and to downtown and mid-city jobs.[27]

By the late 1980s, Pico-Robertson was an Orthodox enclave. Its Orthodox population was—and still is—different from that in the older Los Angeles Orthodox neighborhoods near the synagogues and religious schools on La Brea Boulevard and Beverly Boulevard three miles to the northeast. The latter area is a center for Chabad and non-Chabad

Hasidic Jews, as well as Ashkenazi Jews loyal to yeshiva-based rabbinic authorities and highly restrictive religious law. Less concerned than the Orthodox Jews in the Pico-Robertson neighborhood about conforming to American cultural norms, many of the men of these communities are bearded and garbed in black coats and hats, and the women's head coverings are distinctly Orthodox in style.[28] In contrast, the Orthodox population of Pico-Robertson, despite the strong Chabad Hasidic element, is dominated by Modern and Centrist Orthodox Jews, who are less distinguishable from "ordinary" Americans by their clothing and who strive to balance secular culture and learning with religious law. Furthermore, Pico-Robertson's Orthodox communities include many Jews from Iran and the Middle East who affirm both Orthodox Judaism and their non-Ashkenazic cultural traditions.

Among the Pico-Robertson Orthodox, the most frequently repeated story of the neighborhood from the 1940s through the 1970s foregrounds its "inauthentic" Orthodox Jewish religious life. It emphasizes the laxity of Orthodox Jews in obeying *halakhah*, Jewish religious law.

Orthodox rulings prohibit Jews from using electricity and fire, including internal combustion engines, on the Sabbath. Only men are obligated for communal prayer, and they must not be distracted by the sight of women. Furthermore, *halakhah* requires gender segregation during communal worship. This must occur through the use of a *meḥitzah*, a room divider that hides the women from the men's gaze, either behind or on the side of the men's area, or by a separate women's prayer space in a room behind, above, or on the side of the main room of the males.

However, at midcentury in Pico-Robertson and nearby Beverly Hills, Orthodox congregations were not that different from Conservative ones. Reform and Conservative Judaism, which originated in order to modernize Judaism, eliminated or modified these rules. Their synagogues, with "mixed seating," enabled families and any males and females to sit next to each other. Conservative rabbis permitted using electricity on the Sabbath and driving to the synagogue for those who lived a distance from it; and because Reform rabbis did not regard ritual law as obligatory, Reform Jews generally did not restrict themselves on the Sabbath from using electricity or driving. Yet, in western Los Angeles, Orthodox congregants, too, were driving on the Sabbath to Orthodox synagogues, sitting in "mixed" pews, and listening to an electronically amplified rabbi and cantor. A Los Angeles Jew writing about Orthodox synagogues in the 1950s wrote, "There were plenty of members who drove to the synagogue to attend services on the Sabbath. . . . When there was a bar mitzvah—and there were plenty—there were large crowds, but attendance on the Sabbath without such a ceremony was sparse."[29] Today Orthodox Jews call such congregations "traditional," which, in this case, is a term of mild disparagement.

The turning point occurred about two decades later. Beginning in the late 1960s, a religious awakening among non-Orthodox American Jews became evident. College-age members from Conservative, Reform, and secular backgrounds adopted religious rituals and adapted them to their tastes, developed creative and innovative Jewish cultural expressions, and advocated an expanded role for women in communal prayer.[30] American Jewish ethnic pride surged after Israel's victory in the 1967 Six-Day War, and Jewish identity became closely linked to Zionism. Wearing a yarmulke all day long, no matter one's activity, became the standard practice for Orthodox and the most observant Conservative Jewish men; they favored the colorful, patterned crocheted kind worn by Israelis in nationalist religious circles.[31]

By the 1980s the "return to Judaism" was having a major impact on Orthodox Jewry in all US metropolitan centers. A movement of young people raised in Conservative, Reform, and secular families embraced Orthodox Judaism. The Hebrew term for a newly religious Jew is *ba'al teshuvah* (*ba'alat teshuvah* for a female; *ba'alei teshuvah* is the plural), literally, "master of repentance." The 1980s cultural mood swing granting greater prestige and power to traditional religious culture probably contributed to the *ba'al teshuvah* phenomenon. Another crucial factor was the Orthodox Jews' investment in *kiruv*, outreach. Chabad Hasidic rabbis were the first seriously devoted to *kiruv*, but since that time a number of non-Chabad Orthodox organizations have established outreach programs. The *ba'al teshuvah* phenomenon continues. According to 2013 data, about 30 percent of self-identified Orthodox Jews were raised in non-Orthodox homes.[32]

Another Los Angeles–born Orthodox Jew noted that this narrative gives more credit to newcomers than they perhaps deserve. She recalls an Orthodox rabbi who arrived in the 1970s who liked to claim, "Before I came here there was no Yiddishkeit (Jewishness)!" and followed that with mention of the hundreds of new members during his first years. She points out that prior to his hire, he had been rabbi of a struggling East Coast synagogue that, since his departure, added hundreds of members, too.[33] Despite the appearance of numerical increase during the 1980s, the absolute numbers in the overall Orthodox population dropped in some periods. The older generation, which had been a large portion of the whole, was dying.

On the other hand, Jewish young adults raised in Orthodox homes also infused special energy and visibility into the Orthodox community in the 1980s. Sociologists observed that the retention rate was rising after decades of decline. For years, more than half of young Orthodox Jews abandoned Orthodoxy when they became independent adults, but this changed in the 1980s. Although the retention rate for Orthodox Jews as a whole was still under 50 percent, more than two-thirds of those born in the 1960s and after were still committed to Orthodox religious observance when they were marrying and raising children in the 1980s.[34] This cohort was more likely than their parents to have attended all-day Orthodox schools. Both groups included Jews native to Los Angeles and new settlers. In sum, the younger cohort of the Orthodox community, consisting mostly of Jews who were either Orthodox from birth or enthusiastic neophytes, was determined to live according to "authentic Orthodoxy."

The change was especially obvious among the Orthodox Jews in Pico-Robertson. Orthodox schools and programs, nursery through high school levels, proliferated. New synagogues formed. Chabad, which had an outreach center next to the UCLA campus, established itself in the neighborhood in at least two locations and eventually built the large Bais

Bezalel near the main intersection. A small Orthodox minyan (informal prayer group of at least ten men) that started in 1976 in a rented hotel room shortly thereafter moved into a larger space on Pico Boulevard and then purchased a nearby building in 1982 to become the Young Israel of Century City synagogue. "Storefront" congregations appeared. All the rabbis hired to lead Los Angeles Orthodox synagogues, with one exception, were raised and ordained on the East Coast, in the Midwest, or in Israel. This is the case even today. The rabbis' arrival with their wives and children further augmented the local Orthodox population and its need for religious schools, kosher food, and the like. In 1988 a Southern California Chabad rabbi, Rabbi Eli Hecht, wrote an account of the area's transformation:

> For the past six years the Jewish demographics of Los Angeles and surrounding areas have begun to change. More of our Jewish population areas are returning to the ways of the old, but true form of Yiddishkeit Orthodoxy. Just should think [sic] for a moment of the many new Shuls that have opened all over the city and outlying areas. There are even rabbis who are leaving their Shuls to create new and authentic Orthodox places of prayer, leaving comfortable positions in order to upgrade to true Orthodox Torah standards.[35]

Orthodox Jews who applauded the introduction of religious stringencies and who arrived in Los Angeles in the 1980s repeat slight variations of this foundational narrative.[36]

Stricter standards were instituted in older Orthodox synagogues, such as B'nai David (whose name was changed to B'nai David-Judea after a merger in the 1970s). For years Rabbi Phillip Schroit, the congregation's Orthodox rabbi, had urged the synagogue board to institute gender segregation during communal worship, but it was not until 1988 that they agreed. According to Rabbi Hecht (quoted above), Rabbi Schroit "made a quantum leap forward when he decided to install a new Mechitzah and to rid the Shul of its Shabbos microphone, this after being Rabbi there for over 40 years! . . . He had the new beautiful Mechitzah installed with heavy cement! As Rabbi Schroit told me personally, 'This is for real.'"[37] Although a sizeable portion of the membership left the synagogue in response, more strictly observant Orthodox Jews took their places, and the board was able to replace the retired Rabbi Schroit with the kind of rabbi who could attract devout young families.[38]

The larger number of strictly Orthodox residents changed Pico-Robertson in other ways. Orthodox Jews will not use their cars on the Sabbath or permit other Jews to transport them, and they must live within walking distance of the synagogue. In Pico-Robertson, most of the synagogues are located on Pico or Robertson Boulevard. Orthodox Jews moved into Pico-Robertson's approximately one hundred residential blocks filled with single- or two-family houses and two- to four-story apartment buildings; about three-fourths of these are rented units.[39] Wealthier families augmented the original small houses, bought homes in Beverlywood, or rented or bought on adjacent Beverly Hills streets. With the increased demand, housing costs rose. Orthodox Jews became a visible presence on the sidewalks, walking together to and from synagogues, in contrast to the typical Angeleno who travels by car.

In response to the greater halakhic strictness, food businesses opened or reshaped themselves to accommodate kosher needs. Many of the existing food businesses were purchased by immigrants who entered the food trades to supply others from their homeland with familiar tastes. During the 1970s an influx of Israelis opened eateries offering falafel and other Middle Eastern dishes, and Jewish South African immigrants established catering services and opened Pat's. When Persian Jews from Iran moved to western Los Angeles during the 1980s, the number of customers seeking kosher food multiplied. Persian businessmen became proprietors of grocery stores, restaurants, and food import and distribution companies.

It is difficult to determine whether the increased availability of kosher groceries and eateries was a cause or an effect of the stricter *kashrut* standards, since both became evident in the 1980s. Orthodox Jews could no longer justify eating at nonkosher restaurants—even if they limited themselves to vegan food—or eating nonkosher food when there were so many kosher options. In any event, by the late 1980s Pico-Robertson had established its reputation as a kosher food scene. More pharmacies, dry cleaners, tailors, beauty salons, gift shops, repair shops of all kinds, and medical offices appeared, along with wig and clothing stores catering to the modesty standards of Orthodox women. The *mikvah* (ritual pool) was upgraded, and the separate *mikvah* for immersing new kitchen items was built. Pico-Robertson became what urban planners call "a walkable neighborhood": traversable by foot, compact, safe, and filled with physical attractions.[40] Orthodox Jews from all over the city would drive in on Sundays and weekdays for the specialty shops and schools. People began walking in the area because now there was something to walk to.

Occupying just a bit over a square mile, the neighborhood is hammer shaped, the longer part consisting of a narrow length of about two miles with the east-west Pico Boulevard as its central core and a fuller area alongside the north-south Robertson Boulevard. The intersection of Pico and Robertson is near one end. Calling Pico and Robertson "boulevards" is misleading: they actually consist of three lanes in each direction, with the lane closest to the curb usually reserved for parking, and there is no greenery down the middle and little on the sides. During work hours, driving on these streets is a stop-and-go, stuttering progression. Traffic lights halt the flow every two blocks, buses angle in and out of the side lanes, and cars may stop in the driving lane to drop off or pick up passengers or enable them to load up the vehicles' trunks. The only feature that makes these boulevards a bit more inviting than most retail streets is that many sidewalks are twelve to fourteen feet wide and are filled with more than the usual pedestrians who stop and socialize. The area "is neighborhood-y," one woman explained, "and that is unique for L.A. I can walk outside and know people. My husband and I take long walks up Pico and see people we know."[41]

Another physical feature of the area that makes it amenable to living as an Orthodox Jew is the *eruv*, ritual fence, that was created in 2003 around a sixty-mile perimeter of West Los Angeles. The *eruv* provides a ritual boundary that defines the area within as a private space, as if it

Figure 3. Los Angeles *eruv*. "Boundaries," Los Angeles Community Eruv, https://laeruv.com/boundaries/

were a home.[42] The *eruv* is composed mostly of freeway boundaries, fencing, walls, and thin wire strung high up between utility poles. One of the tasks forbidden on the Sabbath and certain holidays is carrying anything or anyone, including a baby, or pushing a stroller or a wheelchair outside of one's home. Circumscribing the Pico-Robertson neighborhood and even beyond, the *eruv* allows those who follow the proscription of carrying on the Sabbath to attend the synagogue with their family, to bring with them those who cannot walk on their own, and to bring food to share with others in the community. As a project of the Orthodox community, it is checked and maintained on an ongoing basis to make sure there are no gaps in it. Its intention is to strengthen the community as a whole, and it does, but there are still some ultra-Orthodox who do not trust that there are no unknown gaps in it.[43]

A description of the Pico-Robertson neighborhood would be incomplete without taking note of the commercial alleyways that form narrow corridors behind its two boulevards. Commercial alleyways are reputed to look ugly and to provide cover for devious and criminal deeds, and no doubt this judgment is accurate for these alleys. But it is certainly not the entire story, for Pico-Robertson's commercial alleyways and back lots also provide essential space and privacy for respected cultural activities. They establish moral boundaries and extend social control into the liminal areas between public and private life.[44] Like commercial alleyways in other US cities, the alleys were originally laid out for utilitarian reasons: trash disposal, sewage and electrical lines, deliveries, private parking, and the like. The back doors serve as an emergency escape route, because the buildings on Pico and Robertson Boulevards butt against each other with no space in between. While the residential blocks have a suburban look—houses with driveways and grassy front yards and backyards, balconies on low apartment buildings, and tree-lined streets—the commercial area is definitely urban and lacks open spaces.

Businesses and synagogues alike have developed ingenious ways to expand their activities into the rear lots. For very little cost, and even before the COVID-19 pandemic prohibited indoor socializing, congregations have utilized their back lot areas for serving refreshments, lunches, and evening meals. They accommodate dozens of people by renting or purchasing event tents, portable tables, and chairs. Some food businesses have added sales areas in the back. One uses its back door to hand over phone orders to customers who pick up their packaged food by driving up through the alley. The back lot of one kosher grocery store is relegated on weekdays to customer parking and a valet service. On Sunday mornings the asphalt is covered with shaded picnic tables and benches, several portable grills, and a counter with beverages and condiments. Latino men in white chef outfits and gloves cut up beef, chicken, fruit, and vegetables; rotate them on kabob skewers; and serve the kabobs to customers. The grocery store remains open, enabling diners and other customers to do their shopping.[45]

The alleyways provide much needed privacy and seclusion in this densely populated area. In response to antisemitic violence, synagogues and Torah study centers began to favor back door entrances, keeping their front facades unmarked while enabling access through the rear for Jewish community insiders. The back entrance to the Los Angeles Mikvah is essential to its design and its mission. Jewish law requires that husband and wife must cease all physical contact during the woman's menstrual period plus another seven days. She then immerses herself in the *mikvah* and the couple can resume physical and sexual contact. Were anyone to see a woman walking in or out of the *mikvah* building, they would know that she and her husband have recently completed at least twelve days of abstinence and will soon have sex. The Los Angeles Mikvah's back door is said to ensure both the privacy and the holiness of the couple's marital life.[46] Furthermore, back door entrances guard women's modesty in another way. A back entrance may keep women out of the close proximity and uncomfortable gaze of the men entering and sitting inside the synagogue.[47] One small storefront synagogue recently took special pains to enhance its back door women's entrance with a decorative and calligraphed Hebrew and English sign.

THE ETHNIC AND RELIGIOUS DIVERSITY OF PICO-ROBERTSON

Orthodox Jewish enclaves such as Pico-Robertson are not homogeneously Orthodox. Ethnic data for the neighborhood shows that 6 percent of the approximately nineteen thousand residents in 2008 were Asian, 6 percent were Black, 7 percent were Latino, and 8 percent were other; so the 74 percent who are white make this region "not especially diverse for Los Angeles."[48] The most commonly reported ancestries were Iranian at 15 percent and Russian at 9 percent, and these people as well as those grouped or identified as "white" were likely to be Jewish. The neighborhood's rate of 34 percent foreign born (37 percent of these were from Iran, 6 percent were from Israel) was average for the city as a whole.[49] There are three non-Jewish centers of worship: St. Mark's Coptic Orthodox Church, St. Mary Magdalene Catholic Church, and Guru Ram Das Sikh Temple. On Christmas Eve, a few houses or apartments on each block are decorated with holiday lights and Christmas trees.[50] Jewish demographic surveys indicate that about half, or ten thousand, of its about nineteen thousand residents are Jewish. While there is no data indicating how these Jewish residents identify themselves, it is likely that more than half consider themselves Orthodox, leaving a significant percentage of Jews who affiliate with non-Orthodox denominations or do not define themselves as religiously Jewish.[51] There is a small nondenominational synagogue and a large Conservative synagogue in the neighborhood, although most of its members live outside Pico-Robertson. The leadership and teaching staff of the Kabbalah Centre on Robertson Boulevard is dominated by Israelis and Jews, but the facility attracts people from many religious backgrounds, and many of them drive there.[52]

Most of the people one encounters on the streets and in the stores, service centers, and offices are not Jewish or Orthodox. Just under half of the eateries on Pico Boulevard are not kosher. These are small businesses or fast-food eateries that likely have only a local clientele or attract customers driving through the neighborhood, unlike the kosher eateries, which draw Jews from the city at large and outside of it. Most residents do not keep the kosher laws. The one supermarket, the small grocery stores, and stores like Walgreens or gas stations with limited groceries sell foods that are unquestionably *treif*. Even the kosher food businesses employ and serve non-Jews. "We would all go broke," the kosher gourmet sausage shop owner told me, "if our partners, customers, and workers were exclusively Jews."[53] Kosher eateries have an overwhelmingly Latino workforce; the kosher grocery stores employ non-Jewish cashiers, stock clerks, and custodians; and guards hired for security purposes are typically not Jewish. Because of the high cost of housing in the neighborhood, these workers likely commute from the more affordable parts of Los Angeles. Non-Jews, whether they are actual neighbors or present in the neighborhood as employees or business owners, are part and parcel of local life—and yet, they are "others." Orthodox norms teach that one should be respectful and friendly to non-Jews, but not close and certainly not intimate. Non-Jews are not potential converts to be befriended for purposes of persuading them to accept Judaism. For centuries Jews have frowned upon proselytizing and have discouraged people who want to become Jewish.

From the Orthodox perspective, humanity consists of two groups: Jews, who are subject to the Torah's laws and have a special bond with God; and non-Jews, who, although they too are God's children, are less treasured by God and less obligated to serve God. According to rabbinic teachings, non-Jews are considered prone to hate Jews, be jealous of them, and persecute them; Orthodox Jews believe that the historical persistence of antisemitism is proof of this. Aside from the safety concern, aloofness from non-Jews is important because their freedom from constraint may tempt devout Jews who wish to be *frai* (free, in Yiddish), and to throw off "the yoke of the Torah." For all these reasons, Jews who wish to live safely and serve God must keep separate from non-Jews and even from Jews who are not committed to Orthodox religious practices. Community norms prevent social mixing. Fidelity to community norms of all types is of paramount importance, and these norms are not always equivalent to religious law. In the Orthodox community as a whole, people watch, assess, encourage, and pressure each other to behave, dress, and voice allegiance to group standards.

Orthodox foodways are designed to build Orthodox separateness and strong boundaries. Orthodox Jews recognize that "for thousands of years of exile, the biblical and rabbinic kosher laws have formed a natural fortress that prevented the assimilation of the Jewish people into many different cultures of the world."[54] The laws of *kashrut* do not merely dictate which animal species may not be eaten; these laws also mandate that only Orthodox slaughterers produce the meat and prevent its mixture with certain foods, and they require that much of the food preparation is in Orthodox hands. The participation of non-Orthodox Jews and non-Jews in the kosher food realm is socially managed so that their visibility is reduced and their dominion is secondary to that of the Jews in charge. Consequently, Orthodox Jews who obey these laws and have non-Jewish friends, neighbors, and relatives will only very rarely sit together with them in a social exchange over food or drink. These restrictions are designed to prevent the level of intimacy and familiarity that could easily lead to Jews imitating the ways of the "others" or inter-marrying with them.

VARIETIES OF ORTHODOX JUDAISM IN PICO-ROBERTSON

Orthodox Jews in the Pico-Robertson neighborhood are not organized as a single religious denomination and have no single leader. A highly frag-mented community in terms of their Orthodox foodways practices and teachings, they support a total of thirty synagogues within this neighbor-hood that includes approximately ten thousand Orthodox Jews. The larg-est groups among them in this neighborhood are Ashkenazic Modern and Centrist Orthodox, Sephardic, Persian, and Chabad Hasidic Jews. What they all share, and what differentiates them from non-Orthodox Jews, is their commitment to obeying *halakhah*, religious law, as defined by rabbis who understand that law to be divinely revealed and faithfully transmitted by previous rabbis. Non-Orthodox Jews such as Conserva-tive, Reform, and Reconstructionist may also follow *halakhah*, but they and their rabbis attribute a far greater human influence to the origin and development of the law, and they tend to regard it appropriate for the individual to decide her own ritual behavior.

Scholars generally claim that there are three types of Orthodox Judaism: Hasidic, Yeshivish, and Modern Orthodox. These three have internal sub-affiliations. However, there are Orthodox groups who do not find these ideological labels relevant to themselves, choosing instead to identify themselves according to their ethnicity and inherited regional traditions. Nevertheless, my description of the Pico-Robertson Ortho-dox starts with these three types.[55]

Hasidic Jews, or Hasidim (literally, "pious people"), trace their spir-itual roots to late eighteenth-century Eastern European rabbinic figures who valued personal piety and experiential devotion more than Talmud study. Their religious philosophies relied heavily upon kabbalistic con-cepts. The leaders, "rebbes," established brotherhoods around themselves for men to engage in intensive religious experiences or to share in the rebbe's piety, hear his teachings and stories, and pray and celebrate with him by sharing food together, singing, and dancing. A devotee aimed to behave in accordance with his rebbe's interpretation of *halakhah* and to adopt mannerisms and behaviors not dictated by Jewish law that signaled loyalty to the rebbe. Prior to the appearance of Hasidic groups, Jewish governance, religious authority, and religious life had been localized within each town, and smaller settlements were, at least theoretically, under the authority of the nearest bigger community. Where Hasidism spread, Hasidic communities crossed communal boundaries.[56]

The Hasidic movement has always been highly decentralized. Variant forms of Hasidism were named according to the locale of the rebbe, such as Satmar Hasidism, founded in 1905 by the rebbe in Sate Mare (as the town in Romania is now called) or the Hasidism of Ger (which originated in Gora Kalwaria, Poland). No matter their internal differences, Hasidim accept the divinity of the Torah and the duty of the Jew to obey *halakhah* as defined by their community. Strongly resistant to rationalist and modern liberal outlooks and deeply committed to raising large families loyal to their inherited traditions, Hasidism has served as a defense against secularism and acculturation. While the surviving remnants of European Hasidim immigrated to the United States and Israel, many Hasidim are ideologically opposed to the concept and actuality of a Jewish state that provides a home for all Jewry within the framework of modern secular law. Distinctive Hasidic men's clothing is also a sign of resistance. On Sabbaths and special occasions, men's outer garments may even signal loyalty to a specific Hasidic heritage. For example, Chabad Hasidic men today can be distinguished by their round, wide-brimmed, black-felt Borsalino hat, the style preferred by the seventh Chabad rebbe.[57]

The Hasidim who live in the Pico-Robertson neighborhood are associated with Chabad, also known as Lubavitch, a name derived from the Lithuanian town in which the earlier rebbes resided. Chabad is best known for its outreach to non-Orthodox Jews, an activity not generally shared by other Hasidic groups. Today, with its headquarters in Crown

Heights, Brooklyn, Chabad sends its emissaries to all parts of the world where Jews are found. Chabad is no longer led by a rebbe; the seventh and last leader of the Lubavitch dynasty, Rabbi Menachem Mendel Schneerson, died in 1994. Nevertheless, it is a very active and creative movement. Schneerson's dedicated followers disseminate his and his predecessors' conviction that God's special love for the Jewish people is expressed in the *mitzvot*, the Torah's commandments, and that Jews must reciprocate this love by joyously performing the laws and teaching them to other Jews. To ensure the continuity of its unique approach, Chabad establishes synagogues, schools, day care centers, youth programs, and charities independent of other Orthodox institutions.

Food and eating are key aspects of Hasidic practice, but Chabad has made foodways pivotal. When the seventh Lubavitcher rebbe made religious outreach to nonreligious Jews a central component of the Chabad mission, feeding others became an important tool of outreach. He elevated to a very high level the mitzvah of hospitality performed by individual Chabad Hasidim—in particular, inviting Jews, including nonreligious ones, to Sabbath and holiday meals. He described this as an act of love toward God and toward the guest, whose soul would be uplifted in joy and who would be moving closer to becoming a devoted servant of God. Even outside the context of hospitality, however, he taught that there is great spiritual power in a Jew's recital of the proper Hebrew blessing over kosher food (a short phrase even Jews uneducated in Judaism or Hebrew language can master). The act of blessing and eating the food infuses the food with holiness, helps "repair" the world, and makes one a partner with God.[58] Chabad synagogues and emissaries excel at bringing disparate Jews together to share food. This book's next chapters describe some kosher laws specific to Chabad and demonstrate the role of Chabad foodways in preserving and increasing the number of community members.

A different type of Orthodox Judaism opposed Hasidism, and this type also makes itself felt in the Pico-Robertson neighborhood. The Hasidim called their challengers Misnagdim (opponents), but today this sector of Orthodox Jewry identifies itself as Litvish (Lithuanian, where the earliest leaders resided) or Yeshivish (from the word *yeshiva*), after the values embodied by this institution. The yeshiva was a new kind of school that arose in early nineteenth-century czarist White Russia. An elitist academy serving large numbers of intellectually promising older teenagers and unmarried young men, it was independent of the local Jewish community and was supported financially by outside donors. The head of the yeshiva and his professional teaching staff, all of whom were Talmud scholars, created an insular environment that enabled the study of Torah for its own sake. This approach to Torah study, in which it did not serve as a means to earn a living later, permitted them to ensure students' proper behavior and, in some yeshivas, to nurture the students' personal religious development. In contrast to Hasidism, these institutions promoted a more sober and exacting religiosity and fostered a more rationalistic approach that, nevertheless, fortified its followers against secularism.[59]

This sector of Ashkenazic Orthodox Jewry managed to recreate itself after World War II in Israel and the United States. A Lithuanian-style yeshiva was established in New York at the start of the twentieth century, but more followed in the 1930s when yeshiva students and teachers fled Nazism and after World War II.[60] The heads of the important yeshivas in New York, Baltimore, and Lakewood, New Jersey, wield their influence not only by shaping students but also by establishing halakhic rulings regarding their standards for *kashrut*, clothing, prayer, Shabbat holiday observance, and so on. They make public pronouncements that promote conservative values and disdain for Zionism, feminism, and much of modern culture. Yeshiva graduates marry and raise large families in Orthodox communities around the country, where they are respected for their Torah knowledge.

While the greatest concentration of Yeshivish Jews in Los Angeles resides in the Beverly–La Brea neighborhood, people who call themselves Yeshivish dominate the teaching staffs and full-time student population of the Pico-Robertson kollels. Local religious Iranian Jews respect rabbis trained in the Lithuanian-style yeshivas. Despite not being Ashkenazic, these graduates have successfully inculcated Yeshivish values alongside pride in their Persian Jewish heritage. Yeshivish men and women overwhelmingly make up the Judaic studies teachers in the Pico-Robertson non-Hasidic religious schools, even those schools whose student body consists mainly of Modern and Centrist Orthodox families. They, along with Hasidic Jews, hold the positions of *kashrut* agency inspectors, who examine the inventories and operating procedures in the local kosher restaurants, fast-food eateries, catering companies, and grocery stores.

The label "Modern Orthodox" refers to Orthodox Jews who see great value in modern, secular culture and wish to participate in it while faithfully adhering to *halakhah* and Torah values. They believe a balance is possible. Within this group, individuals and congregations can be situated on a spectrum from those who enthusiastically engage in secular academic learning and partake of secular literature, entertainment, and the arts to those who are more cautious and selective with regard to these activities. In this book, I use the term "Centrist Orthodox" for those on the cautious end of the Modern Orthodox spectrum, who accept a maximalist interpretation of *halakhah* closest to the rulings of Yeshivish rabbis; some define themselves as a combination of Modern and/or Centrist Orthodox and Yeshivish. People who prefer the term "centrist" explain that it implies the *proper* balance, in contrast to those on the other end of the spectrum, who, in their eyes, have gone too far by embracing feminism, associating too closely with non-Jews and non-Orthodox Jews, and devoting too little time to Torah study and the performance of the commandments. Yet even the local congregations that define themselves as Modern Orthodox do not agree on fundamental issues; for example, one hired a woman rabbi, and another went on record declaring the illegitimacy of ordaining women as rabbis.[61] Within a single congregation there may be deep-seated divisions. Yet in the Pico-Robertson neighborhood a significant number of families in the Modern-Centrist Orthodox cohort are comfortable in and even pay membership dues to more than one congregation.

The high economic status of Modern Orthodox Jews is a factor in their ability to enjoy and support Pico-Robertson's kosher food culture. According to the data collected in the 2013 Pew Research Forum Survey of US Jews, there are minimal differences among Jewish denominations with regard to annual household incomes, but Modern Orthodox Jews are the wealthiest cohort: 37 percent of self-identified Modern Orthodox Jews report an annual household income of $150,000 or higher (Reform Jews are the next highest group, with 29 percent reporting their earnings at that level). Of course, there are Modern Orthodox who are needy: 30 percent of Modern Orthodox earn household incomes of $50,000 or less, compared to 43 percent of other Orthodox Jews.[62] Yet this means that many Modern Orthodox families have the means to patronize kosher restaurants, cafés, and fast-food eateries; engage kosher caterers for their celebrations; and invite guests to eat at their well-laden Sabbath and holiday tables. Although kosher meat is far more expensive than nonkosher, it is also far more available today in comparison to past eras. Certainly this is a factor in explaining why contemporary American Orthodox rabbis, in contrast to those of the past, agree that meat consumption is essential for honoring the Sabbath and the joy of sacred festivals.[63]

The labels Hasidic, Yeshivish, and Modern Orthodox are not necessarily pertinent or relevant within the lives of many Orthodox Jews. Consequently, the ideological and behavioral distinctions outlined above are not always determinative of congregational affiliation. In Pico-Robertson, Jews who identify by their non-Ashkenazi identity—Persian, French, Yemenite, Mizrachi ("eastern")—have established ethnically identified congregations. Theoretically, the congregations are open to all, and some are noticeably from multiple communities. Also, non-Ashkenazi Jews are members of Ashkenazi and other congregations. There are congregations that cater to *ba'alei teshuvah*, in which prayer leaders and many of the congregants are "veteran" Orthodox Jews who enjoy giving support to and being collegial with the newly religious. The kollels may open their regular daily communal prayers to outsiders. There are congregations organized to distinctive worship styles, like the Happy Minyan's melodious and extended singing, and there is a congregation for young marrieds of Sephardic and Mizrachi ancestry.

Anyone may walk into any of these synagogues for prayer and Torah lectures and for *simhahs* (common plural form of the Hebrew *semahot*, meaning joyous events like a Bar Mitzvah or wedding-related events).

The Hebrew word for synagogue, *beit keneset*, means "house of assembly," and synagogues are social institutions and not simply places of prayer. Furthermore, social gathering and prayer are conflated. For example, although males age thirteen and older can pray individually or at a private home with nine other men, thus forming a *minyan* of ten men, the minimum number required for communal prayer and Torah chanting, such prayer is considered less than ideal because it is a withdrawal from the larger community.[64]

As I have shown, a common way of differentiating Orthodox Jews according to the strictness with which they fulfill Jewish law is inadequate. Neither Hasidic nor Yeshivish Orthodoxy can be compared on this basis. There are Modern Orthodox Jews who feel justified in asserting that their stance, which appears to be the most lenient, is actually the strictest in adhering to Jewish law because it rejects the newer, extreme, and extraordinary rules added by Hasidism and high-demand Orthodoxy. Furthermore, Jewish law and Jewish tradition have never been monolithic; already centuries ago there were deep differences between Jewish religious communities based on conceptual outlooks, regional customs, and the tendency of some groups to emphasize particular Torah commandments more than others. In the words of a scholar of modern-era Jewry, "There is no single characteristic by which Orthodox groups can be compared to one another."[65] They must be differentiated not only by religious outlook and halakhic stances but also by sociological and behavioral features. Examining Orthodox communities according to their foodways, as I am doing in this volume, highlights the variations as well as the shared elements of their religious outlooks and daily experiences.

2

Proper Food, Proper Jews

"Will you eat in my home? I won't serve you anything I cook in my kitchen, and I do keep kosher, but not like you—your rules are more complicated," I said to a new friend who is Orthodox. "What are you talking about?" he responded. "I keep kosher, period. There are no 'multiple versions' of *kashrut*!" I knew better. I'm not Orthodox, but I keep kosher, and I knew there were differences in our standards.

The most obvious one was his practice of eating only *yashan* (old) grains and grain products. This little-known restriction is based on the biblical command to bring an offering from the springtime barley harvest to the priest before consuming the rest of the crop. Leviticus 23:14 states, "You shall not eat bread or flour made from parched grain or new grain, until this very day, until you bring your God's sacrifice." It was understood that the barley offering "gives God His due," and, thus, all the newly harvested grains—barley, wheat, spelt, rye, and oats—were rendered old, that is, permissible to eat. But when it was no longer possible to bring a barley offering after the cessation of the sacrificial system in 70 CE, how could Jews eat grains? Did this law apply to grains grown outside the Land of Israel? There were multiple answers, but eventually the medieval Ashkenazic consensus was that the restriction could be waived for Jews living in Europe, where the short growing season would make the restriction onerous.[1]

My friend is an independent-minded Ashkenazic Jew attentive to the rulings of yeshiva rabbis, and some of them recently declared that the leniency no longer applies. He found their reasoning compelling, and he explained why he found the rule meaningful: "We don't want to eat our produce until we have first offered it to God. I figure it's like a husband not biting into the Shabbat challah [braided Sabbath bread] until his wife gets a piece first!" Now, challenging his claim that there were not multiple ways of keeping kosher, I reminded him about his practice of eating only *yashan*. He responded, "Yes, I forgot about that, but if you want, you can find *yashan* at some Pico Boulevard bakeries." We agreed I would serve a simple late afternoon Sabbath meal, the "third meal" of the Sabbath.

Today, when there is a long time between grain harvest and the production of flour and manufacturers print the production dates on the packaging, people can ascertain whether the flour is permissible according to the stricture of *yashan*. The vast majority of flour sold in stores is *yashan*. The prohibition was regarded both by Rabbi Karo, the Sephardic author of the *Shulḥan arukh*, and by Rabbi Isserles, the author of the Ashkenazi glosses on the *Shulḥan arukh*, to apply to grains produced even outside the Land of Israel. The latter authority, however, ruled leniently, suspending the requirement, because of the onerousness of the restriction. Some argued that the date of harvest could not be ascertained. Currently there are no doubts: US labeling regulations require the harvest date to be noted on packaging, and many other countries require this too.

Prior to the Sabbath I bought rolls and cookies at a *yashan* bakery and cold salads at the kosher grocery. My friend walked over on Sabbath afternoon and we talked for hours, and then I said, "Let's eat."

"I can't," he responded. "It's too late in the day. The sun has already set, and because we didn't start eating the third meal before sunset, we have to wait to eat after Shabbat is over. But I won't have time to wait here—I have to go elsewhere." Later that night, contemplating the untouched foods, I wondered if this had been his way of not eating in my home.

The system of *kashrut* does far more than dictate what one may or may not eat. *Kashrut* exercises a powerful unifying force. It binds Orthodox Jews together into a separate community. Despite the minor variations in kosher practice that prevent some Orthodox Jews from eating each other's foods, Orthodox Jews know that they are the only segment of American Jewry that takes these food laws seriously. Only they can be trusted to prepare kosher food. Because the dietary laws are taught as decrees with no obvious rationale or health benefits, these stringent demands make one's adherence a matter of religious devotion and group membership. Members who disobey the rules or who are suspected of disobedience are kept at a distance.

This chapter will explain the system of *kashrut* in its social and historical contexts, highlighting its function in community formation and continuance. Examples of contemporary practices are drawn from the United States in general and Los Angeles in particular. I am following the lead of anthropologists in showing the importance of foodways for community maintenance.

Kosher is a Hebrew adjective that means "proper," and today it applies to food that meets the standards set by Jewish religious law and custom. *Kashrut* or *kashrus*,[2] the word designating the food rules as a whole, has at its core three dietary demands: the sort of fish, land animals, and fowl that may be consumed; the way these creatures and other nonmeat foods are to be prepared for consumption; and the prohibition against mixing meat with milk products. According to Jewish tradition, these rules are a divine mandate from God's revelation at Mount Sinai meant only for Jews. Some details were first enumerated in the book of Leviticus 11:2–45, where the application of the laws and the holiness associated with them are explicit:

> The Lord spoke to Moses and Aaron, saying, "Speak to the children
> of Israel, and say 'These are the beasts you may eat, of all the animals
> that are on the land . . . but this you shall not eat. . . . For I am the Lord
> who has brought you up from the land of Egypt to be for you a God,
> and you shall be holy, for I am holy.'"

Yet the system of *kashrut* is far more than the several prohibitions found in Leviticus or elsewhere in the Bible. The postbiblical rabbis, whose teachings were first written in the Mishnah and Talmud between the first and sixth century CE, provided hundreds of details not included in the Bible. They also insisted that even if the ingredients were proper, foods prepared by outsiders (idolaters, Gentiles, or even Jews who did not accept rabbinic authority) were not considered kosher. Even properly prepared foods were not to be eaten in social settings with outsiders. Anthropologists call these "commensal rules," that is, norms that establish with whom one may eat.[3] Anthropologists have long recognized that sharing food leads to social intimacy; eating together with other groups of people is a necessary first step toward conjugal relations with them. The laws of *kashrut* block this first step. The rabbis lived at a time and in an environment where Jews were a demographic and religious minority highly vulnerable to cultural assimilation. They explicitly linked eating with people of other religions to forbidden relations: the Talmud succinctly explains that such activities are forbidden "because of their daughters" or "because of marriage."[4] For the Orthodox Jews, religious endogamy, that is, marrying another Orthodox Jew, is crucial for perpetuating and ensuring the future of their religious group and its practices. Intermarriage was considered to lead directly to the Jew violating Torah laws, and it was a grave offense in and of itself. The rabbis assumed that an intermarried couple cannot reproduce Torah-observant Jewish offspring. In biological terms, the Jew would not be perpetuating the species.

Demographic data on American Jews certainly shows a correlation between keeping kosher and maintaining tight community bonds. According to 2013 research data, less than 14 percent of non-Orthodox Jews say they keep kosher, 50 percent are married to non-Jews, and less than 27 percent say all or most of their friends are Jewish. In stark contrast, about 83 to 98 percent of Orthodox Jews say they keep kosher, almost all—98 percent—married Orthodox Jews have Jewish spouses, and about 84 percent say that most or all of their friends are Jewish.[5] Obviously, Orthodox Jews are a socially insular group. A local Orthodox rabbi explained the role of *kashrut* in achieving such a tight-knit group: "*Kashrus* helps define our identity as a community. It promotes togetherness and keeps our people close."

Although *kashrut* differentiates its practitioners from people who do not keep kosher, it does not mean that everyone in the community practices the same way. Variations were already in place when the first rabbis were synthesizing both the recorded biblical laws and the oral teachings they believed were passed down from Moses, and more have been added over the centuries. Such variations in religious beliefs and practices over time are characteristic of lived religion, as described by David Hall, Robert Orsi, and Nancy Ammerman.[6] In many cases, the variants remain permitted practices and are understood to originate in authentic traditions passed down from teacher to disciple or from regional and ancestral norms. Rabbinic disciples are expected to follow and teach the traditions of their respective teachers.[7] The food prepared in accordance with the permitted variant traditions is still kosher, although it should not be eaten unless it is part of one's own tradition. Holders of different traditions may socialize at the table and marry into each other's families. Among the Orthodox today, there are diverse ways to keep kosher to the extent that some might not eat in the homes of other Orthodox Jews or they would do so only after some negotiation or agreement to serve only certain foods. My friend who honors the *yashan* rule warns his hosts ahead of time so that they serve *yashan* foods, or he eats selectively at their table so as not to violate his principles.

One cannot simply place the dietary practices of different groups of Orthodox on a spectrum from most strict to most liberal. For example, the Orthodox communities that are the most stringent in some aspects of *kashrut* do not concern themselves with *yashan* grains. Neither is avoidance of new grains a practice of Orthodox Jews who share the same extent of cultural insularity. One might think it should be honored more by Sephardic Jews, whose medieval rabbinic authorities never waived the restriction, but they do not generally appear to care about the rule. Rather, it appears to be honored by those who align themselves with the yeshiva rabbis who insist on it as well as others who have heard about and find value in the practice.

Today, as in the past, religious law is not found by referring to biblical verses. Rather, a person relies on the opinion of a rabbi or an elder.

Even for rabbis, the starting point is not the Pentateuch (Torah) but post-biblical writings. The classical writings are the Mishnah, additional early legal statements called *Tosefta*, and a few hundred years of commentary called *Gemara*. These three sources were published together as the Jerusalem Talmud in the fifth century CE and the Babylonian Talmud in the seventh century CE.[8] Within this corpus, the most authoritative laws are Torah laws—the term for these in Aramaic is *d'oraita*—which consist of the rabbis' renderings of Pentateuchal laws and the orally transmitted traditions believed to have originated with God's revelations to Moses. The rabbis defined a second category of law of their own making called *derabbanan*, meaning "from the rabbis," that is, of lesser authority than Torah laws. Some rabbinic laws are "fences around the Torah," that is, supplementary prohibitions guarding against the violation of Torah laws. Some are statutes that have no direct biblical basis but were promulgated for other reasons, such as the concern to keep Jews socially separate from non-Jews.[9]

The Talmud is a scholastic text that presents fundamental principles and legal reasoning but does not, however, actually present practical law, *halakhah*. For that, one consults a law code or, more likely, asks a rabbi, who will adopt the decision of the man he regards as the prevailing rabbinic authority and ties his opinion back to a code of Jewish law. Codes state clearly how a Jew ought to behave and how a community should function. The most widely respected code today is the sixteenth-century *Shulḥan arukh*. Its Sephardic author, Rabbi Joseph Caro, summarized the *halakhah* that prevailed in his circles, and the code was published with a commentary by Rabbi Moses Isserles, a leading Polish Ashkenazic scholar, whose views were influenced by his own non-Sephardic community's norms. The *Shulḥan arukh* eventually was accepted as a decisive guide for all Jewry, with a Sephardic or Ashkenazic option.[10] Its precedents and structure were the basis for halakhic codes for later centuries—for example, the nineteenth-century codes *Mishnah berurah* and *Arukh hashulḥan*, relied upon by Ashkenazi Orthodox rabbis; *Shulḥan arukh harav*, attributed to the first Chabad rebbe; or the twentieth-century *Yalkut Yosef* code, widely respected by Sephardic rabbis. Despite these divisions, the leading *poskim* (singular, *posek*)—rabbis who specialize in making decisions about practical law—communicate or take account of each other's rulings. They wish to keep Jewish practice relatively uniform across Jewry's different ethnic groups and Orthodox sub-affiliations in order to avoid the evolution of different "species" of Torah-observant Jews.

Rabbis did not always lead the way in expanding or modifying *kashrut*. We can assume—and in some cases rabbinic texts admit this—that some of today's *kashrut* rules originated in women's application of them in their homes. Many of these practices were later affirmed by rabbinic authorities as obligatory *halakhah*.[11] Women purchased and made food for the household, and they learned from other women—not from husbands or rabbis—how to perform many of the laws dealing with food preparation. This is still the case. Some common practices did not gain the status of law and are simply labeled as *minhag*, or custom. These are usually associated with variations stemming from a regional norm. Custom is less authoritative than Torah or rabbinic law, although some customs may be considered obligatory.[12] When serious food needs arise or at times of crisis, rabbis may justify ignoring both rabbinic injunction and custom. In matters of life and death, they insist that the Torah laws of *kashrut* may be violated, too. Torah laws cannot be changed, so the changes in *kashrut* over the centuries—the additions, variations, and preventative measures—are in the category of custom and rabbinic law. More recently, community standards have been altered by the kosher certification agencies, which are innovations of the twentieth century. Mass migrations have brought diverse traditions together within a community or produced new syntheses. Additionally, larger cultural factors may play a role, such as when modern principles of hygiene are conflated with the idea of kosher. Some Jews and non-Jews, for example, think that kosher foods are healthier or that the rabbinic supervision assures a higher standard of cleanliness in packaging facilities.[13]

In sum, today's *kashrut* is the result of a centuries-old layering of traditions, and only some of these are actual *halakhah*, practical Jewish law. Orthodox Judaism is not the same as halakhic Judaism. Being recognized as an upstanding Orthodox Jew by other Orthodox Jews necessitates conforming to community norms whether or not they are dictated by *halakhah*. When I asked my interviewees how they choose between diverse *kashrut* standards, they—including the rabbis—responded, "I do what others in my community do." I learned that congregational rabbis and their wives do not formally teach *kashrut* to their congregants, even in the counseling sessions required for couples about to marry. "My congregants know what to do," they tell me. The rabbis will answer specific *kashrut* questions from congregants, and they will establish the *kashrut* policy for foods served in their synagogues, but even in these cases they are likely to insist upon community standards rather than what they believe *halakhah* actually requires. Classes on *kashrut* for newly observant Jews, which are offered in outreach synagogues and organizations, are typically taught by women (non-rabbis) to other women, with minimal direct rabbinic involvement. The subject is taught in the schools, with the greatest attention paid to the subject at the high school level for girls. Most Orthodox Jews know very little about the fine distinctions in Jewish law and custom described above, yet they tend to label their congregational standard as *halakhah*.

Over the centuries, community standards have fluctuated between stringency and laxity, even within the same community. Observers note a shift since the 1980s in Orthodox practice in the West toward greater strictness regarding *kashrut* and Orthodox practice as a whole. Earlier leniencies have been rejected and abandoned stringencies have become the norm. Academic scholars have offered theories explaining the phenomenon, and many are quite convincing.[14] Additionally, I suggest here that the greater selectivity is a natural response—in biological terms this would be called an adaptation—to the abundance of kosher food and the ease in acquiring it; that is, proper eating must be "costly" so as to demonstrate the value of the practitioner relative to others. This response could likely occur among those who follow the *halakhah* stringently, who wish to exhibit serious devotion to God and choose to do so by adopting more challenging food standards.

THE COMPONENTS OF KEEPING KOSHER

It is easiest to comprehend the scope of the dietary laws when they are divided according to their three components: the type of fish, land animals, and fowl that may be consumed; food preparation; and the separation of meat and milk ingredients.

Prohibited Species and Foods: Animals

The most obvious deprivation a kosher diet imposes is the restricted number of animal, bird, and fish species that may be consumed. These prohibitions originally appeared in the Pentateuch with no explanation. Prohibited animals are simply designated as *tamei*, a term indicating ritual unfitness that is commonly and erroneously translated as "unclean." The term *tahor*, often translated as "pure" or "clean," refers to the permissible category. Today the terms for prohibited creatures and food are *asur* (forbidden) and *treif* (literally, "torn apart"), as in animals found dead and therefore forbidden, but today "*treif*" refers to any nonkosher food. The rabbis did not supply reasons either; they simply described these Torah laws as inscrutable divine decrees. Later

Components of *kashrut*

- prohibited animals of the land, sky, and sea
- foods prohibited by agricultural and priestly laws
- food preparation
- no mixing of meat with milk

FIGURE 4. Components of *kashrut*

Prohibited animals of the land, sky, and sea

- mammals that do not chew their cud or have cleft hooves
- some bird species
- sea animals lacking fins and scales, such as shellfish, octopus, eel
- amphibians and insects

FIGURE 5. Prohibited animals of the land, sky, and sea

commentators attributed symbolic and ethical interpretations for the animal categories while humbly admitting that these were merely conjectural. Academic scholars over the last century have advanced compelling theories for these taboos.[15] Orthodox Jews today, both rabbis and laypersons, affirm the opacity of the dietary laws and adamantly reject ethical rationales and academic theories alike as merely human inventions.

Meat has been the most frequently tabooed category of food in cultures worldwide and across time, and prohibitions around meat make up most of the laws of *kashrut*.[16] The food limitations in Jewish law began with the Hebrew Bible's list of prohibited and permitted species of animals that live on land and in water and that fly. The permitted land species are mammals that chew their cud and have hooves completely cloven into two. These animals, by definition, are herbivores. Postbiblical rabbis listed the actual species that were permitted: cattle, goats, sheep, deer, bison, gazelles, antelope, ibex, addax, and giraffe. Their milk is permitted, too. Unacceptable are pigs, camels, horses, rabbits, squirrels and other rodents, monkeys, bears, marsupials, dogs, cats, and the many other land animals that neither chew their cud nor possess fully cloven hooves. Regarding animals that live in the water, only those with fins and scales are permitted. Missing from the kosher diet are all shellfish, eel, octopus, and sea mammals, such as whale and dolphin. Prohibited also are all reptiles, amphibians, rodents, and insects, although four species of locust are permitted.[17]

Birds are more complicated. Because the Bible does not mention specific attributes for permitted birds but merely lists twenty-four prohibited species and subspecies, the Talmudic rabbis taught that all birds *not* on that list are permitted. The problem is that it is sometimes difficult to associate the named birds with actual species. The rabbis' conclusion was that a questionable bird was permitted only if regional tradition allowed it. In other words, from this early date, variations of *kashrut* among Jews could prevent shared eating.[18] There was consensus that most varieties of chicken, duck, geese, sparrow, and doves were permitted. Prohibited birds included ravens, eagles, vultures, hawks, falcons, owls, pelicans, and storks. However, the status of birds such as pheasant, peacock, guinea hen, some varieties of quail, and swan was not clear, and so these were only permitted if local tradition allowed it. Turkey, a New World species, was included in the dubious category for some time until a consensus permitting it was reached, although there are still some Orthodox communities that will not eat it.[19] Whether the milk and eggs of a species are permitted or prohibited depends on the status of the animal.

Kosher food production companies today provide a wide variety of permitted meat and fish. Stores with a kosher clientele, like those in Pico-Robertson but also in other parts of Los Angeles, offer fresh, frozen, packaged, and precooked kosher meat and fish foods. The premier Pico-Robertson kosher butcher shop sells beef, lamb, veal, turkey, chicken, and bison in dozens of different cuts and grinds. Sushi has become quite popular among local Orthodox Jews. The five neighborhood kosher sushi bars offer tuna, salmon, yellowtail, and sea bass but not octopus, eel, or shellfish. Jews who keep kosher in Pico-Robertson know that they are especially well-off in terms of variety. "You can find anything you want in the neighborhood," they say. At least locally, Orthodox Jews do not admit to feeling deprived by their diet.

There are also kosher versions of explicitly prohibited meats and fish. The Pico-Robertson kosher sushi shops offer imitation crab and imitation shrimp made from pulverized white fish or pollack mixed with starch and seasonings. The kosher Chinese restaurant offers dozens of familiar westernized Chinese specialties, such as mu shu dishes, made with chicken, beef, or vegetarian ingredients. A "bacon" chipotle sauce was served at the local kosher Mexican restaurant.[20] Enjoying such foods, when they are clearly kosher, confers no shame upon the consumer, although some might hesitate to serve them at Sabbath and holiday meals. The existence of these options raises the question of how the consumer knows whether the imitation is close to the original, unless he or she had actually previously tasted the forbidden foods, or whether these imitation foods are a result of the presence of the newly Orthodox Jews in the neighborhood who long for their old favorites. Yet, this phenomenon is not at all new: the Babylonian Talmud and later rabbinic rulings report Jews simulating *treif* food options out of innocent curiosity. The rabbis permitted kosher versions as long as the kosher status is made obvious to onlookers, thus preserving people's reputations and the honor due to the law.[21]

Prohibited Sacred and Profane Nonanimal Foods

There are foods limited by Jewish law whose restriction is not, technically speaking, about what is kosher or not. Because they are currently considered in kosher certification, I include these foods here. These rules stem from ancient Israel's agricultural produce tithes owed to the poor and managed through the priests and Levites, who administered sacrificial worship rites. Because they are Torah laws explicitly written in the Pentateuch, the rules cannot simply be abandoned but must be either temporarily suspended or substituted with analogous practices that fit a post-priestly religious system. These food practices remind American

Jews that they are not residing in their divinely promised land and are still awaiting the coming of the Messiah. They signal the exceptional status of Jews demographically and geographically.

These five food restrictions relate to agricultural practices in the Land of Israel. They originated in the Pentateuch, and the postbiblical rabbis expanded them to pertain to other contexts.[22] First, the entirety of one's fruit crop is proscribed unless a tithe (*ma'aser* [tenth] or *terumah* [gift]) is donated to the priests and the poor; the prohibited crops—those that did not have the *ma'aser* or *terumah* separated from it—are called *tevel*. Second, newly harvested grains are permitted only if a portion of them was included in the springtime *omer* sacrifice (this is the *yashan* rule). According to rabbinic law, this applied to barley, oats, rye, spelt, and wheat.[23] Third, fruits from the first three years of a tree's production (*orlah*) may not be eaten, only picked and discarded or left on the tree

Foods restricted by agricultural and priestly laws

- crops that were not tithed
- grains from which *omer* was not sacrificed
- first three years' fruit tree produce
- sabbatical year farmed products
- crops from a mixture of seeds
- crops grown too close to grapes

FIGURE 6. Foods restricted by agricultural and priestly laws

for birds and animals. Fourth, during the seventh, sabbatical year, agricultural fields are to lie fallow, and one may eat only plants that grow of their own accord. In addition, the produce at the corners of the field must be left for the poor, and the poor may take the gleanings left by the harvesters. After the cessation of sacrificial worship and the migration of most Jews to lands outside of biblical Israel, rabbis debated whether these prohibitions are still obligatory, whether they apply to food outside of the Land of Israel or produced by non-Jews, and whether new adaptations should be practiced.

Except for the law on tithing for the poor, which was transformed into the general obligation for Jews everywhere to give at least one-tenth of their income to charity, most of these food laws today are considered obligatory in a modified form only in the State of Israel. Jews who lived outside the territory of ancient Israel may not have had access to these foods and were likely not farmers.[24]

In terms of Israeli-grown fruit, vegetables, and nuts, American Orthodox rabbis advise that it is best to purchase them only when the food bears a stamp of approval by Israeli rabbinic authorities.[25] Otherwise, America's predominant kosher certification agency, Orthodox Union, warns, "it may not be eaten, just as one may not eat any non-kosher food." American Jews who have an abundance of regionally grown fruits, vegetables, and nuts—such as those who live in the Pico-Robertson neighborhood—can avoid this difficulty. Yet the Orthodox Union argues that the strong tie between Orthodox Jews and the Israeli state precludes a blanket prohibition:

> It would be unfortunate if Jewish consumers, believing this separation to be a complicated procedure, declined to purchase Israeli produce. There is no need to withhold this revenue from the Israeli economy. In truth, the actual procedure is a simple one and can be mastered in but a few moments of time.

Yet the formula to be recited is a complex one: an eight-step procedure that includes making a mathematical calculation, separating minute portions of food from the whole, reciting a text, and discarding a separated, wrapped portion of both a small portion of the food and a coin.[26] Orthodox Jews who enact this are expressing their self-identity as foreigners residing outside their natural habitat. They are compensating for the loss of sacrificial worship and acknowledging that loss as a spiritual deficit.

Preparation of Food for Consumption: Meat

Acquiring the proper species and permitted nonanimal foods is the first step in preparing food for consumption but hardly sufficient. Before consuming meat or fowl, the animal must be properly killed. An animal must be dead before it is eaten, but it must be deliberately put to death by a devout Jew following a specified procedure. Carrion—that is, an animal found dead because it was killed by another animal, by an accident, or by disease—is prohibited. For millennia, Jewish law has prohibited killing animals for food by hunting them. The kosher mode of killing animals for food, then, differs markedly from the methods used by most people and, in particular, by animals. Defenders of kosher meat production often make a special point to highlight this difference. They declare that

Food preparation rules: meat and fowl

- *shehitah*
- inspection and selection
- removing blood and specific animal parts
- salting, rinsing, and roasting

FIGURE 7. Food preparation rules: meat and fowl

their mode of killing animals elevates them and suppresses the animalistic elements within the human personality.[27]

Biblical texts say unequivocally that whether the animal is designated for sacrificial worship or for profane consumption, it must be intact before slaughter. The postbiblical sages clarified that the animal cannot have broken bones, be castrated, or have serious wounds or diseases, and it must be fully conscious.[28] Disqualified animals may be given or sold for food to non-Jews because they have no obligation to follow these rules. This is the first of many instances within the dietary laws that involve the outsider in food matters while keeping oneself separate from them.[29]

The blood of the animal is prohibited. Although the text of the Hebrew Bible describes this taboo as a universal prohibition, rabbinic tradition regards it as a Torah law incumbent only upon Jews.[30] There is no suggestion that the reason for this is the unhealthfulness of the blood; rather, the blood is considered the life of an animal and therefore reserved for God alone. The concern for eliminating blood from meat perhaps dictates the method of animal slaughter first fully described in postbiblical writings. In the process called *shehitah*, the animal's major neck artery must be neatly severed, a procedure enabling the quick draining of much of the animal's blood onto the ground.[31] *Shehitah* is required for birds and land animals but not for fish, for which no manner of killing is specified. During *shehitah*, the animal needs to be restrained in a position that enables the proper cut. The slaughterer, *shohet*, utters a short prayer and then kills the animal. The *bodek*, a supervising *shohet* or expert in the procedure, watches to see that five disqualifying knife actions spelled out in medieval law codes do not occur: hesitating, pressuring, digging, slipping, and tearing. Done properly, there will be a massive outflow of blood and the animal's nerve center in the brain will shut down; that is, the animal would suffer very little, if any, pain. *Shehitah* certainly sounds like it might be the least painful mode of slaughter, and medieval commentators explained that the compassionate concern for animals and the desire to drain the blood lay behind the commandment. However, because there is no explicit biblical statement about animal pain while killing it for food, rabbinic authorities did not consider animal pain when they determined whether *shehitah* occurred properly. The rabbis of the Talmud taught that there are categories of commandments for which the reason is impossible to fathom, and the dietary laws are among these, although they agreed that the rules were for the benefit of all God's creatures.[32] The rabbis acknowledged that the animal may suffer pain during the process, but this is permitted as long as it is considered necessary for the final procurement of the meat. The question of what is necessary and what is not has been a subject of passionate debate within the Orthodox community and certainly outside of it.[33] In today's industrialized agriculture, prolonged suffering occurs when animals are raised in factory farms, with all the conditions that this entails, and during the handling and positioning of the animal prior to the slaughter, far more so than during the actual knife cut of *shehitah*. However, Orthodox rabbis do not consider the pain suffered during the animal's life or during *shehitah* as a factor in *kashrut* as long as the animal is intact prior to slaughter. This unwillingness to prioritize or even consider animal pain in the determination of kosher meat differentiates the Orthodox from the non-Orthodox advocates of an ethical *kashrut*.

Rabbinic law dictated that the slaughterer must be Jewish, pious in behavior, and trained.[34] The *shohet* was typically male. In rabbinic texts there was no explicit prohibition on women slaughterers, but historically we know that informally trained women and men in rural areas did this work too.[35] The requirement for Jewish status was not based on the assumption that the non-Jew is ignorant or untrustworthy, for even one fully conversant with the law or under the direct guidance of a knowledgeable Jew cannot slaughter a permitted animal according to the rules. This is a social, preparer-based rule: the identity of the person in control of the food helps determine final status of the food, and the non-Jew by definition cannot render the meat kosher. Meat slaughtered by a non-Jew is prohibited and deemed carrion, as if killed by other animals or disease. Non-Jews may *assist* Jewish slaughterers, and historically they often did so. However, if they play more than a secondary role, for example, by pushing the animal's head toward the slaughterer's knife, the meat is not kosher. When meat production was industrialized in twentieth-century America, requiring many laborers to ensure the efficient quick slaughter of numerous animals, the involvement of non-Jews increased too. One responsibility of the kosher supervisor is to ensure that the actual slaughtering occurs at the hands of the Jewish slaughterer.[36]

There was general agreement about the method of slaughter until the modern era. A major schism over meat appeared within the Eastern European rabbinate in the mid-1700s with the rise of the Hasidic movement. Hasidic rabbis insisted that *shehitah* was valid only if the *shohet* used a honed knife rather than the forged kind of knife that had been the norm. The customary knife is forged, that is, made from a single bar of metal that is heated and pounded into shape. It is not very flexible but keeps its edge for a long time. The alternative is a blade cut out from a large sheet of metal and honed, or sharpened, and heat treated. This kind of blade has a sharper edge but gets nicked more easily, and a nicked blade will produce an invalid cut.[37] Even though the sharper honed knife potentially enables a cleaner and deeper cut, the non-Hasidim argued that such knives were more prone to becoming nicked—and besides, changing the type of knife meant modifying a tradition. The difference between their practices produced a deep rift within Ashkenazic communities containing both Hasidim and non-Hasidim; they could no longer eat the same meat. This schism had serious financial consequences for the community because kosher meat was taxed by the community that organized the slaughtering. By requiring their separate *shehitah*, Hasidic Jews now had an independent source of income and non-Hasidic communities bore a loss. Another major change occurred in the United States in the early nineteenth century: kosher slaughterers became independent agents, and local communities ceased benefiting. This remains the case today. Some kosher certification agencies are nonprofit, while others are not. Profits from kosher slaughtering flow to a specific community only when kosher certification agencies, which appeared gradually over the following hundred years, donate their earnings to them.

In America today, the distinction between Hasidic and non-Hasidic meat has diminished, but divisions have not. Kosher meat production companies and the *shehitah* supervisors they hire may or may not be Hasidic, so a person seeking "real *hasidishe shehitah*" in a grocery store looks for a package label with a specific company name associated with Hasidic communities. I asked a Chabad Hasidic rabbi to explain what this distinction means to him, and he explained:

> It is not just because of the *hasidishe* knife. It is because it is so important that the *shohet* has *yir'as shamayim* [fear or awe of God]. We believe that by virtue of a person studying *Hasidus* [Hasidic philosophy] he will definitely have *yir'as shamayim*. Without that, the quality of the meat is not the same. And such a *shohet* will not succumb to the pressure of the meat producer to hurry up, but he will continually check and recheck the blade. If there is a nick, even a very tiny one that cannot be seen, it changes the [spiritual] quality of the meat.[38]

In practical terms, however, the situation is more complicated. In the United States today, virtually the only Jewish men who work as *shohtim* are Hasidim using Hasidic knives. I told a salesperson in a Pico-Robertson grocery store that I was researching whether stores stocked both "*hasidishe*" and "non-*hasidishe*" meat, and a man nearby guffawed and said, "All *shehitah* is *hasidishe* because all the *shohtim* are Hasidim. The label can say what it wants. The only people who work as *shohtim* are Hasidim!" This may be true, the Chabad rabbi conceded, but only a Hasidic *shohet* working under a Hasidic producer will have the time to do the job properly.[39]

Even after *shehitah*, more needs to be done before the meat is considered acceptable. Some parts of the animal cannot be consumed, so they are separated out and either discarded or sold to non-Jews. Animal innards must be inspected for blemishes before the meat is pronounced kosher. This is a source of significant divisions within Orthodox Jewry and between Orthodox and Conservative Jews. Rabbinic texts do not describe these blemishes as matters of the animal's health or as indicative of the healthfulness of the meat—in contrast to some contemporary marketing, apologetic, and pedagogical claims—but as violations of the halakhic rules.

In the matter of internal lung blemishes for mammals, a major difference in regional norms appeared. Ideally, according to the Talmud, the mammals' lungs should be smooth (the Hebrew term for this is *halak*, and the Yiddish term is *glatt*) and free of internal adhesions (scabs). Talmudic rabbis permitted a leniency for cattle, however, deeming kosher those cows whose lungs contained adhesions removable without perforating the lung. In other words, the lungs were not naturally smooth, but they could be made to appear more so. Other mammals—sheep, goats, and deer—had to have naturally adhesion-free lungs. Medieval rabbis in northern Europe and Germany permitted the leniency for cattle since only a small percentage of slaughtered cows had naturally smooth lungs, while the rabbis of medieval Spain held to the stricter standard.[40] The distinction between Ashkenazic and Sephardic practice was preserved in the *Shulhan arukh* law code. To serve Ashkenazic and Sephardic Jews meat at the same meal, Sephardic beef would suffice unless a participant insisted on a specific, different *shehitah*, such as did the Hasidic Jews.

In 1990, the differences increased. That year the Orthodox Union, the leading US kosher meat certification agency, adopted an Ashkenazic standard requiring smoother lungs than in the past, although not necessarily naturally smooth like that specified in the Talmudic *glatt* standard.[41] It is a unique American rule, not found in Israel or elsewhere. The new requirements decreased the number of cattle slaughtered that can pass muster, and it is one factor accounting for the higher cost of *glatt*-labeled kosher beef compared to the cost of non-*glatt* kosher beef that used to be the Ashkenazic norm.[42] The rabbis of the American Conservative movement did not approve this newer stringency. The new rule did not render non-*glatt* beef forbidden—it is still technically kosher for Ashkenazic Jews—but grocery stores and restaurants in Los Angeles that wish to receive kosher certification must stock and serve only *glatt* beef. A major kosher meat scandal occurred in 2013 in the Pico-Robertson neighborhood when secret videotapes showed the owner of a high-volume butcher shop unloading unmarked boxes of meat from a delivery truck into its back-alley entrance. These boxes were later labeled *glatt*. In his defense, the owner claimed that the substituted meat was kosher but not *glatt*. Of course, the owner lacked credibility, and even if his explanation were true, it did not assuage people who considered non-*glatt* meat *treif*.[43]

The present use of the term *glatt* is another indicator of the diversity within the Orthodox community. In America, Orthodox Jews use the term *glatt* both to describe standards for lung adhesions and, less technically, to convey careful and exacting *kashrut* standards—this had been, and still may be, conveyed by the term *lemehadrin*. In other words, there is kosher and then there is "really" kosher, and neither may actually refer to differences in Jewish law. A chicken cannot be *glatt*, since *glatt* is a term for the lungs of mammals, yet product labels may proclaim that it is *glatt* kosher. Nor can the term be applied to nonmeat food, but it is customary to do so. For example, I asked a young Orthodox woman whether the two of us could meet for lunch in one of the neighborhood's kosher dairy (nonmeat) restaurants, and she responded, "As long as the place is *glatt* kosher."

Ironically, producing the food that differentiates Jews from each other and from non-Jews has for centuries required collaboration with non-Jews. A viable kosher meat business must have two commercial streams for its products, kosher and nonkosher. When an animal's innards are found with disqualifying blemishes or when the slaughtering is done incorrectly, the animal owner will bear a great financial loss unless the meat is sold to non-Jews. Aside from the financial loss, it is terribly wasteful to simply discard the rejected animal or the prohibited animal parts. Partnerships are arranged ahead of time so the meat may be purchased while it is still fresh. Rabbinic law prohibits Jews from selling nonkosher food as a regular part of their income—this is a legal "fence around the Torah" to minimize the temptation to eat such foods—but some situations cannot be avoided, and this is one of them.[44]

Partnering with non-Jews led to another variation within *kashrut* with regard to animal parts. There is a Torah law, stated in Genesis 32:33, against eating the sciatic nerve of a mammal, associated with the patriarch

Jacob's injury at the hands of an angel. Removing the nerve—the term for this is *nikkur* in Hebrew or *traybering* in Yiddish—is a rare skill that is also time-consuming and delicate. Because of the availability of non-Jewish partners, Ashkenazic slaughterers in nineteenth-century Europe ceased removing the sciatic nerve and instead sold the hindquarter cuts of the animals to non-Jews. Ashkenazic slaughterers no longer learned how to remove the sciatic nerve, and rabbinic authorities issued a prohibition against eating the hindquarter cuts. In the United States, where kosher meat production is under Ashkenazic Jewish management and most kosher consumers are Ashkenazic, the entire back half of the slaughtered cow is automatically relegated to the nonkosher commercial stream. The blemishes that disqualify meat from being kosher do not necessarily render the meat unfit for consumption, and there is no point in it going to waste. The matter of the hindquarters involves economics and the availability of slaughterers who can perform the removal.[45]

Jews from southern Mediterranean and Middle Eastern lands had a different meat economy and retained the skills of removing the thigh sinew. A number of Persian Jewish women informed me that in Iran Jewish women have been and still are in charge of this task. The *shoḥet* slaughters the animal; the innards are checked for blemishes; and the removal of blood, veins, and sinews is handled by the women at their homes. One woman who spent her childhood in Iran told me, "My mother and grandmother taught me how to remove the sinew, and we did it there." She believes she would still know how to do it today if she had the opportunity. "It's dangerous here," her husband said, dramatically. He recalled a time when he lived in the US Midwest and knew Iranian Jews who tried to start a business supplying kosher hind cuts. "The Mafia intervened," he told me. This was not the Italian Mafia, he explained, but other Jews with vested interests in conventional kosher meat production. His Iranian acquaintances eventually gave up because "the trucks would drive off with the meat and never arrive where they were supposed to go."[46] Jews who wish to eat kosher hindquarter cuts may purchase them privately through an internet-based business. The local kosher certifying agencies in Los Angeles will not grant approval to kosher butchers, stores, or restaurants who sell or serve such cuts, however, lest Ashkenazic Jews violate their tradition.[47]

Modern industrialized methods pose many challenges to the production of kosher meat. *Shehitah* requires especially skilled employees, careful positioning of the animal, and time-consuming and difficult procedures after the slaughter. The rules were written and applied at a time when slaughter was locally controlled and only one or two large mammals would have been slaughtered at a time. The procedure was designed to be carried out in a relatively unhurried manner. Today, factory methods prevail, and business owners favor quick and efficient procedures. Government regulations influence the treatment of animals, the health and safety conditions for workers, and the handling of the meat and by-products. This does not ensure humane treatment of animals. Animals typically bred in factory-farm settings proceed to their final moments in unnatural and painful conditions, and government regulations allow much of this.[48] Orthodox kosher certifiers have adapted *shehitah* to the industrialized setting by prioritizing the rules about the animal's consciousness and the slaughtering cut. They feel the need to consider animal suffering only in response to public concerns, and these are minimal. Consequently, Orthodox *shehitah* faces criticism from people—including Orthodox Jews—who believe that minimizing animal pain should be a higher priority.

There are a few more steps necessary to prepare the meat before it can be cooked, and these have to do with removing the blood. Shortly after the animal is slaughtered, someone must thoroughly rinse the meat with water. It must also be sprinkled with coarsely ground salt (often called "kosher salt") to draw out more blood before rinsing again. This last step may be avoided by broiling the meat—all liver requires broiling.[49] The women of the household used to perform the second rinsing and salting. This changed in the United States in the last third of the twentieth century when meat production ceased to be local. Instead, it was located in rural areas, and the meat was transported to the markets by truck and train. To conform to the kosher rules, the meat-packing companies salted and rinsed at the killing factory and during transport.

Only in select Orthodox communities do women conduct an additional salting and rinsing as an act of great piety; most, however, no longer even know how to do it and are not aware it was an activity their grandmothers considered central to Jewish homemaking. This constitutes a change in American practice, especially with regard to poultry.

Nonmeat Food Preparation: Ingredient-Based and Preparer-Based Rules

Fresh and unprocessed fruits, vegetables, grains, legumes, and nuts are permitted foods, but when they are changed by heat, they invite religious scrutiny. Additionally, when foods are heated they are often combined with other ingredients, and care must be taken to ensure that permitted foods are not mixed with or in contact with prohibited foods. Ingredient-based rules of preparation dictate what to do when permitted food is accidentally contaminated by prohibited foods. The general principle is that contamination occurs only when flavor may be transmitted, and this is assessed by the relative quantities of the ingredients involved and the heat of the foods. For example, contamination might occur if a piece of

Food preparation rules: ingredient based and preparer based

- cooked and processed foods
- milking animals
- making cheese, bread, and wine

FIGURE 8. Food preparation rules: ingredient based and preparer based

prohibited meat falls into a pot of kosher stew, but if the contaminant is less than one-sixtieth of the total amount or if both items are cold, one may be able to consume the stew. The pot and the knife may also play a role in contamination because heated food within a pot conveys its status to the pot. That is, a pot in which nonkosher food has been cooked will convey nonkosher status to the kosher food cooked in it. Knives may also be considered "heated" because of the force exerted upon them while cutting certain foods.

Because these are rabbinic and not Torah rules, there are many details and variances in both legal writings and actual practice. These are the types of questions a layperson would ask a rabbi. In a series of Torah lectures on the subject of "permitted and prohibited food mixtures" presented for men only at a local Orthodox synagogue, the curriculum included such subjects as permitted ratios of accidental mixing of kosher and nonkosher foods, the rabbinic definition of "taste," and the transference of taste through ovens, upon heated surfaces, and by way of steam and aroma. The fact that the course was not even open to Orthodox women, the ones making the decisions in the kitchen, indicates the gap between *halakhah* and actual practice. Food preparation typically occurs within a tight schedule, and when there are accidents, women are most likely to follow the practices they learned from other women or simply to follow their own intuition, both of which are likely to be stricter than *halakhah* requires. A woman in this congregation who consults with the rabbi's wife when she has had such problems with kosher food preparation told her friend, "You should always ask the rabbi or *rebbetzin* [rabbi's wife]. I've learned that it's actually a lot easier than we think it is."[50]

One way to guard against improper ingredient mixing is to prohibit all foods prepared by non-Jews. Indeed, there is a rabbinic injunction called *bishul akum* (the cooking by non-Jews) that forbids dishes cooked by anyone not a Jew.[51] These laws of commensality—that is, rules restricting with whom one may eat and by whom the food one eats is produced—appeared only in the late biblical era and afterward, when Jews increasingly dwelled in religiously and ethnically heterogenous societies. One approach within the earliest rabbinic writings that explains *bishul akum* regards it as a guard against improper ingredients. The other approach regards it as primarily social, for even if the ingredients are proper, the food itself would be forbidden because of the preparer's religious status.[52] As mentioned above, prohibiting "their" food is a way to prevent close personal contact between Jews and outsiders, and requiring Jewish-prepared food, or *bishul yisra'el* (the cooking by Jews), keeps Jews more insular. The social perspective predominates today. The Orthodox Union *kashrut* agency explains it as follows:

> This [*bishul akum* prohibition] was based on the realization that bonds of friendship are established by eating together, and breaking bread with a stranger is the first step to developing a closer relationship. For thousands of years of exile, the biblical and rabbinic laws of kosher have formed a natural fortress that prevented the assimilation of the Jewish people into many different cultures of the world. Today, with spiraling assimilation wreaking havoc at a frightening rate, the prophetic vision of Chazal [our rabbis of blessed memory] is all the more apparent. It is significant that even for secularized Jews, a kosher kitchen often remains the last bastion against intermarriage and assimilation.[53]

The *bishul akum* rule draws a straight line from eating their food to befriending them, acting like them, and marrying them.[54]

Of course, this concern related to socializing around food leads to far more restrictive eating. Cheese is an example. It must be made of milk taken from a permitted mammal by a Jew or by a person under Jewish watch—this milk is called *ḥalav yisra'el*. Some rabbis insisted that a Jew merely has to supervise the cheese-making process to ensure proper ingredients, whereas some insisted that the Jew would actually need to add the rennet (the enzyme that hardens the ingredients into cheese). The requirement to consume only *ḥalav yisra'el* is found in the Mishnah law code, without explanation. The Talmud's explanation that the non-Jew might have mixed in milk from a nonkosher animal such as a pig, implying that the issue was an ingredient-based concern and not a social matter, was essentially ignored; that is, even if one was certain that the milk was from a cow, goat, or sheep, it was still not permitted. Kosher cheese would need to start with *ḥalav yisraʾel*.

The norm over the centuries was for Jews to consume only *ḥalav yisraʾel*, until the industrialized food production economy of the twentieth and twenty-first centuries made this essentially impossible.[55] Rabbi Moses Feinstein, the leading American *posek* of the twentieth century, stated that US regulations on food purity serve the same purpose as a Jewish supervisor in the case of milk. No farmer would risk an enormous fine in order to mix nonkosher animal milk into the cow milk she or he sold, nor would it make sense in the factory-farm economy. While this position has been highly controversial since its first appearance, most Modern and Centrist and many right-wing Orthodox Jews rely on it.[56]

Historians know that the preparer-based requirement was not honored as consistently as the law demands. Jews have rarely lived in purely Jewish societies, and food preparation occurred often between women at the local level with shared equipment. It was common for Jewish families with the means to hire non-Jewish male and female servants to help in the household. When Jews know that a food has no *treif* ingredients or improper mixtures but it is forbidden to eat because of the social concern that they may become too friendly with the non-Jewish preparers and intermarry with them, the Jews may reason that the social concern does not apply to them. So as not to render people into sinners because of this demanding rule, rabbinic authorities permitted *bishul akum* on a limited basis. It was not applied to foods that could be eaten raw, and it only applied to foods that have some prestige and would potentially be served for one's guests. These are subjective judgments that may vary from place to place, however, so rabbinic rulings on specific foods vary as well.

Furthermore, rabbis permitted prepared foods to be designated *bishul yisraʾel* if the outsiders were secondary to the Jews in control. We have already seen this in kosher animal slaughter, where a non-Jew could be involved but only in a subordinate role. In the cooking and baking of the affected foods, the non-Jew could even do the bulk of the work as long as a Jew supervised or started the process, stirred the pot, or made other gestures of control.[57] For some rabbinic authorities, the Jew involved in the preparation must be one who is strictly obedient to *halakhah*. In most Pico-Robertson kosher eateries, the kitchen staff is not Jewish, so the kosher certifier specifies when and how Jewish control is performed. For example, the Jewish owner of a Pico-Robertson kosher pizza shop or his Jewish employee (preferably an Orthodox one) must turn on the gas oven at the start of the workday, and only then may the non-Jewish workers start the baking process.[58] The *halakhah* for Sephardic Jews is stricter and requires direct Jewish contact during the cooking or baking, not merely at the start of the production. One Sephardic rabbi explained, "Theoretically, if a Sephardic Jew walked into a restaurant and asked to mix the items in the cooking pot, the owner should let him. It probably doesn't ever happen in Los Angeles because the *Sephardim* here are unaware of these rules. Really, they shouldn't be eating in LA kosher restaurants!"[59]

Another important leniency in the *bishul akum* prohibition is with bread. Rabbinic law insists that bread should be made by Jews—this was called *pat yisra'el* (or *pas yisra'el* in Ashkenazic Hebrew or Yiddish). Making such bread was the duty of women, who were also specifically commanded to recite a blessing, remove a little piece of dough as a symbolic performance of the ancient tithe, and burn it.[60] Bread was an essential daily staple, and making it could be time-consuming and labor-intensive. In the premodern era there were no ingredient-based concerns about bread (one could presume it was made only with grain), so rabbis permitted Jews to eat the bread of non-Jews if there were no other options and if the bread was not meant for a Sabbath or holiday meal. Kosher restaurants and bakeries in Pico-Robertson that serve only "Jewish bread" are doing this because they want to appeal to the largest customer base. They indicate this high standard of *pat yisra'el* on their signs and in their kosher certification documents.

When food became mass-produced in mechanized factories, the *bishul akum* prohibition became far less relevant. After all, if the prohibition was designed to hinder the development of close relations between Jews and non-Jews during food preparation, this outcome was hardly possible when, for example, foods were boiled and canned by a machine. Yet here, too, there have been divisions of opinion about the need for preparer-based rules, as shown below.

Wine and grape juice are also restricted by the *bishul akum* prohibition, but much more severely. In ancient Israel, wine—mildly fermented grape juice—was the principal daily beverage. It was essential at sacred feasts and joyous celebrations, and it served as a liquid sacrifice. Rabbinic authorities interpreted the biblical warnings against consuming the sacrificial offerings of idol worshipers to apply to drinking even the nonsacramental wine of idolaters. They defined beverages made from grapes as kosher only if from the time that the grapes were crushed it was made entirely by Jews. When rabbinic authorities conceded that Islam and Christianity were not idolatry, they still declared their sacramental wine forbidden. Italian rabbis permitted their nonsacramental wine, *stam yeinam* (meaning "their wine"), because wine was such an essential daily beverage. In Germanic lands, where other fermented beverages were the norm, the rabbis still frowned upon *stam yeinam* out of concern that drinking "their" wine would lead to intimacy between Jews and non-Jews. Rabbinic tradition did not apply such rules to alcoholic beverages made of grains, vegetables, or other fruit.[61]

The rabbis ruled that Jews should not drink any wine, even kosher wine, with non-Jews. The stated social reason for this was to protect Jews against too close social relations with non-Jews, and there was also the concern that Jews could inadvertently be drawn into foreign religious libation rites. The rabbis declared that even kosher wine, after it is made and bottled, becomes nonkosher and forbidden to Jews when it has been touched by non-Jews. (They did not extend this principle to other types of liquor.) The only wine that would not be rendered nonkosher from contact with non-Jews is "cooked"—*mevushal* (Hebrew)—kosher wine. This is wine that is made entirely by Jews and is brought to near boiling temperature prior to bottling. After this point, it may be handled by non-Jews without impairing its kosher status. The assumption was that such cooked wine was, to some extent, spoiled, and it would not be used for religious rites. These rules about all-Jewish handling and *mevushal* wine are still honored, even in factory settings and in social settings. The prevailing rule today is that kosher certification for wine requires the involvement not just of Jews but of Jews of Orthodox practice.[62]

In Los Angeles, catering businesses and restaurants that want rabbinically recognized kosher status are required to serve only *mevushal* wine. The rationale for this is that non-Jews will likely be present in such places. The kosher wines, which are not *mevushal* and which are usually the better wines, are drunk only in private homes and settings. Kosher wines may be labeled "*mevushal*" or "not *mevushal*" so that one buys the wine appropriate for the situation. Supermarkets in Los Angeles that are licensed to sell liquor will stock the most popular kosher wines, such as Manischewitz (which are all *mevushal*), and some kosher grocery stores carry a larger variety of kosher wines of both kinds. There is even a boutique liquor store on Pico Boulevard, The Cask, that boasts "an extensive inventory of wine and fine spirits," a tasting room, and an event room—but there only *mevushal* wine and liquor made from non-grape products would be served.

Prohibition against Mixing Meat and Milk Products

The third aspect of *kashrut*, the prohibition against mixing meat with milk and milk products, complicates even further the daily lives of Jews who keep kosher. Putting this in positive devotional terms, this aspect of *kashrut* provides yet another way of showing devotion to God's Torah. Were the other two requirements—to eat only permitted species that are slaughtered appropriately and to follow the rules about ensuring religious control over food preparation—to stand alone, an individual Jew could simply acquire permitted foods and eat. However, the no-meat-with-milk prohibition adds more foods that cannot be combined into a recipe, more foods that cannot be served together in a single meal or over the course of several hours, and more foods that must be kept away from some of one's pots, cooking utensils, dishware, and appliances.[63] Violating these rules may render otherwise kosher food unkosher and unusable.

The violation may render a "meat" appliance, like a blender, unusable or may change its status from *pareve* (neutral) to "meat" or "dairy." In the case of an accidental mixing of meat and dairy, there may be the possibility that the food may still be consumed as long as a number of conditions apply, and typically in these cases a rabbi would be consulted about the mixture and about the consequences of the error for one's kitchen items.

The numerous detailed rules in the no-meat-with-milk decree have their source in a terse biblical command: "Do not boil a kid in its mother's milk." It appears three times in the Pentateuch with no explanation or elaboration.[64] Historians have shown that the no-meat-with-milk decree expanded during the postbiblical era and was only gradually adopted by Jews as a whole. The rabbis in the Mishnah described it as a Torah law that prohibits cooking together the meat and milk from kosher domesticated mammals, not simply goats, and the prohibition extends to any mode of cooking and to any benefit from such a cooked mixture. Around this Torah law they made rabbinic injunctions, including prohibiting cooking milk with any permitted kosher mammal and prohibiting consuming (not only cooking) meat and milk at the same time. The Talmudic rabbis agreed that the taboo even applied to fowl, even though they do not produce milk.[65] Yet for centuries there were regions where fowl and milk foods were eaten together, until the inclusion of fowl in the no-meat-with-milk prohibition became a universal Jewish practice in the 1500s.[66] Keeping meat separate from fish was mentioned in the Talmud, but the reason for this was that the rabbis believed it is unhealthful to eat the two foods together. This has led to some separation between meat and fish at a single meal. For example, some Jews today put the foods in separate courses of the meal or use different plates or utensils.[67]

The no-meat-with-milk rule created an entirely different category that is neither meat nor milk that consequently may be mixed and eaten with both. Commonly designated by the Yiddish word *pareve*, this neutral category includes foods grown from the ground such as grains, legumes, vegetables, and fruits, as well as permitted fish and eggs and nonbiological foods like water and salt. When *pareve* foods are combined with meat or milk foods or heated in meat or milk cookware, they take on the status of that food. Rabbinical authorities have defined what is permitted when accidental contact occurs, how to avoid the transfer of meat or milk flavor to *pareve* foods, and other such questions. Today, kosher food labeling of store-bought foods includes symbols or words indicating whether the item is meat, dairy, or *pareve*. Kosher restaurants are not permitted to have both meat and dairy on their menus unless they have separate kitchens, and there are regulations for kosher caterers to ensure that there is no such mixing.

The second aspect of the no-meat-with-milk prohibition deals with serving and eating these foods together. Whereas in the Talmudic era the rabbis proscribed in broad terms eating the two foods at the same meal and rinsing or wiping one's mouth and hands after eating meat prior to consuming milk, medieval authorities specified the number of hours to wait. This rule applies after eating meat; waiting after consuming milk is not limited to the same extent.[68] Local variations in the length of the temporal pause developed. For example, the American Orthodox standard is currently a six-hour pause, and Jews from the Netherlands accept a seventy-two-minute pause.

"Serving together" was also interpreted to apply to one's eating implements. Not until late medieval Europe did it become common for people to eat with individual plates, forks, and knives. Once such implements became the norm, Ashkenazic Jews began to insist on acquiring these in separate meat and milk sets. Historians surmise that the women of the household were the ones insisting on these distinctions.[69] Over the last few centuries, and especially in well-to-do families and communities, it became the norm to maintain separate dishware and kitchen items to be used for contact with meat, milk, or purely *pareve* foods. The older practice of eating directly from a common serving platter—what today is called "family style"—lasted longer in Middle Eastern and North African lands, but eventually Jews in those lands, too, began to eat from individual plates. Then they, too, insisted on separate meat and milk plates, cutlery, and flatware. Rabbinic law requires ritually immersing certain kinds of newly acquired dishware and kitchen items in a *mikvah* (ritual bath) or in the "living waters" of a lake, ocean, or river.[70]

We know today that Orthodox women insist upon greater separation of meat and milk in their homes than what the *Shulḥan arukh* requires. A local rabbi told me, with admiration in his voice, "If a piece of cold meat is on the counter, and cold milk drips on it, according to the *Shulḥan arukh* all you have to do is wash it off with cold water—but not according to today's women, who will throw the meat away."[71] A kosher home in the Orthodox community will have for daily use at least two sets of dishes, pots and pans, cutlery, and cooking utensils—one for meat and one for milk—as well as pieces designated for *pareve* foods. It may also have separate milk and meat sinks or sink liners, washcloths and dish towels, working surfaces, dish drainers, dishwasher racks (unless they use the appliance only for milk or only for meat), and—if they are Chabad—separate refrigerators for milk and meat. People who study the halakhic texts know these practices go far beyond the law. Orthodox women follow the standards set by other Orthodox women, and they regard the codified laws as far too lenient.

The third part of the no-meat-with-milk rule, the prohibition against benefiting from their mixture, is understood to apply to commerce or gift giving. Whereas other foods prohibited to Jews, such as designated parts of a slaughtered animal, may be sold to people who are not subject to the dietary laws, selling any food that contains a combination of both meat and milk ingredients is considered an additional and separate prohibition.[72] While this has an effect on one's occupational choice, it has no real effect in a kosher home or kosher food business.

Contemporary Multiple Standards and Strictures

Although the basic contours of *kashrut* are the same for Jews throughout the world, in many American Orthodox communities today—certainly this is the case in Los Angeles—there is no presumption that all Orthodox Jews permit the same foods and will eat at each other's tables. The meat may be an obstacle: Is the kosher beef Hasidic *sheḥitah*, and is it

> ## No mixing meat with milk
>
> 1. Do not cook together.
> 2. Do not serve together.
> 3. Do not derive benefit from
>   their mixture.

FIGURE 9. No mixing meat with milk

Sephardic *glatt* or the less demanding Ashkenazic standard? Is the milk used in the dairy dishes *ḥalav yisraʾel* or just the conventionally produced kind? Is the bread *pat yisraʾel*, and is the flour *yashan*? Is the Jewish cook too liberal in religious observance to be trusted? The refusal to eat at the table of a Torah-observant Jew is not a statement denying the person's Jewish status, and it might not be even a statement saying the person is violating *halakhah*. Certainly, though, it is an assertion of the importance of one's own standards—the standards of the individual, the congregation or sub-affiliation, or the circle within the community. Sociologist Iddo Tavory recounts a joke he heard about the difficulty of bringing two Orthodox children to a kosher pizzeria: The Chabad child cannot eat the pizza because the cheese is not *ḥalav yisraʾel*, and the Yeshivish child cannot eat it because the flour is not *yashan*.[73] To satisfy a wide clientele, certain restaurants and caterers have adopted standards that would unlikely exist within a single household. In fact, there is at least one venue in Pico-Robertson, The Mark catering hall, that can meet the requirements necessary for enabling various Orthodox groups to eat together in one place. Some people find a way to adjust their regular rules in order to attend the meal at a wedding, Bar Mitzvah, or circumcision hosted by other Orthodox Jews not in their own congregation. What is notable is that the level of collegiality is high despite the distinctions in foodways.

Before describing the social impact of these distinctions, it is necessary to explain some basic features of today's kosher certification systems that influence food choices. In the premodern era, because Jews ate food that was locally produced or purchased, the kosher status of the food could be easily verified. The cooks, bakers, and animal slaughterers were known, and the preparation could be directly observed. This changed when Jews moved to large cities and to places where food was produced at a distance from the consumers. The factory production of food also presented new dilemmas of ascertaining whether the ingredients complied with kosher laws. Initially, Jewish women who followed the dietary laws checked the labeling or advertisements or sought word-of-mouth information to determine whether the products were kosher, but this was not sufficient for scrupulous women and rabbinic authorities. Kosher meat produced outside the local arena and in mass volume also posed a challenge. To verify that foods were genuinely kosher, *hashgaḥah* (supervision) was devised. It was a novel system for signaling that the kosher claim of the food could be trusted. This form of supervision requires that an outside expert associated with a specific rabbinic authority inspect the inventory and the production process to verify the kosher status of the products. Producers permit *hashgaḥah* and add the cost of the service to the food (although some claim they do not) in order to garner the kosher market. There may be more than one kosher certification kosher agency, each with different standards and consumer bases. Each has its own symbol or recognizable stamp of approval that is printed on the label or attached to the food.

After World War II, kosher certification agencies increased in number and expanded the scope of their activities. They established many common halakhic standards among themselves, improved reliability, and sold their services to food companies that wanted to develop products for kosher consumers. Orthodox, rather than Conservative, rabbis had greater credibility as inspectors, and kosher certification soon became a niche Orthodox field.[74] Orthodox Jews gradually became persuaded not to rely only on food ingredient labels to determine whether they could purchase the food. Kosher certifiers taught them that synthetic ingredients and vaguely defined additives such as stabilizers, emulsifiers, and preservatives might not be kosher; and they convinced them that professional verification was essential when ingredients in a single food might be acquired from multiple vendors spread across the world. Eventually four major kosher certification agencies ("the Big Four") dominated the field of dozens that provide such services; the largest today is Orthodox Union, with its trademarked "OU" symbol.

By the 1990s, the number of kosher-certified foods began to increase exponentially. Industrialized-food manufacturers realized that products marked with kosher symbols signaled quality and purity to consumers of all backgrounds. It may be, as some argue, that this narrative was invented by kosher food production companies; either way, there is no doubt that kosher certification expands the market for a food product.[75] When nearly all types of nonmeat factory-produced food could be found with kosher certification, Orthodox consumers decided that there was no good reason to choose uncertified products when certified ones were available, and this is the present norm. A rabbi involved in a Los Angeles kosher certification agency admitted that this has distorted what kosher certification means: "First, it is no absolute guarantee. Second, a food that lacks *hashgaḥah* is not necessarily *treif*, like many people think!" Kosher certification has, for some Orthodox Jews, created more restrictive criteria for industrially produced foods than Jewish law requires. People mistakenly think that "as soon as [a fruit] is cooked, canned, frozen, freeze-dried, or packaged—as soon as it is changed in any way from its natural state—it becomes subject to rabbinic oversight."[76] This is certainly the norm for much of the Los Angeles Orthodox community, but it is more than what is required by *halakhah*.

Kosher certification of restaurants, caterers, hotels, and the like is also a new phenomenon. This type of certification enables Orthodox Jews of all types to eat at the venue and perhaps even to eat alongside each other at the same meal. This form of *hashgaḥah* verifies that the food served accords with ingredient-based and preparer-based rules. It is likely to be locally based and operated by a board of Orthodox rabbis who set halakhic standards, determine a management system, and hire inspectors. Approval is indicated by certificates posted on retail food businesses and in caterer and hotel documentation. It is not unusual to have more than one kosher certifier in a single town. There are at least five in Los Angeles, some locally based and some national.[77]

The existence of this kosher certification system means that the authority of the local rabbi over *kashrut* has diminished considerably. Kosher food certification is in the hands of regional or national kosher certification agencies. There are "boutique" kosher certifiers for factory-produced food, called *heimishe hashgaḥah* (Yiddish for "trustworthy supervision"), with the name of a particular rabbinic authority honored by Yeshivish or Hasidic communities. Furthermore, some smaller Orthodox groups arrange for their own kosher slaughterer and establish their own food brands. Yet when these are on packages marked by other kosher certification symbols, it may even indicate that the *heimishe hashgaḥah* was not even the result of an independent inspection process. There is much discussion of this online. The loyal followers of *heimishe hashgaḥah* claim that the standards of the big certifiers are too lax, whereas their detractors insist that the *heimishe* certification is less competent, dependent upon the kosher certification of the national certifier, and simply a sign of belonging to a particular "in" group. One forum organized by and for Orthodox women on the central and right side of the Orthodox spectrum includes many discussions of *hekhshers* (kosher certification symbols).[78]

Local rabbinic guidance in *kashrut*, then, expresses itself when a rabbi answers his congregants' specific questions and when he establishes the *kashrut* policy for congregational events. He will also tell his congregation which kosher certifiers to trust, a judgment based on the kosher certifier's respect for the community's *mesorah* (tradition), its social ties to the group, and its reputation.

The changes to women's role in *kashrut* are great. Their *kashrut* work now occurs primarily in the grocery store, and their food preparation in the home requires far less religious consideration. For example, they no longer salt and rinse meat, they are unlikely to bake bread, and much food preparation involves opening food packages and combining the contents. Perhaps the many additional safeguards that they have added to their kitchens and food preparation routines are a way to fill the void.[79] Women still decide whether they and their family may eat at the homes of other women. They also are the ones who determine whether other women's homemade or purchased foods—for example, when brought as gifts—will be consumed at their tables. These are often not halakhic decisions but ones based on an assessment of whether the host or gift giver is sufficiently pious.

Kosher certifiers are businesses that market their services to producers, and they determine their kosher standards by financial considerations as well as *halakhah*. For example, very high kosher certification standards attract a larger consumer base and enhance the certifier's religious prestige. This is one obvious contributor to the increasing strictness of *kashrut* regulations today. Yet, the more demanding the *kashrut* requirements, the fewer food producers there are who agree to follow them. Most *hashgaḥah* for nonmeat industrially produced food involves many initial visits to clean the equipment and establish protocols but then requires only occasional visits by an inspector to investigate the purchases and the processes. People who want factory-produced foods to be prepared by Jews (a particularly demanding interpretation of the *bishul akum* prohibition, given that the food is machine produced) require a far greater Jewish presence and involvement. Even the best system of *hashgaḥah* cannot prevent all corruption, carelessness, and errors. Kosher certification involves shareholders, wage-earning employees, cost-bearing food producers, and supervisors who may not always be present, making it possible to cut corners or cheat. Certification agencies have to deal with competition and to foster their brand with kosher consumers and food producers, and this, too, may lead to ethical and halakhic breaches.

Thus, while kosher certification has tremendously expanded the availability and ease of providing kosher food, it has not eliminated the diversity in *kashrut* standards, and to some extent it has simply made them visible. Nor have the standards eliminated the purely social aspects of *kashrut* pressures; these simply appear in different forms. Many Orthodox Jews are savvy to this and can be cynical. Across the community, local rabbis and laypeople told me that the kosher certification system—especially for kosher meat and restaurants—"is all political" and "is a dirty business," and they hinted darkly about a multitude of sins they would not divulge. Online forums repeat this also. Among the neighborhood's Persian and Middle Eastern Jews who prefer kosher food, a sizable number care little about kosher certification. One indication of this is that more than half of the restaurants in the neighborhood that feature Persian and Iraqi specialties and declare on store signs that they are kosher actually lack kosher certification certificates.[80] Some Orthodox Jews told me they refuse to pick and choose eateries on the basis of one or the other *hashgaḥah* because "they are all just as good or bad as the other" or "they all hire the same inspectors anyway." Some believe that the agreement of the certification companies to provide unnecessary kosher certification for foods and household products—such as bottled water and soaps—fosters ignorance and fear among the Orthodox and is another sign of the industry's venality.

Awareness of how kosher certification has diminished women's agency in *kashrut* is most apparent when people discussed the recent *kashrut* preoccupation with bugs. Medieval rabbis were the first to address the practical challenge of finding fruit, vegetables, and water that were entirely free of infestation, even after washing and inspection. They agreed that one may consume food that might contain bugs or vermin too small to be detected by the naked eye, for, as one rabbi wrote, "the Torah was not given to angels."[81] This lenient stance prevailed even after the widespread availability of microscopes in the nineteenth century. Since the 1980s, however, the fear and horror of eating prohibited insects has dramatically escalated. It was initiated by rabbis rather than the women of the household, if one believes the writer whose article is posted on a kosher certification website. She quoted one of the businessmen who made it their mission to provide bug-free kosher food:

"I was speaking to Rabbi Shlomo Gissinger and Rabbi Dr. Yitzchok Sokol, who had begun an intensive campaign to educate kosher consumers," says Mr. Gartenhaus. "They realized that people weren't aware of the issues. The average head of lettuce contains as many as 30 thrips and aphids, and certain vegetables, like broccoli and cauliflower, are so infested, they are practically impossible to clean by hand. The rabbis were making presentations in schools and yeshivas and waking up people to the problem. It was incredible—eating an insect is six times worse than eating *treif*, and people just didn't know."[82]

This businessman was one of the founders of a kosher food certification agency known as Bodek (inspector), which sells their own bug-free fresh and frozen produce.[83] Responding to the concern about bugs, some rabbis now prohibit the eating of fresh or frozen foods such as romaine lettuce, asparagus, broccoli, brussels sprouts, and strawberries, or they only permit it when foods are labeled as having undergone a check against bugs and worms. Foods with this kind of *hashgahah* are far more expensive and are often hard to find, even in Pico-Robertson grocery stores. For a while, a local kosher certifying agency posted an English, Hebrew, and Farsi sign on the wall in the produce section warning consumers to clean and inspect bagged salads and vegetables.

The reactions to the bug issue fell into three categories: those who expressed strong concern about bugs; those who regarded bugs as a matter taken care of by normal kitchen hygiene; and those who called it fearmongering, condescending toward women (food preparers), and a business scam. Rabbis were represented in each group. One in the first category lamented that some of his congregants who ate at noncertified vegan restaurants were likely eating bugs, while another suggested that the reason previous rabbinic writings paid so little attention to the problem is that "there must be more bugs in our food nowadays than there were before." Those who call it fearmongering were the angriest. One such person, a woman who called the "first book on bugs in *kashrut*" the "downfall of Orthodoxy," still remembers hearing a mother publicly shame her daughter at a grocery store when the daughter put lettuce that was not Bodek branded into their grocery cart. "The mother screamed at her, 'That lettuce is not kosher!' Lettuce is always kosher!!"[84]

A teacher of newly Orthodox women told me she teaches them how to take greater control over the *kashrut* of their foods and save money at the same time. She teaches them the careful process of washing food in cold soapy water and then checking for bugs. "Anyone can do this. The young women today do not like to take the time to do things," she said, but she is determined to give them the knowledge they need. She told me,

> It's ridiculous what is happening: people hear of an opinion that is way out there, and then suddenly everyone feels compelled to follow it. In fact, the *klal* [general principle] of the *halakhah* states that you don't even have to check for bugs in food that is not likely to have bugs, for example, in apples. People have stopped looking at the *klal*—they've stopped using their heads.[85]

The teacher described her observance of *halakhah* as "strict but eclectic," noting that she and her husband, a rabbi, find it utterly pointless to purchase kosher-certified (*ḥalav yisra'el*) milk ("that is a Chabad and Yeshivish concern") or to differentiate between *hashgaḥah* providers. Commercial food businesses, however, have less leeway on how to deal with bugs. The owner of a kosher Chinese-style food business, a mainstay of Pico-Robertson for decades, recently switched to another kosher certifier when the previous one decided to prohibit scallions because of a potential bug problem. He explained, "I make Chinese food—how can I not use scallions? I've been using them for years and I'm not going to stop now."[86]

The fact that there are many regulations about food is, in itself, not an issue that divides or perturbs Orthodox Jews. All areas of their lives are bound by commandments, from the moment they awake until falling asleep at night, and they appear to value that reality and do not question it—certainly not publicly or to an outsider like me. An oft-repeated rabbinic statement connects the large number of rules to the extent of God's love for the Jewish people: "The Holy One, praised be He, desired to benefit the people Israel; therefore He gave them the Torah with an abundance of commandments."[87] According to this teaching, the profusion of rules not only indicates God's great love; it also increases the opportunities to be reminded of God's love as well as for an individual to demonstrate obedience to and love for God.

Yet over the centuries there has been considerable disagreement about the extent of regulation, the multiple variations in practice, the supplemental customs, and the addition of stringencies. Historians and sociologists have shown conclusively that American Orthodox Judaism has shifted to the right, meaning that as a group they are strictly following *halakhah* and adopting rabbinic injunctions and customs that are more demanding than they were in the past. Historians and sociologists have given compelling explanations for the increase in strictness and in standards.[88] This change has contributed to the multiplication of standards because individuals and whole communities resist accepting some changes they regard as too restrictive or too idiosyncratic and unnecessary, whereas others adopt them to greater degrees. I add to these the idea that proper eating must be "costly" so as to demonstrate the value of the practitioner relative to others. This can enhance the sense of being special and of having strong individual and group identity.

Orthodox Jews who grew up in or managed households during the 1950s and 1960s and were members of Modern Orthodox congregations then and up until the mid-1980s are the most conscious and resentful of the changes and the increase of standards. The older ones might mention that it used to be acceptable to eat nonmeat foods at restaurants that served nonkosher foods or to eat at vegetarian or fish restaurants that had no kosher supervision. This level of permissiveness actually violates long-standing preparer-based rabbinic rules described earlier in this chapter. Eating permitted foods at nonkosher establishments, once—and still—acceptable for travelers, is no longer respectable for Orthodox Jews in a city like Los Angeles with its many kosher-certified restaurants. Nowadays, those who patronize such restaurants do so out of the sight of their rabbi and their congregation's more devout members. During my interview with an elderly couple who fondly remembered the older, easier era, the wife interrupted and silenced her husband as he began admitting that they still ate dairy foods at nonkosher restaurants.[89] Perhaps they did not want to trust me with their secret, or they were ashamed of their behavior. In any case, they knew their behavior was inconsistent with *halakhah* and their community standards. A person pleased with the current stricter rules told me, "The era of leniency is over. Now are the conditions in which we can do it right."[90] A rabbi in a congregation with such "oldsters" lamented their lax behavior: "Some of my congregants eat at [noncertified kosher] vegan restaurants!" They have not admitted this to him, but he knows who they are, and he will not eat at their homes.[91]

Other new practices were forthrightly criticized by Modern Orthodox Jews because they know they lack universal rabbinic and communal support. The *glatt* kosher meat standards are a case in point. A woman proud to have fed hundreds of guests at her Sabbath dinners and lunches over the past four decades observed ruefully, "The kosher meat back then was not *glatt* and it was just fine—but no longer. Some people think if it's not *glatt* it's not kosher!"[92] As I explained above, the Ashkenazic non-*glatt* standard was a leniency that dates back to the Talmudic era, and today's "new" *glatt* standard represents a slightly stricter version, although still more lenient than the Sephardic standard. The non-Hasidic rabbis I interviewed described the new requirement for Ashkenazic Jews as a practice largely driven by non-halakhic factors; they explained that kosher meat production companies adopted it to expand their market share to stricter kosher consumers, that the animal's lungs are not really naturally *glatt*, and that the term *glatt* is being used to indicate scrupulous adherence to *halakhah*. Younger adults among the Modern Orthodox know little about these issues and understand *glatt* kosher to mean "authentically kosher." When older and knowledgeable Modern Orthodox Jews disparage the *glatt* meat standard, they demonstrate that they—not the younger and stricter Orthodox whose knowledge and authority are nowadays granted more respect—actually have greater knowledge.

Lamenting the difficulty of keeping kosher and ridiculing current stringencies are markers of belonging to the Modern Orthodox cohort. This group is on the left end of the cultural insularity spectrum and, more than other Orthodox groups, engages in secular academic learning and culture. As such, their routine activities would be most impaired by stricter dietary laws. In addition to their group's loss of cultural authority due to the shift to the right, they are also most aware of what historians, sociologists, and Modern Orthodox rabbis have written about the turn to the right and stringencies in *halakhah*. From the Modern Orthodox I frequently heard the quip, "Anyone who is more lenient than me is violating the law; anyone who is stricter than me is an extremist." Orthodox Jews across the spectrum may make these observations and jokes and use the phrase "the *ḥumrah* of the month," but Modern Orthodox Jews were the most likely to criticize the increasing *kashrut* strictness. A *ḥumrah* (plural, *ḥumrot*) is supererogatory behavior, that is, a practice that goes beyond the requirements of the law, although some rabbis acknowledge it has some merit for individual practice.

Technically, a *ḥumrah* is different from a rabbinic ruling that can be identified as *maḥmir* (strict) or *makel* (lenient). In Talmudic sources there is consensus that in terms of public policy—that is, when rabbis delineate in their rulings the standards of acceptable behavior and when communal judges rule on specific cases—there should be moderation and avoidance of the strictest position. A *ḥumrah* goes beyond *halakhah* to a standard that is not embraced by the community. It is just this aspect of it that is valuable to people who want to stand apart, either in their private practice or in their public persona. In rabbinic tradition, this elevated standard was justified only for Talmudic scholars. Less learned and devout individuals who wanted to adopt a more demanding and ascetic standard would be scorned for adopting a *ḥumrah*, and there are cases when the rabbi would intervene to prevent them from doing so.

One Los Angeles rabbi cited Talmudic support for his description of *ḥumrot* "as a way of outdoing the other, of egocentric competitiveness, and of putting down others."[93] One reason for the initial opposition to Hasidism was that Hasidic leaders permitted lay Jews to add *ḥumrot* as expressions of their piety. Such behaviors had been previously only permitted to great scholars and recognized masters of kabbalistic wisdom.[94] I asked a Chabad woman if she was bothered by the diminished enjoyment resulting from a standard she adopted that was an obvious *ḥumrah*. Smiling, she responded, "It's okay. It's my *mesiras nefesh*" (Hebrew [Ashkenazic] for "self-sacrifice").[95] She was referring to a concept in Chabad Hasidic religiosity that teaches that true devotion requires a person to negate his or her ego.

I heard a Yeshivish man, when learning about a Chabad standard, ask in exasperation, "Why are people doing all this extra? When you do all this extra, you're not focusing on what you are really required to do!"[96] Of course, I imagine that Modern Orthodox would regard this Yeshivish man's practices in the same light. Scorning *ḥumrot* puts them "in the know." For them, calling a practice a *ḥumrah* is pejorative, signaling its dubious authenticity. Many stated that the stringencies were a sign of ignorance: "People simply do not know what is *halakhah* and what is not, and that's why they get so strict," I was told. Several rabbis, some of whom were not Modern Orthodox, pointed out that the desire for strictness comes from people who are less knowledgeable. "It takes greater learning to rule leniently," they said.

Some practices known in the community as *ḥumrot* are actually norms followed in one community—a community *mesorah*—that are being imposed on others without their direct consent. This imposition occurs today through the kosher certification system. "It's the Hungarians," a local rabbi of Lithuanian Jewish heritage resignedly explained in reference to the increase in strictness. Through most of the twentieth century, the prevailing American Orthodox *kashrut* norms were in accordance with long-standing traditions from Central European and Lithuanian non-Hasidic rabbis who ruled moderately and with some flexibility. The post–World War II immigration of Hungarian rabbis, both Hasidic and non-Hasidic, brought to the United States traditions that were comparatively more stringent and inflexible. Although this group was (and still is) smaller in number than the non-Hungarians, it was still sizable, and its rabbis now hold greater prestige. The new *glatt* requirements in beef are derived from Hungarian precedents, and kosher food producers seeking the largest share of kosher consumers have found it more profitable to meet the Hungarian standards.[97]

The insistence by some Orthodox that one should only drink *ḥalav yisraʾel*, the milk deemed kosher because a Jew watched the milking of a kosher animal, is another example of a contested practice that, depending upon one's community, could be regarded as a stringency or normative *halakhah*.[98] In pre–World War II Europe and Mediterranean and Middle Eastern lands, where Jews farmed, owned dairy livestock, or lived near Jewish dairy producers, it was not difficult to obtain milk from Jewish farmers and employees. Jews who kept the kosher laws purchased such milk as a matter of course and would only eat cheese and dairy products made from it. In the United States, however, Jews were not involved in dairy farming, especially in the twentieth century, and after American dairy farming became highly industrialized, *ḥalav yisraʾel* was expensive and not widely available.

In 1954, the leading rabbinic authority Moshe Feinstein, who was learned in Lithuanian halakhic traditions, permitted regular milk by ruling that US federal laws and inspections of commercial dairies are even more effective than Jewish supervisors in guaranteeing that the milk sold is from cows and not pigs because there would be serious financial disincentives for such cheating.[99] For decades his opinion was accepted within Orthodox society. Consequently, his loyalists and the force of recent tradition render *ḥalav yisraʾel* as an unnecessary *ḥumrah*. Those Orthodox who prefer the Hungarian standard, as well as Chabad Hasidic Jews, reject what they regard as Feinstein's overly lenient and flawed ruling. Currently, Jews who describe themselves as Yeshivish also prefer *ḥalav yisraʾel*. The amount of passion generated by *kashrut* issues is tremendous, and the *ḥalav yisraʾel* question is a case in point: a 2009 article in an online Orthodox newspaper discussing Feinstein's ruling prompted 184 comments debating its merits.[100] The issues transcend the milk itself. What the participants were debating included the extent to which one can trust non-Jews to comply with the law, the authority of another community's rabbinic leader, the legitimacy of American law and the probity of its regulators, the extent of God's concern for the minutiae of Jewish practice, and the responsibility of Jews to be role models for non-Jews.

Financial concerns play an important role too. Restaurants and caterers who do not serve *halav yisra'el* dairy foods are eliminating these Orthodox Jews from their clientele. Two Chabad rabbis told me, "It's almost as important to us as the prohibition against eating pork," even though they do not declare that Jews who drink regular milk are actually sinning.[101] One educator in the Pico-Robertson Modern-Centrist Orthodox girls' high school takes pains to instruct the students to honor each other's standards. He tells students, "Don't go around advertising your *humrah*, and don't judge others for not practicing it!" He recalled a time when some girls arranged a surprise birthday party for their classmate from a Chabad family and purchased a *halav yisra'el* cake because that was her—but not the majority's—standard.[102]

The Chabad Hasidic community does not always favor the most restrictive rules; Chabad insists on *halav yisra'el* and only Hasidic *shehitah*, but it permits regular kosher bread (while acknowledging that *pat yisra'el* is best), does not believe *yashan* flour is required, and has not elevated the threat of bugs over other matters.[103] It is more accurate to say that Chabad promotes its distinctive set of practices, some of which are known *humrot* and some of which are particular to Chabad, such as encouraging people to have separate refrigerators for milk and meat in their homes. An Orthodox man asked me why I asked a kosher grocery store clerk about the store's single refrigerator case holding separate packaged meat and dairy foods: "What do you think—that the milk cells are going to jump into the meat?" I told him that Chabad teaches people as an ideal to have two separate refrigerators in their home, one for milk and one for meat. He said, "Don't get me started on them."[104]

One Chabad rabbi explained the phenomenon of unique standards as a type of cultural pluralism: "People stick to their own community. That is natural because every congregation has its own customs: in the foods, the melodies, and so on. What could be objectionable in such communal diversity? It enriches everybody."[105] He applied this to the Orthodox community as a whole. He admitted that there are Chabad families who do not accept the standards of other Chabad Jews. He attributed the problem to the many *ba'alei teshuvah*, newly religious, in the community, but "down the road, the children of these newly Orthodox Jews will be following the same [Chabad] standard." Other Chabad members I spoke to were not as optimistic, such as the older woman who lamented what she saw as a liberalizing trend among the younger women in her congregation, in whose homes she would not eat.[106]

Expecting that all Orthodox Jews should aspire to share the same table, I learned, betrays one's outsider status or position on the liberal side of the Orthodox community, who are the least culturally insular. Those who define themselves as Modern Orthodox believe there should be a community Orthodox *kashrut* standard—not just on occasions but on a regular basis. They were most likely to praise halakhic leniency and compromise and were the most likely to indicate that they would unqualifiedly eat at the table of others in their congregation.

The Modern Orthodox admiration for a whole-community approach and for the prioritization of Jewish community solidarity is consistent with their unabashed nationalistic Zionism—that is, their support for a Jewish state inclusive of religious and secular Jews—a political position that is not shared across the Orthodox spectrum. They were more likely to describe *kashrut* as a way to "connect to your ancestors" rather than as a response to a divine directive. One left-leaning Modern Orthodox rabbi in the neighborhood will eat at the home of any of his congregants, no questions asked. According to his congregants, he tells them, "You all know my standards, and if you invite me I assume you are following them."[107] Another rabbi, who serves a Centrist Orthodox congregation, has a policy of not eating at any of his congregants' homes unless the meal is catered or the food is from kosher packages or from kosher-certified producers, lest he insult them. But he does not follow this practice with rabbinic colleagues who are members of his congregation.[108]

Yet I learned that even in Modern Orthodox congregations, people may refrain from eating at the tables of fellow congregants whose *kashrut* practices are less strict than their own.

The desire for a communitywide *kashrut* standard has been a theme within the kosher certification arm of the Rabbinical Council of California (RCC), whose member rabbis are drawn from the Modern and Centrist Orthodox cohort.[109] Its most influential leaders live in Pico-Robertson and the San Fernando Valley, and RCC *hashgahah* has been the one used most frequently in Pico-Robertson food businesses. Yet the RCC's past efforts to bring unity to Los Angeles's kosher certification by holding a monopoly on local kosher certification demonstrate that unity to some means oppression and lack of choice to others.

In 1997, the RCC's effort to dissuade two rabbis who resisted RCC control and were known for a more lenient standard provoked open and angry resistance. The two rabbis' supporters included laypeople and rabbis across the Orthodox spectrum, even the most liberal. They publicly denounced the RCC for defaming the integrity and Torah knowledge of one of the kosher supervisors, and they engaged an attorney to complain to the Federal Trade Commission about the RCC's unfair business practices. The RCC abandoned its effort. Perhaps it is characteristic of the "mixed origins" and Modern Orthodox dominance of the Pico-Robertson community that the initiative even occurred, one observer suggested. He pointed out that two of the pro-monopoly rabbis had *ba'al teshuvah* origins—they came to Orthodoxy as young adults—and may have sought one supreme, rigorous Torah authority for the entire community for the purpose of showing devotion to God and diminishing Orthodox "internecine warfare." He explained that "had they encountered such rigor when they were first exploring Judaism, they probably would not have continued with their Jewish journeys."[110]

Today in the Orthodox enclave located in the Beverly–La Brea neighborhood, however, RCC *hashgahah* is scorned for being too compromising, on the one hand, favoring its upscale and acculturated clientele, and for being too strict, on the other hand, being overly focused on bugs.[111] Disdain for the RCC increased after the 1997 kosher meat scandal because the business was under RCC *hashgaḥah*. The owner was not an Orthodox Jew, and for some time there had been rumors that his meat was not genuinely kosher. A private investigator not associated with the RCC videotaped the owner sneaking non-*glatt* or nonkosher meat into his Pico-Robertson store. Newspaper coverage revealed that the owner had been accused of *kashrut* fraud two decades earlier and that the RCC had known of this. Because he was dealing with meat, his business was under constant (*temidi*) supervision. Critics argued that even constant supervision is not foolproof and his status as a non-Orthodox Jew and his past bad behavior could have—and, for many, should have—been cited as reason not to certify his business. Community reactions to the event fell along existing social and community lines. Beverly–La Brea neighborhood Jews heaped scorn on the perpetrator and the RCC, but in Pico-Robertson some supporters of the accused kosher business insinuated that the incident was the underhanded work of a competing kosher certifier. The situation was resolved satisfactorily when a local Orthodox philanthropist purchased the discredited kosher meat distribution business and retail store and handed it over to someone else to manage. People urged him to put the butcher shop under the most scrupulous Los Angeles standard. However, he thought it was best for the Los Angeles community to have multiple kosher authorities, and he arranged with the now-chastened RCC to continue to supervise.[112]

Five years later the memory of this event remains and still has repercussions. Although the Beverly–La Brea neighborhood contains kosher grocery stores, bakeries, and restaurants, there are far more on Pico Boulevard, and proprietors have switched their kosher certifier in order to secure a greater market share of consumers. An agent for a kosher food distributor who lives in the La Brea neighborhood, who overheard my questions to a clerk in an RCC-approved grocery store, voiced his disdain:

> The sign on the door and the RCC food labels [on the meat] don't mean anything. In this part of town, you can't find out anything unless

you ask! They just label the store and the meat "RCC" and that's supposed to tell you anything? In La Brea, the labels actually tell you
something. . . . I will only buy according to the [meat company] name.
My wife knows who to ask for.[113]

He is implying that anyone who places trust in a group of rabbis, especially this group, is bound to be deluded. In 2017–18, two national kosher
certification agencies started certifying restaurants in the neighborhood,
purchasing an existing agency and supplanting some of the market share
of the RCC.

Some individuals' and groups' attitudes toward the trustworthiness of food are not related to the food itself. A nonreligious Jewish chef
trying to gain clients in the Orthodox community was exasperated by
the questions that potential customers asked about her Sabbath observance and synagogue membership: "What does it matter that I attend
an Orthodox synagogue?" she complained. "I am committed to following the rules of *kashrut*; otherwise I wouldn't be doing this. But they
don't trust me."[114] A local rabbi explained the logic: if Jews violate the
laws in one major aspect of *halakhah*, "they have lost their *ne'emanut*,"
their trustworthiness regarding other aspects of Jewish observance, like
kashrut.[115] Orthodox women demonstrate trustworthiness in a number
of ways. A woman who is a member of a Centrist Orthodox synagogue
told me that when the women arrange food for community or home
events, she is relegated to bringing in something from the kosher bakery
or kosher deli. "They won't accept my food because I don't wear a wig or
cover my hair outside of the synagogue," she told me.[116] I found these
kinds of judgments to be widespread in Centrist and Chabad congregations, where modesty may also include length of sleeves and hem, type
and thickness of stockings, and tightness and color of clothes. Establishing trustworthiness for a person in one activity by looking at another
aspect of his or her behavior in another activity is part of Jewish tradition appearing as far back as the Talmud, yet—typical of rabbinic
law—there are opinions that such generalized guilt has no legal foundation because the judgment is based on data from another setting.[117]

One aspect of today's stringencies is an outgrowth of a different and distinctly modern socio-intellectual phenomenon. New household cleansers and technology that permit detection of food sources and eliminate food residues at a higher level than in the past have become identified with ritual purification. Certainly, this particular stringency results in part from kosher food companies that conflate hygiene and purity with *kashrut* when marketing their food to Jewish and non-Jewish customers.[118] Modern education values precise measurements, scientifically verified research, and commonsense logic. While past rabbinic authorities also valued these, they valued halakhic precedent and their own rabbinic logic more. They demanded less purity than what is demanded today, permitting some contact and mixing of permitted and prohibited foods, especially after-the-fact inadvertent adulteration, and even allowed the use of animal ingredients that were no longer considered "food" according to rabbinic standards. These animal ingredients include powdered enzymes or catalysts whose animal origin is not apparent without chemical testing.

To people unfamiliar with rabbinic logic and precedents, these standards are too lax. They have what I would call a "germ theory" of *kashrut*, that is, the notion that all residues of *treif* food or improper mixtures may infect one's kosher food. Soap is a case in point.[119] According to rabbinic law, soap is not food, so the laws of *kashrut* do not apply to it. Furthermore, food that comes into contact with soap has been made inedible, so the laws do not apply to it either—therefore, any kind of soap is kosher. Theoretically, one could use the same soapy dishwater to clean milk and meat dishes. These halakhic points, however, do not affect normative practice: most Orthodox women and men simply do not accept them. Some seek a kosher certification symbol on dishwashing liquid, and others apply the same germ theory logic even to laundry detergent because it indirectly may come into contact with food residues. According to one woman, writing on an internet forum for religious women, "I decided I saw value in the *hekhsher* on my laundry detergent when I added some to a pot of BOILING water in order to remove all the burnt-on rice that slid right off afterwards." Her logic is drawn from some rabbinic reasoning—namely, that heat transmits kosher status—and some of her own that ignores rabbinic tradition.[120]

Today, modern ideas of free choice and mistrust of rabbinic-led kosher certification can express themselves in demands not rooted in Jewish law. My interview with a former *mashgiah* (hired *kashrut* inspector) is illustrative. A *mashgiah* does not need to be a rabbi or even know much *halakhah*, I was told by a local authority; what is important is that the person is devout, is attentive, and knows what should prompt a question to the supervising rabbi. I spoke to one such *mashgiah* who had previously worked in a kosher warehouse under RCC supervision. He told me of an incident when, for the Sabbath before a big catered event, the containers of milk had to be stored in the meat refrigerators—a violation of the usual rule but, for various reasons, necessary. When he entered the meat refrigerator on Sunday morning, he saw that the milk had spilled onto the floor, shelves, and the prepared platters of cut meat. He did not know what caused the accident—perhaps a small earthquake or an unstable shelf? He immediately phoned the RCC, and the rabbinic authority there told him to thoroughly wash off the meat with cold water and use it. He told me,

> That was it—I did what they wanted and then quit. Yes, I've heard that you can just wash it off if everything is cold, but would you eat that meat? Shouldn't the people have been told? And if they had been told, would they ever trust that *hashgahah*? These are excuses made just to save money.[121]

He may not have recognized his preference as a *humrah*. Based on my perusal of comments after online news articles and in online forums, neither would many other Torah-observant Jews. Labeling it as a *humrah* may have made no difference anyway.

So much of what makes food kosher takes place in the privacy of one person's kitchen, and today it also occurs behind closed doors at the rear of a restaurant and in a factory hundreds of miles away. Modern conveniences, technology, and business practices have made it easier to keep kosher but also have added new concerns. In addition to the other factors generating the innovations and revived traditions, I suggest that these may be regarded as adaptations. They keep the act of keeping kosher a high-demand religious practice that is not only a sign of authentic individual devotion but also an effective marker of one's community.

Through the observance of *kashrut*, the Torah-observant community and the subcommunities within Orthodox society display their boundaries internally and externally to others. For Orthodox Jews, the adage "you are what you eat" says more than whether one is Orthodox or whether one's internal religious quality matches one's outward behavior. A person's way of keeping kosher indicates membership in a particular Orthodox denomination or in a class of people who are distinct for their style of religious devotion and for their level of knowledge. An Orthodox Jew's *kashrut* practice merely hints at whose religious authority she or he considers paramount because the authority today is not likely to be a particular rabbi or set of rabbinic rulings. Familial tradition and congregational norms are more important than rabbinic opinions. Even these may go by the wayside in the face of the continuous carving out of smaller groups within the larger and growing Orthodox community. People who differentiate themselves in terms of *kashrut* are asserting their allegiance to a community within the larger whole. By choosing a particular combination of *halakhah* and custom within *kashrut*, Orthodox Jews create community with others, and individuals can forge a unique personal identity while affirming loyalty to the whole.

To outsiders, these rules of *kashrut* seem impossibly complex and tremendously restrictive. When queried, Orthodox Jews typically respond that it is not difficult and in fact rather automatic and natural. This response belies the extensive decision-making and labor needed to obey these rules. These foodways would certainly not feel so natural and would not be as carefully maintained and perpetuated except for the fact that Orthodox Jews choose to live in concentrated proximity to each other. Their enclaves supply the social support necessary to reinforce the performance of the laws. Living near each other makes it far easier to observe the Sabbath and holiday rituals and to obey the prohibitions, organize communal worship, and arrange the schooling and youth activities essential for raising the next generation of Orthodox Jews.

3

Pedagogy and Public Relations

In the 1970s a teenage boy who had been raised in Los Angeles and attended American Judaism's Conservative movement synagogues, afternoon Hebrew school classes, and summer camp was introduced to Orthodox Judaism and decided to utterly change the course of his life. His befuddled parents gave him permission to go to Israel and enroll in an Orthodox yeshiva in Israel designed for post–high school age *ba'alei teshuvah*. Like all such schools, this provided courses in Jewish law and a daily and Sabbath routine of religious life. Much time was devoted to exploring questions of meaning, explanations for the individual *mitzvot*, theology, and reflections on the value of religious commitment. All these constitute what Orthodox Jews call *hashkafah*, or religious worldview. *Hashkafah* is crucial to Jews who are making such fundamental changes in their lives because they need to explain their radical transformation to their families, friends, and themselves. Yet Orthodox Jews as a whole follow a tradition that insists that the primary reason for performing God's commandments is that God commanded them. Finding personal meaning and wisdom in the laws is good but nevertheless secondary and certainly not a prerequisite to the performance of the commandments. Years later, I interviewed this man, now a rabbi, author, and teacher in two local Orthodox high schools. He now minimizes the value of *hashkafah* by arguing that his students need to learn the value of performing inexplicable *mitzvot*, ones that have no obvious reason. He recalled the yeshiva director's guiding directive to him and the other *ba'alei teshuvah*:

"The rabbi said to us, 'Start slow. Every week take upon yourself one mitzvah that you find meaningful, and one mitzvah that you do not. Accustom yourself to being God's servant.'"[1]

Being a servant of God is a theme I heard often in my interviews with Orthodox Jews about why they keep kosher and how they teach their children to do so. A woman who became Orthodox soon after marriage told me, "My husband and I chose Orthodoxy because we wanted to pass on a substantial heritage to our children. I wanted to be a servant of God."[2] *Kashrut* is the law that most exemplifies servitude to God because it is considered a decree, an incomprehensible divine law. It makes many demands on the time, finances, and appetites of today's Orthodox Jews, regulating all snacks and meals, without any claim that the rules are reasonable or will benefit them. Chabad Hasidic Jews I interviewed also invoked the theme of servitude, but they were likelier to affirm the inner logic of the dietary laws and describe them as acts of *partnering* with God.

The field of social psychology is useful for clarifying why Orthodox Jews accept or reject certain types of religious reasoning. Jonathan Haidt argues that within the human brain there are five innate prosocial impulses that make people bond to each other as kin and as members of the same community. These inclinations optimize the individual's survival and the group's preservation and reproduction. The first is a concern to care for and not to harm another; the second is a sense of fairness and a disdain for cheating; the third is a desire to be part of a group and a sensitivity to signs of group betrayal; the fourth is a deference to legitimate authority, rank, and status and an aversion to people who flaunt their disregard for these hierarchies; and the fifth is a sense of disgust for things or behaviors considered harmful to self and community and an attraction to those things or behaviors that preserve and strengthen the self and group. A person's temperament, experience, and culture temper and shape these five foundational reactions.[3]

Orthodox Jewish children, like all children, are imprinted with the impulse to respect authority, but they are also socialized to extend parental respect to God and to fear God's punishing power. Secular American children today are born with the same proclivity to respect authority, but they are taught to favor scientific authority rather than religious authority, and it is unlikely that many parents even teach them about divine authority. Depending on their upbringing, many secular American children are also taught to be skeptical of political authority.

Social psychologists assert that behavior or preference for a particular behavior starts from one's intuitive response, which is shaped by one's upbringing and community; intellectual reasoning comes afterward to justify the initial response. This is why explanations and rationales may sound inadequate or unconvincing on their own or why people have difficulty articulating their moral convictions.[4] Religious Jews are taught that the proper and holy way to produce, prepare, and eat food is in accordance with God's will as defined by rabbis. They also are taught that intellectual reasoning, in its very essence, differs from faith, comes from a different source, and is far less important. Some, like the yeshiva director mentioned above, even regard the desire for explanation as a sign that one's religious faith is weak.

Orthodox Jews treasure most those values that strengthen their community and its perpetuation. Haidt found that people on the conservative side of the political and cultural spectrum give greatest importance to group loyalty, submission to authority, and concepts of holiness and disgust. They situate the care/harm and fairness/cheating principles within the context of their own community rather than within universal humanity. In contrast, people on the liberal side of the political and cultural spectrum give greatest importance to the care/harm principle and tend to regard group loyalty, submission to authority (though not scientific authority), and disgust for the unconventional as leading to oppression and discrimination.[5] Orthodox Jewish modes of teaching and talking about *kashrut* and Jewish food rituals fit the conservative pattern. Despite their disinclination to put religious faith into intellectual terms, the Orthodox do so because they live among others who do not share their viewpoints, and they live within a society that regards human reason as a good basis for decision-making. They are asked by outsiders and insiders how to explain their choices, and they ask themselves these questions. Consequently, they learn to explain *kashrut* as a response to divine authority that requires them to be a holy people, that is, to be a distinctive community attesting to God's majesty.

The Orthodox recognize that a high regard for human reason and individualism are distinctively American values and admirable to some extent, certainly in a professional context. But they also recognize that the survival of Orthodox Judaism and the Orthodox community are at risk if too much importance is placed upon individualism, ethics, and reason. This resistance to the prevailing culture around them explains why Modern and Centrist Orthodox, the groups who are the most engaged with and integrated into American secular society and its favorable regard for human reason and individual freedom, may recoil from portraying *kashrut* in rational and ethical terms. They do not explain *kashrut* as arising out of compassion for animals. They prefer instead to describe it as deference to divine authority, a means of preserving the group, and a way to live in a holy manner. Yet, Orthodox Jews may appeal to reason and rationalism when reaching out to non-Orthodox Jews who are considering stricter religious observance or when trying to fortify the commitment of Orthodox Jews who may be wavering. When speaking with non-Jews, they also employ the language of ethics to describe the kosher laws, especially the laws of kosher animal slaughter.

OBEYING AND UNDERSTANDING GOD'S COMMANDS

Jewish rabbinic tradition has long been ambivalent about the effort to explain the Torah's laws. The rabbinic outlook takes its cue from the Pentateuch, in which nearly all laws lack explanation and many are preceded or followed by the statement "I am the Lord [YHWH] your God." Most of the dietary laws follow this pattern.[6] Biblical authors prioritized behavior—the doing or following of the law—over the understanding of the law, and they highlighted the consequences for obedience or disobedience. For example, in the first biblical episode involving a food taboo, God's prohibition of the fruit of the Tree of Knowledge is followed by the warning "on the day you eat it you shall die." When the serpent presents Eve with the reason for the prohibition, namely, "on the day you eat it, your eyes will be opened, and you will be like God, knowing good and evil," she violates the rule. This story implies that when human beings seek understanding of God's laws, they are signaling their resistance to God's authority.[7]

The classical rabbis, whose teachings are in the Mishnah (ca. 200 CE), Talmud (200–600 CE), and other writings from the same era, agreed to some extent with prioritizing behavior over understanding the laws. They disdained the human desire to supply rational explanations for individual divine precepts, even to account for their good sense from the perspective of human logic and wisdom. For the rabbis, God's laws should be respected because they are a result of God's will, not because their content is in accordance with our understanding of what is good or wise.[8] Of course, many demands made by religions, Judaism included, fail the test of reason. For the past two thousand years, however, Jewish religious leaders have not only asserted that the dietary laws could not be explained but also insisted that their opacity is a key aspect of these rules' importance and a sign of their divinity. Many secular people disdain this attitude, labeling it with adjectives such as childlike, mindless, and submissive. Anthropologist Roy Rappaport observes that attributions of sanctity are given to matters that are unverifiable but are essential to human organization. Social psychologist Haidt quips that "sacredness binds people together, and then blinds them to the arbitrariness of the practice."[9] Orthodox rabbis and teachers are well versed in the Talmudic sources asserting the legitimacy and value of decrees. The rabbis I interviewed uniformly regarded it as problematic to connect faith with reason. One local rabbinic author, using some sarcasm, chose the following passages to compare the faith (*emunah*) of Jews, which is "complete" (*shelemah*), to the partial religious faith of non-Jews:

> Some people come to believe through their investigation and comprehension. This is not the belief that is appropriate to a Jew. A firm conclusion one day can turn into an equally firm different one the

next. Reasoned, investigated belief is appropriate to the finer people of the nations of the world [non-Jews]. It is not the *emunah shelemah*, the completed belief that a Jew declares each day.

Human inquiry and comprehension are not void of value but are "fragile and plastic," he wrote. The only enduring faith is that "which is predicated on the word of the Torah itself."[10]

Yet, the rabbinic tradition does not regard all divine laws as impenetrable. According to the Mishnaic rabbis, an ordinance, *mishpat*, is a law whose necessity is so apparent that even if it were not found in the Torah, a society would legislate it. An example of this is "do not steal." Ordinances are reasonable, obviously necessary, and not unique to the Jewish people. This makes their performance less an act of faith. The other type of commandment is a *ḥok*, a decree, an inexplicable law. Here is the classic definition of the term:

> Decrees are matters that the evil inclination queries and the idolatrous nations of the world query, such as [the prohibition against] eating pork. . . . Therefore [in response to such queries] it is written "I, the Lord" have decreed them, and it is not for you to call them into question.[11]

Decrees testify to God's sovereignty and majesty, and they are unique to the Jewish people. It is an act of faith to obey a decree, as well as a sacrifice. Decrees require that a Jew stifle his or her evil inclination—that is, the self-centered ego and reasoning capacity—and face the ridicule of non-Jews. Obedience to a decree is far more "costly" than obedience to an ordinance and therefore of greater value. Here and elsewhere in rabbinic writings, a dietary prohibition is cited as the prime example of a decree.

The Talmudic rabbis exerted little effort when explaining decrees. One sage even declared that "reasons for the different commandments of the Torah should be kept secret," as secret as esoteric teachings about creation and the divine chariot.[12] They deliberated over this matter by referring to the law in Deuteronomy 22:6–7, where God requires shooing away a mother bird from her nest before taking her chicks or fledglings to eat. While the law seems to indicate God's compassion for the mother bird, the rabbis of the Mishnah ruled that a prayer leader who chants "God's mercy extends to a bird's nest" must be silenced. For centuries thereafter, rabbis debated why the Mishnah wanted to silence the prayer leader. They wondered, for example: could it be because the prayer leader implies that God favors some animals over others, or was he making an unauthorized addition to the prayers? One rabbi argued that the Mishnah recognized that shooing away the mother bird is actually a cruel and merciless act. This, he argued, made obeying it an ideal way for a sensitive person to show selfless deference to God's sovereignty. The consensus of this debate is that it is presumptuous to assume that one understands the underlying logic of this or any law. Even laws whose logic appears transparent are actually beyond human understanding and should be valued as such. For rabbis, this principle is fundamental to the proper determination of *halakhah*, applied Jewish law. In other words, one's notion of the purpose of the law must not influence one's obligation to follow it.[13]

The Talmudic rabbis believed that the commandments impart spiritual and moral benefits to a person's character. Even one that appears inexplicable inclines a person to be upright, more aware of God's presence in the world, and more desirous to please God. The goodness of God and God's Torah is a point of faith. This is a theme in the liturgy.[14] An oft-repeated affirmation from the Mishnah says: "The Holy One, praised be He, desired to benefit the people Israel; therefore He gave them the Torah with an abundance of commandments."[15] This divine love and beneficence, however, are nevertheless intertwined with a measure of human discomfort. A frequently repeated teaching is one from the Talmudic sage Abba Arika, known as Rav:

> Were not the commandments given so that man might be refined by
> them? Do you really think that The Holy One Blessed Be He cares
> if an animal is slaughtered by the throat or the nape of the neck?

Therefore, the commandments were only given to purify human beings.[16]

Here the assertion of the laws' positive effect is accompanied by derision for seeking meaning in the specific details of the law. The laws have a refining or purifying effect.[17] Rav does not claim that the required mode of slaughtering the animal is better because it is less painful to the animal, removes the blood, or has any other rational reason. For him, refinement occurs not because of something inherent in the details of the laws but in the very act of doing them in accordance with God's will.

The rabbis identified two incentives for obedience that have been central to Jewish spiritual life. The first is *yir'at shamayim*, fear or awe of God. It is the attitude of great reverence for God as Creator, Ruler, and Majestic Presence. Such a feeling of awe toward God's omnipotence should lead a Jew to dutifully and devotedly obey God's will, irrespective of a fear of punishment or desire for reward. A rabbinic aphorism teaches, "Do not be like servants who serve the master on the condition of receiving a reward; rather, be like servants who serve the master without the condition of receiving a reward. Let the fear of Heaven be upon you."[18] Pious Jews should accept the "yoke of the commandments," even if they do not understand or enjoy fulfilling them. A Pico-Robertson rabbi writing to his congregants, many of whom are newly religious Jews, explained, "One must first accept Hashem [literally, 'the Name,' used to avoid using the word *God* in a nonsacred context] and his Torah as a load that you must carry. After practicing 'weightlifting,' our souls become stronger and not only bear the burden but actually enjoy lifting it."[19] This level of piety is a great achievement. Another rabbinic statement underlines the extent to which achieving the fear of God is in itself a mystery: "Everything is in the hands of God except the fear of God."[20] The second concept is *ahavat Hashem*, love of God (or *ahavas Hashem*, Ashkenazic pronunciation). This, too, is fundamental and so important that the exhortation from Deuteronomy 6:5 in the *Sh'ma* prayer, "You shall love the Lord your God with all your heart and with all your soul and with all your might," accompanies the declaration of God's oneness in this prayer. Ideally, Jews perform the commandments out of the desire to please God, recognizing that God gave the *mitzvot* to the Jewish nation as a gift and as a demonstration of His love.[21]

The rabbis considered *yir'at shamayim* and *ahavat Hashem* far more powerful inducements than a person's opinion that the law is good or wise. While the rabbis raised questions and engaged in intellectual inquiry during Torah study—and certainly reasoned logically while deciding applied law—they taught that one should perform the *mitzvot* with wholehearted conviction that these are God's will. Even if a Jew were not fully convinced, he should obey and in so doing would be fulfilling his obligation. A person who struggles to obey a prohibition is to be commended more than the person who obeys it with ease. The effort invested in obedience makes it more precious, more heroic.[22]

This disdain for the specific meaning of the laws did not always prevail. There is a long history for the genre of addressing "the reasons for the commandments" (*ta'amei hamitzvot*)— the genre that systematically explains the wisdom of the specific laws and their spiritual, ethical, and health-related purposes, as well as their symbolic meanings. This genre first appeared in the Hellenistic era to an audience outside Palestine away from rabbinic influence.[23] Jewish philosophical writing, which began to appear in the ninth century CE, insisted that there was significant overlap between reason and revelation. "Reasons for the commandments" were often included in this literature. Although the authors sought to show the wisdom of Judaism from the perspective of human reason, they did not always claim that every law had a discernable purpose; for example, Rabbi Sa'adia ben Yoseph Gaon argued that God deliberately created some decrees to be utterly senseless so that Jews could fulfill them to demonstrate their pure obedience.[24]

The pursuit for meaning was significantly furthered in the thirteenth century. The "secret teachings" mentioned by the Talmudic rabbis, detailing the processes of creation, the divine chariot, and the reasons for the commandments, were put into writing in the *Zohar*, a compendium of mystical thought that purported to reveal the authentic, deeper meaning of the Torah. This work and its subsequent commentaries were later called Kabbalah, meaning "received tradition." Previously incomprehensible decrees were now decoded by being described as having a particular influence on the soul, on the physical world, and on God. This made the practices sound reasonable in that they were described as producing specific results. These results were still rather intangible (e.g., greater divine harmony), however, and the explanations had to be accepted on faith. At first, Kabbalah was studied by and generally restricted to elite Jewish scholars. It eventually was spread to wider audiences in abridged and simplified form. For example, Hasidic leaders in Eastern Europe transmitted kabbalistic ideas to their lay followers in sermons and stories.

Nevertheless, the influence of Kabbalah did not stop the production of non-kabbalistic explanations for the commandments. There were late medieval and modern thinkers who felt the Kabbalah should remain concealed, who preferred more rational interpretations, or who found other ways to address the need for a meaningful philosophy of Judaism. Today's Modern and Centrist Orthodox Jews, even the elite among them, do not study Kabbalah. Chabad Hasidic Jews learn it through the study of *Tanya*, the first Chabad rebbe's interpretation of Kabbalah, and consequently they are more amenable to providing explanations for divine laws.

While there is much traditional Jewish literature available to help a person seeking to develop a meaningful religious view, a *hashkafah*, the quest is not greatly emphasized except, as this chapter's opening story indicates, when one's faith is new or wavering. An individual's *hashkafah* is a private matter, an aspect of the self that is relatively free from social control because of the emphasis on behavior. The active doing of the commandments is emphasized over *hashkafah*. "We shall do and we shall listen," the Israelites declared at the moment of revelation of the Torah. This declaration from Exodus 24:7 is regarded as the Torah principle of prizing performance of the *mitzvot* above the understanding of them. Belief does not come first; the commitment to behave dutifully is the foundation for everything else.

Furthermore, because proper behavior is understood in collective terms, an individual's personal belief is relatively unimportant. An individual who obeys God may be punished for the community's sins. Nowhere is collective merit or guilt more obvious than in traditional liturgy, where confessional prayers and requests for forgiveness are uttered in plural form. The group is responsible for each other's behavior. This collective responsibility makes it imperative for people to be vigilant about their children's and neighbor's misdeeds, and it strengthens community solidarity.[25] Being a member of the Orthodox community means that one's religious conduct is scrutinized by other Orthodox Jews, along with voiced or implied judgment. Sociologist Iddo Tavory emphasizes that Orthodox identity and community are not static but are constantly being created when one is summoned by others into communal participation and religious observance. I would add that attention to others' scrutiny and judgment about one's behavior, especially avoiding criticism, also creates Orthodox identity.[26]

In the Home

Parents do not supply reasons for the *mitzvot* to their children; their young are socialized in such a manner so that observance of Torah laws is a natural part of the fabric of daily life. My question to parents about how they taught *kashrut* would initially draw a blank look. They would then respond, "I don't recall actually teaching them" or "It was a given." One delayed her answer for a few days so she could ask her older children how they had been taught. Prompted by my mention of possible techniques or arguments (ethical rationales or spiritual meanings), most answered, "I taught it as a *ḥok* [decree]." They did not recall offering explanations for why some animals were prohibited and some permitted, why one must separate meat and milk, and so on. After all, a decree needs no explanation. Of course, parents likely reference the dietary laws differently depending on the ages of their children and their own background. When children are raised from birth to be Orthodox (the expression for this is "*frum* [religious] from birth"), *kashrut* is taken for granted and unlikely to be questioned or regarded as a subject of interest. Even when parents came to Orthodoxy later in life, they are not likely to supply

Torah laws with reasons in a familial context. Parents govern the household, and God is master of the world. These boundaries are blurred, as reflected in the liturgical reference to God as *avinu shebashamayim*, "our Father in heaven."

Parents across the Orthodox spectrum take seriously their duty to make their children learn fear of God, love of God, and obedience to religious law. They teach their children that God watches them to see whether or not they are fulfilling the commandments. They would likely affirm the principle that God is good and God's Torah is good. They may also say that *Hashem* loves when they follow His Torah, *Hashem* sees everything that they do, and *Hashem* will reward or punish them depending on their behavior. The child does not stand alone; every Jewish individual is part of the larger Jewish people. Anthropologist Ayala Fader has found that Hasidic women in Brooklyn cultivate a sense of self in their children, but they teach them "to realize fulfillment by independently conforming to a religiously communitarian society rather than to one that promotes pride in individualism."[27]

One Persian father was a bit scornful about Americans' belief in the power of reason, especially in child-rearing. He explained that the most effective way of teaching *kashrut* starts when children are quite small:

> It's easy. You start when they are very little. A little boy will cry for *treif* candy at the grocery store, but once you say "It is not kosher!" [said with great drama] he will instantly stop crying. It is God. There is no other way. Once you don't believe in God, you lose it all. The anchor is *yir'at hashamayim*. Because of that, a child doesn't need explanations. Even later in life, if they don't do anything else, they will be keeping kosher.[28]

Another Persian young woman, who had recently emigrated from Iran, echoed this lesson and also identified a disconnect between American liberal values and religious faith. Like other Orthodox Jews of Persian background, she used the term "traditional" to describe Persian Jews who are not Orthodox but attend synagogues and eat only kosher meat.

These Persian Jews follow certain Jewish traditions as practiced in Iran and are traditional in outlook and practice relative to most American Jews. She explained, "Even the least religiously strict Persian Jew who grew up in Iran is more religious than an American Jew. This is because Iranian society is more God centered. It is a Muslim society, and so everyone has *emunah*." She does not remember ever having a conversation with her parents or teachers about keeping kosher, and she was never and is not now curious about explanations for these laws. She said, "Once you really believe in something, once you know it is the truth, you take its truth for granted."[29] An Ashkenazi Modern Orthodox principal in the boys' high school agreed with her characterization of Persians as a group: "The Persian families are very supportive. They are very respectful of education and of educators, and they give a lot of *kavod* [honor] to the teachers and the school." He did not find the same attitude among other Orthodox Jews. He likened the Persians to the Japanese, who he believes also highly prize the virtue of honor.[30]

Belief in God, understood in personified terms—as a divine Father, Teacher, Judge, Creator—is essential to Orthodox faith. This includes the conviction that God will punish Jews for violating the commandments, if not in this life then in the afterlife. As the ultimate authority of a world characterized by an innate hierarchy, God must reward or punish to preserve this order or exercise mercy if He so desires. Human beings cannot change their subordinate position; they can merely make the proper choices so as to enhance their situation.

My interview with a young man who was both in and out of the Orthodox community put the contrasting American liberal and Orthodox outlooks into sharp relief. He had been raised within a Chabad community and attended the Modern-Centrist Orthodox Pico-Robertson high school, yet his parents were *baalei teshuvah* who maintained strong ties with their secular past. They did not limit their table guests to Orthodox Jews, and they permitted him to attend a university with a low Jewish student population. On the one hand, he rejected the idea that *mitzvot* should be explained in ethical terms. To him, this is a "social justice Judaism" that diminishes theological acts into political statements. He also ridiculed the notion that an individual must find personal meaning in them:

> When you ask, "How do you feel about it?" my reaction is to roll my eyes. It's a selfish approach: Oh, I feel this way, I feel it has meaning, I get a sense of religious ecstasy, I don't do it because I don't feel a connection—that's about your own individual feelings. Just because you don't feel a connection is the *worst* reason to not keep it! The real reason you do it is because you realize it is high-level stuff. If you want to bring God into the picture, any reason you come up with is just skimming the surface. Of course, you can find all sorts of *reasons*, and we talked a lot about that at school. But they are not the real reason; the real reason is beyond you, on a level that you can't understand.

His rejection of human reason echoed the points made by his high school teachers.

On the other hand, he regarded the traditional anthropomorphic notion of God as "personified and limited." He prided himself on being more enlightened than his religious high school friends, who thought it was best not to break the laws so as to avoid God's punishment. He had been influenced by his father's "mysticism," an outlook that erased both authority and hierarchy. I asked him whether his outlook made it possible for him to serve God, and he answered,

> Yes, of course, but what does that even mean? What is God? The Torah personifies God, but is that real? Then you can try to avoid the personified images, and compare God to electricity and waves and forces. People think it is less puerile. But those images are just as limiting as personified images, and just as distant from what God is.[31]

For him, the best reason for performing the *mitzvot* is "because otherwise you are messing with the cosmos." Later, when I spoke to his high school principal, I described this perspective as one I had heard from a school alumnus. The principal did not appear impressed and immediately asked, "Is he keeping kosher?" When I reported that the student was "taking a temporary break" from it, the principal indicated he was not surprised and sadly shook his head.[32]

In the home, snack time and mealtime are occasions for the fulfillment of many commandments and for socially reinforcing proper religious views. The proper way to eat, according to *halakhah*, is to thank God before and after eating through formulaic Hebrew blessings. The ones said before eating are short and are taught to children who are quite young. They all start with the phrase "Blessed are you, Lord, King of the universe," followed by mention of God's role as creator of the food that will be eaten. Foods are grouped into categories for the purpose of these blessings. For example, the blessing over fruit ends with "who creates the fruit of the tree," the vegetable blessing ends with "who creates the fruit of the earth," and the blessing over pastries ends with "who creates various kinds of sustenance." Among the food categories, the most important is bread, whose blessing ends with the words "Who brings forth bread from the earth." Bread is understood to be necessary for a proper meal, and eating bread must also be preceded by a ritual handwashing. Blessings after the meals are also in fixed liturgical form and are longer. A lengthy prayer of praise and thanksgiving is recited after a meal that includes bread. A meal without bread requires a shorter prayer, several sentences long. Additional words or paragraphs are added on the Sabbath and holidays, and these reinforce the importance of the holy days. When a child is young, her mother is likely to hold out a snack and remind her, before handing her the food, "Say the *berakhah*." The lips of a more independent or older child may be watched, and if they are not moving, she may be asked, "Did you say the *berakhah*?"

A sense of sacredness is inculcated by these rules: God is holy, and the people who follow His laws are witnessing God's sanctity and associating themselves with it. The formulaic blessing uttered prior to performing a mitzvah praises God, who has "sanctified us with Your commandments." It seemed to me that this desire for holiness was behind the words of a woman who became Orthodox in her twenties and explained why she began to follow *kashrut* in a strict manner. She said, "First, I love saying *berakhot.* If the food is not kosher, I can't say a *berakhah.* And I want to say *berakhot!* Saying *berakhot* is very important to me, I can't explain it, I just love doing it."[33] She also likes the discipline that the practice gives her, as well as the bonds with other Jews. She remembers being in high school when she did not keep kosher, and because of that she now treasures the sense of specialness and the strong feeling of community that were missing then. A shared sense of sacredness enables people who are not otherwise related to cooperate and protect each other. Members of such religious communities have an advantage in that more people are willing to make sacrifices and extend themselves on their behalf and have high regard for them simply because they belong to the group.[34]

The daily home context for *kashrut* observance makes it easy to teach it without any commentary. Typically, women teach *kashrut* by focusing on surrounding visual cues. They point out the family's differently patterned or colored meat and milk plates, cutlery, and pans and the separate drawers and cupboards for their storage. Milk and meat dishcloths and sponges vary, too—typically, patterns with red or pink for meat and blue or white for dairy. Advertisements for *treif* food and forbidden mixtures are teaching moments. Walking through the grocery store aisles, the mother points out the permitted and prohibited foods and scrutinizes the food labels. Indeed, a parent's facial and verbal reaction to prohibited foods and mixtures may be the most memorable. One informant, remembering some of her parents' strategies that continued even through her teen years, gave the following examples:

> They used to say, "Oh, think of the little baby calf being boiled in its mommy's milk!" We were horrified. I don't know why we didn't think about the little baby calf when we ate the meat alone. They did it for other foods, too: eating lobsters was like eating big bugs, octopus was slimy, pigs eat poop and pork gives you a disease.

Disgust, as this woman noted, is used selectively to keep people from the category of the forbidden; the fact that it may not be rational is not noticed. Without much conscious effort or reflection, parents can teach disgust for nonkosher food. This may prevent a person from being tempted by appetite or reasoned analysis to eat *treif* food. Treating some and not other objects, people, places, and principles as sacred helps bind communities together.[35]

Older Orthodox children are shown how to find acceptable food when they are outside the home. They are taught to look for a kosher certification (*hashgahah*) symbol. During family trips, when their pre-assembled food supplies are inadequate, they learn which uncertified foods they may purchase from gas station markets and fast-food outlets. "We could eat churros at amusement parks like Disneyland," one woman remembered, "if the seller could produce the box or tell us he was using Tio Pepe's, the brand with kosher certification."[36] Before kosher certification became widespread in the late twentieth century, longing for popular American nonkosher treats was a regular feature of American Orthodox life. This changed in the 1990s when many candies, cookies, and other manufactured baked goods received kosher certification. In 1998, when Nabisco adjusted its manufacture of Oreo cookies for kosher certification purposes, Orthodox Jews touted it as a watershed moment and a sign that "they had finally made it" in America and could be full participants in American life.[37]

However, something is lost when keeping kosher is so easy: it is no longer an act of selfless obedience or religious heroism. Sacrifice strengthens a religious community by suppressing individual selfishness. Indeed, according to anthropologist Richard Sosis, who studied two hundred religious and secular American communes, the more sacrifice that a religious commune demanded, the longer it endured.[38] A central principle of Chabad religious piety is *mesiras nefesh*, negating one's ego and self-centered desires, in order to leave more room for God. A Chabad rabbi referenced this type of personal sacrifice to justify making *kashrut* more challenging: "It is now so easy to keep kosher, so making people drive a bit farther to buy *halav yisra'el* is not difficult and gives them the opportunity to show *ahavas Hashem*."[39]

Idealized methods for parents to foster religious obedience vary according to Orthodox affiliation, and some of these are associated with a particular *hashkafah*. Hasidic forms of Judaism stress the experiential elements of observance, particularly the importance of serving God in love and joy. A Chabad teacher was alarmed to hear my report that Chabad parents are teaching their children only that *kashrut* is a *ḥok* and are not supplying reasons for the practice. She said, "But that is fear-based learning!" She told me that this is not representative of the community. "There must be love, warmth, and openness in the home in order for children to learn *ahavas Hashem* and Torah," she insisted. She mentioned the regular practice around the table of fathers explaining the wisdom of the *mitzvot* and of children being asked to report what they learned in school. To her, a decree does not mean that no reasoning is possible but rather that the reasons are "not the whole picture—Hashem's wisdom is not fully known to us."[40] The religious Jew who performs God's commandments should know that she is engaged in a loving relationship with God, Who created the world for just that purpose. Love, here, is not about duty: God chose to create the opportunity for connection, and Jews choose to reciprocate.

Non-Hasidic Orthodox Jews, especially those who call themselves Yeshivish and are associated with Lithuanian traditions, are associated with a more sober piety, an emphasis on duty, and a greater concern for performing to exact halakhic standards. They are also referred to as Litvish, the Yiddish term used by the Yeshivish Orthodox. Not needing explanations is an element in this *hashkafah*. Orthodox Jews joke about these contrasting styles or tease each other about acting Hasidish or Litvish. People who self-identify as Centrist Orthodox lean toward the stereotyped Yeshivish style. A teacher who self-identifies as Centrist Orthodox told me that the norm is what he calls "the rational approach": simply calling *kashrut* a decree, without any embellishment. He admitted that his practice of sometimes talking to his children about the wisdom of the dietary laws stems from his background as a child of *ba'alei teshuvah* and his lapse from observance during high school before returning to strict Orthodoxy—both are situations in which belief plays a decisive role. He told me, "It is important to me to straddle the line" between saying the law is a *ḥok* and supplying a spiritual reason. For example, when he taught his children about the taboo against eating animal blood, he told them it is because "the blood is the life force of a creature, and when you eat it, you're bringing its essence into you. This reason is metaphysical." Nevertheless, he cautioned them that this explanation is not at the same level as God's wisdom.[41]

For some, explanations are loving adornments of the Torah and essential for mature devotion to God. This has been the case in Modern Orthodox Judaism, whose religious ideology affirms the desirability of engaging with secular culture and learning Jewish philosophy and traditional explanations for the commandments. This group still emphasizes, however, the Talmudic ideal that the commandments should need no justification. For the other Orthodox non-Hasidic communities, however, it has been a point of pride and piety not to need reasons. One could say that their *hashkafah* of obeying unembellished divine law is the highest level of devotion. A frequent response to questions from outsiders about the burden of following all the requirements of the dietary laws is "It never bothers me" or "It is natural." To some extent this response is part of an "insider-outsider" discourse: insiders are those who easily follow the Torah, while outsiders are those who regard it as a huge challenge. It does not fully represent the reality that some Orthodox Jews, even the most insular Haredi (those who most strictly adhere to Jewish law), struggle to resist tasting forbidden foods and are bothered, as the definition of *decree* signals, by the inexplicable nature of these rules.

A milestone on the way toward becoming Orthodox is when the newly religious Jew sets up a kosher kitchen. He or she will be directed to a rabbi who provides guidance over the phone or who personally does the work: using a blowtorch to make an oven kosher, advising which kitchen items need to be replaced, bringing to a *mikvah* the items that can be made kosher, and providing basic instruction on separating milk and meat. The rabbi may suggest his wife or another woman to offer practical advice on kosher meal preparation.[42] A Pico-Robertson Chabad rabbi described a later stage in this initiatory process. When newly religious people invite him to a meal in their home, he tells them, in a friendly manner: "On one condition: that I inspect your kitchen and inside your cupboards first."

When he arrives, the hosts give him a tour of their kitchen and show him how they have differentiated between meat and milk. He opens the cupboard doors, and sometimes he finds a can that is marked with kosher certification that is not reliable. He says to them, "See this: I'm not saying that this is not kosher, but the certification is not trustworthy so it *might* not guarantee you." It has never happened that he would not stay and eat, because the people who permit such inspection are the ones who make a sincere effort to keep the rules. He said, "You know, it's a way to get to know people. The women [his wife and the other women in the household] talk to each other about how they do things." I pointed out that it seemed a rather intimate act to go into someone's kitchen cupboards. He smiled and agreed: "It brings broader camaraderie." The camaraderie is with other Jews who keep kosher.[43]

In the Schools

Orthodox Jewish parents enroll their children—girls as well as boys—in all-day Orthodox schools, and in the Pico-Robertson communities, those who do not do so feel shame and are socially marginalized.

Intensive religious schooling is considered essential for ensuring that children become Torah-observant Jews, not only because of the Torah knowledge imparted in the schools but also because the insular environment minimizes the influence of secular and non-Orthodox culture and reinforces the Jewish identity of the children. The curriculum, teachers, and student peers are considered partners in raising the next generation of Orthodox Jews. Family and school boundaries are blurred, but at times the two are in tension with each other. School rabbinic leaders—there may be several in positions of authority and others who serve in the role of spiritual guide for students—tell parents how they expect them to teach Judaism and reinforce school lessons at home. When the rabbis hear that parents are not following Orthodox norms or that they allow their children to violate *halakhah* outside the school setting, they contact parents. This depends on the school, and, even then, this kind of over-sight happens only sometimes. A family's level of religious observance is typically a criterion for the child's admittance to and ability to remain in the school, and parents choose the school partly on the basis of the school's assessment of its families. Most schools, however, are aware that many students' families are not observant at all or only partially observant.

Despite financial aid for the high tuition, some parents, however, cannot send their children to these schools. In cases in which parents believe the schools cannot meet their children's special educational or social needs, the parents may provide a Jewish education for their children through tutors or through afternoon or Sabbath programs. These options are not considered optimal, and parents and children who use them may feel shame. Jewish education ideally continues beyond high school for at least a year of intensive study in a male-only or female-only yeshiva. For parents who can afford this option and who wish to choose it, this continued study ideally occurs in Israel or, for Chabad children, in Crown Heights, Brooklyn.

In my observations and interviews with principals and school-teachers, I sought to learn how they taught religious food practices, especially the extent to which they made an effort to give meaning to the dietary decrees. Conveying meaning by learning "reasons for the commandments" and religious philosophy occurred far more in the school than in the home. I found that in the local all-day middle and high schools attended by Pico-Robertson Orthodox Jews, the schools that focus on meaning and *hashkafah* are Modern Orthodox, on the liberal side of the Orthodox spectrum, that is, more accepting of American culture. Except for Chabad, which teaches the Rebbe's *hashkafah* front and central, the other schools that include *hashkafah* in the curriculum do so far less for the boys than for the girls.

Pico-Robertson Orthodox parents have many options for all-day religious elementary and high schools within walking distance or a short drive out of the neighborhood.[44] In Los Angeles as elsewhere, Orthodox schools offer a range of pedagogical approaches and outlooks. All schools are required by state law to provide the secular material demanded by national and state standards, but they are permitted to do this in the ways they see fit. For example, the Orthodox schools opt, legally, to schedule secular studies in the afternoon hours or to concentrate them into fewer hours than in the public school. A school's religious outlook may be apparent to the observer by the number of hours it devotes to secular studies. Gender separation is also an indication. Today in western Los Angeles, the most liberal Orthodox high school is the only coed one. In the rest of the Orthodox schools in western Los Angeles, starting at the elementary level, boys and girls learn separately in the same school or in entirely separate school buildings.

There is some blurring of lines within the Modern and Centrist Orthodox schools because of the teaching staff: Modern Orthodox Jews generally do not encourage their young men and women to become high school teachers, so their schools may employ teachers whose religious outlooks are more conservative than the stated mission of the school; the schools that identify themselves as Centrist (that is, not Modern Orthodox) may also employ teachers who are more religiously conservative than their mission indicates; for example, these schools may offer college preparatory courses for their students but hire Judaic studies teachers who did not earn a bachelor's degree.

The Los Angeles Orthodox community is distinctive in the country for its high number of Persians. One estimate is that about a third of the student population in the religious non-Hasidic Orthodox schools are children or grandchildren of Jews born in Iran. In addition to the Persian cohort, there are students whose parents emigrated from Israel, the former Soviet Union, and North Africa. Furthermore, a significant portion of the parents and grandparents have a *ba'al teshuvah* background.[45] Consequently, most of the Los Angeles Orthodox schools find themselves with students who are ethnically and culturally diverse among themselves and from the teaching staff.

Ethnically and culturally diverse school populations can be disruptive. The most liberal Orthodox high school includes students from families that do not self-identify as Orthodox. One school parent, who is a member of a Conservative synagogue and keeps a kosher home, described an incident that reveals the blurred boundaries between home and school. The school rabbi called to tell her that her son's Orthodox classmates had confessed that her son had brought them to a *treif* restaurant. She questioned her son and then reported to the rabbi that it was the Orthodox students, not her son, who had insisted they go to the nonkosher eatery. The rabbi did not doubt her, but he asked her to fulfill her promise as a school parent to make her son uphold school norms.[46] Most Orthodox parents will not enroll their children in a school where they would face such temptations. I heard a teenager in the boys-only Modern-Centrist high school tell his parents that in comparison to the year before, his school had enrolled only "serious" students—that is, those who come from strictly observant homes and who espouse strictly Orthodox values. He reported that he was now learning more and better, and his parents nodded approval.[47]

In the past two decades there has been an increase in the public discussions about the role of schools in preventing young people raised in religious families from abandoning Orthodoxy. The common phrase for this is "going off the *derekh*" when they became independent. The defectors even include *ba'alei teshuvah*, formerly non-Orthodox Jews who had enthusiastically adopted religious observance and breathed life into Orthodox communities. Some informed onlookers from within the Orthodox community claimed that the number of Orthodox Jews leaving Orthodoxy is increasing and the defection is starting at an earlier age. The actual data on the phenomenon is scant. In one study on the effect of Orthodox upbringing and attendance in all-day Orthodox schools, researchers found that Sabbath observances are obeyed in the range of 90–97 percent but that the practice of *kashrut* lags behind that. Of those surveyed, 88 percent observe strict *kashrut* at home, but outside the home, 25 percent report following the dietary laws only moderately and 8 percent do not follow them at all.[48]

In 2005, Faranak Margolese, an Orthodox Jew who researched the subject at length and whose book is highly regarded as authoritative, summarized the changing situation:

The last few decades have seen an almost unprecedented return to Judaism, with thousands of secular Jews becoming observant. But while many secular Jews return to Judaism, thousands are casting off their religious upbringing for an alternative way of life. We are not too surprised when that occurs in secular, Reform, or Conservative Jewish families; but today, more and more yeshiva-educated children from classically observant homes are abandoning their tradition.[49]

She also noted that the phenomenon is evident among those who, from all appearances, remain Orthodox but who have lost faith or heartfelt conviction. While this is troubling in and of itself, it may presage a future loss of their children. Even though Margolese stresses that the Orthodox are flourishing, she captures the anxiety of losing anyone from the fold.

The surveys and interviews of "off the *derekh*" Jews conducted by Margolese, which include former Hasidic as well as other Orthodox Jews, reveal that more than three-fourths of them mentioned disillusionment with the Orthodox community as a reason for their exodus. They pointed most frequently to the community's fixation with conformity, its judgmental stance, excessive stringency, disdain for other Jews, and tolerance of ethical abuses by rabbis, teachers, and community members. More than half were victims of sexual or physical abuse by family or community members.[50] She pointed out that they do not seem to have left the community because of lack of faith in God or disbelief in the Torah's divinity; most still affirmed these beliefs. Some reported that they were unable to find intellectual value and spiritual meaning in the commandments.

Margolese does not directly address the ethical community-based abuses that contribute to the phenomenon, although she does suggest better modes of parenting. Instead, she focuses on how the community could prevent the problems by permitting more discussion of values and questions of faith. Margolese suggests that the model for Orthodox religious education should be the yeshivas designed for *ba'alei teshuvah*, which first and foremost address *hashkafah* before turning to the demands of the law. She disagrees with the temptation to sequester young people from potentially heretical ideas or to minimize their exposure to non-Orthodox ideas, culture, and people. Margolese is confident that freer discussion will strengthen, not weaken, commitment to Orthodoxy.

Teachers who specialize in outreach and those who focus on the challenge of keeping Orthodox Jews "on the path" share Margolese's belief that the weakness of *hashkafah* education in schools is partly to blame.[51] A popular educator explains that "both the religious dropout and the *ba'al teshuvah* must cross the same gate—the *hashkafah* barrier; one contemplates whether to get out through that gate, while the other deliberates whether to go in through that gate."[52] These specialists fault Orthodox schools for their single-minded focus on conveying knowledge and fostering loyalty rather than on building students' individual religious outlook that includes passion for a Torah-driven life. That is, *hashkafah* education cannot simply consist of the study of theology or the reasons for the commandments. It must include intellectual learning, but this should be integrated into a larger program designed to enable individuals to develop his or her own deep convictions and emotional satisfaction. One educator described a survey of Hasidic high school seniors showing that most say they are religious "because my parents told me." By that age, he believes, they should say that they are religious "because it is true." He developed a *hashkafah* program for the Orthodox schools that includes special lectures conveying excitement and proof of Torah wisdom and, in addition, provides specialists to schools who help deal with troubled students. While initially only the Modern Orthodox institutions signed up for it, eventually some Centrist Orthodox and Haredi schools also accepted the need for his program.[53]

In the Pico-Robertson Modern-Centrist Orthodox girls' high school, students learn about food-centered commandments in a yearly core course that systematically covers practical religious laws pertaining to women: prayer, *kashrut*, laws specific to women, and Shabbat.[54] In contrast, boys in the corresponding high school spend less than an hour a day on contemporary practical Jewish law, and during these minutes, they hear about a broader range of subjects than those taught to the girls. The boys' Jewish studies curriculum includes hours of Talmud study consisting of the explication and derivation of legal principles by rabbis living in the third to sixth century CE. Class discussions deal with current practices, including *kashrut*, but those are peripheral to the subject at hand.[55] Consequently, graduates of the girls' high school leave with a greater knowledge of practical Jewish law and the ability to discuss its meanings.[56] According to their principal, "The girls know far more about *dinim* [practical laws] than the boys. When they are dating and talking together, the girls tower over the boys in terms of their knowledge." Furthermore, girls are given the opportunity to discuss meanings of the law. They know that *kashrut* is a *ḥok*, the principal said, but "they are not happy with that answer; they love to talk, they love to push further. That is in their nature. It's the responsibility of the teacher to engage them at that level."[57]

The nature and depth of the *kashrut* curriculum at this girls' high school was obvious in the textbook, a photocopied and bound anthology of texts, including forty-five pages from the Talmud, biblical commentaries, codes, and responsa (rabbinic halakhic correspondence) explaining practical laws and their underlying moral and spiritual meanings. Studying about *sheḥitah* is not included. The course has a practical focus, and the topics were chosen to help the future homemaker purchase foods and arrange her kitchen routine according to *halakhah*.[58] Kabbalistic and Hasidic teachings were not included. During the unit's first meeting, the teacher pointed out that while *kashrut* is a *ḥok*,

> we do not believe in blind faith. We see that the great *Rishonim* [rabbinic authorities dating from the close of the Talmud until the *Shulḥan arukh*] address what they think are the reasons for this mitzvah, and they believe it is a good thing to question and reason.[59]

As an introduction to the unit, the class read an excerpt from a contemporary Orthodox rabbi's book on *kashrut*. The author explained why the Hebrew word for *reason* in the Hebrew phrase for "reasons for the commandments" (*ta'amei hamitzvot*) is the same as the Hebrew word for taste, *ta'am*: "the reason makes the mitzvah appetizing and 'tasty' to the heart and mind so that not only the body but the totality of the Jew—body, mind, soul and emotions—serve Hashem."[60] Servitude to God need not be blind faith.

The teacher emphasized that a kosher diet does not physically affect a person but that it changes their soul and character. For example, eating *treif* food may make a person coarse or brutal. The textbook elaborates on this theme by referring to a medieval explanation for the prohibited mixture of meat and milk:

> There is no need to ask the reason for this prohibition, because it is hidden from the eyes of the wise, but perhaps it was because it makes a heart cruel to cook a kid in the milk of its mother, similar to [the prohibitions against] slaughtering a cow and its calf on the same day (Leviticus 22:28) and taking the chick from the presence of its mother (Deuteronomy 22:6).[61]

It is important to note two things about this explanation. First, the explanation is regarded as a mere suggestion; and second, the reference to cruelty about cooking is not about hurting the animal, since the kid was already slaughtered, but about harming the character of the Jew. Nevertheless, the language and passion in some renderings of this explanation do make it sound like an ethical critique of meat eating. For example, the following view, which is that of Abraham ibn Ezra, is from a lecture given in a Modern Orthodox yeshiva:

> There is an obvious incongruence in this practice [of mixing milk and meat]. The milk was produced by the mother in order to give life to the kid, and now we seethe the calf in this same milk after its death. The milk produced by the mother to nourish her offspring is now feeding the very person who slaughtered that offspring! It is as if we were seeking to nurse the forces of death and cruelty (the slaughtered calf and the human who took it from its mother), rather than nourish life and loving-kindness![62]

One of the problems with such an explanation is that it implies that meat, associated with death, is morally deficient, a perspective that is contrary to Orthodox Judaism today. Only among the Modern Orthodox did I hear this rationale. Most other rabbis I asked had not heard of it and did not find it convincing. "I don't get it," said one teacher in response to my more moderate version of the above interpretation. "The animal is already dead, so how does this change anything?"[63]

Because of the Talmud-centered curriculum in the boys' high school, the teachers I interviewed had less experience with and less enthusiasm for teaching reasons for the commandments. Those trained in Yeshivish rabbinic seminaries may have less knowledge of *hashkafah* literature. One such rabbi, who teaches in the Modern-Centrist Orthodox boys' high school, said, "I don't recall that I ever learned *ta'amei hamitzvot* in yeshiva," and he also never remembers even asking such questions when he was young. He added,

> It was very easy for me. I was a kid who had no problems accept-ing the truth of the Torah. Of course, look at me, I became a rabbi. And these questions still do not trouble me. I'm fine with the realiza-tion that I cannot know.[64]

He said that he tells his students that questions are proper as long as the students start with the "fact" that the Torah is true. The truth of the Torah and the truth of the *Shulḥan arukh*, the most authoritative code of Jewish law for Orthodox Jews today, are fundamental. According to him, it is acceptable for a student to request reasons if that student accepts these truths, because then the student is not rebelling but simply hungering for an explanation. Whatever explanation satisfies the student, he said, "hardly scratches the surface" of the deep truth of the Torah.

However, if a student is asking for a reason because he is not sure he wants to do the mitzvah, he is really asking whether the Torah or the mitzvah is true. In such a case, "no reason is going to be good enough," the teacher said, and he would turn the student over to someone better equipped to deal with such cases. He also advises the boy's parents to send him to a sheltered Jerusalem yeshiva. Students who go there full of questions and doubts, he asserts, no longer have any upon their return. In other words, the more one lives within an Orthodox social and intellectual cocoon, the more the truth of the Torah becomes obvious. A rabbi whose background was more liberal and whose training was broader offered a variation on these themes. He has taught in Centrist and Modern Orthodox schools and is more practiced at discussing *ta'amei hamitzvot*. He tells students that a *ḥok* has a reason, but because it is "in God's worldview," which is outside of our worldview, we cannot discern the reason.[65] He knows that these students' proximity to the secular world leaves them unsatisfied with this response. He may offer reasons, then, but he is convinced that they must learn the value of a decree that has no discernible explanation. For him, the desire for logic and explanations is a sign of weakness, an affliction produced by secular culture.

The same desire to distance students from the lure of secular culture prevents this high school teacher from offering ethical rationales for kosher meat slaughter and for *kashrut*, such as the above explanation for the prohibition against eating meat with milk. The teacher told me that some ethical arguments have medieval origins, but he objects to the secular context in which they have been revived. First, he finds them in modern academic writings—a mark against them. Presumably he is referring to the biblical scholarship of people like Professor Jacob Milgrom, whose contention that biblical dietary laws are ethically driven is now fundamental to liberal Judaism.[66] Second, he believes these reasons are a defensive reaction to People for the Ethical Treatment of Animals (PETA), "who are anti-Semites and anti-religious." Third, he maintains that ethical reasons were generated by Conservative Jews "who are genuflecting to the outside world." A devoted Jew should not need the approval of outsiders. Furthermore, he explained, Conservative Jews were also reacting against Reform Judaism, which had eliminated many *mitzvot* because they were "merely" ceremonial and had no spiritual value. His historical location of some ethical rationales is accurate, but it is surely not the sole or original source of Jews' desire for ethics-based religion. Nevertheless, he fears that resorting to ethical explanations would make his students too much like Conservative Jews or non-Jews. It may be that he was concerned about possible slippage by young people already positioned close to the secular and non-Orthodox world. This teacher emphasized the importance of being selective about secular culture and "the world." A genuine Modern Orthodox Jew, to him, is one who does not simply call the world nonsense. Instead, he values what is good in it—even lets it enhance his understanding of Torah—but rejects views and behaviors contrary to Torah.[67]

In the Modern Orthodox high school that is coed and the most liberal of the local all-day options, intellectual query and discussion of ethics are highly valued. The school provides an identical curriculum for boys and girls as well as greater breadth and variety in the general and Jewish studies courses than the gender-segregated Modern Orthodox schools offer. Its mission includes guiding students toward democratic values and building skills to create "a just community" within the school and in the public at large. Given the limited hours of a school day, the broader curriculum relative to the other Orthodox schools results in less time learning practical Jewish law and Talmud. Students may choose more classes on these subjects by signing up for an intensive Talmud track within and after the school day, and twelfth graders may choose a yearlong elective in practical *halakhah* that includes the laws of *kashrut*. Study of *kashrut* is also possible through a shorter mini-semester course offered to all students.

The principal and teacher I interviewed from this school regard it as part of their mission to fully address ethical issues and *hashkafah* for all students. "We teach the students that we must keep the *mitzvos* because they are commanded by God," one of the teachers explained to me, "but we also tell them it is important to look for meaning because it enhances our observance."[68] He believes that one learns the truth of the Torah by finding meaning in it, and this meaning is the primary means by which adults create a lifelong commitment to following Jewish law. Nevertheless, he is careful to encourage humility with regard to seeking reasons by emphasizing that one can never know for sure. Avoiding ethical rationales for *kashrut* and kosher animal slaughter because that is

how Conservative Jews approach these, or because that is what the secular world expects, "seems like a Haredi [very strict Orthodox] *hashkafah*
that deals with modern and secular outlook by building walls." This is
a valid approach, he said, but not for him or his school. Neither he nor
his school insists (as Haredi Jews do, he implied) that *halakhah* never
changes. Students are taught that it has changed in response to cultural
influence but that this does not impair its authority.

His views about ethics and community echoed those of the school's
former principal, to whom I spoke several years earlier. He likened teaching *kashrut* alternately to a boat and to a three-legged stool: "We need
to observe these laws because first, we are commanded to be a holy and
separate nation; second, to bind us together as a community; and third,
because we find them to be wise and ethical." To stay afloat or in balance, explanations (the third element) must support the obligation to be
kadosh (holy), which is primary, and the explanations must not undermine community:

> We're on the same boat, and it has to carry all the [Orthodox] Jews.
> There are lots of elements of *kashrut* that do not make sense: why
> is the meat and milk prohibition extended to eating chicken? You can't
> just drop that, because you won't be on the boat. The three-legged
> stool will topple.[69]

Caution is necessary, then, when teaching students to seek explanations. Teachers must inculcate humility within that quest and the all-
importance of obeying God.

The principal pointed out that the larger Orthodox community
reacts badly to hearing the word *ethics* in reference to Jewish law; they
understand ethics as something from the outside culture and extraneous to *halakhah*. He, like some other Modern Orthodox rabbis I met, is
not absolute on this point. They admit that Talmudic rabbis and Jewish
tradition gave some respect to natural morality, and they give it a role
in their halakhic decision-making.[70] He is convinced that the method
of *shehitah*, believed to be the least painful way of killing an animal,

was motivated by ethics: "The concern in *shehitah* about how hard you push the knife against the animal's neck is of course an ethical question, but they [rabbinic authorities] use other language." Yet, he admitted that using the term "ethics" "conjures up liberal Judaism, and you will get *big* resistance from the [more conservative] Orthodox, who say, 'Oh no, there is nothing here that smacks of ethics!'" He believes that caution is necessary when advocating changes in practice that may be permitted by *halakhah* but which appear to be motivated by ethical considerations. In those cases, there will be a hardened insistence that the current practice is the only halakhic possibility.[71]

In sum, Modern and Centrist Orthodox Jewish rabbis and teachers believe that it is best to teach children decrees like *kashrut* as an inscrutable divine command, although the Modern Orthodox affirm the importance of meaningful explanations for a teenager and adult, as long as these are understood as merely speculative. Explanations that bring in the issue of causing harm to the animal, however, are discouraged; they are associated with liberal forms of Judaism or secular thought, and as such they violate the boundary around the Torah and the Torah-centered community.

Chabad families take a different approach regarding explanations for following the laws. Chabad schools are distinctive among the local schools not only for their particular religious ideology but also for the consistency of their curriculum. The teachers are trained in separate male and female Chabad seminaries, and many of the movement's educational materials come from the denomination's national education department or from other Chabad sources. That those raised from birth within Chabad do not attend secular college ensures a minimum of outside intellectual influence on religious ideology and in the schools.[72] Compared to the Orthodox schools described above, the student population is more homogeneous. I was told that students and their families are fully committed to Chabad and the schools do not have to deal with religious dissension.

Of central importance to the community and curriculum is *Hasidus* (*Hasidut* in Sephardic Hebrew). *Hasidus* refers to the spiritual teachings associated with Hasidism, published as discourses, stories, theological tracts, Torah commentaries, and halakhic commentaries taught by past Hasidic leaders—in this case, Chabad leaders. These teachings include reasons for the commandments. The schools seek to invest the younger generation with the enthusiasm and skills to achieve the goal of the seventh Chabad rebbe, Menachem Schneerson, of transmitting love of God and the Torah to other Jews, particularly secular or non-Orthodox Jews, and ideally bringing them to lives of performing God's commandments:

> The vision and mission of the school is to harbor and foster an envi-
> ronment where the students will a) understand the Rebbe's vision
> of reaching every corner of the earth, b) realize their responsibility
> for impacting their environment and the world around them, and
> c) acquire the necessary tools, academically, emotionally, and socially,
> to complete this mission.[73]

Such a mission cannot be successful without including the meaning behind individual *mitzvot*. In Chabad, the distinction between educa-tion for insiders and outsiders is often blurred. Vocabulary, rather than concepts, differentiates educational material designed for people firmly ensconced within the Chabad community and those outside of it.

As in the Centrist Orthodox schools, the boys and girls are educated separately. Students are not encouraged to attend secular universities, although the girls' high school provides a college preparatory curric-ulum. Girls are taught that their primary duty is to prepare for being wives, rearing their children as devout Jews, managing their household, and ideally choosing a career as teachers in Chabad schools.[74] The local Chabad girls' high school curriculum includes a detailed course in the ninth grade on the dietary laws. One teacher explained that the girls are taught to differentiate the legal distinctions among *halakhah*, custom, stringencies, and distinctive Chabad traditions. They also learn what the teacher called "the *neshamah*"—the heart or soul—of the law, that is, its deeper meaning:

The fundamental reason [for *kashrut*] is that this is Hashem's will, but there is no hesitation whatsoever to talk about reasons. Of course, you would teach about the impact of eating *treif* on the soul—the animal's blood becomes our blood, for example. The reason for only eating animals with split hooves is because it teaches us to split the world; that is, to differentiate between the material and the spiritual. The reason for eating animals that chew their cud is because we, too, chew over and ruminate on things.[75]

Explanations such as these are considered essential for nurturing love for God and for character development.

The issue of *kashrut* and ethics is a particularly fraught one in Chabad schools. When I asked a Chabad teacher whether one could connect the dietary laws and ethics, she assumed I was asking about the highly publicized evidence in 2004 that the Chabad kosher meat company AgriProcessors had engaged in cruel animal slaughter.[76] She said, "This is not a minor matter. This is what we are facing. We have to teach them that the Torah defines reality." I asked whether she would mention the findings of scientific research about animal pain, and she responded, "You can make anything true using human reason and logic. The Torah is divinely inspired. The Torah tells us *shehitah* is the best way and that it is painless—*that* is truth, not human reason."[77] A Chabad teacher in another school assured me that there are many resources for explaining *mitzvot* and then warned, "But you cannot depend on logic. [We always teach that] the most cultured country in the world was Germany, and through their own logical reasoning look what they were able to justify!"[78]

In contrast to the girls' schooling, much of the boys' schooling at the high school level consists of learning Talmud and *Ḥasidus*, and their formal study of *kashrut* occurs through their daily study of law codes and occasional guest speakers.[79] The principal explained that the rationales for *kashrut* that were taught at the Chabad girls' high school might be taught to boys during Torah sermons but not in their courses. "It's a really grueling schedule we have here," the principal explained, "so students who enroll are serious and have great *yir'as shamayim*," but they do not care much or talk about such topics.[80] They will likely hear about them during Torah sermons, youth programs, and *farbrengen*, which are joyous mass gatherings where men and women are seated separately and where a rabbi teaches words of Torah and everyone sings melodies, eats refreshments, and offer toasts over drinks. In their last years at the high school, the boys are trained for outreach work. They focus on a single and relatively simple mitzvah like *tefillin* or mezuzah, not on a complex matter such as *kashrut*, and are sent to local public places (e.g., a shopping mall) to approach Jews, teach them how to perform the mitzvah, and explain its meaning and importance.

EXPLAINING THE DIETARY LAWS

Health and Hygiene

When reasons for the commandments began to appear in medieval Jewish writings, one claim advanced for the kosher diet was that it was God's way of warning His beloved chosen people about the ill effect of eating certain animals and food combinations. For example, Maimonides, a physician as well as a rabbinic scholar, declared that forbidden animals contain more pathogens than permitted ones and that eating meat and milk together causes digestive distress. Some medieval rabbis objected to this argument on empirical grounds. Many insisted that whether or not there were any health benefits, God commanded the dietary laws for the spiritual, not the physical, health of the Jews. Their viewpoint prevailed.[81]

The claim that forbidden animals and mixtures are unwholesome persisted over the centuries and still can be heard today. The health claim implied by the well-known marketing slogan of the Hebrew National kosher hot dog and beef company, "We answer to a higher authority," is successful because many people do believe that kosher food is more pure—although it is unclear whether this is because of the animal species, ingredient mixture, or sanitary procedures followed.[82] Among the

Orthodox, the health claim is most often found within the literature and teachings presented by Chabad and Aish HaTorah, a non-Hasidic outreach organization. These present "expert testimony" from doctors and nutritionists who identify specific diseases and ailments likelier to appear in a nonkosher diet.[83] They may also mention that kosher meat comes from animals that are inspected beforehand for fitness and that the slaughtered animal must be free of internal blemishes.

These arguments are misleading, for although downed, wounded, and obviously sick animals are excluded from kosher slaughter, Jewish law permits meat that government health inspectors may disqualify. Others who offer the health claim present a case that seems scientific but in fact privileges religious tradition over science, such as in the following:

> Modern medicine has only recently discovered that the DNA present in every cell controls the nature of that organism. Similarly, every cell possesses a spiritual nature which is carried through the food chain. One who eats any particular animal ingests its nature and characteristics as well. The fact that this is not recognized by current medical knowledge is of no moment. Science has only begun to scratch the surface of the mysteries of the human body and knows little of the unquantifiable spirit. It requires no great leap of faith to speculate that in due time science will discover the truth that Jews have accepted as faith for 3,000 years.[84]

This kind of reasoning is common in New Age or "spiritual metaphysical" circles and sources. People drawn to these are receptive to such claims and invoke them when they explain their adoption of *kashrut*. I did not hear this claim or anything similar among Modern or Centrist Orthodox Jews who had actual training in the physical sciences. I suggest that Chabad and Aish HaTorah also disdain the health claim because it is so easily turned against *kashrut* by secular Jews who scorn the dietary laws on the grounds that they are merely an outmoded system of hygiene.

An obvious reason for why the association between prohibited food and ill health persists is that it reinforces the brain's reflexive fear of pathogens. An expression of visceral disgust for *treif* food by parents is a strategy for ensuring compliance. Even when the inner logic is revealed, it can be effective. According to Rabbi Moses Hayyim Luzzatto, the eighteenth-century author of a popular manual of Jewish spiritual behavior who rejected the ill health claim, "Anyone with a little bit of sense will consider prohibited foods as poison or as a food that has poison mixed in it."[85] That is, a person may not actually believe that nonkosher food is poison, but associating *treif* food with poison may inhibit the desire to eat it. The health argument preserves the hierarchical system important to the religious community, in which sacred objects and behaviors are granted devotion and prohibited items and behaviors are considered sacrilegious or disgusting.

Ethics

Most Orthodox Jews do not currently favor describing the dietary laws and kosher animal slaughter as motivated by concern for animal suffering. The Modern Orthodox are a notable exception. As noted above, the primary reason for the resistance to ethical explanations is that these are considered an appeal to secular or liberal Jewish notions, rather than to Torah principles, of what is right and wrong. Relying upon secular ethics could just as easily lead a person to reject Jewish law or to commit grievous wrongs. Yet, in the non-Jewish public sphere, Orthodox Jews defend kosher slaughter as a humane mode of killing animals for food. Indeed, they often argue that kosher slaughter is governed by the Torah law *tzaʾar baʾalei ḥayyim*, the concern for and prohibition against causing suffering to animals. If so, why not make this same argument in the home, in schools, and in congregations?

Ethical rationales are spurned in some contexts and highlighted in others. In rabbinic legal texts concerning *sheḥitah*, when the context is one in which rabbis are in conversation with other rabbis, animal pain is not a consideration. There are several explicit biblical laws requiring compassion toward domestic animals and wildlife, such as forbidding the yoking of an ox and a donkey together, not muzzling an ox on a threshing floor, requiring one to rest one's work animals on the Sabbath, and shooing away the mother bird before taking her fledglings. *Tza'ar ba'alei hayyim* is a principle that is not actually explicit in the Pentateuch but is part of the oral tradition of laws and teachings thought to have originated in God's revelation at Sinai. As such, it has an elevated status, with greater authority than Talmudic-era rabbinic rulings.[86] Because it has the appearance of a principle, however, rabbinic authorities must apply it to specific situations. So, for example, they understand *tza'ar ba'alei hayyim* to prohibit tugging a donkey's lead for no reason or beating an animal in anger. One might reasonably conclude that *tza'ar ba'alei hayyim* would apply to aspects of animal slaughter, but rabbinic authorities do not bring it to bear in this case. The Pentateuch does not explain proper animal slaughter or present rationales for the procedure; it merely assumes that the correct and divinely ordained procedure is known.[87]

The rabbis of the Mishnah and Talmud make no claim to know God's reasons for requiring this type of slaughter. They focus on the basic requirements for *shehitah*: the place on the animal where the cut is made, the depth of the cut, the proper kind of knife stroke, and so on. Whether the animal feels pain is not a factor.[88] When medieval rabbis engaged in the enterprise of providing reasons for the commandments, they made the case that God designed *shehitah* in order to minimize animal pain. The thirteenth-century text *Sefer hahinukh*, the earliest written example of this argument, explains:

> We would say furthermore about the reason for *shehittah* being done at the throat and with an inspected knife, that it is in order not to cause living creatures undue suffering. For the Torah permitted them to a man, in his superior state, to use them for food and for all his needs, [but] not to cause them needless pain. Long ago the Sages greatly discussed the prohibition against pain for living creatures, in the tractates *Bava M'Tzi'a* (32b) and *Shabbath* (128b), whether it is forbidden by the law of the Torah; and they concluded, as it seems, that it is prohibited by Torah law.[89]

In his passage, the author explicitly connects *tzaʿar baʿalei ḥayyim* with kosher slaughter. Even here, however, the text refers to "needless" pain. Causing pain to an animal while getting it into position for kosher slaughtering may be necessary, as would pain resulting from the cut itself, and these would not be a violation of *tzaʿar baʿalei ḥayyim*.

The distinction between necessary and unnecessary suffering and its connection to *kashrut* were clarified by Rabbi Moses Feinstein, a respected Orthodox authority on applied *halakhah*, who showed in 1982 how the application of the Torah prohibition could be applied in the case of rearing animals for food. He was asked whether it is permitted to raise calves in a painful way but one that produces a better (whiter and more tender) meat. Is such a mode of raising the animal "necessary" pain? The following is the core of his answer:

> On the matter of calves who, in this new method, are fattened, each calf living alone in its separate place, very narrow, so much so that they have no room to walk even a few steps, and they are not fed anything that is usually fed to calves, never tasting even its mother's milk, but they fatten it with very oily liquids that are not fit for animals—just the opposite of what is explained in Talmud *Beḥorot* 39 where it is said it is permitted to give different food to animals to improve it, etc. Also these calves get sick from the liquid and need all sorts of medications. . . . For the matter of human need one is permitted [to cause an animal pain] when there is need such as slaughtering an animal for food, when one is using an animal for work, for plowing and for carrying loads and the like. . . . And thus it is permitted to give them food that is better [than normal] in order to enhance the taste of the meat, fatten the meat in a manner so that people who eat the meat will enjoy it better than if it had eaten fodder. But not something that will deceive and fool people . . . or to cause sorrow to the animal by feeding it food that does not add a [real] benefit and which causes such pain through the eating, and also they get sick from it and suffer torments from the disease, all for the sake

of this outcome, that is, so you can deceive people—this is prohibited, a violation of *tsa'ar ba'alei chayim*.[90]

Feinstein is not making a general statement here prohibiting suffering that occurs in the normal course of animal agriculture. Rather, he is restricting his words to pain and cruelty inflicted for cosmetic and marketing objectives. In the case of white veal, there is also the sin of fraud. However, eating such meat is another matter. He wrote that the meat would be kosher if the calf was slaughtered properly and was free of blemishes. Feinstein insisted on far more extensive checking of the calf's innards than would have ordinarily been performed (increasing the likelihood that the meat would be found to be *treif*). People "of scrupulous standards" would refuse to eat this meat, he wrote, but they would not be eating *treif* food, nor would they be guilty of actually violating the *tza'ar ba'alei ḥayyim* prohibition. In sum, the principle of *tza'ar ba'alei ḥayyim* does not figure in the judgment about the correctness of the slaughter, and consequently the meat will be kosher if the animal was slaughtered properly.[91] This judgment about the meat being kosher is not an innovation. The medieval *Sefer haḥinukh* states with reference to a slaughterer who uses a dull knife: "But if he slaughters with a bad knife, even if he goes back and forth the whole day, his slaughter is fit [to eat]" if the knife cuts were appropriate and the animal's innards pass inspection. The entire passage reads as follows: "If, however, someone does *shehittah* with a bad [dull] knife, even if he moves it back and forth the entire day, his *shehittah* is acceptable—unless he thus moved it back and forth after severing the greater part of only one organ in an animal. If in the remaining small part of it he moved a bad [dull] knife back and forth for the duration of a [disqualifying] pause, his *shehittah* is disqualified."[92]

Feinstein's declaration that *tza'ar ba'alei ḥayyim* is distinct from *kashrut* echoed what all Orthodox rabbis already knew. The most basic level of Orthodox rabbinic ordination requires learning the laws of *shehitah* as laid out in the *Shulḥan arukh*, and these do not include the issue of animal suffering: *tzaʾar baʾalei ḥayyim* does not apply to *sheḥitah*, and neither does it apply to how animals are raised.

A mention of animal suffering would be out of order for another important reason. Orthodox rabbinic students learn that decisions in *halakhah* are not to be influenced by assumptions about the reason behind the commandment. This much-repeated Talmudic axiom applies in all areas of religious law. A ruling must be made by analysis of earlier hallowed halakhic texts and their application to the presenting situation. Only in this way can the decision be pure, that is, entirely in accordance with God's will. Outside observers may discern that a rabbinic authority is influenced by his own understanding of the law's purpose, his perception of the public good, or public pressure, but a decision maker who explicitly references these "extraneous" concerns would be violating the professional standards and thereby mark his decision as invalid.[93] In contrast, rabbis from the Conservative movement have broken with this rabbinic tradition. They explicitly reference Jewish nonlegal sources or non-Jewish ethics in their decision-making.[94] When a Modern Orthodox rabbi told me, "The concern in *sheḥitah* about how hard you push the knife against the animal's neck is of course an ethical question, but the rabbinic authorities use other language," he was referring to their adherence to the accepted discourse of Orthodox rabbis that preserves their status as legitimate authorities.[95]

However, ethical rationales are mentioned in public, non-Jewish contexts. When rabbis or spokespeople for the Orthodox address governmental agencies or a secular American audience or when they conduct religious outreach, they emphatically connect *sheḥitah* to the biblical law prohibiting suffering to animals. Rabbi Yosef Dov Soloveitchik, a leading Modern Orthodox rabbi who was involved in the US congressional effort in the 1950s to establish regulation over meat slaughtering, spoke out forcefully about the concern in Jewish law for causing minimal pain in animals.[96] He, like others testifying to this close connection between *sheḥitah* and biblical law, relied upon the "reasons for the commandments" literature like the one quoted above. Because the final version of the US law actually declared *shehitah* humane, defenders of *shehitah* declared it as a simple fact that *shehitah* is humane.[97]

In the aftermath of the 2004 revelations of cruel treatment of animals at the AgriProcessors kosher slaughtering plant and the recent increase in European legislation against *shehitah* and halal, Orthodox spokesmen have become adept at describing scientific research testifying to the near painlessness of kosher animal slaughter. Some might blur the lines between *tzaʾar baʾalei hayyim* and *shehitah*, such as the following statement on the Aish HaTorah website: "Slaughtering animals is never a pleasant topic, but the kosher method ensures that the Jewish injunction *tzaʾar baʾalei chayyim*, the prohibition to cause pain to animals, is preserved."[98] Chabad, which was associated with the AgriProcessors kosher meat company, declares on its website that "*Shehitah* is the Jewish religious and humane method of slaughtering permitted animals and poultry for food."[99] Perhaps because of its supervisory role over AgriProcessors, the Orthodox Union (OU) kosher certifying agency emphasizes the close connection between humane treatment and *shehitah*: "The OU and AgriProcessors are committed to the Torah principles of humane treatment of animals. At the OU we constantly review our procedures, evaluate them, and if necessary, improve or correct them. We don't want ever to be wedded to a mistaken procedure."[100] The reader could assume from this statement that the methods of kosher slaughter are being continually updated to conform to humane standards. This is certainly not the case.

Jews raised in secular or liberal families approve of a link between ethics and religion, and unlike Orthodox rabbinic leaders, they do not associate ethics with anti-Torah attitudes. Lessons designed to bring such Jews to Orthodox religious observance, consequently, describe *shehitah* as an act of kindness to animals. One young newly religious woman who was educated in Aish HaTorah programs explained that she followed the dietary laws because they were commanded by God. Another reason was that "you are what you eat," a theme that appears frequently in rationales for *kashrut*. For her, the principle refers to eating only meat from humanely raised and slaughtered animals:

The whole of the animal will be incorporated into your body, and that includes the trauma that the animal goes through during its slaughtering and really, all of its life. Since kosher *sheḥitah* is the least traumatic for the animal, that's best—they don't let the animals see each other being killed, [and they require] the most humane way of raising the animal. And kosher chickens, too. They let the chickens roam around.[101]

These details about required humane methods of animal husbandry may have originated in her imagination rather than in the actual words of Aish HaTorah teachers. Certainly, it is a good public relations technique to explain kosher meat in this way to non-Jews and to the non-Orthodox. In an explanation written for such potential customers, a Pico-Robertson owner of two kosher restaurants made this false claim on their restaurant websites: "If an animal . . . is injured or slaughtered in a way that brings it pain, any ingredient derived from that animal is non-kosher."[102]

Other Orthodox groups are more moderate in their language and claims and take greater care not to equate ethics with *halakhah*. One kosher certification agency posted an article on its website clearly differentiating between scientific standards, Jewish law, and public relations:

Scientific findings in support of *shechitah* have value when engaging in dialogue with lawmakers and rational advocates for animal protection. Nevertheless, for Jews who turn to the Torah for direction in all matters, they are only nominally relevant. Proper treatment of animals is a concept originally introduced to humanity by the *Torah*. The same Creator who created the animal kingdom and enjoined us to treat animals compassionately is also the One who commanded us how to *shecht* [slaughter] them.[103]

In other words, scientific research on the humaneness of *sheḥitah* is important for maintaining the legality of *sheḥitah*, but Orthodox Jews do not need such research. For them, it is simply a tenet of faith that *sheḥitah* is the best procedure. These distinctions are usually made explicit within

Orthodox high school settings, as noted above. Teaching that divine authority and wisdom are more authoritative than ethics preserves Jewish law.[104] One high school teacher told me, "I don't know whether *shehitah* is humane. But if the *Shulḥan arukh* says that it is more humane, then I don't care what any scientist says. I accept that it is more humane because it is written in the *Shulḥan arukh*."[105]

The "Spiritual Refinement" Explanation

Modern and Centrist Orthodox rabbis and teachers are most likely to explain the dietary laws by quoting the Talmudic sage Rav, cited earlier in this chapter, who declared that the commandments were given "to refine human beings." This refinement is a spiritual and moral, not a physical, condition. The Talmudic rabbis taught that God breathes into each human a soul that not only animates the body but is the element enabling a person to restrain bodily impulses in order to behave morally.[106] Animals are not capable of morality; they have no divine soul and are prompted only by instinct and impulse. The rabbis taught that God revealed his moral expectations for humanity after the flood when He mandated seven universal precepts: prohibitions against blasphemy, idolatry, sexual perversion, bloodshed, robbery, and tearing a limb off a living animal and an enjoinment to establish courts of justice.[107] These laws foster human morality by requiring people to suppress their animalistic desires.

More accurately, the dietary laws are meant to refine *Jews*. Only Jews who obey the dietary laws can truly be refined.[108] According to rabbinic tradition, when God imposed the hundreds of Torah laws upon the Jewish people, He meant to refine them even more than the rest of humanity. Jews would be more moral than other peoples and also holy. Yet their morality and holiness are not entirely innate; they require discipline, and some rabbis claimed that Jews must make a greater effort than non-Jews to control their bodily impulses.

The language of battle is frequently used to describe the struggle between body and soul. The rabbis taught that every person contains a *yetzer hara*, an evil (or self-centered) impulse rooted in the body, and a *yetzer hatov*, an impulse for good located in the soul. The refining process may be explained as the individual's development of good attributes, *midot*. The young, especially, need to learn self-discipline and refine themselves, but the struggle is considered a lifelong one.[109] Another metaphor for moral and spiritual transformation is healing or repair. According to the Torah commentary of sixteenth-century rabbi Isaac Abravanel, "The Divine Torah did not come to heal the body or to promote physical health but rather to foster the health of the soul and to heal its afflictions."[110]

Only Jews who keep the dietary laws can hope to have good enough souls so that their eating rises to the level of holiness. A more positive way of expressing this, one that focuses on Jews' potential rather than their weakness, is implicit in the formulaic blessing uttered prior to performing a commandment: "Blessed are you, Lord our God . . . who has sanctified us by his *mitzvot* and commanded us to [perform this specific act]." When Jews utter the blessing prior to eating, they are also exercising restraint and bringing God into their mundane activities.

Reasons for the kosher diet that emphasize its effect on the inner life of a Jew are of two types. The first appeals to human reason by stating that the kosher diet stimulates the intellect and imagination in order to develop better personal qualities. This approach prevails in Modern and Centrist Orthodox settings; it also appears in Chabad, but less so. A second approach is to regard foods and the eating processes as actual metaphysical forces that operate outside of the human will. The implication is that they hold power over a person's soul or overall character, regardless of the person's awareness. For example, a Jew who eats *treif* food impairs her soul and then may have difficulty performing *mitzvot*. In contrast to the first approach, the second must be held as an article of faith. This approach appears in Chabad circles. Each method harbors distinctive understandings of the human being, nature, and the purpose of the Torah.

The concept *timtum halev* (obstruction of the heart) illustrates these distinctive approaches. At the end of the list of prohibited animals in

Leviticus 11 is the statement, "Do not impurify yourselves with them, so that you should not be thereby impurified." A Talmudic sage suggested that the second word, *venitmetem*, impurified, could be read as *venitamtem*, stupefied or obstructed. The result is *timtum halev*, an obstructed heart or soul.[111] In context, it is hard to tell exactly what the obstruction entails, but over the centuries, and certainly in the *Zohar*, *timtum halev* indicates that the Jew's soul and physiognomy have been impaired. The result is that the Jew has become captive to bodily urges, more animalistic, and therefore less able to fulfill *mitzvot*.[112] This belief in the metaphysical-physical power of kosher and nonkosher food first appeared in the Talmud and then was adopted wholeheartedly in later kabbalistic writings, where it was reinforced and elaborated upon with vivid images.

Because of the Talmudic origin of *timtum halev*, it is included in the curriculum of Orthodox schools. Rabbis and teachers referenced *timtum halev* in their discussions with me about *kashrut*, yet it was clear that the concept made some of them uncomfortable. In the Modern Orthodox girls' high school I observed, texts about *timtum halev* are positioned at the start of the photocopied source book used in the *kashrut* unit. Among the interpretations of *timtum halev* was one by the rabbinic commentator Abravanel, who wrote that forbidden animals have "a deleterious effect on the pure and intelligent soul, breeding insensitivity . . . and corrupting its desires."[113] He emphasized that the harm was on the soul and did not constitute physical damage. A contrary opinion appears in the same source book with a paraphrased warning attributed to the kabbalist Moses Hayyim Luzzatto (although not identified in the book as such): "*All* sins obstruct the mind, but the mind is dulled in particular by the consumption of non-kosher foods, which become a part of one's body."[114] The teacher taught the concept and demonstrated its veracity with a story from an outreach teacher who believes that the reason he attracts more *ba'alei teshuvah* in Israel than in America is that Israeli Jews are eating kosher meat more than American Jews are ("even if they don't go out and purchase it, it's so prevalent there"). The teacher explained that Israelis are "closer to Hashem"; that is, their hearts are less obstructed, making them more receptive than American non-Orthodox Jews toward a life of *mitzvot*.[115]

The school's principal, a rabbi who described himself as Modern Orthodox, admitted his dismay at the popularity of this particular interpretation of *timtum halev*. He likened it to the belief he disdains: "You are what you eat." He told me about a student who confessed to him, "I couldn't concentrate on my prayers this morning, and I realize that it must have been because the gum I was chewing yesterday was probably not kosher!" The principal called this approach *narishkeit*—Yiddish for "nonsense." He favors more rational approaches to the *mitzvot*, and although he knows that the source for this one is the Talmud, he believes that "it's a way of abdicating responsibility." He counseled her to think differently and give her food less power.[116] Another Modern Orthodox rabbi in the neighborhood, when asked about *timtum halev*, did not explain the concept but instead emphasized that in Jewish law, an inadvertent violation of law is called *shogeg*, and one can be cleansed of that by repenting. The person can specifically mention that accidental sin in the daily prayer, and on Yom Kippur the prayer for accidental sins should make them feel cleansed of the misdeed.[117]

People with intellectual outlooks like the Modern Orthodox much prefer the more rational approach to spiritual refinement that emphasizes free will. The power of the food is explained symbolically. An example of this is the lesson that teaches that just as predator birds are not kosher, Jews should not be predatory but rather should shun violence and treat others with kindness and respect. This kind of reasoning also conveys the "you are what you eat" logic, but it operates only on a metaphoric level. There is no claim here that eating predatory birds alters a person's soul or body. Another popular example of this more rational approach is when people explain *kashrut* as a regimen of training in the internal battle between one's good and evil urges.

At the start of this chapter, I described a method of teaching newly religious Jews to accustom themselves to obeying seemingly meaningless *mitzvot*. *Kashrut* has been described similarly as a regimen of training in the internal battle between one's good and evil impulses, and military and competitive language are used to stoke enthusiasm. An interpretation from the *Zohar* is cited to support this point. Rabbi Binyomin Forst, author of a popular manual of *kashrut* published by the Haredi ArtScroll publishing house, writes:

> Thus, the act of eating . . . is the place where the combatants engage, where the ongoing struggle to forge a productive relationship between the physical and the spiritual is at its fiercest. . . . Perhaps this helps to explain why the *Zohar* refers to the time of eating as a "time of war." This primal desire is the "front line" in the ongoing battle between body and soul. This may explain the connection between the words *lechem* (bread) and *locheim* (warrior).[118]

The same lesson surfaces in the teaching materials of the Orthodox outreach organization Aish HaTorah. Both excised a crucial principle within the original *Zohar* text insisting that forbidden food has power over a person's soul.

Representing a classical example of Modern Orthodoxy, Rabbi Samson Raphael Hirsch (1808–88) developed a rationalistic interpretation of the dietary laws. Hirsch disregarded the tradition that *ḥukim* (plural of *ḥok*, decrees) must ultimately remain a mystery. Instead he decodes them through linguistic analysis and identifies the details as meaningful symbols. Hirsch taught that God gave the Torah for human understanding, and this ensures that Jews find meaning in the *mitzvot* and appreciate them as evidence of God's love and wisdom.[119] His interpretation of *kashrut* is a singular version of the spiritual refinement theme.

Hirsch argues that the Torah's classifications of physical nature were designed to train Jews to honor crucial distinctions and respect God's order. In doing so, he appeals to the human sense that hierarchy and rank are crucial for survival. Hirsch notes that the first chapter of Genesis shows God separating elements of creation and repeatedly creating plants and animals "according to its kind" (*lemineihu* in Hebrew). This phrase signals the duty to preserve God-given distinctions, Hirsch explains. The Torah prohibits many kinds of mixing, such as wearing a garment woven from wool and linen, grafting trees of diverse kinds to each other, yoking different species of animals to each other for work, and sowing diverse seeds together in the same field. One of the most problematic mixings is the marriage of a Jew and a non-Jew. Living at a time when people were demanding and receiving equal rights and when Jews were abandoning their distinctive religious practices and blending into the majority, Hirsch understood that this mixing would result in the disappearance of the Jew and the Jewish way of life. He directed attention to the many forbidden mixtures to show that violations of status and hierarchy are contrary to God's will and to divine order. By guarding their own separateness in multiple ways and acting as a sanctified nation, he believed that the Jewish people model respect for God's orderly creation and preserve the imperative of "according to its kind."[120]

Furthermore, when Jews are faced with food choices, they must realize that these are symbolic of desired Jewish traits. Prohibited animals, Hirsch observes, "have more vigorous and defiant habits and are not so submissive to man," and their meat diet makes them much closer to the carnal world. In contrast, permitted animals possess a "passive quality of dependence and impressionability," and eating them teaches the Jew that the human body must be "the willing instrument and servant of the mind." The Jewish mind, trained in Torah and reason, will then understand the duty to obey God and stand firm as part of a distinct, Jewish, holy nation that honors God's design.[121] The prohibited mixing of meat and milk does this, too. Milk, "the substance that mammals come equipped with to nourish their young, symbolizes this plant-like facet of the animal world," whereas the meat is the muscle tissue that enables the animal to locomote from place to place. The problem with this combination, Hirsch argues, is that "the uniquely animal part, the ability to locomote, is pressed into the service of the more basic functions of reproduction and nourishment. It is an example of a higher, more advanced potential [animal] serving a lower one [vegetative], rather than the reverse"—which is the proper way of the world.[122] Instead of casting the forbidden foods as possessing inherently negative qualities, Hirsch uses naturalistic descriptions drawn from the natural sciences.

Rational and humanistic arguments such as these may suit audiences seeking a more modern outlook. Jews or adult *ba'alei teshuvah* who are attracted to Modern Orthodoxy are most likely to find them appealing. A teacher in the Modern-Centrist Orthodox boys' high school thought they are too abstract for students and would not be persuasive. "The boys don't even know the source of their food," he said. "They just think it comes from boxes and cans."[123] He believes it is more effective to warn students that *treif* food has intrinsic destructive power over their souls or that God will punish them for infractions. Hirsch is respected and is studied in Modern Orthodox seminaries and yeshivas, but not necessarily those further to the right. When I mentioned one of his modern-sounding explanations of kashrut to a teacher who had trained in a Haredi seminary, he responded skeptically, "I never heard that before—what is his source?"[124] Nor does Chabad educational material include any writings from Hirsch.

Kabbalistic Explanations

Although Chabad parents, teachers, rabbis, and authors agree that *kashrut* is a decree that signals servitude to God and cultivates spiritual refinement, they favor explanations showing Jews as partners of God and attributing metaphysical power to food. Both are rooted in Kabbalah. Kabbalists claimed that their teachings, which include the deep meaning of the laws and other divine matters, were revealed to just a few and were meant to be kept secret; hence they were merely hinted at, but not explained, in the Talmud. Yet, even in the medieval era there were kabbalists who believed that these teachings should be disseminated widely, and this broader approach was affirmed in the Hasidic movement.

Schneur Zalman, the founder of Chabad Hasidism, recorded his interpretation of Kabbalah in the book *Tanya*. He favored the creation narrative of the sixteenth-century kabbalist Rabbi Isaac Luria, who taught that God formed the universe by first withdrawing inward to create a vacuum (*tzimtzum*). God emanated divine light into the vacuum in varying intensities to create the universe. The excess of divine light caused a breakage radically separating God from His creation. Elements (sparks) of divinity that remained embedded within the physical universe, as well as elements of evil, account for the struggle between good and evil and humanity's alienation from God. God designated the Jewish people to be His partner in restoring the sparks of divinity to the spiritual realm and thereby bringing greater harmony between the earthly and spiritual realms. Jews do this by living in accordance with the Torah and practicing the *mitzvot*. The restorative process is called *tikkun* (repairing). The ultimate stage of *tikkun* is redemption, or the Messianic Age, or *tikkun olam* (repair of the world).

According to these teachings, Jews' sanctified eating—that is, their consumption of kosher food, accompanied by blessings before and after, with proper table comportment—is a form of *tikkun*. The foods and beverages are made from the lower levels of materiality (minerals, plants, and animals). When they are included in sanctified Jewish eating, they are elevated with the Jew to a higher, spiritual level. This may also be expressed as a rescue of the trapped divine sparks and a restoration of them to the divine realm.[125] Kabbalistic teachings place religious Jews in the center of a cosmic drama in which they exercise spiritual power and are partners with God.

Chabad.org is the repository for many essays and audio lessons on *kashrut*. The following is the Chabad explanation of the power of eating kosher meat: "Thus, one who eats a piece of kosher meat and then uses the energy gained from it to perform a mitzvah, thereby elevates the spark of divinity that is the essence of the meat, freeing it of its mundane incarnation and raising it to a state of fulfilled spirituality."[126] Chabad teachings emphasize that the kosher slaughter of the animal, not simply the eating of the meat, is part of this process. *Sheḥitah* "draws the animal out from its beastly state" and enables it to be "sublimated as an accessory to the life of the spirit."[127]

> Plants, too, can benefit from being eaten by a religious Jew: When a Jew takes a kosher food and recites the blessing over it, he uplifts that spiritual essence and provides the "nutrition" that the soul needs.

> This is what it means that "man does not live on bread alone," rather
> the energy that keeps him alive is the G-dly spark hidden within that
> feeds the soul.[128]

For the Jew, food is transformed from merely a mundane source of nutrition into spiritual, divine energy.

Another Chabad essay focuses on the redemptive aspects of this process. The author points out that when the animal is slaughtered through *shehitah*, a "crucial spiritual cycle is completed, helping to perfect the universe" and benefiting all of humanity.[129] Within Chabad, the Talmudic concept of *timtum halev*, the obstructed heart, is interpreted through Kabbalah. The divine sparks within prohibited animals are encased in especially hard *kelipot*, "husks" of negativity. God prohibited them to Jews because people who eat these creatures will become enmeshed in the creatures' negativity. Forbidden mixtures of kosher food are harmful for a different reason. According to Chabad teachings, kosher milk contains the divine attribute of mercy, while kosher meat incorporates the divine attribute of judgment. Milk and meat embody opposite spiritual energies and therefore cannot mix.

These teachings are central to Chabad's religious philosophy and are taught widely in simplified non-kabbalistic language through stories, sermons, aphorism, and songs. I heard the following at the local Chabad girls' high school: "The animals have the *zekhus* [merit] to help us serve God" or "Through our eating we are raising up plants, animals, and ourselves to a higher level."[130] Explicitly kabbalistic terms tend to be reserved for advanced study in post–high school yeshivas or in materials designed for Chabad outreach to nonreligious Jews. Yet, in Chabad the distinction between education for insiders and for outsiders is unclear, especially because young people are educated for outreach. The seventh and last rebbe made outreach a central concern, yet some of his interpreters insist that he regarded the term *kiruv*, from the longer phrase *kiruv rehokim* (bringing near those who are far away), as insulting and paternalistic because it implies that nonobservant Jews are the *rehokim*, in need of repair by the ones who are already perfect. They maintain that the Rebbe taught that any material designed for outsiders is "also meant to bring even closer those who are already close to God."[131] I have found that vocabulary, rather than concepts, differentiate educational material designed for people firmly ensconced within the Chabad community and those outside of it.

Kiruv teachers have discovered that people who are seeking an exotic and exciting religious practice are drawn to Kabbalah. The Aish HaTorah outreach organization, which is not Hasidic and whose leaders are associated with Centrist Orthodoxy, references Jewish mysticism and offers explanations based on Hebrew numerology and other unusual ideas associated with Kabbalah. However, when the people involved with Aish HaTorah become more deeply integrated into the Orthodox community, their mentors provide them with a study program consisting of classical, non-kabbalistic rabbinic writings.[132] Chabad, too, may draw in nonreligious Jews with kabbalistic teachings and then provide newcomers with more basic and how-to lessons, but kabbalistic teachings are at the center of Chabad *Hasidus* and are not kept from them.

Jewish Essentialist or Ethnic Explanations

Every explanation above assumes that the proper, ideal Jew is part of a holy nation distinct from all other nations of the world and that Jews are members of the winning team. This implication is fundamental to Kabbalah, but it is also present in non-kabbalistic Orthodox teachings.

Kabbalistic teachings about food, for example, insist that food enhances the inborn and differing natures of the Jew and the non-Jew. Unlike the Talmudic rabbis, kabbalists sharply differentiated between Jewish and non-Jewish souls, maintaining that Jewish souls have inborn spiritual powers that non-Jewish souls lack. Jews' intrinsic powers make their performance of the *mitzvot* efficacious in *tikkun*, and for this reason non-Jews were not given the Torah laws and should not attempt to follow them. Jews, through obedience to the dietary and ritual laws, elevate themselves to holiness; likewise, they can descend from their inborn higher spiritual level by eating *treif*. The non-Jew, for whom God did not provide a special diet, remains at the lower level; yet that, too, is in accordance with God's design. A non-Jew who eats kosher food gains no benefit and has no effect on the cosmos. These ideas reinforce Jewish ethnic solidarity, social separatism, and the rule against eating "their" foods (*bishul akum*).

An Iraqi Jew, a member of a Sephardic congregation whose rabbi teaches Kabbalah, told me he learned that the souls of errant Jews are reincarnated into animals, and when a kosher animal is slaughtered according to the rules of *shehitah* and a Jew eats the food with a spiritual intention and utters the proper blessing, the soul trapped in that animal can be repaired and elevated to a higher level. Only Jewish souls are punished and redeemed in this way, and the power to elevate souls is unique to Torah-observant Jews.[133] Eating kosher food in a kosher manner marks one as a Torah-observant Jew and not a sinning Jew, and it extricates the soul of the sinning Jew from its punitive nonhuman reincarnation.

Chabad teachings are particularly disparaging toward non-Jews. The first Lubavitcher rebbe taught that non-Jews' souls are minimally higher than animal souls and lack capacity for significant spiritual elevation, and this teaching is part of Chabad *Hasidus*. The moral foundation that pits disgust against sanctity is here extended to group membership: insiders are holy, and outsiders are barely human.[134] This perspective is rarely made explicit in lectures, audio lessons, and writings available to the public, but since it is so fundamental it is still transmitted. An example of this may be found on the Chabad.org webpage that displays a free translation of a letter by the sixth Lubavitcher rebbe, Rabbi Yosef Yitzchak Schneersohn. In it he tells the story of a simple, unlearned Jew who eats only kosher food, contrasted to a non-Jew who speaks Yiddish perfectly and also eats only kosher food. The latter's diet cannot transform his essential nature, and when asked his goal in life he responds, "to take a swig of vodka and have a bite to eat."[135] The seventh Chabad rebbe, even so, was notable for emphasizing the need to extend charitable activities to everyone, and the movement's leaders take pains to establish good public relations with non-Jewish leaders. Belief in the inborn differences between Jewish and non-Jewish souls does not preclude righteous and generous behavior toward non-Jewish people.

Belief in Jews' essential and superior natures is found in non-kabbalistic sources as well. By definition, group identity always includes affirmation of the group and rejection to some extent of nonmembers, but boundary making does not need to include biologically essentialist claims. When Orthodox Jews describe eating *treif* as "acting *goyish* like a non-Jew," does this necessarily mean contempt for non-Jews? As I showed in chapter 2, the food laws' function as social glue was enshrined in Jewish law through the rabbinic prohibition *bishul akum*, forbidding the consumption of certain foods prepared by non-Jews, even if all the ingredients were kosher, "because of their daughters."[136] This is not an intellectual concept but a social one, and at times it is dressed up with intellectual rationales. Many Orthodox people I interviewed recognized that explaining it as something other than a social construct is inconsistent with their own ideas (e.g., a belief that all humans are God's creation and therefore deserving of respect) and offensive to non-Jews. The Orthodox people I interviewed who mentioned *bishul akum* said they would not mention it to non-Jews because it sounds insulting. Instead, they would explain these kosher laws by saying, "It is what my religion teaches," "It is Jewish tradition," "It is my family's heritage," and the like.

I have found that Modern Orthodox Jews are the most likely to explicitly define *kashrut* to their children as an expression of Jewish ethnic belonging or as a device to strengthen the community. One mother told me, "I teach them that it connects you to your ancestors, it is our tradition, and feeling good about Jews and being Jewish can't be transmitted unless it is connected to ritual, whatever that may be." A Modern Orthodox rabbi described the reason for separate Jewish eating in ethnic terms also: "Kashrut promotes togetherness, keeps us close to each other. It defines our identity as a community."[137] Eager to defend the prohibition to me in terms he thought I would respect, a Chabad rabbi said, "Aside from the fact that it is *halakhah*, buying only *bishul yisra'el* is good for Jewish businesses! It's good to help each other."[138]

Faranak Margolese expresses the tension between individualism and community loyalty facing modern Jews, the Orthodox among them. She argues that explanations for observing *mitzvot* that put individuals in the center are the most effective:

> This is particularly important in the modern age. . . . With the rise of the Enlightenment, man became the measure of what is right and good. This fundamental shift in mentality has affected the Jewish world as much as the world at large, the result being that today it is more difficult for people to accept God's word as the measure of what is good. Today, to experience something as good or right and therefore meaningful, it must be good in one's own eyes. Moreover, it must be good for me, the individual. . . . The more we see *mitzvot* as helpful to us, the more likely we will experience them as a privilege, to value and perpetuate them.[139]

Margolese is referring to that portion of the Orthodox world that is highly impressed by secular, individualistic values. She recommends that instead of trying to undermine the humanistic and pragmatic outlook of those who are wavering in their commitment because of their allegiance to these modern values, the teacher or parent should discuss the *mitzvot* as tools for self-actualization. However, individuality cannot be all-important in Orthodox society, so Margolese makes it one part of the triad of self, the Jewish nation, and the world at large. She argues that even Jews who are influenced by modern culture still want to "become connected to something greater, first to ourselves, then to our nation, then to the world at large. This broader perspective provides an understanding for *mitzvot* that transforms each individual deed and greatly magnifies its significance." Individual fulfillment for religious Jews occurs when that individual independently conforms to "a religiously communitarian society rather than to one that promotes pride in individualism."[140] They freely choose servitude to God and communal authority.

• • •

Orthodox Jews believe that their adherence to the kosher laws is essential to living in accordance with God's will. More than that, keeping kosher is tantamount to being a religious Jew. Devotedly performing these laws and regarding them as inexplicable decrees means that the Jew who obeys them is truly a servant of God. Some may also regard this servitude as having an element of partnering with God. The laws' inexplicable nature demonstrates that Jews who obey them value selfless devotion to God and are not going to be swayed by certain destructive modern and American ideals: secular ethics, the primacy of reason, the pursuit of individual expression and happiness, and suspicion toward religious authority and tradition.

Orthodox Jews today also believe that keeping kosher is crucial for community perpetuation. Because of the requirements of the laws, Jews who keep kosher are far likelier to marry Orthodox Jews and produce Orthodox Jewish children. The dietary laws interpreted in Orthodox terms promote a culture in which Orthodox Jews eat with other Jews. Jews who become too much like Americans reject *kashrut* as superstitious and unethical, and they become more and more like non-Jews. Breaking bread with non-Jews and non-Orthodox Jews leads to marrying them and to the fading out of the Jewish tribe.

Nevertheless, living within modern American society, Orthodox Jews cannot simply deny the attractiveness of the values they explicitly reject; some have effectively integrated these values into their individual religious philosophies. The explanations favored for pedagogy and public discourse are those that best reinforce deeply ingrained cultural beliefs, and these rest upon innate human senses of what is right and good. Outreach educators recognize that evoking American values in defense of *kashrut* may strengthen the religious convictions of Jews who are situated near the margins of Orthodox society. Finally, good public relations sometimes require something more than "We do it this way because of God's will." People and governments that revere religious authority may respect such a conviction. However, governments required to guard public health and ensure a measure of humane animal treatment cannot always let religious beliefs prevail. Neither will religious considerations bring any advantages in a competitive food market. In these public contexts, it would undoubtedly be advantageous for Orthodox spokespersons to emphasize the inherent goodness of the laws.

4

You Shall Eat Meat

Hot, spicy cuts of grilled beef and lamb lure people of all types to this gourmet sausage deli. The kosher certificate on the plate-glass window facing Pico Boulevard in West Los Angeles signals that Orthodox Jews may eat there, and a ritual handwashing cup and laminated prayer cards are set on a table at the back wall. Customers are sitting in small groups at the little round tables. Most wear Orthodox dress: yarmulkes on men and boys, white strings of *tzitzit* hanging from under the shirt of the teenager cleaning a table, and women wearing long-sleeved blouses and long skirts in the summer heat. Others are clearly not Orthodox and perhaps not Jewish: the two women in sleeveless blouses speaking Farsi to an elderly man, the bareheaded dad and two teenage boys, and the three men wearing Los Angeles Fire Department uniforms. The smells of fried onions, garlic, and roasted meat infuse the room's air. A man enters the deli, greets the owner, and cheerfully announces, "My plane leaves in a few hours, and the friend picking me up at the Baltimore airport threatens to abandon me on the curb unless I bring him three orders of your Polish sausage."

• • •

The ancient Israelites believed that God cares deeply about the human diet. This is obvious in the creation narratives in Genesis. Immediately upon creating the first humans, God tells them what they and the animals will eat. God's first prohibition is the rule against eating the fruit of the tree of knowledge of good and evil. The first quoted conversation, between Eve and the serpent, focuses on a dietary taboo, the first divine rebuke is about Eve and Adam's violation of it, and the first punishment includes new hardships in procuring food. Nine chapters into Genesis, after the world has been destroyed by flood, God inaugurates a new era by permitting people and animals to kill animals and eat them. Generations later, as described in the books of Exodus, Leviticus, and Deuteronomy, God makes a covenant requiring the Israelite nation to follow laws that include a sacred diet not imposed upon the rest of humanity. In particular, the holy diet restricts the sacrifice and consumption of certain animal species and animal parts. Orthodox Jews take these biblical narratives very seriously. Even Jews in liberal religious denominations connect food choices to morality.

In the modern era, the state intervenes in food production to an extent never before seen, and discussions about the morality of eating meat are far less shaped by religion in present times than they are in the biblical books mentioned above. By the mid-nineteenth century, European governments guarded public health by regulating meat production. Citizens advocated for legislation to require humane treatment of animals before and during slaughter, and they insisted that stunning animals into unconsciousness first is the most compassionate way to slaughter them. Food producers were restricted by these new requirements, of course, but the Jewish minority was uniquely burdened because *halakhah* requires the animal to be intact and conscious during slaughter. Unless *halakhah* were to be radically changed, it would be impossible to produce kosher meat.

Jews also felt the brunt of growing antisemitism, with popular demagogues vilifying Jews and *sheḥitah*. Lobbying to keep *sheḥitah* legal became a necessary duty for Jewish communal leaders in the early twentieth century, and in many places it still is. Furthermore, modern thinkers and new scientific research challenged traditional views about humans' relation to animals. Scientific theories of human evolution undermined the bibliocentric religious belief that humans are entirely different from and superior to animals.[1]

Orthodox Jews rightly see these political and intellectual develop-
ments as a threat to their outlook and way of life. This chapter shows how
they respond to the moral and conceptual challenges of eating meat in
today's world. My focus in this chapter is not on their approach to kosher
meat but on their views of meat eating in general. There are Orthodox
Jewish vegetarians, but those who have chosen this path for ethical
reasons are rare. I focus primarily on the prevailing outlook, which is
heartily supported in the Pico-Robertson Orthodox communities living
in their kosher food hub. I explain why so many Orthodox rabbis and
teachers argue that meat eating is important for humanity and, from a
moral viewpoint, better than vegetarianism.

THE FIRST HUMANS AND THEIR DIET

The foundation for their ideas is the biblical account of God's directives to the first humans, found in the first nine chapters of Genesis.
These tell the origin story of humanity, what Jews later called "the (other)
nations of the world." Later, starting with chapter 10 of Genesis, Abram
the Hebrew appears. With him, God lays out His laws for the small nation
of Hebrews, later known as the Israelites and as the Jews. Orthodox
Jewish beliefs about humanity's proper diet cannot be found through
a straightforward reading of the biblical chapters. From the Orthodox
viewpoint, the Hebrew words of the Pentateuch, or Torah, presented to
Moses on Mount Sinai and over the course of his life, form the sacred
core of God's revelation, but they must be read through the oral teachings that Orthodox Jews believe God revealed to Moses and that were
recorded only millennia later in the Talmud. Moses transmitted both the
written Torah and oral teachings to the next generation of sages, and each
generation's teachers passed them to the next. In other words, Orthodox
Jews depend upon rabbinic interpretation to reveal the true meaning of
the revelation. They learn this fuller version from their parents, in school,
and throughout their lives while reading the weekly Torah portion in the
synagogue, listening to rabbis' sermons, and studying rabbinic texts.[2]

In the Torah's narrative of creation, God speaks to the first humans about their relationship to the animals and to food: "Be fruitful and multiply and fill the earth and subdue it, and rule over the fish of the sea and over the fowl of the sky and over all the beasts that tread upon the earth." God then says,

> Behold, I have given you every seed-bearing herb, which is upon the surface of the entire earth, and every tree that has seed bearing fruit; it will be yours for food. And to all the beasts of the earth and to all the fowl of the heavens, and to everything that moves upon the earth, in which there is a living spirit, every green herb to eat.[3]

Meat is not mentioned as a food for either humans or animals. Reading the biblical text alone, one could reasonably conclude that God decreed a vegetarian diet for the first humans and animals.[4]

However, Jews who read the Bible through the lens of rabbinic tradition may conclude otherwise. The absence of an explicit prohibition against meat and God's clear statement that humans are to dominate animals permit a range of rabbinic opinions. Three different positions appear: first, that meat was prohibited until after the great flood; second, that meat was permitted but then prohibited after Adam and Eve's sin; and third, that meat was never prohibited.[5] Rashi (Rabbi Solomon ben Isaac, 1040–1105), whose line-by-line commentary is considered authoritative for all Orthodox Jews, endorsed the first view that people were not permitted to kill animals for food until the post-flood era. This was the prevailing view over the centuries. Chabad Hasidic tradition teaches the third view.

Before turning to the Chabad outlook, it is worthwhile to examine the thinking of those who believe God prohibited meat eating and whose reasoning points to the limited nature of the first humans. According to Rashi, humans were more like animals in the Garden of Eden than they would be later since they lacked the discernment they would acquire by eating from the tree of knowledge of good and evil. Adam and Eve are

not idealized even before they ate from the tree. While they had dominion over animals, they did not have the constitution to fully exercise it.
They were obviously permitted to kill animals for sacrificial worship,
because Adam and Eve's son Abel brings a sacrificial offering from his
flock. God accepts Abel's animal offering and rejects Cain's grain offering.[6] Generations later, before God permits humans to eat meat, Noah,
too, made animal offerings upon leaving the ark. In sum, God's initial
preference for a vegetarian diet is not because it is the better, more elevated way to eat.

According to the Chabad version of events, which is consistent with
the seventh rebbe's interpretation of Rashi, the first humans ate meat but
did not themselves kill the animals.[7] Being the pinnacle of creation, Adam
was permitted to consume the lower forms of life, and God kept Adam's
arrogance in check by forbidding him to kill animals. Adam was also
humbled by the awareness that, like the animals, he needed food to sur-
vive. In this perspective, also, Adam and Eve were not idealized. It was
not until after the flood that human beings were given a more refined
spiritual nature.[8]

It is hard to deny a link between diet and human morality in the
biblical narrative of the world-destroying flood. Looking over the deeds
of the people He created, God admits dismay about the human heart
being evil from birth (Genesis 8:21). When the survivors—Noah, his
family, and the animals they care for on the ark—emerge onto dry land,
Noah offers an animal sacrifice, and God is pleased and repeats his earlier judgment: "And the Lord smelled the pleasant aroma, and the Lord
said to Himself, 'I will no longer curse the earth because of man, for the
imagination of man's heart is evil from his youth.'" God then dictates a
new set of rules for humanity, including a prohibition against eating the
flesh of living animals:

> Be fruitful and multiply and fill the earth. And your fear and your
> dread shall be upon all the beasts of the earth and upon all the fowl of
> the heaven; upon everything that creeps upon the ground and upon

all the fish of the sea, [for] they have been given into your hand[s]. Every moving thing that lives shall be yours to eat; like the green vegetation, I have given you everything. But flesh with its soul, its blood, you shall not eat.[9]

The permission to hunt, capture, and kill animals for food, coming after God's realization that human beings are evil at heart, might lead to the conclusion that eating meat is not ideal. Yet the biblical text does not make this explicit, and throughout the Hebrew Bible meat eating is associated with economic and physical well-being. Abstention from meat is a temporary gesture for times of mourning and for short-term ascetic displays. Rabbis who regard meat eating with dismay and distaste are few and far between. Generally, as a group they regard meat eating as a sign of prosperity and fitting for times of celebration, if it is enjoyed in moderation and in accordance with divine law.[10]

The meaning of the exception, "flesh with its soul, its blood," is not obvious, but the rabbis teach that it means an animal must be entirely dead before it is consumed; that is, people may not tear off and eat the flesh of their living prey. The rabbis called this prohibition *ever min hahai* (limb from a living animal).

Aside from ruling that humans must not eat flesh while it is still alive, God did not decree at this stage a specific way of killing an animal or prohibit eating any species of animal life or vegetation. Humans are even permitted to eat the blood.[11] Animals are also permitted to eat everything except humans. An omnivorous diet is the new natural way of eating. The biblical text continues with God's statement that when human beings are killed, the perpetrator deserves the punishment of death at the hands of other humans: "Whoever sheds the blood of man through man shall his blood be shed, for in the image of God He made man."[12]

According to rabbinic oral teachings, the dietary prohibition against tearing off and eating from a living animal is one of the seven universal laws. These laws are called *sheva mitzvot benei No'ah*, the seven commandments for the children of Noah, or Noahide laws, because God decreed them for Noah and his offspring. The other six Noahide commandments prohibit blasphemy, idolatry, sexual perversion, bloodshed, and robbery and enjoin the establishment of courts of justice. Through these seven laws, God established his baseline standard of moral behavior and religious probity for humanity.[13] Later, He will give the Jewish people their additional and much more extensive commandments. These include the dietary laws described in chapter 2.

MEAT EATING: THE CHANGED MODERN DISCOURSE

Although there is a long history of Jewish reflections on the human diet, modern cultural changes in Western Europe and the United States prompted new interpretations. Nineteenth-century urbanization removed a large portion of society from animal husbandry. Most people's livelihoods were no longer bound up with breeding, feeding, maintaining, and selling animals. People who bought cuts of meat in stores were unaccustomed to seeing animals raised, slaughtered, and butchered for a meal. The animals eaten by city dwellers were more likely to exist in their imaginations than in plain sight. Still, they may have witnessed the poor treatment of animals in nearby stockyards and slaughterhouses.

Urban reformers pressured governments to move these to the edge of cities for public health and aesthetic reasons. However, the need for business owners to make a profit and the vast quantity of meat involved made it nearly impossible to keep these activities humane for animals and out of the public eye. In 1824 the Society for the Prevention of Cruelty to Animals was founded in Britain, and by the next decade similar advocacy organizations appeared in Germany and the United States. Their members campaigned for laws to ameliorate what they saw as callous treatment of animals under human control, especially in meat production.[14]

It is not surprising that a movement for secular vegetarianism emerged around the same time. Like animal welfare advocacy, vegetarianism represented a new kind of sympathy toward animals. In England, the first-ever vegetarian organization was established in 1847. Vegetarians argued that killing animals brutalizes human beings, that it is an unnecessary destruction of life, and that meat eating is unhealthful. Promoters of vegetarianism were not typically associated with religious denominations. One exception to this was the leader of a marginal "Bible Christian" sect who pointed to the diet in the Garden of Eden as proof that vegetarianism was more spiritual and closer to God's will than meat eating.[15] In any case, the vegetarian cause was not very popular, either in Europe or America.

Advances in scientific research provided other novel perspectives. During the 1840s, evolutionary theories about the development of animal species became a subject of popular writing in England. The 1859 publication of Charles Darwin's *On the Origin of the Species* and especially his 1871 *The Descent of Man* showed that humans share a common ancestry with apes and evolved from lower life forms in a gradual and sometimes accidental process. Some thinkers believed that the same natural causes shaped human mental and moral faculties. These ideas challenged long-held religious beliefs, especially those dependent upon a literal reading of the Bible. Of course, there were Christians and Jews who interpreted the creation narrative in Genesis less literally to reconcile it with science. Most people were ignorant of Darwin's claims or simply dismissed them.[16] For the rest, evolutionary science undermined key principles in the biblical account of creation: God's instantaneous creation of humans, a hierarchy that gives more value to humans than other life forms, and an anthropocentric view of the universe. The most serious conflict, however, is the religious tenet that God created human beings as a life form fundamentally distinct from animals.

Evolutionary theories certainly came to the attention of a German contemporary of Darwin, Rabbi Samson Raphael Hirsch (1808–88), mentioned in chapter 3 in regard to his rationalistic interpretation of dietary laws. Hirsch received a university education as well as rabbinic training, and he urged Jews to acquire secular learning and become full members of civil society while maintaining strict obedience to their religious law. He adamantly opposed the nascent Jewish movement to reform religious practice, an effort he characterized as simply a way to bring Judaism "up to date" according to the latest fashions.[17] In his books, articles, and commentary on the Pentateuch (all written in German), Hirsch affirmed the wisdom of rabbinic tradition and highlighted the ways Jewish beliefs, halakhic practice, and moral teachings contribute to modern society. Passionate and eloquent, defensive of tradition, and polemical against modern ideas he saw as threatening, Hirsch was read widely in his day and for decades after.[18] Because he addressed the new intellectual and social challenges so squarely and clearly and through the prism of rabbinic values and traditions, Hirsch is still favorably regarded by Orthodox Jews.[19] While Jews listen to the chanting of the Torah during the Sabbath service in Pico-Robertson Orthodox synagogues, they may be reading from a volume of Hirsch's commentary on the Pentateuch, or they may find excerpts from Hirsch included in other synagogue-supplied Pentateuch volumes.

Hirsch's adamant defense of rabbinic views of creation was clearly a response to evolutionary theory. His discussion of the biblical creation narratives appears in his commentary to the Pentateuch, published in several volumes between 1867 and 1878, as evolutionary research was emerging. In his interpretation of God's creation of Adam in Genesis 2:7, Hirsch highlighted the essential differences between animals and humans. Unlike animals, humans were created "by the breath of God Himself" and were endowed with a soul that can resist physical urges. According to Hirsch,

> The difference between man and animal is the touchstone of human morality and at the same time the rock on which human morality can founder. . . . Animals are endowed with an instinct; this instinct is the voice of God, the will of God as it applies to them. . . . Not so man. Man must opt for the good and shun evil out of his own free will and sense of duty. Even when he gives his physical nature its due, he must do so not because of the stimulus of his physical appetites but out of a sense of duty. . . . Nowhere, and under no circumstances, may [man] ever be an animal.[20]

Hirsch believes that it is essential that humans see themselves as above and distinct from animals. If humans identify too closely with animals, they will listen too closely to their inner appetites and deafen themselves to the voice of God calling them to dutiful and righteous obedience.

The way meat is procured may preserve or destroy the human-animal distinction. This is evident, Hirsch says, from the prohibition against eating "the flesh with its soul, its blood," which he understood as the rabbinic prohibition against removing a limb from a living animal. Hirsch finds it significant that God's words to Noah after the flood, in which God permits humans to eat meat, are immediately followed by a warning that anyone who sheds human blood is deserving of death, "for in the image of God He made man." According to Hirsch,

> This sentence, attesting to the higher, godly dignity of the human body and of human life, seems to hold the motivation for all the legal provisions cited here regarding the assignment of the animal world as food for man, the prohibition against absorbing the animal soul into the human body (*ever min haḥai*), the subordination of man's physical existence to God, and God's role as defender of that existence against any attack.[21]

Just as Hirsch earlier emphasized that humans, unlike animals, came into being with "the breath of God," here he stresses that they are "in the image of God." Both statements, according to Hirsch, differentiate humans from animals. God permitted humans to kill animals for food, but "*Jedoch Fleisch, dessen Blut noch in seiner Seele ist, sollt ihr nicht essen,*" literally, "flesh whose blood is still in its soul, you may not eat."[22] This enigmatic phrase Hirsch understood as a prohibition against absorbing the essence or soul of an animal into a human body. If the flesh or limb is removed while the animal is alive, the animal's soul still permeates it, according to Hirsch; once the animal is dead, its soul is not in the meat.[23]

Lest one think that the best way to avoid absorbing the essence of animal is to avoid meat, Hirsch explains that the animal's flesh is not a threat to the human once it is dead: at that point, its soul has relinquished control over its blood. The body tissues of an animal may become part of the human body, for the animal body is passive, inert, but the soul of an animal can never, and must never, become part of the human soul.[24]

Because "soulless" meat does not pose a danger, the Torah "does not recoil from the consumption of meat." Hirsch does not explain the prohibition of meat eating before the flood in terms of the morality of the act; instead, he bases it on the pragmatic reason that vegetarian food was abundant:

> We already have discussed the view of our sages, which is consistent with geological findings, that before the Flood the Earth's temperature was stable and vegetation more luxuriant. Thus, vegetarian food always was available in sufficient quantity, and there was no need to derive sustenance from living creatures.

After the flood, the climate changed, as did the human body, he argues: "If we had remained in our original physical condition, the eating of meat might never have been permitted to us, whereas now it may be necessary."[25]

Hirsch sees no contradiction between the mandate to be compassionate toward animals and the permission to kill them for food or sacrifice. For him it is axiomatic that animals may be used for human needs, and one of these needs is worship. As Hirsch explains, the fact that Cain and Abel brought offerings to God shows that this act is "a natural expression of pure human thoughts and emotions." In Hirsch's day, Jewish religious reformers were dismissing sacrificial worship as a holdover from polytheism and the primitive notion that God needs to be fed, and they proposed excising prayers for the restoration of the priestly rites from the liturgy. Hirsch, an adamant opponent of religious reform, argued that sacrifice is a timeless act in which the animal is offered as a substitute for the offering up of one's own self to God. He writes, "It is in fact our own blood, our own mind, our own muscular strength which we symbolically offer up to godliness, surrendering ourselves completely to the all-conquering power of God's will as He has set it down for us."[26] By sacrificing the animal, humans affirm the essence of their distinctive humanness: they are servants of God and not ruled by their instincts. In short, the Torah's directives for killing animals for food or for sacrificial offerings are not only just and proper; they are designed to foster human morality.

Vegetarianism was a marginal phenomenon during his era, so Hirsch gave very little attention to it. In contrast, the movement to improve animal welfare in meat production was gaining attention. Among other improvements, reformers advocated stunning large animals so they would be unconscious prior to slaughter. The first legislative proposal to require initial stunning came in Baden, a German dukedom, in 1864, but it was defeated. Twenty years later, similar laws were proposed and not passed, and in these debates the practice of *shehitah* became an issue. Some animal welfare activists described the Jewish procedure as terribly painful for the animal, although other experts disagreed. Legislators also considered the principle of religious freedom in their deliberations, but they made no legal changes. These public debates may account for Hirsch's greater attention to the Torah's concern for compassionate treatment of animals and for his emphatic declarations on this topic in his Pentateuch commentary and other writings. According to Hirsch, God obligated all of humanity, not only Jews, to avoid inflicting pain upon animals.[27]

With the increase of antisemitism at the end of the nineteenth century, the alleged "brutal treatment of animals" by Jews in kosher slaughter became a central theme in public discourse.[28] While parliamentary debates in favor of mandating stunning and outlawing *shehitah* were held in northern, central, and eastern European lands in the pre–World War I era, only Switzerland adopted a ban on *shehitah* that was not repealed despite appeals from the Jewish community.[29] Jews were shocked to hear kosher slaughter disparaged, for they had always considered it the most pain-free way to slaughter animals, and the stunning of animals seemed brutal in comparison.[30]

With the formation of the National Socialist Party in the 1920s and the spread of antisemitism in Europe, proposals for laws requiring stunning (which meant banning kosher slaughter) were accompanied by fabricated descriptions of Jews reveling in the torture of animals. Days after Hitler became chancellor of Germany in 1933, it became obligatory for the entire Reich to stun animals prior to slaughter, with no exception for kosher slaughter. Over the next few years, severe anti-Jewish measures became law alongside legislation mandating gentle treatment of domesticated animals. The Nazi leadership publicized its humane animal policies, knowing the cause was dear to German society. Few people, including Orthodox rabbis, were aware, then or even now, that the actual treatment of domesticated and wild animals under Nazi rule had either changed little or was harsher or that the Nazi regime outlawed vegetarian advocacy organizations in countries under its control.[31] By the 1930s, European Jews would see an obvious linkage between animal welfare advocacy and antisemitism. After the Holocaust, efforts to restrict *shehitah* were often seen by Orthodox Jews as the first step in a larger anti-Jewish campaign.[32]

JEWISH VEGETARIANISM IN POST–WORLD WAR II AMERICA

The defense of meat eating in general and *shehitah* in particular became an issue in the United States soon after the end of World War II. In 1954, the American Humane Society promoted humane industrialized meat production by objecting to the way live hogs were being handled before slaughter. This concern hardly could be construed as antisemitic. The US Congress responded to public pressure by addressing the treatment of all large animals in meat production. Not only preslaughter stunning but also preslaughter handling of animals came under review. At the time, the standard practice for restraining large animals in position for slaughter was to shackle and hoist them in the air. When Jewish communal leaders, including Orthodox rabbis, were forced to confront the shackle-and-hoist method, they were divided: the shackle-and-hoist approach appeared to traumatize the animal and was not required by *halakhah*, yet changing the method would make kosher meat far costlier to produce.[33] An organization of Eastern European–born Orthodox rabbis declared that "any type of law dealing with *shehitah* brings great danger that, in the end, will produce—Heaven forbid—an evil decree for the community."[34]

The prominent Modern Orthodox rabbi Joseph Ber Soloveitchik, mentioned in the previous chapter regarding the 1950s US congressional effort to regulate meat slaughtering, stepped forward to ensure that *shehitah* was not imperiled. After his work with a US Department of Agriculture advisory committee and extensive lobbying by other Jewish leaders, the final version of the 1958 Humane Slaughter Act was favorable toward kosher meat production. Although the law required an initial stunning of animals for nonkosher meat businesses, it declared *shehitah* humane and permitted it to function as it had in the past. The final law contributed to the widespread view within the Jewish community that kosher animal slaughter was a painless, humane mode of killing animals.

As concern for animal welfare in mid-nineteenth-century Europe had been accompanied by the emergence of vegetarianism, a similar connection occurred in twentieth-century America. At the start of the century, Jews made considerable efforts to promote vegetarianism, but it became noticeably more popular in the 1960s, when it gained wider respect as an ethical ideology in some culturally sophisticated urban communities.[35] As before, proponents denounced meat eating as unethical and harmful to human health as well. At this time, however, they also argued that increased consumption of meat and the growth of industrialized agriculture damaged the environment and contributed to world poverty. In addition, college-age critics of Western culture pointed to the exotic religious vegetarianism in Hinduism, Buddhism, and Jainism as a source of spiritual value.

One of the most important challenges to meat's pride of place in the Jewish diet came from inside the Jewish community. Ironically, it was the Conservative movement's defense of the Jewish dietary laws that challenged long-held rabbinic approval of meat eating. The Conservative movement is the American Jewish religious denomination that, although affirming that *halakhah* is obligatory, promotes a more flexible and permissive version of it. Although it is conservative relative to the more liberal Reform Judaism because of its commitment to Jewish law, the Conservative movement's outlook is more indebted to secular thought than all forms of Orthodox Judaism. This is apparent in its discussion of vegetarianism.

Rabbi Samuel Dresner, a Conservative rabbi, published an essay in 1959 on the meaning of the Jewish dietary laws, which was republished a few years later by the educational arm of the Conservative movement. Dresner drew upon rabbinic teachings to connect *kashrut* to the larger story of God's will for the human diet. The Hebrew Bible's origin story, Dresner wrote, focuses on "Adam, the perfect man, . . . an inhabitant of the Garden of Eden, which represents the divine order of creation, the perfect, ideal society, [who] is limited to [eating] fruit and vegetables. He is clearly meant to be a vegetarian." In sum, vegetarianism is the ideal diet in the ideal society.[36] Dresner argued that the prophet Isaiah imagined the same ideal diet for the perfect society at the end of history, when the world will return "to the original state: 'And the wolf shall dwell with the lamb, and the leopard shall lie down with the kid; . . . Their young ones shall lie down together; *And the lion shall eat straw like the ox*.'" If this were true, Dresner wrote, "can we, therefore, not draw the inference that if the carnivorous animal will disappear at the end of time, how much more so the carnivorous man? . . . At the 'beginning' and at the 'end' man is, thus, in his ideal state, herbivorous."[37] Dresner was not reading these biblical narratives as actual human history, but as the ancient Israelites' thoughtful answers to fundamental moral questions. To him they regarded vegetarianism as an eternal ethical ideal.

Yet, according to Dresner, while the Bible shows the Garden of Eden as an ideal, it also describes the post-flood era as man "in his real state." For the "real" human, God permits a more reasonable but still ethical diet: One may eat meat as long as it is not eaten with the animal's blood, which is the animal's soul. The following is how Dresner summarized this transition:

> The permission to eat meat is thus seen to be a compromise, *a divine concession to human weakness and human need.* The Torah, as it were, says: "I would prefer that you abstain from eating meat altogether, that you subsist on that which springs forth from the earth, for to eat meat the life of an animal must be taken and that is a fearful act. But since you are not perfect men and your world is neither a Garden of Eden nor the Kingdom of God, since your desires cannot be stopped nor your nutritional requirements altered, they must at least be controlled . . . with one restriction—that you have reverence for the life you take."

This restriction, Dresner writes, is expressed in the biblical command: "The flesh with the soul thereof, which is the blood thereof, shall ye not eat" (Genesis 9:4).[38] In other words, God prefers that humans not kill animals for food, but humans lack self-control over their appetite for meat and their physical needs require it for health. Dresner does not explain this proviso of Genesis 9:4, and he ignores the rest of humanity and its laws. Instead, he presents the Jews and their dietary laws—specifically, kosher animal slaughter and the steps taken to remove blood from the meat— as God's compromise, albeit one that shows reverence for life and hallows the everyday needs of human beings.

The booklet, written for a lay audience of Jewish adults and high school students, was reprinted and distributed during the 1970s and 1980s in the youth groups, summer camps, and synagogues of the Conservative movement. Although it was written to encourage observance of *kashrut*, not vegetarianism, it might have inspired idealistic young Jews who learn about "the Bible's vegetarian ideal" to reject meat. After all, *kashrut* is described as second best, whereas vegetarianism is the diet of the past and future Garden of Eden. In an idealistic era when young people aspired to "get back to the garden," it seemed possible to do so by one's diet. These ideas spread to other Jewish denominations and to secular Jews. In 1973, the highly popular *Jewish Catalog: A Do-It-Yourself Kit* made the case that keeping kosher is one step short of the Jewish ideal of eating vegetarian. Two years later, the Jewish Vegetarian Society of America was founded, and its director explained, "In a real sense, vegetarianism is the highest form of Judaism. . . . Intrinsic values in Judaism—compassion for animals, concern about world hunger and ecology—are exemplified by vegetarianism."[39]

These positive statements about vegetarianism and criticisms of meat eating soon came to the attention of Orthodox rabbis and teachers. Young Jews who became Orthodox, a phenomenon that became more common in the 1970s, brought with them what they learned about Judaism from secular culture and liberal Jewish denominations, sometimes including the notion that a vegetarian diet is the most ethical diet and superior to a kosher one. Even Jews raised within the Orthodox community began to make this and similar points. In particular, these included Modern Orthodox Jews, who, in contrast to the more culturally insular Orthodox, attended American universities.

One such person was Richard Schwartz, one of the founders and later the director of the Jewish Vegetarian Society of America. Schwartz demonstrated his facility with biblical and rabbinic texts in his public speaking, teaching, and writing. His book *Judaism and Vegetarianism*, which showcased rabbinic sources that could be construed as favoring vegetarianism, was one of two books published about Jewish vegetarianism in 1982.[40] That year, Rabbi Alfred S. Cohen, a prominent Modern Orthodox rabbi, noted, "There are many, many Jewish vegetarians, and more than a few are quite Orthodox in the full sense of the word." Writing and publishing the first extensive Orthodox refutation of ethical vegetarianism, Cohen admitted he was motivated partly by "an increasingly familiar phenomenon [of] . . . vegetarians putting meat-eaters on the defensive."[41]

ORTHODOX RESPONSES TO VEGETARIANISM

It is important to clarify that most Orthodox rabbis and teachers do not pay much attention to whether their congregants are vegetarians. Yet, rabbis understand their role as guardians of proper religious outlook, *hashkafah*, and they would feel it their duty to respond to and correct congregants and students who assert false statements about Torah principles. Chabad rabbis began to systematically engage in outreach to unaffiliated or non-Orthodox Jews in the 1960s, and their congregations and classes included many *ba'alei teshuvah*, their offspring, and non-Orthodox Jews who attended for other reasons. These rabbis were probably the first to tackle the subject of vegetarianism and to do so with references to distinctively Chabad perspectives. Published works were first produced by Modern Orthodox rabbis. Rabbi Alfred S. Cohen, mentioned above, and Rabbi J. David Bleich, both highly respected scholars and teachers with ties to Yeshiva University, the Modern Orthodox rabbinic seminary in North America, each wrote articles that appeared in Modern Orthodox journals. Each elevated rabbinic texts that regard meat eating as necessary and beneficial. Over the following years, these were reprinted in both full and abridged formats. The points still appear in Orthodox outreach materials, sermons, curriculum, and modern Torah commentaries, and they have also been incorporated into Chabad educational materials. When abuses in the kosher meat industry came to light at the start of the twenty-first century, Cohen's and Bleich's arguments were revived and augmented to meet the new challenges and audiences.[42]

Much of the discourse about meat eating and morality is ostensibly about humanity's diet, yet the rabbis address a Jewish audience. The arguments are built around the narrative that starts with the Garden of Eden and culminates with God's commandments to Noah and his family after the flood. There are three main components to this discourse: the moral defense of meat eating, the claim that meat eating promotes human morality and vegetarianism leads to immorality and antisemitism, and the insistence that Jews who wish to be upright and devoted in their religious observance should eat meat.

It Is Moral to Kill Animals for Food

The primary response to the question of the morality of killing animals for food is that God has permitted it. It is a fundamental principle of rabbinic thought that God's laws are good, and the good is defined by reference to God's laws, not to independent human judgment. This, then, is a statement of faith, not an argument. Of course, non-Jews might not accept the Torah as revelation, but according to Orthodox Jews, all Jews certainly should. Already in 1973, a rabbi responding to Jewish vegetarians succinctly identified ethical vegetarianism as a direct challenge to centuries of Jewish tradition: "For a Jew to adopt vegetarianism because he objects to killing animals for food is to introduce a moral and theological idea which suggests that Judaism has, in fact, been wrong all the time in not advocating vegetarianism."[43] A decade later in his article, Cohen stated this point more emphatically:

> Let us bear in mind the concomitant question of whether a religious Jew may accept moral values which are not found within Torah or *halacha*, or approve standards which might oppose the Torah's standards, or which imply, at the very least, that the Torah's standards are inferior or less humane. Is it not presumptuousness bordering on blasphemy to call an act sanctioned by the Torah (and perhaps mandated by halacha), an act of cruelty, of inhumanity? We must first of all respond to this challenge to Jewish tradition, for if there is indeed any lèse majesté in accepting the vegetarian credo, that would automatically preclude acceptance of that system for an observant Jew. Where the standards of vegetarianism condemn the values of the Torah or denounce its *mitzvot* [commandments] as immoral or distasteful, we must categorically reject vegetarian ideology as aberrant philosophy. We believe that the Torah's ways "are paths of pleasantness" and

righteousness; any belief which seeks to negate the Torah's truths is misguided.[44]

Cohen signals here that he is assessing vegetarian principles in terms of their compatibility with Torah principles, and even a mild claim that they are superior is offensive. A Jew should know the good by learning from the Torah.

The idea that only moral opinions already divinely revealed in the Torah are legitimate represents a particularly narrow approach to Jewish ethics. It is not characteristic of Modern Orthodox thought.[45] Nevertheless, both Cohen and Rabbi Bleich insisted on this stance in their articles. Bleich stated this point more concisely than Cohen:

> In Jewish teaching, not only are normative laws regarded as binding solely upon the authority of divine revelation, but ethical principles as well are regarded as endowed with validity and commended as goals of human aspiration only if they, too, are divinely revealed.[46]

Perhaps the two took this unusual stance because of their defensiveness in the face of Jewish vegetarians. Not surprisingly, this narrow point of view is taught in Chabad. In the words of a Chabad high school teacher, "We have to teach them that the Torah defines reality. You can make anything true using human reason and logic. The Torah is divinely inspired." Another teacher expressed the larger issue as a matter of belief that "the Torah is *yashar*," meaning "upright" or "good." That is, even if a commandment is not identified as being about ethics or goodness, it is *yashar* because it is in the Torah.[47]

At other times, however, rabbis and teachers do use logical reasoning. Utilizing the concept of *ta'amei hamitzvot* (reasons for the commandments), they explain *mitzvot* in terms of how they enhance the wisdom and beauty of the Torah. Rabbis' reasoned defense of meat eating starts with the concept summarized today among Orthodox teachers as "the hierarchy of creation." It is essentially a Jewish version of the ancient Greek idea of the chain of being.[48] In class at a Pico-Robertson Orthodox synagogue, my teacher expressed it in the language of the medieval Jewish philosopher Moses Maimonides, who had been highly influenced by Aristotelianism. She explained the hierarchy as four levels ascending in spiritual importance. The bottom level is *domem*, silent or inanimate creations; above it is *tsome'ah*, growing things; above that is *hai*, the animal world; and the top level is *medaber*, the human level, which was thought to be unique for its ability to communicate through speech.

"We now know that animals do have language," she told us, "but human speech is unique because it can create and destroy worlds." The hierarchy of creation is implicit in the first two chapters of Genesis. The position of humans on the top level is what permits them to use and even destroy the lower orders for human needs. It is not an absolute right, she pointed out, because "we are not allowed to waste the lower levels and certainly not permitted to cause animals unnecessary pain."[49] Both the hierarchy and the avoidance of waste and animal pain are what renders the human use of animals a moral act.

Indeed, discussions about the morality of eating meat invariably refer to the Torah's mandate for the compassionate treatment of animals. Cohen's approach is typical. After quoting a spokesman for vegetarianism who praised a Buddhist precept equating reverence for life with refusal to kill animals, Cohen mentions the Torah prohibition *tza'ar ba'alei hayyim* against causing unnecessary suffering to animals, the rule against destruction of nature for trivial reasons, and the procedures in *shehitah* that cause a quick and painless death to the animal. Cohen writes, "In embodying the concept of compassion for all living things into actual practice, I do not think there is anywhere a legal or religious system which can compare to the Torah's teachings."[50] That is, Judaism, more so than Buddhism or any other religious tradition, Cohen argues, insists on minimizing animal suffering and inculcates reverence for animal life. Today, Orthodox Jewish schoolteachers, rabbis, and community spokesmen are practiced in reciting the many Torah laws requiring care for animals. They point out that these concerns were already evident among Jewish teachings long before the rest of humanity discovered the importance of animal welfare.

AgriProcessors, the corporate identity of the slaughterhouse and meat-packing factory in Postville, Iowa, has used this argument to defend its practices. In response to the request by PETA that AgriProcessors improve its slaughtering methods, Nathan Lewin, the attorney for AgriProcessors, responded:

> Long before the rest of the world showed any "common decency" to animals or had the slightest concern for the treatment of animals, the laws of the Torah and rabbinic teachings commanded the Jewish people to treat all living creatures humanely. Secular society—including your organization—has still not caught up with the precepts of Jewish law in this regard.[51]

The mandate to be compassionate to animals has one important limitation: humans must be able to use animals, and using the animal may cause it pain or even cost it its life. The pain involved must be *necessary* pain, with steps taken to cause as little pain as possible. To deny this entitlement is wrong, from the perspective of the Torah; it is a distortion of the divine hierarchy of life. If eating meat is necessary for a person's health or for a Jew to fulfill a religious obligation, she must permit the animal to be killed on her behalf and consume the meat.[52] The principle *tza'ar ba'alei hayyim* is not absolute. An animal does not have the right to be unharmed and unused by humans.

Because of this principle, Bleich argues that the medieval Jewish rabbinic approval of the vegetarian diet places the person, not the animal, as the object of concern. This preserves human supremacy. He explains:

> A number of medieval scholars . . . regard vegetarianism as a moral ideal, not because of a concern for the welfare of animals, but because of the fact that the slaughter of animals might cause the individual who performs such acts to develop negative character traits, viz., meanness and cruelty. Their concern was with regard to possible untoward effect upon human character rather than with animal welfare.[53]

That is, the individual who consumes meat reasons, "My desire for meat will cause the slaughterer's character to worsen." Bleich does not dwell on the implications of the medieval scholars' ruling: If they are correct in believing that the act of slaughtering animals may harm the *shohet*'s character, is not this an admission that the act is morally problematic? Instead, Bleich cites their opinion to emphasize humanity's position at the top of creation. In his other arguments, Bleich states his belief that ethical vegetarians refuse meat because they believe that animals are equivalent to humans. This is not an accurate characterization of ethical vegetarians. Many of them regard themselves as a higher species than animals but refuse to eat meat because they, unlike animals, can choose their food, and they choose what they believe is a more ethical diet.

Meat Eating Promotes Morality, and Vegetarianism Leads to Immorality and Antisemitism

Not only is human ascendancy over animals the basis for the morality of meat eating; it is also the basis of human morality. The latter point was already advanced by Rabbi Samson Raphael Hirsch. Hirsch rested his conclusion on the creation narrative's categorization of species and its prohibition against humans consuming a live animal. Bleich, however, bases his reasoning on an argument advanced by the medieval Jewish philosopher Rabbi Joseph Albo (Spain, 1380–1444) in his book on the fundamentals of Judaism.

According to Albo, human beings from Adam and Eve until the flood were confused about their status compared to that of animals. To them, God's prohibition against eating animals meant they were equivalent in value. Consequently, Cain chose vegetation, not animals, as his offering to God. When it was rejected and Abel's animal sacrifice was accepted, in Bleich's paraphrase of Albo, Cain "remained confirmed in his opinion that man and animals are inherently equal, yet he was led to the even more grievous conclusion that just as man is entitled to take the life of an animal so also is he entitled to take the life of his fellow man."

In other words, Albo reasoned, "if I may kill an animal, then I may also kill a human, which is the same as an animal." Albo is arguing that had God permitted the first humans to eat meat, Cain would not have made this error; he would not have been led astray by his reasoning. Abel, too, was trapped by his independent thinking, according to Albo. Although Abel understood that humans were superior to animals, he erred in supposing that human superiority was based on their reasoning power. God therefore permitted him to be murdered by his brother.[54]

It may be instructive to stop at this point and consider Albo's interpretation. His reading of the Cain and Abel story is idiosyncratic. Rabbinic commentators taught that God rejected Cain's grain offering because he offered the least and not the best of his harvest. Others pointed to Cain's egocentric and irreverent character, but no one criticized his employment of reason. Bleich could have highlighted Albo's critique of vegetarianism without censuring the use of reason, but the latter point served to critique contemporary Jews' trust in their rational deductions and their engagement in secular culture that was leading them away from Jewish tradition. He could have cited Hirsch on the importance of the hierarchy of creation and meat eating as a foundation for morality. Hirsch, however, was known for celebrating the newly granted opportunity in the West for a Jewish male to enroll in advanced institutions of learning and "to devote himself to all true progress in civilization and culture—provided, that is, that he will not only not have to sacrifice his Judaism but will able to bring it to a more perfect fulfillment."[55] Bleich, writing from the vantage point a century later, was less optimistic about Jews' abilities to preserve Torah values under the pressures of modern culture.

Bleich blames the false equation of humans with animals for the evil behavior of the generations after Cain. Because people believed they were equal to animals, they acted like animals, and eventually society became so degenerate that God brought the flood. This is why Albo concludes that the "renunciation of the consumption of meat for reasons of concern for animal welfare is not only morally erroneous but even repugnant."[56] Vegetarianism can be adopted for other reasons—for example, if people have no desire for meat or find it disgusting. But, Bleich declares, when people adopt it out of concern for animal welfare, they are denying the fundamental doctrine that humans stand above animals in the hierarchy of creation, and this is bound to lead to immorality. God gave people an omnivorous diet, says Bleich, to fully eliminate the false beliefs "that animals are somehow endowed with rights and that man's obligations vis-a-vis animals are somehow rooted in such rights rather than in a concern for the possible moral degeneration of man himself." Animals are important only insofar as they serve human needs.[57]

Bleich also found support for his critique of vegetarianism in the writings of Rabbi Abraham Isaac Kook (1865–1935), a widely respected pre-Holocaust Torah scholar whose disapproval of meat eating was celebrated by Jewish vegetarians.[58] Bleich disagreed. He admitted that Kook taught that vegetarianism was the norm in the Garden of Eden when Adam had high moral awareness and that humans during the future eschatological epoch would be vegetarians again because their awareness would also be high. Bleich insisted, however, that Kook frowned on widespread vegetarianism during the intermediate era in which we live and did not think vegetarian advocacy was warranted until the more serious problems facing the world were rectified. When most human beings cannot sublimate their desire for meat, unrelieved cravings for meat would be dangerous for most people. They would channel their "natural moral instincts" toward being scrupulously concerned about animal welfare, leading them to ignore human welfare. If a person believes that killing animals is as abhorrent as killing humans—Kook, like Bleich, assumes this motive for vegetarians—then that person will conclude "that he is bound by standards of morality no different from those espoused by brute animals" and may even resort to cannibalism.[59]

Bleich responded to Kook's extreme prediction by introducing Nazism into his disparagement of vegetarianism. He believed Kook showed great psychological insight in recognizing that people with skewed moral priorities often take up "moral" causes. Knowing that Kook had died just as the National Socialist Party came into power, Bleich comments on what occurred in Nazi Germany:

With almost prescient knowledge of future events, Rabbi Kook argues that, were vegetarianism to become the norm, people might become quite callous with regard to human welfare and human life and express their instinctive moral feelings in an exaggerated concern for animal welfare. These comments summon to mind the spectacle of Germans watching with equanimity while their Jewish neighbors were dispatched to crematoria and immediately thereafter turning their attention to the welfare of the household pets that had been left behind.[60]

Bleich is doing more here than repeating the modern adage about animal lovers caring more for pets than people. His argument draws a straight line from some streams of modern secular thought—with its elimination of differences between humans and animals, its concern for animal welfare, and its faith in human reason—to violent antisemitism. Bleich's moral critique of vegetarianism and animal welfare advocacy points dramatically to the horrors that he believes will occur when people abandon religious tradition. Here, non-Jews are shown to be the ones whose morality is damaged by modern secular thought, and Jews are their victims. The implication is that Jews who adopt these modern ideas for themselves are contributing to their own persecution.

Years later, the Nazi trope appeared in a different way in the rhetoric of animal welfare advocates. Novelist Isaac Bashevis Singer, a Polish Jewish immigrant who had recently adopted a vegetarian diet, wrote in 1968 that animals living near human society experience "an eternal Treblinka." Singer observed that humans justified the exploitation, torment, and extermination of animals because of a conceptual hierarchy comparable to the Nazi racial hierarchy in which Aryans were entitled to exploit, inflict pain upon, and murder Jews.[61] Singer's point was amplified by historian and animal welfare activist Charles Patterson in *Eternal Treblinka: Our Treatment of Animals and the Holocaust*. Published in 2002, the book compared the victimization of Jews with the use of animals as resources for human needs or the perception of them as threats to humanity.[62] Adopting this metaphor, in 2003, the organization PETA created a photo exhibition called "Holocaust on Your Plate." It consisted of photographs of animals in various phases of industrial farming and slaughter juxtaposed with images of concentration camp inmates and piles of human corpses. The photo exhibit essentially likened meat eaters and fur wearers to Nazis and their collaborators and onlookers. It received enormous publicity, some of it from the many people and organizations who denounced it as insulting to Jews and a trivialization of the Holocaust.[63]

In 2004, PETA and its animal advocacy came into the full focus of the Orthodox community. After receiving tips about maltreatment of animals in meat slaughtering plants, PETA arranged a secret videotaping of seven weeks of handling and slaughtering animals at AgriProcessors, the leading kosher meat company in the United States. Its huge distribution network brought kosher meat to places where it was previously unavailable, and its prices were lower than those of other brands. The company was owned and operated by Sholem Rubashkin, a member of an influential Chabad Hasidic family who was known to distribute company profits widely within the Chabad community. PETA published a short video culled from the weeks of filming. It showed that AgriProcessors was following painful procedures not used in other kosher slaughterhouses. These speeded up *shehitah* so that more meat could be produced per hour. In addition, immediately after the *shohet* cut the main neck artery, and often before the animal apparently lost consciousness, the *shohet*'s assistants pulled out and cut the esophagus and trachea of the cattle. This second cut is not required by Jewish law and appeared to cause the animals terrible pain and delay their death. The video gave the impression that *shehitah* was as brutal as antisemitic propaganda claimed it to be.[64]

Kosher meat scandals had occurred before in American history, and they typically involved the business owner deceiving kosher customers by selling nonkosher meat as kosher. These events cause great distress in the community of those who keep kosher, and they shake up the relationship between kosher consumers and business owners. Unlike the typical *kashrut* scandal, however, the scandal about AgriProcessors did not remain within the Jewish community but was disseminated on TV and in the national press.[65] The unapologetic, belligerent response of Orthodox spokesmen likely increased the media coverage. One widely published editorial by Rabbi Avi Shafran, director of public affairs for the Haredi organization Agudath Israel, treated the accusations as an attack on *shehitah* and on Judaism and included the Nazi theme. "The 'PETA Principle,' the moral equating of animals and humans, is an affront to the very essence of Jewish belief," he declared. He highlighted the Torah's laws mandating compassion toward animals, declared that these are scrupulously followed during *shehitah*, and closed with the warning:

> *Shehitah* was attacked and outlawed by the Nazis when they came to power in Germany. Today, animal rights activists have succeeded in banning it in several European and Scandinavian countries. If PETA's misleading campaign is not seen for the partisan salvo it is, our own country may be next.[66]

Because of the videotape, the Orthodox Union, the kosher certification agency for AgriProcessors, insisted that the company cease performing the second cut on the animal. Subsequent video evidence indicates that the practice resumed later. No charges were filed by the government, and there were no serious efforts in the United States to end *shehitah*.[67] Four years after the video appeared, FBI and Department of Homeland Security investigators raided the meat production plant and offices, and more than a hundred charges were filed for violations of immigration and child labor laws, money laundering, bank fraud, and tax evasion. In 2010 Rubashkin was found guilty of eighty-six criminal counts and sentenced to twenty-seven years in prison.

A segment of the American Orthodox community regarded the entire matter as antisemitism originating in a false accusation by PETA. In their minds, people who advocated vegetarianism and veganism were likely to hate *shehitah* and Jews. A rabbi in a Pico-Robertson high school who described himself as Centrist explained the specific ethical issue to me as follows:

I don't think *sheḥitah* is cruel. The claim that it is cruel—this is an old tactic. You know, it was the first thing that the Nazis outlawed. Hitler came to power in January and prohibited *sheḥitah* in March. It's always been the first move on the road to persecuting the Jews. It's the easiest thing to pick on. Arabs don't do it because they, too, have a type of *sheḥitah*. And it's well known that PETA had a vendetta against Rubashkin, that's the only reason why they went after him. You know, Rubashkin was the largest *sheḥitah* company in the world, I think.[68]

Among my interviewees, Modern Orthodox Jews were the most likely to concede that *sheḥitah* might not be the most pain-free slaughtering method, but even they referred to animal welfare advocates as antisemitic.

At the time of the scandal, Chabad Hasidic Jews, the most fervent and vocal defenders of Rubashkin, appeared united in the opinion that he was the victim not only of the antisemitic organization PETA but also of antisemitic judges and investigators. They regarded Orthodox Jews who spoke out in defense of PETA's investigation, such as Rabbi Shmuly Yanklowitz, as duped and guilty of collaboration. In the Pico-Robertson neighborhood, Chabad Jews boycotted the kosher food establishments that supported Yanklowitz's labor ethics initiative.[69] In 2012, I asked one of the teachers at the local Chabad girls' high school, "How would you respond if a student asked you whether *sheḥitah* is ethical?" She said, "I would tell her that we believe that *sheḥitah* is painless for the animal, that it is the most sensitive way to kill an animal. I would also tell them that *sheḥitah* was one of the first acts outlawed by the Nazis."[70]

Jews Should Eat Meat

The claim that eating meat promotes human morality, while vegetarianism leads to human immorality, reinforces the insistence that a Jew should eat meat. Most Orthodox rabbis today, if pressed, would have to admit that Jews are not, strictly speaking, *required* to eat meat. However, in religious life the letter of the law may be less important than community norms. Community norms favor meat eating and look askance at people who have chosen vegetarianism or veganism out of ethical conviction.

It is important to realize that the daily, weekly, and yearly rites that are central to Orthodox Jewish life are built upon the Torah's framework of sacrificial worship, mostly involving meat. About one-third of the Torah's laws deal with the animals and foodstuffs donated by lay Israelites or owed by them to the Tabernacle and later the Temple. Some of what was offered was consumed by the priests, their families, and the person bringing the offering. The only meat a lay Israelite was required to eat was the Passover offering, *korban pesaḥ*. According to the Torah and later rabbinic law, this once-yearly consumption of meat was incumbent upon the entire nation during the era when sacrificial worship was in place. A rabbi who counsels students in the Pico-Robertson boys' high school put it this way:

> If a student tells me they really do not like meat, you can't argue with that. Even on Shabbos and festival. They don't want to eat it, they won't eat it. But if someone says, "Eating meat is not ethical," I'd have to disagree. I'd respond, "Hashem tells us we must eat meat. It's a mitzvah to eat *korban pesaḥ*."[71]

In the biblical era, when Israelites wished to eat meat outside of the context of sacrificial worship, they were required to follow rules similar to those given for animal sacrifice, including eating only permitted animals, removing the blood, and removing certain fats. When sacrificial rituals ceased with the destruction of the Jerusalem Temple in 70 CE, rabbis taught that the sacrificial commandments were suspended, not abolished, and they anticipated their revival in a later era when the altar and Temple would be rebuilt. Meanwhile, Jews continued to pray for the restoration of the Temple and sacrificial worship, and Orthodox Jews still do so today.[72]

The rabbis democratized the priestly duties to some extent by transforming them into communal and domestic obligations and voluntary acts of piety. In the place of daily, Sabbath, and holiday offerings, men were obligated to participate in morning, afternoon, and evening prayers at the same hour the sacrifices had been offered. Torah study could be regarded as a substitute for sacrifices, in line with the expression from Hosea 14:3, "We offer the bullocks of our lips." Meals, too, could serve this function; for example, serving the Sabbath and holiday bread with a sprinkling of salt was likened to the requirement in Leviticus 2:13 to add salt to every grain offering. The table at which pious Jews dined was compared to "the table before God," that is, the altar at the Temple, if three of them shared words of Torah during the meal. The blessing of thanks after a meal, like many other prayers in the daily, weekly, and holiday liturgy, included a prayer beseeching God to rebuild the Temple and restore the sacrifices there.

The duty to honor the Sabbath with three meals cannot be traced back to the ancient sacrificial rites, but their presence in the weekly lives of Jews dates back two thousand years. Ideally, the Friday evening and Saturday midday meals are the best of the week, featuring wine, bread, delicacies, and choice foods. Eating these meals meets a separate obligation called *oneg shabbat*, making the Sabbath pleasurable. Eating meat and drinking wine were considered activities bringing pleasure. However, the rabbis ruled that if an individual finds meat disgusting, would be sickened by eating it, or is very pious and has reason to believe that the kosher meat available does not meet fastidious halakhic requirements, he or she could refrain from eating meat and not violate *oneg shabbat*. Certainly, there were people who could not afford to buy meat or fish. They were not, on that account, guilty of sin, but it was meritorious for the well-to-do to invite the poor to their tables or provision them so they, too, could fulfill the duty of *oneg shabbat*.[73]

Choosing to abstain from meat on the three religious festivals is a more serious matter. Deuteronomy 16:14–15 teaches, "You shall rejoice in your festival, with your son and daughter, your male and female slave, the Levite, the stranger, the fatherless, and the widow in your communities. . . . You shall only be happy." Rabbis teach that the obligation to be joyous is a positive duty whether one feels like it or not.

They debated whether the obligation necessitates drinking wine or eating meat or both. A few ruled that Jews must eat meat, but there is greater consensus among them that only drinking wine is obligatory. In their 1980s articles summarizing the challenges vegetarianism poses to Judaism, Rabbis Cohen and Bleich do not unequivocally state that *halakhah* requires meat eating on the festival. However, in Cohen's words, "Vegetarianism would be antagonistic to the *spirit* of Jewish thought on *Yom Tov* [the festival], even if not to the actual letter of the law."[74]

It is also "antagonistic" to Orthodox Jewish life. Today's American Orthodox Jews, like Americans as a whole, depend a great deal upon meat for their weekly caloric intake. Meat is central to the American diet, and the Jews who immigrated to this country were delighted to enjoy the bounty. Because of the greater availability and affordability of kosher meat, not only in the United States but also in the other lands in which Jews reside, meat probably plays a larger role in Jewish religious culture than it did in the past. Orthodox Jews hold a virtual monopoly on kosher meat certification and kosher food businesses. These are not only places of employment but also crucial sources of revenue for communal educational, religious, and social institutions. The ubiquity of kosher meat in the heart of the Pico-Robertson neighborhood may intensify its importance for its Orthodox communities. There are few vegetarians among the Orthodox Jews in Los Angeles. They have learned it is easiest to claim they have chosen the diet for health reasons and yet are often asked, "Even on Shabbat? Just a little?" One man, whose obvious Torah knowledge and strict halakhic practice provoke questions from rabbis about his refusal to eat meat, told me how he deals with their challenges: "They know I am not violating *halakhah*, so if they make that claim I correct them. And then I tell them, 'When *Moshiaḥ* [the Messiah] comes and the Temple is rebuilt, I will gladly eat *korban pesah*,' and they leave me alone."[75]

The Chabad community takes a different approach, which is that Jews are essentially duty bound to eat meat. The obligation is rooted not in *halakhah* but in *Ḥasidus*, the spiritual teachings of past Hasidic leaders. Some Chabad synagogues, which are places of adult education, also teach—sometimes more emphatically—that for Jews, eating meat is a responsibility. For example, a photocopied handout of short insights and commentaries provided to attendees at one of the Pico-Robertson Chabad synagogues identified vegetarianism as an abrogation of responsibility:

> With regard to vegetarianism: Generally speaking, according to *Kabbalah* and *Chassidus*, such conduct has no place, as each of us is obligated to refine and elevate his quota of food. By denying oneself a certain type of food, one is unable to refine and elevate it. The only exception to the above are unique and particularly holy individuals.[76]

A Jew is justified in refusing to eat meat only by claiming extraordinary holiness, and this status is so rare that it is not even explained. The source for this teaching is the venerated seventh Chabad rebbe, Menachem Schneerson, who everybody knows ate meat. Another source, an article on Chabad.org, makes meat eating a universal obligation:

> After the flood, G-d laid down a new world order. People needed to recognize the moral obligations and divine purpose entrusted to humankind. To make this clear, G-d told Noah that humankind can—indeed, must—eat the flesh of animals. Our dominion over animals highlights our superiority and reminds us that we are charged with divine responsibility to perfect the world.[77]

Human beings must eat meat to fulfill their duty to God and the world.

Just as forceful an imperative was voiced in a Pico-Robertson congregation by a rabbi who made his point through kabbalistic principles of reincarnation. He started with the principle that Jews who have sinned in a particular way are punished after death when their souls are reincarnated into living animals. Trapped in a lower level of existence, they can be freed and elevated to a higher level only when a kosher animal is meticulously slaughtered and eaten in a devout manner by a pious Jew.

A member of the congregation, after making a disdainful remark about vegetarianism, explained it as follows:

> When a person dies . . . if your soul is so bad that when it approaches Gehinnom [the first, purgatory-like stage of the afterlife], all those souls say, "You're too dirty for us, go away," then . . . your soul wanders to and fro, and you are captured and then torn apart or burned up, all into little pieces and have to get put together again, and then you wander to and fro, and the same thing keeps happening. There are four levels of life, and you will be put at the bottom of them, and you have to work your way up, from *domem* [stones], *tzomeah* [vegetation], *hai* [animals], to *medaber* [humans]. When an animal is slaughtered, and it is done correctly [very sharp knife, smooth cut with one stroke], and a Jew eats the food with a spiritual intention, says the *berakhah* [blessing], the soul trapped in that animal can be fixed.[78]

Eating meat is a noble act, then, comparable to the redeeming of a captive. Vegetarians do not realize this, and they cannot do this work. Indeed, they might be reincarnated as a lower creature and be dependent upon meat-eating Jews for their release.

Hierarchy as a concept and a reality is fundamental to Orthodox Jews. The hierarchy of creation that places humans above animals, long an element of Jewish thought, has assumed for them greater importance with the widespread acceptance of evolutionary scientific views that appear to refute it. The prevailing Orthodox view is that a disproportionate concern for animal welfare and a growth in human depravity are a consequence of these modern ideas. If non-Jews, even the seemingly gentle-hearted vegetarians among them, forget the distinction between humans and animals, they will invariably turn against each other and the Jewish minority in their midst. Jews, too, require what meat eating provides: the valuable message that they are above animals and must obey God's commands and do their part to repair the world. Jews who accept the principles of ethical vegetarianism may lose sight of their fundamental obligations. Living in homes devoid of meat, they will not need to perform many of the dietary laws, such as the myriad ways of separating meat and milk, that govern the normal Orthodox household. They will have fewer reminders at the times when their daily life is related to food and at every meal that they are part of a community bound together by special laws and a unique devotion to God.

5

Feeding Others

The thick large plate-glass window of the big room in the community center faces the street, letting in Southern California's sunshine while blocking out street noise. The center's open spaces, tables, and comfortable chairs serve as the site for an organization that teaches Torah and Jewish values to newly religious young men and women. The students typically eat Shabbat Friday night and Saturday lunch meals at the homes of local Orthodox families, but they assemble here during the week and for praying, learning, and singing connected to the third and final Shabbat meal. A coffee machine, cups and napkins, and snacks occupy a counter at the back wall next to a door to the office, which has its own back door leading to the alley. While the rabbi and I sat talking in the big room, a man the rabbi did not recognize came from the office into our room, fingered the pamphlets on a table, and quickly exited out the front. The rabbi sighed and said, "I really need to learn to lock that back door." He walked into the back office, locked the door, and upon returning told me a story.

During an evening program the previous week, someone had entered through the unlocked alley door and stolen his laptop from the office desk. On Saturday night he received a phone call from a local woman friend. She is a generous woman, so much so that she regularly hosts a Jewish man who is living on the street at her Shabbat lunch meal. The rabbi doesn't know anyone else who does this. The woman told the rabbi that this guest had been very excited when he arrived for lunch that day. He had found a laptop while scrounging through an alleyway garbage bin, and he hoped she would help him restore it to the rightful owner whose name—a rabbi's!—was on the laptop screen. "Yes, it's your laptop," she said to the rabbi. He showed me the text message she sent him consisting of a photo of an unkempt man holding open the laptop, a wide smile on his face.[1]

This chapter focuses on two Jewish commandments to feed others. Unlike the laws of *kashrut*, these commandments are not decrees but mandates that are intended to enhance society. The first, hospitality, *hakhnasat orḥim*, is understood today to mean hosting out-of-town visitors in one's home for meals and, if necessary, lodging them. The second is charity, *tzedakah*, understood as an obligation to provide for the needy.[2] In the biblical tales and until the present day, providing hospitality for visitors and food for the needy are regarded as righteous and essential acts. Nevertheless, they have changed over time, and there have been disagreements about how to perform them. Today there is no single authoritative opinion regarding either mandate.

For example, some believe that nondiscriminatory hospitality entails a social as well as a physical risk that should be avoided. Others use Sabbath hospitality as a loving means to promote Jewish religious observance to non-Orthodox Jews, yet some scorn these overtures not as a genuine act of love or community but as a means of winning supporters. The distinction between normal socializing and religiously motivated hospitality can be unclear; that is, when does one's hosting of a meal really "count" as the fulfillment of a mitzvah? The extent of an individual's—or, more often, a group's—cultural insularity, religious ideology, and community culture influences whom one invites to the home or helps, how one does it, and whether one expands or narrows the scope of these commandments.

Determining how to give *tzedakah* and to whom to give it also differs among rabbinical authorities. For example, some religious authorities teach that it is best to give *tzedakah* anonymously and without even knowing the identity of the recipient to preserve the dignity of the poor. Others reject the ethic of anonymity and try to erase the boundaries between the well-to-do and the needy by embracing the latter as part of the family and community table. There are diverse rulings on the maximum one may give to the needy and on which poor should be included.[3] This chapter explores the variations within the Pico-Robertson neighborhood in how people view and fulfill these mandates, the explanations that people give for their mode of practice, and the effects these have on shaping and sustaining communities.

Of course, the variations in practice are not always simply, or even primarily, a result of religious ideology or a principled approach toward cultural insularity. Many social psychologists maintain that intellectual reasoning follows, rather than dictates, a person's emotional response to choices and to life situations. From birth, humans possess the capacity for empathy as well as a natural curiosity, and the intensity of these within the individual varies according to temperament. Cultural training has an influence on the development of these capacities: children can be taught to regard outsiders indifferently or suspiciously or to assess the stranger according to specific criteria before showing concern and warmth. Orthodox Jews teach their children in multiple ways to avoid social intimacy with non-Jews and non-Torah-observant Jews. Boundary making occurs between different types of Orthodox Jews, too, although the barriers are not as high. In a neighborhood like Pico-Robertson, where there are many Orthodox synagogue options, people gravitate toward those congregations that share their approach to "outsiders" as they have defined them.

In this chapter I focus on tendencies within congregations. Drawing on interviews with congregational rabbis, lay leaders, and members, as well as my own participation and observations, I describe how home hospitality and food charity are performed. Both commandments are considered central to a Torah-defined life, and both take place or are partly performed in public settings. They are a key element of what a community advocates and facilitates, especially around proper Shabbat observance.

Tradition dictates that the Sabbath should be experienced communally, with worship at a synagogue, Torah study, bountiful meals with family and guests, and the assurance that all members of the community can enjoy it. On Thursday afternoon and Friday morning the grocery stores are full of people making last-minute purchases. On Thursday night the local Orthodox food charity sends out its food disbursements, and it is customary to give charity prior to lighting the Sabbath candles. No one wants to eat Friday night dinner alone on a regular basis. Meal invitations are a sign of acceptance and popularity, and eating together at Sabbath meals is an important Orthodox social activity. In the Orthodox community, invitations may be offered weeks in advance and the guest list may lengthen up until the hour before the meal starts. When the Friday night and Sabbath day worship service ends, hosts and guests gather to walk together to the meal, and afterward guests walk home while chatting and crossing paths with others. People are taught that they may enjoy the Sabbath meals and rest with a clear conscience only if they have done their part to provide for the poor.

FEEDING OTHERS: THE COMMANDMENTS AND TRADITIONS

The written Torah does not explicitly command people to offer home hospitality, but it includes stories indicating that such an act is both essential and a great virtue. For Jews of the past and Orthodox Jews today, the biblical patriarch Abraham is the model for hospitality. After receiving God's blessings and undergoing circumcision, Abraham sat in the door of his tent in the midday heat. Noticing three travelers in the distance, he ran toward them, bowed, and called out, "My lords, if I find favor in your eyes, please do not pass away from me, your servant." He sat them under the shade of his tree, bathed their feet, and served them a feast prepared by his wife, Sarah, and their servants.[4]

Orthodox Jews understand this story from the perspective of rabbinic commentaries. These say that Abraham would open his tent on four sides to see travelers from all directions. Pointing out that in the previous verses God was telling Abraham what was in store for him, the followers of one tradition insist that he saw the wayfarers in the distance while listening to God's message, and Abraham's words were not an invitation to the strangers but a request of God, that is, "My Lord, if I find favor in your eyes, please do not pass away from me, your servant, [while I tend to these travelers]."[5] Abraham knew that God would be honored by his generous treatment of the strangers. He ran to greet the travelers, served them the entire day, and afterward resumed his conversation with God.

"Hospitality to wayfarers is greater than receiving the Divine Presence," the Talmudic sages declared. Such acts confer God's benevolent treatment in this life and the next, they wrote:

> There are six matters a person enjoys the profits of in this world, and nevertheless the principal exists for him for the World-to-Come, and they are: Hospitality toward guests, and visiting the sick, consideration during prayer, rising early to the study hall, raising one's sons to engage in Torah study, and one who judges another favorably, giving him the benefit of the doubt. . . . Hospitality toward guests and visiting the sick are in the category of acts of lovingkindness [gemilut hasadim].[6]

Hospitality is one way to fulfill the comprehensive commandment known as gemilut hasadim. These are personal acts that involve physical or emotional closeness. Other acts in this category include visiting the sick and dowering a poor bride. Commentators linked hospitality and visiting the sick with Abraham when they noted that God appeared to Abraham that day as an act of "visiting the sick" because shortly before this episode Abraham had circumcised himself at God's command. Despite his pain, Abraham ran to the travelers and exerted himself on their behalf all day. The rabbis portrayed him as a hasid, a hero of graciousness who emulated God's hesed, grace.[7] Today among the Orthodox, hospitable people are compared to Abraham and Sarah. For example, a Pico-Robertson rabbi described a husband and wife renowned for their hospitality by saying, "They are paragons of this midah [attribute], like Abraham and Sarah."[8]

In the biblical tale Abraham offers hospitality to strangers whose nation or religion is not known to him, but rabbinic writings portray the deed as one extended only to Jews. An Orthodox Jew finds applied Jewish law, *halakhah*, not in the Bible but in the postbiblical Talmud and law codes, and these do not encourage the universal hospitality shown by Abraham. Classical rabbinic expressions of the virtue of hospitality, such as the exhortation in the Mishnah, "Let your house be wide open to strangers, and treat the poor as members of your own family,"[9] were narrowed and understood as referring to Jews hosting Jewish strangers. Indeed, some Talmudic discussions of hospitality describe rabbis who are so selective that they only invite Torah scholars or well-born Jews to their homes, although these stories may have been included to show that one should not be that discriminating.

Although the rabbinic admonition links hospitality and charity, rabbinic law differentiates the latter from the former. "The poor" are the needy; their identity and their poverty are known, and helping them is *tzedakah*, a separate commandment mandating a specific percentage of one's income or a specific amount given to or left for the poor. The rabbis did not affirm Abraham's nondiscriminatory hospitality as an option for regular Jews. As I showed in chapter 2, the Talmudic rabbis believed that commensality forges close social ties and that eating socially with non-Jews leads to intermarriage and Jews' violation of the Torah laws. Rabbinic law prohibits Jews from eating bread, cheese, and cooked food produced by non-Jews, and even wine produced by Jews that has been merely touched by non-Jews is unfit to drink.

In short, the rabbis introduced the consideration of social risk into the performance of *hakhnasat orḥim*. Consequently, hospitality in the Jewish tradition, in contrast to the early Christian tradition, is not a subversive or countercultural activity, for the strangers at one's table are not actually strangers but merely unknown Jews. It is not an act of universalism but an affirmation of the group.[10] This kind of hospitality reinforces Jewish community bonds and hierarchies and is designed to perpetuate Jewish togetherness.

Because the rabbis insisted upon Jews maintaining social distance from others, they interpreted Abraham's nondiscriminatory hospitality as an aspect of his effort to dissuade polytheists—that is, nearly the entire population—from their false beliefs. Abraham, who had several conversations and a personal covenant with God, could dine with such people. The rabbis read the textual references to Abraham and Sarah's growing band of accompanying servants as referring to new proselytes, for "Abraham would convert men and Sarah would convert women."[11] While Jewish proselytizing appears to have been common in the first centuries of the Common Era when these rabbinic traditions appeared, it was never made into a communal agenda.[12] Perhaps as a way to show the futility or undesirability of proselytism or to show the singularity of Abraham and Sarah's family line, rabbinic commentaries note that the descendants of these proselytes reverted back to idolatry.

Orthodox Jews today do not proselytize or encourage conversion to Judaism. There is a tradition that a non-Jew should be dissuaded and turned away three times before being permitted to convert. The dissuasion is not law, and practices vary. Orthodox rabbis across the spectrum frown upon interfaith theological dialogue as impermissible sharing, and they know that the erosion of Jewish religious observance is most likely during the times of positive interaction and friendship between Jews and Gentiles. Proselytes, too, can be a force for internal division and erosion of faith.[13]

Late antique and medieval literature, consequently, associated hospitality with love of Israel, *ahavat yisra'el*, rather than love of humanity. The medieval philosopher and legal scholar Maimonides regards hospitality as an expression of the Torah law "love your neighbor as yourself," where "neighbor" means "another Jew."[14] Hospitality retained its link to proselytism but in a reversed way: contrary to Abraham employing it as a tool to convert others, Jewish hospitality functioned in Christian lands as a defense against Christian proselytism. By the ninth century CE Jewish men nearly everywhere worked in trade, and many journeyed away from their homes for their livelihoods. When they arrived at inns owned by Jews or in towns inhabited by Jews, they could count on lodging with people who would protect them and not try to convert them. Their hosts would supply them with kosher food and, if their stay coincided with the Sabbath, would help them enjoy and observe the day's rituals and keep its rules. In sum, the commandment was understood as providing Jewish travelers who arrive in one's town with lodging and meals.[15] Jews' hospitality toward other Jews was a means of group survival, and only in the late twentieth century did it again become a tool for Jews to promote Judaism, albeit to non-religious Jews.

The commandment to provide hospitality did not specify the kind of Jewish guests to host and precisely how to serve them. Unlike other expressions of lovingkindness for which Talmudic rabbis provided specific directives, such as visiting the sick or comforting mourners, medieval codes praise *hakhnasat orḥim* but provide details mostly about what other obligations may be deferred in the performance of this commandment. The Ashkenazic commentator on the *Shulḥan arukh*, the sixteenth-century Sephardic law code considered authoritative by all Orthodox Jews, states that *hakhnasat orḥim* is distinct from feeding one's friends and family members, that is, from regular socializing. While some authorities disagreed with this narrow definition, the consensus is that the mitzvah implies that the recipient must face some real need so that the host is conferring out-of-the-ordinary generosity.[16] The assumption is that were the person situated within a normal context, he or she would be supplied food and lodging by kin. The vagueness in this commandment helps account for and permits the variation in approaches today.

In contrast to home hospitality, helping the poor is far more defined. The English word *charity* implies a voluntary act, but the Hebrew *tzedakah*, literally, "justice," indicates that giving is not optional. Biblical texts teach that God expects people to provide for the needy, an ever-present group within society. The rabbis teach that God is partly (or fully) responsible for financial success and that a portion of a person's earnings must be given as *tzedakah* or else God will not permit success to continue. A Jew owes a minimum of 10 percent, equivalent to the biblical agricultural tithe. This may take the form of funds for the purchase of food and other basic needs, actual food, or service to others. The rabbis discuss how to calculate the percentage, when the percentage varies, how to prioritize recipients, when and how to give, and so on. They teach that love for God's creatures should play a role in the giving. Emotion is not relevant to the fulfillment of the duty, but it is crucial to give in a manner that preserves the dignity of the poor.[17]

The breadth of the biblical exhortation to help the poor, like that of home hospitality, was narrowed in rabbinic law. The postbiblical rabbis designed the laws of *tzedakah* so that Jews would take responsibility for other Jews as opposed to society at large. The ideal stated in the Mishnah, cited above, "Let your house be wide open to strangers, and treat the poor as members of your own family," was limited to Jews not only for hospitality but also for the poor. At face value it could be read as an ideal to feed the poor at one's family table, but it is also interpreted as an admonition to hire the Jewish poor, not the non-Jewish poor, as household servants.[18] Jews had no government of their own at this time, and the states in which they lived generally did not aid any of society's poor. Concerned for Jewish well-being and the preservation of the group as a distinct entity, the rabbis insisted that Jewish individuals were obligated to help support needy Jews outside their own family and establish a community organization on behalf of their own poor. In the words of scholar Meir Tamari, rabbinic charity laws were designed to create a separate "religio-national group."[19]

The rabbis envisioned the individual adult Jew and his financial obligations at the center of concentric circles. He (the laws assume male authority) must support his immediate and perhaps also extended family, but this is not considered *tzedakah*. *Tzedakah* is the duty to help needy Jews who are not kin. The first concentric circle, where *tzedakah* obligations begin, is inhabited by the poor Jews in his locale. They have a claim on his earning by way of his direct donation or his contribution to a community fund. According to some authorities, at a further distance are the local Torah scholars, who require assistance so they can devote their time to study. Others disagree with this placement of Torah scholars. The outermost circle is occupied by the Jews of the Land of Israel; although they are not local, they are considered part of the Jew's social group and so are entitled to his *tzedakah* obligation. Within these separate circles there are priorities about who receives first (or instead of, if there is a shortage of funds): the neediest more so than the less needy, women prior to men, Torah scholars before the less learned, and the poor Jews of one's own region before those living in the Land of Israel. Poor non-Jews living in one's locale are considered outsiders. Nevertheless, their requests for assistance should not be entirely ignored.[20]

According to Jewish law, when a non-Jew is in danger and asks for immediate assistance from a Jew, the Jew must ignore his other Jewish claimants and respond positively. Some authorities argue that any direct request, from any beggar, non-Jewish or Jewish, should not be entirely refused. That is, giving charity to non-Jews fulfills the mitzvah of *tzedakah*. However, while giving to a non-Jew is considered *tzedakah*, it is understood as emanating from a different principle than that of giving to a Jew. Whereas the Jewish poor have the right to be supported "in accordance with the Torah," the non-Jewish poor have the right to be supported "for the sake of peace" (*mipnei darkhei shalom*). This distinction can be confusing since both forms of giving are regarded as fulfillment of a mitzvah, and it leads to the belief among some Orthodox Jews that *tzedakah* for non-Jews can be avoided or "does not count."[21] Even Jews who understand that such charity "counts" may understand that it is less of a priority than giving to other Jews.

In short, the laws of giving charity, like the commandment to provide home hospitality, have a social function outside of providing aid: the rules define and create the community in which the individual Jew lives. The donor is a member of a community that includes the recipients of its largesse. The laws show who matters most, whose economic distress deserves the most amelioration, who is more entitled to receive the individual's and the collective's finite resources, and who is peripheral. Whomever an Orthodox community or Orthodox individuals exclude from receiving *tzedakah* is outside communal bounds. It is not considered necessary or wise to verbalize these boundaries, for doing so might be rude or in violation of the principle to give "for the sake of peace."

Today, the most widely recognized rules for how to give charity are those of Maimonides. These are not original to him; rather, he consolidated certain Talmudic statements about disbursing *tzedakah* into a list of eight ranked ways of giving.[22] The lowest level is giving grudgingly when asked, and a higher step is giving directly to the poor without being asked. The value of the giving ascends when the giver honors moral principles such as preserving the dignity of the poor and when the giver avoids being honored or identified as a giver. Yet the highest level of *tzedakah* is helping a needy person learn a trade or start a business, and this can hardly be anonymous. The second highest is the anonymous donation to a community charity fund. Such a fund should be in the hands of an appointed steward who carefully and respectfully determines who is truly needy. The steward must guard the identities of both the recipients and the givers. In such a case, the giver foregoes acknowledgment for his or her gift and the recipient is not embarrassed. There is no intimacy in this transaction. The rabbinic maxim that a Jew should "treat the poor as members of your own family" means, then, that one's obligation toward them is of highest importance, not that one has a familial relationship with them.

A contrasting approach is to insist that genuine piety requires welcoming the poor to join a meal at one's home. One medieval source illustrates this by describing a burial custom for generous benefactors: their coffin is built from the wood of their tables, as though the tables upon which they hosted the poor testify to their worthiness before God. Kabbalistic and Hasidic writings insist that spiritually elevated men will invite the poor to eat of the finest delicacies they have prepared for themselves.[23] These practices, like those of the woman described at the start of this chapter who regularly invites the poor Jewish man to join her Shabbat meal, simultaneously fulfill the two commandments, *hakhnasat orḥim* and *tzedakah*. Perhaps she would not consider her invitation *tzedakah*, and perhaps he does not consider his inclusion an expression of charity. What is occurring, rather, is an expression of community that puts the poor on the same level as those with more resources.

PICO-ROBERTSON NEIGHBORHOOD PRACTICES

In the following pages I illustrate the variations in how Pico-Robertson Orthodox communities perform home hospitality and food charity, starting with the most broadly inclusive home hospitality and food charity and moving toward the less inclusive expressions of them. Congregations differ in how their rabbis exercise leadership (some small congregations have no appointed rabbi for the group) and how members shape each other's practices. I do not mean to suggest that all members of a specific congregation behave uniformly. In fact, I show that some members dissent from their congregation's stated mission or policies. Nevertheless, there is a correlation between a congregation's stance on cultural insularity or its religious ideology and the way it approaches the practices of feeding others. The group's way of performing hospitality and food charity preserves the kind of community to which its members want to belong as well as whom they wish to include and whom they wish to exclude from their social circle.

Whereas hospitality in the past was defined as providing food and lodging to Jewish people passing through one's vicinity, more recently the interpretation of *hakhnasat orḥim* has been stretched to include Jewish guests who live in the vicinity but who would not otherwise have access to a traditional Jewish Sabbath experience. In this new form, the imagined proselytism in Abraham and Sarah's hospitality reappears as *kiruv* (literally, "bringing near" or "outreach"), that is, bringing non-Orthodox Jews closer to religious practice. Alarmed by the drift of the younger generation of Jews away from Torah observance and the move toward other religions or secularism, outreach specialists consider a Friday night family meal, or a communal meal, to be a "selling point" for bringing Torah observance to nonreligious Jews.

This expanded definition is oddly consistent with the tradition that *hakhnasat orḥim* requires a recipient who lacks a local home or family. In contemporary Orthodox *halakhah*, the term for an adult Jew raised in a nonreligious family who does not fulfill the commandments is *tinok shenishbah bein haʾakum*, a Talmudic term literally meaning "a captive infant raised by idol worshipers." In other words, in matters of obser-vance, a Jew raised in a nonobservant family is comparable to a Jew-ish child who has been kidnapped by idolaters and thus never had the opportunity to learn the practices of Judaism. Such a person is not held liable for transgressions of *halakhah*.[24] For Jews involved in *kiruv*, hosting such Jews is truly an emulation of Abraham and Sarah, who served their guests with food and taught them to believe in one God.

The familial character of Orthodox Shabbat meals is so strong that it is easy to understand why a person lacking a family who eats with an Orthodox family on Shabbat is like an orphan. Jewish tradition regards a household as one headed by a married couple, and Sabbath practices today are shaped around a nuclear family embedded within a commu-nity. On Friday shortly before sundown the presiding woman of the household lights the Sabbath candles alone or with her female family members and guests, while the males of the family are at the synagogue for the communal prayers that usher in the day. When everyone arrives home, they gather around a table set with nice dishes and two covered Sabbath bread loaves. Parents bless their children, everyone sings intro-ductory Sabbath hymns, and the husband recites chapter 31 of Proverbs in praise of his wife, followed by the *kiddush* (sanctification blessing) over wine. Diners ritually wash their hands, the husband or wife recites the blessing over bread, and everyone begins the meal. A proper Sabbath meal includes the singing of Sabbath songs and the presentation of Torah lessons by knowledgeable adults and by children demonstrating their learning. Upon the meal's completion, everyone recites a long post-meal prayer that varies according to one's familial or guest status. In one's own home, the person recites the version that blesses family members, and if one is a guest, she or he recites the version that blesses the host.

The second Sabbath meal takes place on Saturday around noontime after the morning prayer service. A congregation may offer a full com-munal meal for attendees or a more limited fare to be enjoyed before departing for one's real second meal elsewhere. Typically, a family eats this second meal together at their own home or at the home of another family. The third Sabbath meal is less family focused. It may take place at the synagogue between the afternoon and concluding Sabbath prayers, or it may be served at home prior to the prayers concluding the Sabbath. Every Jew is obligated to eat three Sabbath meals even if no family or guests are present. In the Orthodox community, dining alone would be considered a pale version of the real thing. The fact that traditional Jewish prayers are written in first-person plural form, so any individual uttering the prayer positions himself or herself within a community, reflects this commensal ideal of dining. The familial nature of the Sabbath is so strong that some people consider it an act of *hesed*, lovingkindness, to invite unattached single people or Jews who have no observant family of their own, even if they live locally, to the first or second Sabbath meal.

Although there are few generalizations about each other that Orthodox groups agree upon, they acknowledge that the Chabad community is the most committed to both outreach and hospitality.[25] The movement's teachers insist that the obligation to host other Jews is not a rabbinic law but a law of the Torah itself, a fulfillment of the commandment to love one's neighbor (that is, other Jews) and an act more important than showing love for God.[26] From the time he was inaugurated in 1951 as the seventh Lubavitcher rebbe, Menachem Mendel Schneerson, the leader of the Chabad-Lubavitch movement, made the social dimension of Chabad central by repeatedly insisting that love of God is entirely dependent on the love of Torah and love of other Jews. He taught that the substance of the love of God "can only be constructed in the realm of living social reality, via love of Torah and love of the Jewish people."[27] He initiated programs and campaigns inspiring Chabad members to revitalize their performance of ten specific *mitzvot*, including the commandments to love one's fellow Jew and perform *tzedakah*.[28] The *mitzvot* in general and these in particular are to be carried out with joy and should increase the joy of others, for Chabad teaches that "genuine joy comes from profound spiritual awareness of life and an absolute clarity of direction, living for a purpose."[29]

Chabad Jews have regarded secular American culture and higher education with disdain, and yet the Rebbe instructed them to act lovingly toward even those Jews immersed in secular culture. When Chabad Jews show hospitality toward nonreligious Jews, they are hosting in intimate settings Jews who are very different from themselves and from whom they would normally keep socially distant. Suppressing one's aversion to such potentially risky contacts or simply unfamiliar people is made into a great virtue: it is *mesirat nefesh*, literally, "self-sacrifice," understood as denying one's own wishes and inclinations to do what God asks. Chabad Jews are taught that what at first may appear a burden will be the source of great joy for giver and receiver alike.

In Pico-Robertson and all over the world, Chabad rabbis and synagogues can be relied upon to help Jewish visitors and travelers with lodging and meals. It is common for Jewish parents to tell their college-age children before they travel abroad or go to college away from home to contact a Chabad rabbi if they are in an unexpected or urgent situation requiring food and temporary housing. Yet, for Chabad, the mitzvah is not understood as *tzedakah* or as a response to poverty or material deprivation. The ideal hospitality means supplying guests *beyond* their basic physical needs to include what the host discerns they require emotionally.[30] This helps explain why, in practice, Chabad applies the mitzvah to hosting visitors and to feeding local Jews who lack a supportive family with whom they can eat—for example, if the person lives alone, is part of a troubled family unit, or lacks the religious environment a Chabad family meal provides.

A phone call to a local Chabad center or synagogue will elicit a quick, positive response to a request for a Shabbat meal. One does not need to be an out-of-town visitor. The largest Pico-Robertson Chabad synagogue employs a phone receptionist, and she was puzzled by my question about whether she attempted to discern a requester's character or religious observance. "No—just Jewish. We offer hospitality to people who call." In fact, when pressed, she admitted that she does not interrogate callers about their Jewish status because she would not want to embarrass them, and she assumes only Jews would make such a request. After she learns the caller's needs (e.g., the number of people and food allergies to avoid), she sends the request to a "mitzvah group" that communicates by means of the digital WhatsApp social media platform.

Someone accepts the request, or they may alert others not on the platform to do so. The receptionist attested to her community's commitment:
"We have a lot of inquiries, and there are many who feed the people who
ask. Many, many people make these requests. We are very earnest about
this mitzvah. We take it very seriously." She told me that visitors who
attend the Friday evening service without having arranged a Friday night
dinner day in advance will likely be offered to join a family for the meal.[31]

Stories about Chabad hospitality are plentiful. The Chabad.org website has four dozen separate articles and audio lectures about *hakhnasat
orhim* showing that it is deeply rooted in biblical, rabbinic, and Chasidic
sources. One article teaches that hospitality is such an important mitzvah
that a Jew should not simply wait for someone to call and ask for hospitality. Instead, a person should initiate an invitation to a stranger or volunteer one's home to a local organization that places visitors.[32] Some of
the articles append readers' comments that advise how to be prepared for
guests at a moment's notice and how to make guests feel more welcome.

I have seen these recommendations in action. Once, while walking alone through the residential streets of Pico-Robertson one Friday
evening at dusk, I was approached by a group of Chabad teenage girls
who invited me to join their Shabbat meal. I was a stranger to them, yet
my dress indicated I was Jewish and somewhat religious and could adequately fit in at their table. My friendly engagement with Chabad rabbis
and *rebbetzins* is likely to be followed by a Shabbat meal invitation, and if
I accept, I am treated warmly. Non-Chabad Jews who admire this generosity find ways to support it by monetary donations. One woman I know
supports Chabad hospitality by purchasing food. At the local supermarket she showed me the section of her shopping cart filled with meat,
fruit, vegetables, and desserts that will be bagged separately and delivered to a Chabad rabbi for his upcoming Shabbat meals. She provides
Shabbat meals for him this way each week.

Every Chabad congregation in the neighborhood offers a free sit-
down Shabbat lunch to all attendees. Needy attendees are not differentiated from the rest. Long tables are set out, and congregational volunteers
pass around wine for the *kiddush* prayer and other liquor and beverages,

bread, and serving platters loaded with food. The food includes a hot meat stew called cholent, consisting of beef, beans, and potatoes; cold dishes such as salads; casseroles; fruit; and simple desserts. By contributing funds for such meals, congregants fulfill the *hakhnasat orḥim* obligation.

People outside of Chabad are likely to explain or disparage such hospitality as an expression of *kiruv*. These critics regard it as a means of enlarging the Chabad community as if this were a mere game of numbers, prompted by ulterior motives rather than simple love for other Jews. A local Chabad teacher lamented the criticism and explained, "According to *Tanya* [the major work of Chabad *Hasidus*], you should invite a Jew to your Shabbos table because you love him, not because you want him to keep Shabbos. You are obligated to love him, and you have to invite him out of pure *ahavas yisraʾel* [love of Israel]." He sent me a video of the Rebbe criticizing the use of the term *kiruv*, which is part of a longer phrase, *kiruv reḥokim*, literally, "bringing near those who are far." The Rebbe says that it is an error to characterize nonreligious Jews as far from God and religious Jews as near to God or to think that acts of love should be directed to some Jews and not others. The caption on the video quoted the Rebbe's Yiddish words in translation: "There is no such thing as a Jew who is far from G-d. Reaching out to other Jews simply means bringing even closer, those who are already close to G-d."[33] A local Chabad teacher introduced me online to colleagues who pointed out that facilitating other Jews' performance of the commandments is not an attempt to "convert" them to Chabad Hasidism or Orthodox Judaism or to create a Torah-observant Jew or a Torah scholar. They wrote, "Today we have outreach groups that take an 'all or nothing' approach—they're out to make a 'black hatter' sitting in kollel all day or it is worthless. We take the 'every mitzvah is valuable in its own right' attitude."[34] They attribute this approach to Rabbi Schneerson.

The doctrine that "every mitzvah is valuable in its own right" leads to Chabad rabbis' warm relations with nonreligious or non-Orthodox Jews. They believe that when a Jew performs a mitzvah it is valuable and precious to God. Even if he or she is not performing the other *mitzvot*, the performance of this mitzvah is not illegitimate or hypocritical. This view is not widely shared among other Orthodox Jews. A non-Chabad woman explained it as a halakhic conundrum:

> When a Jew invites people to their home for a Shabbat meal, and these people will likely drive, should you do it? Some people—like Chabad—say, "Yes! It is a mitzvah: you are giving them a Shabbat meal." Others say, "Shabbat is Shabbat and cannot be separated into separate *mitzvot*, so it is prohibited to have them over if it involves violating Shabbat."[35]

Others would not invite such a guest based on a rabbinic interpretation of Leviticus 19:14, "Do not put a stumbling block before the blind," meaning that one should not help or tempt another Jew to sin.[36] "The way around this, though it's not really right," I was told by a man with this concern, "is to invite but not ask how your guest is getting to you or ask where he lives."[37] This approach of "don't ask, don't tell" requires both parties to cooperate in hiding personal details. Both these responses highlight Chabad's distinctive religious ideology.

A local Chabad teacher delivered a homily about *mitzvot* to me and a dozen other people at his Shabbat table:

> God loves *mitzvos* [divine laws]. God loves them! We don't know why, but God loves *mitzvos*! This is why the world looks the way it does. He created Jews so people would perform the *mitzvos*. He created fruit trees so that Jews could utter *berakhos* [prescribed blessings] over the fruit. He created palm trees, myrtle, and *etrog* [citron] so Jews could make the *berakhos* on Sukkot.[38]

In this succinct lesson on Chabad theology, the rabbi places Jews and the *mitzvot* at the center of the universe. Jews' fulfillment of the commandments is the purpose for the existence of the world. It is a message of great empowerment to the already Torah-observant Jew and a response to Jews who are asking whether they should take on ritual practice. According to this message, even if Jews are not aware of the *mitzvot*, their souls long for them. Helping Jews fulfill a mitzvah is, by definition, an act of giving love. When Jews perform a mitzvah, their soul is gladdened, they earn more of God's love, and they become more of who they are meant to be. According to Chabad ideas, the guests, along with the family who hosted them and gave them a Sabbath meal, were giving pleasure to God and would be rewarded by Him.[39]

Inviting nonreligious Jews to one's Shabbat family meal involves the whole family in this kind of gift giving. The hosts may coach the guests in the blessings before and after eating, assist them in the mealtime singing, and talk about the Torah at a level that they can understand, but the crucial element is friendly conversation and a joyous atmosphere. When the parents and children regard the event as an opportunity for promoting the guests' performance of this and other *mitzvot*, the relations between the parties change. The host family's children, who have been taught to be "foot soldiers in the Rebbe's army," do their part by befriending the invited children and showing them how to have fun within the parameters of Shabbat rules. A ten-year-old winner of a Pico-Robertson Chabad congregation's essay contest on the theme "What My Rebbe Taught Me" wrote about his role in such a meal:

> The Rebbe has taught me many things. One of the most important things I have learned as a Chassid and a Shliach [emissary] of the Rebbe, is that every Yid [Jew] matters, and is important to Hashem. Each person, no matter how simple, has a special mission to do in his lifetime. You might think "What difference does it make if I act a certain way in front of this person? He is only one person!" In truth how you behave towards that one person, and the *Ahavas Yisroel* [love of Israel] you show him can change the world in a big way!
>
> One Friday night we invited a family for Shabbos dinner. They have a son who is a few years older than me. My brother and I played with him and we spoke for a very long time about many things. After Shabbos, the boy's mother texted my mother to say how much William loved Shabbos and how much he enjoyed the time he spent with

us at our home. Now William loves to come to Shul and participate in Chabad events. The whole family is more involved in Yiddishkeit. But best of all, William decided to put on Tefillin for the first time in his life, and he had a mini *Bar Mitzvah*! One family, one Shabbos, and one boy whose life was changed all because I cared enough to show love towards my fellow Yid.[40]

From this perspective, home hospitality shows loving concern, but it is explicitly instrumental. Meeting others in the context of *kiruv* is not an expression of mutual respect with the possibility of reciprocal religious influence or even about making friends—that kind of intimacy would imperil the Chabad community. The Chabad boy has been taught that although he and the visiting family share the identity of the "Yid," the nonobservant Jews are in a separate class, the object of a specific kind of nurturing care. This kind of home hospitality is designed to increase the number of mitzvah-observant Jews, that is, devotees of *Hashem*. It also reinforces the Chabad sense of itself as a loving and welcoming community that exemplifies the ideals of the Torah.

Other Pico-Robertson organizations and synagogues also promote and support outreach. Among the thirty or so Pico-Robertson synagogues, some are obvious extensions of a larger outreach organization like Aish HaTorah. At least three, the Persian Chabad centers and the Young Sephardic Community Center, are specifically geared toward Persian or Sephardic Jews. Several are independent Ashkenazi congregations known to be especially welcoming to newly religious Jews or to Jews exploring their options. In such places, congregants include former *ba'alei teshuvah* who are involved in or sympathetic to outreach, or they simply enjoy the convivial style of the worship and teaching characteristic of such places. These synagogues are distinctive because attendees are especially warm to strangers, even ones who look different from the norm. Prayer leaders announce pages and offer the type of explanations not necessary in other congregations. Those with websites have mission statements mentioning that the community welcomes Jews of all backgrounds and religious levels. Food is often plentiful after their prayers, and it is not unusual for older members to extend Sabbath meal invitations to strangers in attendance.

Outreach seminaries use home hospitality as a tool for education and socialization. They do not explicitly state that they are promoting Orthodox Judaism; their goals are more vaguely stated as showing people how to "connect to Judaism" or "access the depths of the Torah." Their focus is potential or actual Orthodox *ba'alei teshuvah* among singles and young married couples, and their aim is to foster new family units living in accordance with Orthodox Judaism. Generally, the seminaries offer courses that are gender segregated and taught by practicing Orthodox Jews. Students are invited to Shabbat meals of families established securely within the Orthodox community. In one such Ashkenazi seminary, a staff person finds hosts through her list of contacts who are members of local synagogues, alumni, or the seminary teachers and their acquaintances. Students are asked to find, or are helped to find, local lodging for Shabbat. "It is not difficult to find dinner hosts," the rabbinic director of the seminary told me. Sometimes the regular volunteers decline because they need to give their own children more attention or do not have the time to do the extra cooking, he said, but not because they regard such requests as inappropriate. To the contrary, they regard their hospitality as the fulfillment of a mitzvah.[41]

My interview with one of the students reveals how Shabbat home hospitality facilitates her socialization. The young woman, whose family lives in another state, resides a few miles outside of Pico-Robertson and must stay with her female friends in the neighborhood if she wants to spend Shabbat there. "For meals, the girls are always sent to a different home than the guys," she told me. She appreciates when hosts seat single males and females on different sides of the table or apart from each other so as to avoid awkwardness or inadvertent physical contact. She has been taught that being a female guest requires volunteering to set the table before the meal and helping serve dishes and clear the table. One hostess told her, "I haven't had girls before as guests, and now I see how great it is—all the help!" The young woman enjoys watching how the couples relate to each other and their offspring.[42]

One older couple regularly invites the young woman when they are not spending the meal with their grown children and grandchildren and there are no other men present. On these occasions, the couple speaks to her about marriage, about what they believe makes some marriages successful and others not, and how they have met the challenges of parenthood. She appreciates their role as mentors. Also very special, she told me, are the invitations to a rabbi's home. To her this means she will have a greater connection to Torah just by virtue of the rabbi's presence, plus there will always be words of Torah at the meal and Shabbat singing. She told me, "At one rabbi's home, he actually helped out in the kitchen!" She knows that the married couples and her teachers are crucial for finding her a husband. Although she is completing professional training that could make her financially self-sufficient, she needs to marry and raise children to be a full member of an Orthodox community. She admitted that if she does not find a husband in Los Angeles soon, she would need to leave and find one elsewhere.

The rabbinic leader of her seminary sees Shabbat hospitality in broader terms. He explained that God gave Jews *mitzvot* to make Jews into people who are truly giving. The commandments "develop a person's character" and make them into "givers," he said. Sometimes it is not clear just how mysterious rules such as *kashrut* do this, he said, but one simply has to have faith that they do.[43] In the case of *hakhnasat orhim*, the connection is obvious. By being welcomed at others' tables, the young guests themselves learn to give to others. They will want to marry and raise children—certainly these are acts of giving—and be members of a religious community who love and support each other. The rabbi is delighted when alumni of the program host the students, for it shows that they are living the values they were taught. For him and for those who assist him, home hospitality creates an ever-expanding community populated not only with members of the next generation but also with the fresh faces and energy of Jews newly determined to carry on Jewish traditions.

The Modern Orthodox synagogue down the street also promotes hospitality quite freely but from a different set of principles. Its mission statement declares itself a community "defined and driven by our adherence to *halakhah*, our love of God and *mitzvot*, compassion and justice." It welcomes people "Jewish by birth or by choice, new to halakhic observance or born into it, married, single, divorced or widowed, gay or straight, old or young, whatever . . . level of ability or whatever challenges you face—all are invited to join with us in prayer, Torah study, *tikkun olam* [working for social justice], support for Israel and the sacred work of being a Jew."[44] While it defines Jews as inextricably bound up with obedience to *halakhah*, its mission statement signals that the *halakhah* it follows is more liberal than that of all other Orthodox congregations by virtue of its explicit acceptance of homosexuality. Unstated in its mission statement but known to all is the fact that one of its congregational rabbis is a woman. Some of its programs are obviously liberal in a political sense. For example, on the weekend in 2020 commemorating Martin Luther King Jr., the synagogue offered a guest lecture after the Shabbat morning service by the Catholic priest who directs Homeboy Industries, a nonprofit organization teaching occupational skills to former gang members. Through this type of program, the congregation declares itself as firmly entrenched within the larger and not necessarily Jewish Los Angeles community. No other Orthodox congregation in the neighborhood paid such attention to the commemoration.

Like Chabad, this Modern Orthodox community regards home hospitality as a crucial expression of love for other Jews. The synagogue's senior rabbi pointed out that *hakhnasat orḥim* is a way of acting upon the principle "All Israel is responsible for one another."[45] Unlike Chabad, this congregation does not believe that love for other Jews consists of enabling them to perform *mitzvot*, nor does it have an agenda to turn non-Orthodox Jews into Orthodox ones. The community values Jewish ethnic unity despite religious differences. The congregation, whose link to Israel is strongly Zionist, supports Jewish political nationalism and statehood as important causes in and of themselves. Its relationship to Israel goes beyond the concern for the Jews of Israel and the land's holiness that characterizes Centrist, Hasidic, and other Orthodox Jews. Congregants and rabbis alike admire and possess degrees from secular American universities, and many of the congregation's parents send their children to the coed Orthodox high school. Most striking, the congregation occasionally shares programming with nearby Conservative and Reform synagogues. These alliances and its liberal interpretations of Jewish law are frowned upon by the other Orthodox congregations. The rabbi sadly acknowledges that his goal of building bridges to other Jews is not successful with those to the right of him.

A member of a Centrist Orthodox congregation explained how the scandalous practices of this Modern Orthodox congregation isolate its members from the other Orthodox Jews, "even more than Chabad." The distinct Chabad practices can be overlooked, apparently, because "Chabad people take jobs in non-Chabad schools and take non-Chabad children into their own schools, and they so love Judaism that they do not stay isolated." The Modern Orthodox synagogue has crossed the line, she said, and she's heard the men there do not recite the prescribed blessing praising God "for not making me a woman." Her husband, who prays in different Orthodox congregations and *minyanim* (daily prayer groups of at least ten adult males), refuses to pray there.[46]

The leadership and the congregants of the Centrist Congregation to which this woman belongs embrace the goal of connecting Jews to each other and promote *hakhnasat orḥim* in multiple ways. Individual worshipers are encouraged to invite visitors attending the Sabbath services to the meal following the service. The visitors are easily recognized as "strangers" in Orthodox congregations when members regularly attend the service. At this congregation it is customary at the end of the service for a designated member to make a public announcement inviting congregants with room at their tables and strangers lacking meal invitations to come forward, and the two parties are matched.[47] A former member of the congregation, a man who regularly brings out-of-town visitors to his family's Shabbat lunch meal, recalls that the congregation's requests "got out of hand" in the early years when the emphasis on *hakhnasat orḥim* began:

Synagogue members were coming forward asking for meals because they did not want to prepare for Shabbat, or they felt they were entitled. I remember people saying, "I'm single and I need to have a real Shabbat with others." That's just lazy. I was single but I prepared a Shabbat meal for myself. I invited others to join me if I didn't want to be alone. Every person is obligated to make Shabbat![48]

Current members I interviewed differentiate between *hakhnasat orḥim* and regular socializing. They insisted that simply inviting the same friends time and again is mere socializing and that, in fact, it may damage the congregation's well-being. In this congregation, as in all the other big congregations, "some people can be quite cliquey." Yet the synagogue maintains its reputation for friendliness. "When we relocated to Los Angeles, my husband and I attended a different Orthodox synagogue in Pico-Robertson every Shabbat morning for months without ever being invited to a meal," a woman told me. The first time they visited this congregation, they were promptly invited to Shabbat lunch. After weeks of being hosted, they joined the synagogue and began returning the favor to other visitors.[49] Another couple, who tries to host outside of their regular friendship circle, explained their rationale:

Inviting someone over for a Shabbat meal is about building a community. There are always new people coming in as members, so having a community requires an ongoing effort. If you want the shul to be a good place, then you want to do what you can to make these new people a genuine part of the community. That's true also about the people who have not been that successful at making connections. It is an investment in friendship and an investment in community.[50]

For situations when out-of-town visitors request Shabbat hospitality in the form of lodging, the synagogue made a rule that host families should have guests sleep on mattresses rather than on sofas or in sleeping bags. This rule means that members of the host family may be displaced from their usual sleeping quarters if there are no spare guest rooms. The rabbis and other congregation leaders privately and publicly praise hosts and hosting. At a recent annual gala dinner, a fundraising event designed to attract many attendees, the synagogue honored a couple who was exemplary, like the paragons Abraham and Sarah, for their service as hosts. Finally, two or three times a year, the membership committee reviews the membership list to match those who are new or not well integrated into the congregation with socially better-situated members, who then host them.[51]

Even at this Centrist Orthodox congregation, the leadership cannot count on everyone to step forward to offer hospitality to outsiders. Sometimes, one of the rabbis wryly admitted, it is just "the usual suspects" who host. Despite the rabbis' and lay leadership's advocacy, their religious ideology cannot fuel the type of enthusiasm found in Chabad and the outreach seminaries.[52] Interviewing the wife of the couple honored for their home hospitality, I learned that most of her synagogue friends do not invite strangers to their table, are bewildered by her desire to do so, and think it is bad form to request free meals and lodging if it is not a matter of serious need—which, typically for the requesters, it is not.

The hostess did not think requesters were taking advantage of the synagogue, and she also felt that the difference between herself and her friends was not rooted in ideology: "I think it is a matter of personality and not religious belief." Yet, she and her husband are certainly conveying the importance of the mitzvah to their children and affirming the ideal of Jewish religious pluralism. The hostess admitted that she is not bothered if the guests are not Orthodox, although she knows that such guests often feel they must pretend that they are. She was amused rather than upset about a large family from Australia who was "all over the place." The father seemed to be Orthodox, but his wife was not, and at dessert time one of their sons arrived in an Uber. She does not think it is her role to promote mitzvah performance; rather, her hope is that her hospitality "makes the guests feel good, as a part of the community."[53]

She thinks this is how she conveyed the family practice to their children. "The kids were reluctant at first," she admitted, "saying, 'What if these people are weird?'" But it adds an interesting element to the family's meals. They can hear about the guests' lives, and afterward her family can discuss what they learned. She said, "It can relieve the boredom we would have with the same old conversations about school, shul, parking and traffic, and so on. Instead, it is about someone else and their experiences." This kind of hospitality expands the borders of the local community, but not indiscriminately. "We raised our kids in a bubble," the hostess told me, not unhappily, referring to the family's Orthodox social and educational environment. Their guests, even though they were strangers from other cities and foreign lands, expanded the size of the children's sequestered world. Through this form of hospitality, they met Jews from distant US cities and from Europe and Israel who share their ideal of broad Jewish unity and are comfortable with the Modern Orthodoxy in which her family were raised.[54]

This congregation's focus on Jewish peoplehood, however, does not lead to the denial of giving *tzedakah* to non-Jews; in fact, among the non-Jewish population, it is the most generous of all Pico-Robertson congregations toward the needy. Like many of the others, it supports the local food charity organization, Tomchei Shabbos, and congregants in need may ask for funds from the rabbis' discretionary accounts. In virtually every neighborhood synagogue, the morning prayers are a time when local poor people appear and beseech the worshipers for charity. Many of these mendicants are not Jews, and some are known to be homeless or living in their cars. It is not proper to outright refuse these mendicants, but the local rabbis have made rules about the timing of the requests so that the prayers are not interrupted.[55]

At the Modern Orthodox synagogue, the senior rabbi has done this as well, but unlike the others, he systematically and generously handles the distribution. He explained, "These are the needy in our neighborhood. It's a form of outreach. It's a way of expressing warmth and caring." Supplicants are directed to him, and signs are posted next to the daily prayer room announcing that funds will be disbursed on four days every week after the morning prayers. People who come to the morning prayers to receive funds are shown where to line up in the hall outside the prayer room. If they are Jewish and wish to pray, they may enter and pray first. After the prayers, the rabbi comes out and speaks to them one by one. He greets each by name or asks their name, and he learns what their particular challenges are (e.g., unemployment, homelessness, medical issues) and which men are Jewish so they could be asked to make up the *minyan* for prayers. Depending on the need, he writes a check or hands out twenty-dollar gift cards to the local supermarket. He also may find other help as needed. For example, a synagogue member recounted what the rabbi did when he noticed a festering sore on the arm of one of the "regulars." The rabbi returned to the prayer room, fetched a doctor who examined the man, and arranged for him to be taken to a local hospital emergency room for treatment. Congregants who wish to support this form of food charity are told to donate to the rabbi's discretionary fund. When the rabbi is nearby and congregants are asked for charity, they bring the supplicant over to him personally.[56]

Jewish law requires that Jews are obligated to give if a poor non-Jewish person requests help, but this Modern Orthodox congregation does not wait for non-Jews to take the initiative. Beginning around 2006, a few members joined the work of The Giving Spirit, a nonprofit organization that aids the overwhelmingly non-Jewish population who are homeless in Los Angeles. Started in 1999 by a member of a large Presbyterian church in western Los Angeles that serves as its headquarters, The Giving Spirit raises funds to buy items needed by those who are homeless, organizes volunteers to pack them into large duffle bags, and brings the bags directly to them on the street. There are two giving events per year: one before Christmas with items that will help people endure the winter months and one at the start of June for summer needs. The bags also contain information about organizations that assist the poor. The Modern Orthodox congregation, a cosponsor of The Giving Spirit, takes a special role in the assemblage of the care packages.[57]

I attended a December synagogue event where several dozen members—singles and parents and children—packed twenty or so small items (such as a manicure set, comb, lip balm, soap) into a plastic case to be included in the duffle bags that would be packed the next week at the church. The night before the big packing and delivery day, I joined synagogue members and others at the church to break down a truckload of wool blankets into manageable piles, set up an assembly line of portable tables, and load separate items on them. The next morning, hundreds of volunteers joined with us to pack the items into duffle bags. We listened to speakers and watched a training video explaining the best way to hand out the duffle bags and blankets to the needy in a loving manner. A volunteer next to a huge street map of Los Angeles directed us to target a specific neighborhood.

With six bags and blankets in the trunk of the car, I accompanied a synagogue member to an area just east of Pico-Robertson. The following is how he described our task:

> Look out for a homeless person. We'll park the car. We walk up to the person, keeping a respectful distance, and introduce ourselves, "Hello, my name is Sam and this is my friend Jody. How are you doing today?" Then I say, "Please tell me your name." Then say, "I'm pleased to meet you. (Offer to shake hands.) I'm part of a group of people who have free supplies to give to people who are needy. Would you be interested in receiving it? It includes a blanket, socks, hats—things like that." If the person is interested, or wants to see it first, bring out the duffle and a blanket. They can take both, just the duffle, or just the blanket, or refuse both. If they are willing, engage in a conversation about their lives. Ask, "Where are you originally from? Is this the spot where you stay?" Listen to them. The point is to recognize the person's humanity and membership in the neighborhood.

It took about an hour to have such a conversation with eight people living on the neighborhood sidewalks or standing near stores seeking donations. Among them was a man whom my companion recognized from the synagogue handout line. The man moved in busy and frantic movements in the manner of someone under the influence of drugs, and he was extremely thin and had a wound on his face. "I've seen you before at the synagogue," my companion told him. "Please come back and see the rabbi and get a food card. Do you know we serve a free monthly luncheon?" He told me later, "I'm not sure he's going to live much longer." Months later, he wrote me that the man was still around and looking much healthier. The reason for this outreach to the needy, he told me, is simple: it is the right thing to do. He echoed the message of the rabbi and the motto of The Giving Spirit: "They are our neighbors. They are us."[58]

I understood that in this case "us" does not mean full inclusion; it means that their existence and plight must not be ignored and they must not be labeled as outsiders. It does not mean inviting them into one's home or close circles, however. The synagogue's monthly Tikkun Olam luncheon is an expression of this intermediate position. Attending the luncheon on a cool midweek February day, I joined the 150 people lined up on the sidewalk outside the synagogue. They did not appear to be people living on the street, and I was told that many had arrived via public bus. The crowd included middle and high school students and their teachers from the Orthodox and Conservative day schools who had signed on to volunteer at the luncheon, along with the coed choir of the liberal Modern Orthodox high school that would entertain the group during lunch.

The visitors were guided into the sanctuary, and when they were seated, the smiling senior rabbi welcomed them and announced the standard order of events: first he would distribute the grocery store gift cards in accordance with the list of recipients; then they could stay for the luncheon—either the English-language or the Russian-language luncheon; and only when those events were finished would he talk to people who were new to the program or whose card had been mistakenly omitted from the list. Before distributing anything, the rabbi shared some personal good news: his son had finally received his bachelor's degree after years of interrupted education and had been offered a job. "The lesson here is," the rabbi declared, "never give up!" People clapped, several wanted to know his son's academic field, and a few called out, "Mazel tov!" Attendees then came forward with a card marked with their name and number, and students gave them a supermarket gift card.[59]

The luncheon that followed was designed for a universal, not specifically Jewish, audience. A quarter of the attendees were Russian speakers, and the rest were a mixture of European American immigrants, American whites, Latinos, Blacks, and Asian Americans. Originally the entire group was served together in the same room, but the organizers complied with the Russians' request to have a separate luncheon so they could speak their language freely and enjoy their own community. The organizer, the same man whom I accompanied during The Giving Spirit event, finds the synagogue sponsors who pay for the food purchased from the local kosher groceries, bakeries, and restaurants. Bread (a large challah and individual-sized challah buns), a beefy stew (cholent), pasta with tomato sauce, pita, and oranges were served; later in the meal a large sheet cake was provided in honor of the birthday of a choir member. At the larger English-language luncheon, guests found seats at the long paper-covered tables. After hearing the Hebrew bread blessing, which was then translated, they lined up at the buffet, where students piled their paper plates with food. They sat in their seats eating and talking. The event felt like a celebration. The choir sang, attendees clapped, and afterward everyone was invited to come forward again for cake.

The rabbi, obviously enjoying himself tremendously, circulated the room. After the choir performance, he delivered words of Torah based on the weekly Torah portion. He talked about the passages from Exodus describing how, when the Israelites escaped Egypt and crossed the sea, they found themselves in a desert with no water and no food. God fed them with manna dropped from the sky. It was bread from the sky, the rabbi said, not from the earth as they were used to. The Israelites said, "This is a miracle: bread from the sky!" After forty years of this, when the Israelites were about to enter the Promised Land, Joshua told them, "You'll go to the land, and there will be bread from the earth!" The Israelites were astonished, saying, "This is a miracle: bread from the earth instead of the sky!" The difference between "what is natural" and "a miracle," the rabbi said, is what you are used to—you consider something unusual to be a miracle. He concluded: For some of us, love is a miracle, enjoying lunch together is a miracle, and opening our hearts and eyes is a miracle. He thanked everyone in attendance for being part of a miracle. One of the helpers passed out pamphlets with the Grace after Meals blessings and led the group in the recital of an English paragraph thanking God for providing food for the entire world. The rabbi and organizer bade the group farewell, and the choir sang as everyone exited the room.

I asked the rabbi how he reconciled the public nature of this luncheon with Maimonides's teaching about the importance of anonymous giving and receiving of food charity. He said, "Sometimes Maimonides gets it wrong! It's community! But, of course, some people will not show up because they are embarrassed. There are all kinds of people." Very few congregants attend these luncheons, the organizer told me, even though they are supportive and proud of this project. I asked the rabbi whether congregants who attend the monthly Tikkun Olam luncheons become better acquainted with the needy and invite them to their homes. He looked at me, puzzled, and responded, "That's not the design. It's not designed to lead to home hospitality."[60]

A few doors down Pico Boulevard is a community food charity that, like the Modern Orthodox synagogue, does not distinguish between Jewish and non-Jewish needy. The SOVA Community Food and Resource Program is a project of the Jewish Family Service of Los Angeles. Its inclusiveness is a matter of principle. It is funded by a combination of Jewish community funds, city and federal grants, and corporate and private donations. *Sova* is a Hebrew word meaning "satiation," but the service is equipped to provide only one emergency allocation of food supporting a family for three to five days per month. More important and long-lasting are the one-on-one meetings with staff, who help clients access free "on-site services including legal advocacy, job counseling, nutrition counseling, food stamp enrollment, information and referrals, case management, and counseling."[61] Across the spectrum of the Jewish community, the needy are urged to make use of governmental assistance to which they are entitled, and they generally do so. The director told me that Orthodox rabbis, institutions, and individuals remain aloof from SOVA, although they do enter the Pico-Robertson building to utilize the family counseling program service designed for Orthodox Jews. SOVA makes efforts to accommodate Orthodox needs, for example, by stocking Jewish holiday foods and fresh kosher chicken. These often go unclaimed, however, and then are given to people who do not keep kosher. The director speculated that the Orthodox do not use the food pantry because they do not want to be seen leaving the building with bags of food or standing in the line that snakes down the sidewalk on food distribution day.[62] Certainly, participating in that way would be considered deeply humiliating. This mode of disbursing food reinforces the conviction that SOVA is not a bona fide component of the Pico-Robertson Orthodox community.

Chabad is also distinguished for disbursing funds, food, and services to needy Jews who are not members of its congregations and to non-Jews who request help.[63] This approach is rooted in Jewish law, of course, but also in the social agenda of the seventh Lubavitcher rebbe. He asked his followers to perform the mitzvah of *tzedakah* daily—for example, by putting a few coins into a *pushke* (charity box).[64] Rabbi Shlomo Cunin, director of West Coast Chabad, is responsible for the particularly wide reach of Chabad's charitable activities in Southern California. In 1980, he started the first yearly Chabad Telethon, which raises funds with the help of TV and film celebrities, most of them male and many of them not Jewish.[65] Funds are used to subsidize West Coast Chabad's educational institutions and informal youth groups, summer camps, and campus programs that serve Jews of all backgrounds. However, Chabad's local drug rehabilitation program, an outpatient center, and a residential facility for men serve people of all religious and ethnic backgrounds.

Speaking privately with the Chabad rabbi who hosted a Shabbat evening meal I attended, I requested that he spread the word about a local public mental health agency's free services for indigent families. He told me that it is not unusual for people in the Chabad community to seek counseling and that "you do what you can to make them feel whole again." He revealed that the sullen, silent young man at the table was in drug rehabilitation treatment at the Chabad Treatment Center. Clearly the rabbi had hoped the Shabbat meal would have a salutary effect. In a video posted on the Chabad Treatment Center's website, the director of patient services described how the center's meals serve multiple healing roles: helping people learn to work with others preparing food, giving to others, and learning to receive.[66] At Thanksgiving time, the men at the center prepare and deliver meals to those who are experiencing homelessness. The Chabad Treatment Center offers outpatient services as well through another location two miles away. The Chabad Treatment Center and Chabad Telethon websites show other videos of Chabad-sponsored feed-the-hungry events as well.

While these food charity events are occasional, Chabad's assistance occurs routinely and often informally. Chabad rabbis privately disburse aid to needy Jewish families they encounter in their pastoral work. Chabad congregations that serve food after Shabbat services generally include everyone in attendance. Every congregation includes a few people who are regularly "taken care of" by being invited to meals, by receiving the leftovers from the community repast, or by being handed food packages prepared in advance for them particularly. One Orthodox Jew I interviewed testified that "Jews must give to anyone who asks, without caring if the recipient is Jewish or not. You are not allowed to *not* give."[67] "I hear this all the time in the Chabad shul," said a woman who alternates between a Chabad and a Sephardic congregation. One of the "Charity Basics" lessons on the Chabad.org website reinforces this:

> You're walking down the street and someone asks for food. The mitzvah says, you have to give something. If he asks for money, you're allowed to make some inquiries to determine if he's legit. Nothing in your pocket? Show some empathy, provide some kind and uplifting words. In no case can you just keep on walking.[68]

The website provides dozens of articles and audio lectures that present teachings about *tzedakah* based on distinctive Chabad themes. For example, the belief that each mitzvah has value in and of itself appears in response to the question of whether it "counts" if a Jew unknowingly donates to an unworthy individual:

Even if the person you gave to was not at all needy—and so, you haven't really performed an act of charity—nevertheless, your act was still a charitable act. Charity has two aspects: the giver's sacrifice of self for the sake of a mitzvah, and the receiver actually benefitting from the charity. Even when the actual provision for the needy is not there, you have still made your sacrifice by giving.[69]

Maimonides's hierarchy of eight ways of giving are also endorsed by Chabad, including the principle that the second highest form of giving is to donate anonymously to a community fund that carefully and respectfully investigates recipients. Such a fund would be SOVA or the Tomchei Shabbos food charity. The senior rabbi of the largest Chabad synagogue in the neighborhood advocates that people donate to and volunteer for the latter.

Tomchei Shabbos of Greater Los Angeles is the community food charity that aids local Jews who adhere to the Orthodox kosher laws by requiring kosher certification for any packaged and processed foods, although it does not declare itself Orthodox or demand that its clients embrace that label. The organization name means "supporters of the Sabbath." It does not supply enough for a person's or family's entire food supply, but it provides the extras for Sabbath meals and perhaps some meals during the week: uncooked kosher food, such as chicken, soup, grape juice, and tuna, and foods not requiring kosher certification, such as eggs, fruit, and vegetables. Deliveries are made on Thursday evenings, and special deliveries that include kosher meat and holiday-specific foods, such as matzah and horseradish for Passover, are made prior to Jewish holidays. The organization also provides grocery store credit to individuals and offers a job board for employers and job seekers.

Tomchei Shabbos follows the principle favored by Maimonides about preserving anonymity. The board of directors appoints a rabbi who interviews the applicants. Currently the procedures require that people seeking regular assistance fill out applications detailing their expenses and income. The requirement that applicants must divulge the amount of government assistance they receive implies that the needy should not forgo this help without a compelling reason. Applicants are required to submit a letter of support from a rabbi, who vouches for their truthfulness (and, presumably, their observance of *kashrut*). Tomchei Shabbos purchases food in bulk, and the lot is divided between several Los Angeles packing and disbursement centers. Volunteers place the food into boxes for each household, and these are brought outside recipients' homes or other designated places. Recipients also have the option of driving up to the distribution center and getting their food boxes themselves. They can do this without disclosing that the food is for them. Protecting the identity of the recipients is paramount. Shivering with vexation, a volunteer told me, "Once I recognized the household when I delivered the food!"

Tomchei Shabbos has a reputation for efficiency and integrity. It enables religious Jews to easily fulfill their *tzedakah* obligation with the confidence that it reaches truly needy Jews. The organization advertises its existence and solicits donations in the Jewish press, e-newsletters, and posters. It supplies *pushkes* (collection boxes for coin donations) for the home, school, and workplace. At some kosher grocery stores, customers may donate in the checkout line by indicating the amount to the cashier, who scans a Tomchei Shabbos bar code along with the rest of the groceries. Store owners fulfill their obligation by selling their goods to Tomchei Shabbos at a hefty discount. Individuals can fulfill their *tzedakah* obligation by donating their labor to pack the foods. Some of the packing occurs in the local Orthodox high schools when items such as bakery goods are placed into family-sized plastic bags that are then placed into larger boxes to be brought to disbursement centers. The final packing and the deliveries occur on Thursday night so that recipients have time to prepare the food for their Sabbath meals.

I participated in the packing and disbursement of food at the Pico-Robertson site located at the center of the neighborhood in a space that serves at other times as a yeshiva and synagogue. By 6:00 p.m. on Thursdays, people were walking into the Pico Boulevard entrance, ready to fulfill their obligation. Moms or dads with their elementary-age children formed most of the volunteers. "When these little children gather milk, challot, produce, etc., together to help pack a box, they feel at their best, because they understand that they are making a difference in someone else's Shabbat," wrote one such father in the local Jewish newspaper.[70]

Fulfilling the mitzvah as a volunteer packer takes very little time. Volunteers who arrive to pack are handed a sheet of paper with a specific route's households, each labeled by a meaningless three-letter code. A few paid workers (Spanish-speaking Latino men, who are greeted with familiarity by some volunteers) bring the bulk food into the packing room, help load packed boxes onto dollies, and wheel them to the back alley. There the boxes are placed into the cars lined up to receive them, and the drivers receive instructions for the routes. I was paired with a high school student the first time I volunteered. When we completed assembling all the food for three families in ten minutes, I asked her, "What do we do now?" "Now we go home," she said and walked out the door. Drivers' obligations take longer. After lining up their cars in the alley and arranging for the right boxes to be loaded into their cars, they make their way through Los Angeles traffic to their drop-off places. They may need to carry the boxes of food up a flight of stairs. By late Thursday night, everyone who supports and participates in Tomchei Shabbos can feel they are helping truly worthy and needy members of the Sabbath-observant community.

One of my interviewees revealed that her family receives Tomchei Shabbos aid, and she shared her perspective on how it teaches her about her place in the community. First and foremost, she is deeply grateful for the assistance and the protection of her privacy. Her children are even unaware that their Sabbath and holiday food is not purchased in the normal fashion. It distresses her when they ask why certain foods the family dislikes continue to appear on the table. She knows this is a manageable burden, far better than the one she would experience if the children knew about the aid and worried that their parents are in financial distress. She dislikes being an object of pity, even when friends and acquaintances mean well:

One of the things that is sad for us is that sometimes people send us checks anonymously (occasionally, not so anonymously) or will drop second-hand clothes at our home. Taking that first check written to us for *tzedakah* made me feel grateful, because the money was needed, but also horrible. No one wants to be "a *nebbuch* case" [an unfortunate]. We need these things but accepting them sometimes makes us feel downtrodden.

She believes Tomchei Shabbos is an excellent way to fulfill the mitzvah of *tzedakah* for people who require financial support for their food needs. However, she believes the best action of all would be to invite the needy family as guests. They would not know they are being helped because of need. Instead, they would feel they are invited because they are liked and welcomed. Although her family attends a local synagogue and her children are in Orthodox schools, they are rarely invited to Sabbath or holiday meals. She said,

> Inviting us for a Shabbat meal saves us fifty dollars! And instead of feeling like we're there just for people to dispense *tzedakah* and forget about us, we feel like we're friends or family. When you are going through acute financial struggles, the feeling that you aren't wanted, that people look down on you, that you are left out—those are as painful as the actual financial details.[71]

Such a practice blurs the distinction between *tzedakah* and *hakhnasat orḥim*. From an ideological perspective her family would fit better in a congregation with a different social outlook and dynamic. Clearly, she is affiliated with a congregation that regards Sabbath and holiday meals as occasions reserved for socializing with friends rather than as opportunities for sustaining the community.

Sometimes community charity is entirely synagogue based. "The Ashkenazis are so much better organized than us Sefarads," another woman laughingly told me. She called Tomchei Shabbos an Ashkenazi organization and said, "We could never set up a system like Tomchei

Shabbos, but I think we still manage to take care of people."[72] She is a member of the Pico-Robertson French Jewish community, a relatively small number of Jews whose synagogue base is either the Pinto Torah Center or the French Jewish Community Center, or both. They are American born or immigrants from Paris, Tunisia, Morocco, Algeria, or Iran (sometimes by way of Israel). Very much aware of not being part of the "default" Ashkenazic Orthodox community, she volunteered—unbidden, I believe, by my questions but certainly because of my Ashkenazic ethnicity—this and other comparisons. "Unlike the Ashkenazis," she said, "we don't have a system of synagogue dues, which is nice, but it causes problems later," such as when community expenses need to be paid. English is the vernacular and French is the secondary language of these congregations, and French food, which plays an important unifying role, is a community marker.

Delice, for example, the local kosher French bakery–café–caterer, is a focal point for the French-speaking Orthodox community. Whereas the Pinto Torah Center has supported a charity food market in a sister congregation in Israel, locally the French community provides for the needy in an informal manner, she told me, and primarily within the community. She has not heard about a congregational Tomchei Shabbos delivery route or references to donating to the community fund.[73] Yet the rabbis and her children's schoolteachers remind everyone to give 10 percent to charity, she reported. People know who is in need when they talk or write online to each other, and they respond with money or services. When food or meals are needed, they respond with direct donations or meal invitations. This *tzedakah* occurs within the community. Nevertheless, she still gives food assistance to outsiders. When she is solicited by people on the sidewalks, she gives packages of unopened food that, as a mother of young children, she always has on hand. When people positioned at stop signs and signals request donations from drivers, she gives them snacks and drinks she has stocked in her car. She knows the French bakery owner gives free food handouts to needy people who request them, and typically there are several in the alley at the end of store hours to whom he gives the leftover food or some money. Occasionally a poor person will ask for coffee with his only spare dollar, and the waiters bring him coffee and a pastry.

Shabbat and holiday meals are bountiful, filled with carefully prepared food from the cuisine of Sephardic Francophone Jews. In the woman's community, men are often in charge of the shopping and food preparation. "My husband takes the initiative with the guest list," another woman from the French-speaking Orthodox community told me, because he is very generous and cannot bear the thought of someone not having a place to eat on Shabbat. "He is a person with open arms and always the life of the party," she said.[74] When he chances upon out-of-town French people at the synagogue or at the bakery because they have heard it is French, he will invite them to a Sabbath meal. These are often young couples on vacation, but it may be others he hears about, and of course there are regular family guests. Neither the rabbi nor a layperson makes an announcement in the synagogue about hosting guests; people in the congregation take this upon themselves if they wish.

A man who regularly prepares the well-attended Friday night meal at his home told me that he prefers to eat the second meal, Shabbat lunch, with the community at the synagogue. Later in the day he will return there for the men's Torah class and the third meal. "I'd never invite strangers to my home," he told me. Who, exactly, is a stranger? A woman who attends the Pinto Center Shabbat morning service insisted that the congregation is warm and friendly. I asked, "If I—an Ashkenazi, older single woman—showed up, and no one knew me, would I be invited to join a family's meal?" She responded: "It depends. People would have to know your story. Perhaps the first time you show up, if people know your story, you would get an invitation. And if you actually say you want an invitation, you would likely get one. But, generally, people want to know your story first."[75]

This cautious, insular way of being hospitable is the norm for the neighborhood's Persian Orthodox Jewish population as well. Like the French, their guests are mostly those of their own ethnic background. Having full tables and many courses is not unique to the French or Persians, but both groups pride themselves on their intricately prepared and complex dishes that they believe are far tastier than Ashkenazic fare. It is not unusual for men to handle some or all of the shopping, but women are the cooks. Persians welcome people they do not know to their tables, but they do not consider these to be strangers because they are friends of extended family, relatives of members of the community, or others who have been vouched for. "Last week we had fifteen," one man told me, "and when our children eat here, we have more."[76] He, like most members of his group, belongs to synagogues identified as Persian or Sephardic. The smaller number of Persian Orthodox Jews who have successfully integrated into congenial Ashkenazic-dominated congregations have guests of mixed backgrounds.

The Ashkenazic-Persian divide is, from one perspective, utterly natural and not problematic; many, however, are disturbed by it and explain it as prejudice emanating from *Ashkenazim* or Persians. "All Persians are tarnished by the elderly Persian women who arrive at a synagogue in time for the *kiddush* and fill their purses with food," lamented a young Persian woman.[77] A local Ashkenazic rabbi came to the defense of the elderly Persians: "They need this food! These women are responsible for feeding the people in their families who are housebound."[78]

A large family meal on Friday evening is of crucial importance to Persian Jewish families, even those who are not Orthodox. In secular or so-called traditional Iranian Jewish families living in Southern California, such a meal starts in mid-evening and extends for hours, with multiple courses of food not necessarily kosher. Family members and friends may arrive and depart throughout the evening to pay their respects at different households. Strangers may be included, too, but they are brought to the meal by the hosts' friends or extended family, so their trustworthiness can be assumed. It is a warm, celebratory atmosphere.

Offspring from these families who become *ba'alei teshuvah* and seek a different kind of Friday night experience are criticized for rejecting a generous, tolerant, and loving family tradition. Parents who try to accommodate them—for example, by purchasing kosher meat and separate plates and cutlery—will likely still fall short. The children must struggle to fulfill the commandment to honor their parents and the ideal of *shalom bayit*, achieving domestic harmony. This dilemma often occurs in families of *ba'alei teshuvah* of all ethnic backgrounds. Among Iranians it occurs perhaps more frequently because of the importance of the Friday evening meal. "They just don't understand, or they pretend they don't," a young Orthodox woman said in dismay about her "traditional" parents.[79] Another described the compromises she and her husband made to attend the meal at her nephew's wedding, where, even though they received special kosher meals, *treif* food was served to everyone else. She told me, "It was a real *kiddush Hashem* [sanctification of God's name] for us."[80] That is, although inwardly they disapproved of nearly all the elements of the event, they managed to act graciously in order not to give a bad reputation to Torah-observant Jews.

Like these Persian and Francophone congregations, the predominantly Ashkenazi congregations that are in the center or right-leaning range of Orthodox communities are hesitant to invite outsiders to their tables—that is, non-Jews, non-Orthodox Jews, and people from Orthodox circles different from their own. Their congregational rabbis do not prioritize *hakhnasat orḥim*, whether it is the traditional form reserved for out-of-town guests or the expanded versions distinctive to *kiruv* or to the local Modern Orthodox. They leave the decision to extend hospitality to their members' discretion. Gender plays an important role in the dynamic of hospitality when the act of extending invitations occurs at the synagogue. Only adult males are obligated to attend communal prayers, and they, more often than the female head of the family, invite other men during or shortly after the service while they all are still in the men's section. Women who attend communal prayers can approach unfamiliar women on their side of the synagogue and offer a meal, although from my experience and from what I have heard, this occurs far less often. Women tend to be more discriminating than men. With a single glance they discover an unknown woman's marital status and her religious strictness by the extent to which she covers her hair and how she does so (a wig, a hat, both, or nothing), the length of her sleeves and hems, her neckline, the thickness of her stockings, the style of her outfit, and her jewelry.

These signal an aspect of her "story" and what kind of social disruption she and her family might bring to the meal. In the words of one such unconventional woman, "Those who don't measure up to the communally accepted model of married parents of X number of children [X can vary by neighborhood] are often shunted aside, usually without intention to harm, but in that simple intuitive sense of like seeking like."[81]

One Centrist Orthodox congregation in Pico-Robertson consists largely of families "*frum* (religiously observant) from birth" who received a parochial elementary and high school education. Most of the adults attended college and expect the same from the younger generation, although the rabbi and many of the congregants identify themselves with the Yeshivish outlook that elevates Torah learning above all. Congregants send their children to gender-segregated Orthodox elementary and high schools, and their sons are sent to a post–high school yeshiva before (or if) they attend college. A synagogue leader said about *hakhnasat orḥim*, "Mostly we do it within the congregation." No person stands up and announces that visitors may step forward and request hospitality, but he thinks strangers who attend the synagogue on Friday night or Saturday (particularly the former) will be invited for a Shabbat meal "because individuals in the shul are friendly and reach out a lot." Several times a year, a layperson reviews the membership list and asks people known to welcome guests to invite members who are not well integrated into the community.[82]

A similar but more vital matter is hospitality during the holiday of Sukkot. The weeklong holiday requires eating meals in a *sukkah*, an outdoor booth-like temporary structure. A layperson matches up those who lack a *sukkah* with those who have one in their yard; they may dine together or work out a schedule for separate meals. Another way the congregation fulfills the mitzvah of *hakhnasat orḥim* is when a member needs such hospitality. For example, the leaders regularly arrange Shabbat and holiday invitations for a member who is developmentally disabled, and they send emails to the congregation to take care of meals for a member who became widowed and is going through the process of adjusting to his new situation.[83]

Members of this Centrist Orthodox congregation voice some discomfort about inviting strangers into the home, and they have shown in various ways that they are happy to leave that kind of hospitality to individual volunteers. The synagogue has no general phone number or receptionist. "We are just a mom-and-pop operation," the rabbi's wife told me, "so people who wish to arrange meals in advance would have to contact the rabbi via his personal phone or email. If the rabbi wants to extend such hospitality, he invites them to his own home or calls a few people in the congregation to do so. The usual way such invitations occur is when a member offers it to a new person attending the service."[84] "Sometimes people are a little bit creepy," a member said, explaining why she is uncomfortable with having someone sight unseen be a visitor in her home.[85] Another sympathized with those who held back, telling me of a member who, after having a particular guest at his table, confessed that he was nervous to have this man hang around his kids again. He knows Chabad is less discriminating, but, he said, "Chabad has meals in shul. If we had meals in shul, we wouldn't be so nervous. We've had cases when people freaked out because a guest acted too strangely. And another time a guest pulled out his phone at the table even though he professed to be a *frum* Jew."[86]

Congregants at this synagogue regard theirs as a friendly one. Their Shabbat tables are surrounded by many guests. A couple known for their hospitality regularly invites eighteen to twenty-five people to eat at their Friday night table and about the same number for Shabbat lunch. For the most part, these are members of their own synagogue or another congregation that has similar religious and social characteristics. Their noon meal typically includes two or three other families whose children are friends with their own four school-age children. After the meal, other children from the neighborhood may join the invited group, and the adults stay and talk. "I'm not sure what we do is technically *hakhnasat orḥim*," the mother told me, "but I make sure also to invite singles because I was single for years in the neighborhood and know how it feels." Some of these singles are repeat guests, and others are Orthodox Jews she does not know personally but takes a chance on because they are in town for their work with the school or youth group. Occasionally she is contacted by her own or another congregation's leaders to invite an out-of-town guest or a family, but that does not occur often.[87]

The cautious and insular approach that governs hospitality in this congregation is also evident in food charity. In Centrist Orthodox congregations, the primary focus of food charity is on feeding local needy religious Jews and the secondary emphasis is on helping feed the poor in Israel; helping non-Jews may occur, but it is not a priority. The congregation favors using Tomchei Shabbos and regularly provides drivers for several delivery routes. As in all Orthodox congregations, during the days prior to Purim and Passover, when there is a special obligation to provide food for the poor, members donate funds through the rabbi. He divides these funds between local and Israeli food charities. The rabbi devotes his regular discretionary fund to help member or local Orthodox families. This kind of assistance is not only for food; it may also pay for rent, medical and counseling services, school or summer camp tuition, and the like. Through the congregation e-newsletter or the Los Angeles Orthodox online newsletter, the rabbi and his leadership team may publicize other charitable causes that send funds or services to the much larger circle of Orthodox Jews locally, nationally, and in Israel.

These food charity priorities influence the management of the influx of the many donation-seeking men attending weekday morning worship services at this Centrist Orthodox synagogue. Like virtually all the congregational rabbis in the neighborhood, this rabbi instituted a rule that only after the conclusion of the prayers may worshipers be asked for money. It used to be that the requesters could be non-Jews as well as Jews, but the 2018 shooting at the Pittsburgh Tree of Life synagogue and the 2019 attack on Chabad of Poway altered synagogue entrance policies. Congregations that had not already done so instituted security measures designed to limit entrance to members or to Jews only. For example, at this synagogue the door is equipped with a code pad whose password is revealed only to members, or at times a guard or member stands sentry at the entrance and ensures that people seeking admission are there to join the prayers. Consequently, most of the nonmembers who manage to enter and seek funds are needy Orthodox Jews or, more likely, they are *meshulaḥim*, emissaries, poor Orthodox Jews from elsewhere who ask for support for specific Israeli religious institutions and are permitted to keep half for their own expenses. The local non-Jewish poor or the Jews who do not pray do not get admitted. Of course, they may be assisted at other times. "I always give something to that old Persian man with the white hair and beard who wanders around the neighborhood at all hours," a member told me.[88]

The most insular form of food *tzedakah* that still fulfills the commandment is to reserve one's donations for extended family and friends. One rabbi I interviewed admitted that he—and many other rabbis, he insisted—facilitates this type of charitable giving. In his congregation it works as follows: a person donates to the synagogue *gemakh* (community fund) and directs the rabbi to send a check to the donor's friend or relative needing money. Were the donor to send the check himself, he or she would not earn a tax deduction. "Some accountants are not comfortable about this way of operating the *gemakh*," the rabbi told me, "because technically I am supposed to be acting entirely on my discretion." That technical requirement does not hinder him. He proudly mentioned the yearly dollar amount disbursed this way. On the morning of Yom Kippur, he announces the total to the congregation. "It is an open book," he told me, and "people can walk into the office and ask to see the disbursement record, although they never do." I asked another rabbi whether his synagogue followed that practice. He was insulted I would even ask, and he responded, "That is illegal. That is simply laundering money, a way to avoid paying taxes." Instead, when people come to him and tell him they need financial support (for rent, summer camp, emergencies), he will give it. "*That* is legal. The needy person must come to me to ask for help."[89]

A synagogue's approach to insularity may not be an indicator of whether it is a community that actually welcomes strangers or offers charity broadly. The rabbi's influence and the prevailing sentiments among the members can be more determinative of how the group generally behaves. People with experience as newcomers or who were not well-to-do told me that some congregations are "cliquey" or condescending toward people with fewer means. People who professed to have many friends often did not perceive any problems, unlike those with fewer friends or who are unconventional. An editorial in an Orthodox women's journal addressed these tendencies as follows:

> Avraham and Sarah's story is a strong reminder of another approach, of what openness, inclusiveness, and welcome can look like. Sadly, these are too often lacking in the Orthodox community. I recently heard a phrase that I loved: the "frozen chosen," referring to people who, while seeing themselves as uniquely chosen to serve God and do His will, stay isolated in a cold identity that freezes others out. This illustrates the dichotomy between the Avrahams and Sarahs, who warmly invite in any who want to be a part of the group, and those who, no matter how devout, still develop intractable rules of engagement meant to keep people out.[90]

It is important to point out that there is reciprocity within the hospitality dynamic: people invited may refuse the invitation, leaving the offeror embarrassed.

Some congregations simply do not act as a unified body. One of the local congregations is deeply divided on the matter of hospitality. The staff person answering the phone at the synagogue made her opinion clear when I asked how hospitality requests were handled. "We used to do far more," she said, "but it became a real problem. Visitors, sometimes families who come to Los Angeles on vacation with their four or five children, would call and ask to be hosted. It is not fair! It is an imposition on our families, and it is not right to come and expect to be taken care of for free." She also finds the requests problematic because accepting strangers into one's home is risky behavior. Such a person could be "crazy, dangerous, a schizophrenic, or just 'off,'" she told me. People are expecting too much, she said, adding, "We are not Chabad or Aish!"

Yet when people call or email asking for hospitality, she does not say no. She asks the requester's level of religious observance. She then conveys the information to one of two laypeople designated to call and speak to the potential guest. According to the receptionist, if the requester sounds "normal" and does not have excessive needs, the layperson attempts to find a host from a list of volunteers. However, if the requester requires too much or says something that raises concerns, the layperson in charge "very politely, very discreetly" apologizes for not being able to help. The receptionist directs the caller to the synagogue website page listing phone numbers and addresses for local hotels, kosher restaurants, and restaurants and food businesses that offer "Shabbat takeout." Perhaps, I suggested, such visitors could attend Shabbat services and find meals by responding to someone who announces that people seeking meals should come forward and be matched with hosts. The receptionist responded, "We don't do that anymore—it became a problem. Families would be 'on the rotation' and arrange extra food, and then no one would come forward and they would be put out." I persisted: "At least visitors can enjoy the nice *kiddush* you offer after Shabbat morning services—it can serve as a lunch." She responded, "We don't do that anymore either. We were losing $19,000 per year!" Only when the *kiddush* is sponsored—that is, paid for by a member—is there anything more elaborate than cookies and beverages.[91]

My interview with the rabbi produced similar responses. When I suggested that a visiting family gives the hosts an opportunity to fulfill a mitzvah and to meet Jews from other places, he responded heatedly:

> They make a family vacation to come to LA for a week, and they don't plan how they are going to do Shabbat?! They rent hotel rooms, rent a car, make all sorts of arrangements, but for Shabbat dinner they—say it is a father, mother, and several kids—are going to ask for someone else to feed them?! That's asking quite a lot! No, they can arrange it, along with all their other arrangements, to have a refrigerator in their room. There are these little kitchenettes. No reason to not exert themselves.

Yet the rabbi insisted that his congregation is a welcoming one. He said to me, a nonmember, "Walk into the shul on a Friday night or a Saturday morning, and people will ask you to a meal." I told him this was not my experience when I attended. He sighed, "I've heard that it is different on the women's side of the *meḥitzah* [room divider] from the men's side. It is far friendlier on the men's side, people talk to you, the men will invite a person over, unhesitatingly. But the women are not very friendly. It's been a problem for years." I asked him how he would address it, and he said, with some frustration, "We have all sorts of programs in which people can get to know each other."[92] Clearly, he wants the synagogue to be known as one that welcomes strangers, in consonance with Jewish values. However, by his example and his language, he cares more about fostering self-sufficiency and protecting his congregants' freedom from responsibility.

The congregation's starkly contrasting opinions became obvious when one of the laypersons responsible for finding hosts for Shabbat guests presented his perspective and a biting critique of the rabbi's view:

> A family comes from Chicago with three kids. It shakes my entire being when a rabbi calls that "*ḥutzpah*." All I can respond is to say, in the world we live in today, raising a Jewish family is very stressful. Women in the home deserve way more credit than they are given, and if a vacationing family wants home hospitality, don't be a *beit din* [court of justice]. Go out of your comfort zone! I've had such people at my table, and they may have real broken hearts and are so comforted by the presence of another family.[93]

On the other hand, I said, perhaps Jewish values suggest that one should not risk one's safety, and a stranger could pose a danger, and don't Jewish values teach that we should strive for self-sufficiency and make Shabbat for ourselves? Is not this new way of providing hospitality actually a deviation from the past? "I don't know what religion those words come from," he responded. "That's not Jewish—that's another religion. I've never heard one word of Torah proof for this point of view. Never." As to the matter of danger, he retorted, "I will always do my due diligence. I will speak to the strange guest, ask where they are from, where they *davven* [pray], then find them a place that fits—and that might be my own." He said,

> It goes back to the story of Abraham and Sarah. This is not a fairy-tale story, it is in the Torah. If you believe, you need to emulate what Abraham did in the sweltering heat in the desert. He was more than a hundred years old, she was ninety-nine, and God tested him by sending three idol worshipers who were Arabs. He passed the test with flying colors. He brought them into his tent, not a villa. These were not his best friends. He did not pass on this one.

He insisted that the reason why the Jews are still in exile is because of the closed hearts of the religious, the fact that too few Jews are offering hospitality and too few rabbis take it upon themselves to model the right behavior. "If our rabbis did this, we wouldn't have to depend on Chabad."[94]

Another congregant, a scientist who regularly attends Shabbat services, described the members as strongly divided. He was not surprised by my report of the receptionist's and rabbi's statements, but he did not agree that there was an actual synagogue *hakhnasat orḥim* policy. "Keep in mind," he told me, "people don't always follow what the rabbi says anyway," and some members are quite hospitable. Before the Sabbath he receives email requests from the laypeople in charge of *hakhnasat orḥim*, and "every single Shabbat, without fail," he told me, one of these leaders announces during the service that visitors needing a meal should come forward and will be placed with hosts. "I have guests nearly every week," the man told me, "including families of six. I wish there were more people who did it so it would not fall to us so often, but it's what you are supposed to do. We have met people from all over the world. I now have a colleague overseas who hosts my children when they are there."[95]

On the other hand, generosity in charity may be advocated by leaders and rejected by followers. Despite the divine commandment to give charity when asked, many people I interviewed admitted they could not or would not give when they were individually approached. A Chabad woman told me, "I generally do not give—if it's a woman, sometimes a small amount." She used to donate regularly to Tomchei Shabbos and Chabad, but her family's essential expenses have ballooned, and all funds are directed to their own physical needs and those of their children.[96]

Another woman, who belongs to a Centrist Orthodox congregation and who has ample resources, confessed that she fails in her fulfillment of this mitzvah. She is not proud of her behavior, telling me, "Unfortunately, I have no compassion." She believes that the Jewish woman who lives in the car parked next to Pico Boulevard and asks people who walk by for money is genuinely needy, but she avoids that corner. "The other local beggars? I ignore them. I keep my distance." When her children were younger, the family regularly volunteered to drive a Tomchei Shabbos route, and all of her grown children keep a "10 percent account" to ensure that a tenth of their income is devoted to *tzedakah*. She told me of her husband's discovery that a regular beggar at the morning service had sufficient funds of his own to take a yearly vacation to Berlin and stay in a luxury hotel. "I hope you don't tell the rabbi," the man said to her husband when they met on the flight and he confessed all. Her husband did not tell the rabbi, but he felt very awkward about the matter when the man continued to show up and beg.[97] Some rabbis themselves are disdainful even while permitting the morning solicitations, such as the one who told me, "It's a racket."[98]

Unlike the woman above, other congregants have mixed feelings but give anyway. A young Persian couple who came to Orthodoxy in their teens takes care to follow the demands of Jewish law. They determined that with their income each of them should donate ninety cents per day, so her husband gets fresh one-dollar bills from the bank to hand out to the men who approach him after the morning prayers. She, however, has worked as an assistant in medical clinics and is more grudging. When she worked near the encampments in downtown Los Angeles for those who are experiencing homelessness, she said that she saw attitudes of entitlement among the poor and their up-to-date mobile phones. There were young women who asked her to certify their medical disability so they could receive funds, although they were not medically disabled. "I know I'm supposed to give when people ask," she said. "We have to work hard for what we have, so I resent if my money goes to people who are not even trying." For this reason she directs her food charity to the community fund. Several times a year she will go with her kids to Tomchei Shabbos and pack food or drive a delivery route.[99]

Another young mother's generosity is tempered by the high cost of living as an Orthodox family because of the private school tuition and the costly demands of kosher and appropriate Sabbath and holiday foods. "I learned you can count part of the school costs as *tzedakah*," she told me, "because the schools subsidize the tuition of really poor families." Nevertheless, they do give *tzedakah*, and Tomchei Shabbos is one of the concerns they support. If they did not count some of their school tuition, however, they would not be able to fulfill the obligation to dedicate 10 percent of their income to charity.[100]

I asked a rabbi whether handing over even a part of one's earnings to others is difficult. "Not for me," he told me. He divides his paycheck, depositing 90 percent into an account he labels "Income" and the other 10 percent into an account labeled "*Tzedakah*." He regards the latter account as simply not his own, yet he still feels proprietary about it.[101] According to Jewish law he should, in the sense that he must direct the charity funds to worthy recipients, the vast majority of whom should be other Jews. This ensures that Jews take care of each other, that the stronger look out for the weaker, and that beneficiaries and benefactors regard themselves as an interwoven social organism.

Whereas passionate voices from within Jewish tradition proclaim that God demands that righteous Jews support the needy regardless of their religious identity, the prevailing opinion in religious law regards this assistance as a strategy for Jewish peaceful continuity. This strategy is summed up in the first part of an aphorism attributed to the first-century sage Hillel: "If I am not for myself, who will be for me?"[102] That today there remain followers of Hillel—Torah-observant Jews who study and revere his words—testifies to its pragmatic wisdom. No one among the Orthodox doubts this maxim; rather, they disagree about who constitutes "others," the extent to which they should help them, and how high the barriers between them and others should be erected. These disagreements are constituent elements differentiating Orthodox groups from each other.

Unlike food charity, home hospitality requires intimacy and an openness to being vulnerable. Guests may expose the hosts to foreign and heretical ideas and practices, showing that the ways of the host are imperfect and fragile. While it is potentially risky to share one's table, it is essential for creating bonds. Eating across families is essential for community survival and growth. The flip side of the rabbinic warning "If you eat at their tables, you will marry their daughters" is "You cannot marry their daughters unless you eat at their tables." This is made manifest in the traditional Jewish wedding ceremony when the bride and groom drink from the same goblet of wine and the rite is followed by a meal between both families and the community in attendance. Within the framework of Jewish law and tradition, when a host offers a meal to a guest, the invitation is, at the most, a declaration of potential future family kinship and, at the least, recognition of shared community identity. Whom one should invite and whose invitations one should accept are matters that shape a community and ensure that the community will, in its present form, endure.

Conclusion

The Pico-Robertson neighborhood of Los Angeles is like a fully equipped ethnographic laboratory for studying the wide range of Orthodox approaches to eating and sharing food. With its variety of Jewish ethnic groups and Orthodox communities and its plethora of kosher foods available in stores and restaurants, each of the different Orthodox communities follows its own particular way of practicing *kashrut*, *tzedakah*, and *hakhnasat orḥim*. The cultural and halakhic differences among these groups enable them to serve God in the way each deems proper. The very intricacy, extensiveness, and particularity of the rules of *kashrut* may provide the opportunity for diversity and individuality. At the same time, the Orthodox residents of Pico-Robertson experience the overarching unity inspired by the inscrutable commandments of *kashrut* in order to be servants of God.

Although my research in this neighborhood confirmed a connection between the Orthodox food culture and the neighborhood's vibrancy, my initial vision of Orthodox unity and internal harmony was highly inaccurate. While there was unanimous agreement about the importance of the kosher diet, there were many variations in the details of the diet and internal tension and conflicts about these details. Indeed, I sought long and hard to find one venue in which everybody could eat together without prior negotiations and compromises. Even with negotiation, no home would qualify. Morever (and somewhat to my surprise), I learned it was not important to them to do so.

My research demonstrated that Orthodox subaffiliations use foodways to construct smaller, intimate communities, and individuals use food to fashion personal identities within the larger group. The rabbinic rules have always permitted a variety of standards that enable Jews to differentiate their food practices from each other and, if they wish, to avoid unified Jewish eating as a matter of religious principle.

The evidence presented in this book demonstrates the inadequacy of what Menahem Keren-Kratz calls "the one-dimensional paradigm," that is, the attempt to define Orthodox Jews based on a single characteristic.[1] Typically, people (and even academics) define and differentiate Orthodox Jews on the basis of their strictness and cultural insularity. Distinguishing Orthodox communities on a spectrum from halakhic laxity to halakhic strictness may work within a specific group, but that criterion does not adequately explain the difference between, say, Chabad and Centrist Orthodox. They differentiate themselves by other characteristics such as religious ideology, internal organization, and commitment to Talmud study. Modern Orthodox congregations are typically described as the most flexible and least demanding in matters of *halakhah*. In the Pico-Robertson neighborhood, however, they may be the most diligent about fulfilling *mitzvot* connected to hospitality and charity. It may be helpful to arrange Orthodox communities on a spectrum of their willingness to participate in American non-Orthodox culture, but that misses other defining characteristics. Besides, where does one place the groups engaged in religious outreach, with their *kiruv* teachers highly attuned to outside culture and the non-Orthodox Jews immersed in it? Furthermore, *ba'alei teshuvah* in whatever community they join cannot help but carry with them and act in response to the ideas with which they were raised.

Differentiated kosher laws not only originate in rabbinic law and levels of strictness but are also outgrowths of Jewish communal dynamics, regional identities, and women's practical concerns. The current variety and abundance of kosher food enable pluralism within the Orthodox population—and the development of extreme and novel practices.

At the same time that there is internal diversity among the Orthodox groups in Pico-Robertson, there is an overall sense of community partly because of the shared commitment to the kosher diet. The loyalty of the Pico-Robertson Orthodox Jews to their local kosher resources testifies to a larger truth: the kosher diet is the Orthodox diet. No one "owns" *kashrut*, but today it is the province of Orthodox Jews. Virtually all of them claim to obey the dietary laws, compared to 14 percent of non-Orthodox Jews. The authority wielded in the production of kosher meat is in Orthodox hands. Production of food bearing kosher certification is under Orthodox oversight whether the food is made at a distance in industrial settings or at the local level when food is prepared for hotels, hospitals, schools, synagogues, and the like. Only Orthodox Jews are considered trustworthy to serve as *mashgiḥim*, kosher inspectors, ensuring that the Orthodox rabbinic rules are maintained. The kosher certification agencies, which are owned by Orthodox individuals or organizations, provide community members jobs in administration, sales, and clerical support. In the case of community-based nonprofit agencies, they disburse the profits to worthy Orthodox charities, educational programs, youth groups, and cultural activities. *Kashrut* as it is practiced by American Orthodox Jews certainly keeps the community close not only through commensal, ingredient-based, and preparer-based rules but also through the kosher certification system. Non-Orthodox Jews, even those who obey the dietary laws, participate as consumers.

The shared commitment to the kosher diet creates an overall sense of community. A singular focus on tradition and authority strengthens communal bonds. These bonds, I have shown, are cemented together by foodways, especially the commensal regulations that keep outsiders at a social distance. These ensure the perpetuation of the community and its principles.

Rabbinic *kashrut* rules were designed to bind together the Jewish people who follow them and to exclude and diminish the influence of those who do not. The values and symbols most effective for community survival—authority, sanctity, group loyalty—are favored by the Orthodox as a whole. They define the kosher diet as an inscrutable decree demonstrating servitude to God. Chabad Hasidic Jews augment this with a kabbalistic outlook portraying the kosher diet and religious eating practices as an act of partnership with God. Ethical rationales for *kashrut* are avoided because they are so favored by non-Orthodox Jews and because they are less effective for ensuring obedience and group survival. Orthodox Jews who employ ethical reasoning are thereby indicating their position on the margins of the Orthodox community. Yet because ethical arguments are persuasive to non-Jews, as are hygienic concerns, Orthodox spokesmen use these terms to explain and defend the kosher laws and especially kosher meat slaughter when addressing the non-Jewish public.

The kosher certification system tempers to some extent the inclination to create alternative options. The agencies, particularly Orthodox Union's kosher division, designed an inclusive set of *kashrut* rules to enable the largest market reach and enable Orthodox communities to recognize each other's food as kosher and share the same table. To this end, they created regulations not seen before, such as the new American Ashkenazic *glatt* regulation. Other historic halakhic stipulations were dropped, such as the requirement for *ḥalav yisraʾel* (milk production watched by Jews). These are compromises made in the name of maintaining Orthodox unity.

These compromises were also made in the interest of curtailing food costs. Many people point to the overall expense of living as an Orthodox Jew and wonder whether it is sustainable. Not requiring the special milk keeps the price of milk and milk products lower than it would be, and the new Ashkenazic *glatt* standard is also less expensive than the traditional and more demanding Sephardic and Hungarian *glatt* requirements. A trade-off has been made with kosher meat, surrendering better animal treatment in favor of lower cost. Much of kosher meat production has been moved to Central and South America, where labor costs are lower and the preslaughter animal handling is less humane than permitted by US regulations.

EFFORTS TO SUSTAIN KOSHER FOOD
RESOURCES DURING THE COVID PANDEMIC

The Pico-Robertson Orthodox community's efforts beginning in March 2020 to sustain the local institutions that provided kosher food during the COVID-19 pandemic testify to just how crucial the shared commitment to maintaining these local resources and institutions is to the well-being of the community. At the time of year when Orthodox Jews are most focused on buying and preparing meals and when food businesses make their highest sales, COVID-19 virus began to spread throughout the Los Angeles County population.[2] It was the beginning of March 2020, and Orthodox Jews had already made and accepted invitations to the hours-long, intricate family Seder meals held on the first two nights of the eight-day Passover holiday that would begin six weeks later.

The Orthodox communities in Pico-Robertson were unified in taking very seriously the warnings of doctors and public health specialists. The first cases among the Orthodox appeared in the Beverly–La Brea neighborhood at the end of February. At the beginning of March a wide array of Los Angeles Orthodox rabbis began announcing and publishing warnings against too close contact. Fear of infection already had a major impact on Pico-Robertson street life and kosher food businesses by the second week in March. The Orthodox Union national board organized online teaching sessions devoted to ways to prevent infection and to continue functioning as schools and synagogues. The rabbinic chaplain at the local hospital had worked in a Pico-Orthodox synagogue and had maintained close ties with rabbis of all Jewish denominations. He was "at the vanguard" of those educating the Orthodox about the virus, a *rebbetzin* told me. The rabbis of three large congregations in Pico-Robertson issued a joint statement announcing the closure of their synagogues on Friday afternoon, March 13, and they forbade private quorums for prayer because of the danger of social contact.[3]

In the third week of March, Los Angeles's mayor prohibited dine-in service in all restaurants and eateries. To stop panic buying and hoarding, he held a press conference with leaders of regional grocery stores to assure the city that the food supply chains were intact and that the grocery shelves would remain stocked if people would purchase at their regular rate. For Orthodox Jews, the largest concern was kosher meat. Although the West Coast kosher meat distributor published reassurances that kosher meat production was safe and plentiful, people were still stockpiling it. In contrast, bakeries, restaurants, fast-food eateries, and caterers had too much stock. Restaurants and catering businesses contacted their regular customers, but many were afraid of takeout and delivery.[4] When holiday programs were cancelled and people changed their travel plans and prepared to hunker down in their own houses without guests and without the benefit of dishes prepared by the local trade, wholesale sales plummeted. A public Facebook page called "People supporting kosher restaurants, caterers + event planners in crisis" appeared, describing its mission as follows:

> This group is for us to come together NOW to help our local Kosher restaurants, caterers, chefs, event planners, photographers, videographers, DJ's, musicians, and others facing a real crisis. Let's support these local businesses, so that they are still around after the Pandemic is over. Some ways to support: Buy gift cards, Order Shabbat takeout, Order and freeze food, Order holiday meals, Order birthday meals, Sponsor meals for needy, Sponsor meals for frontline workers. Order for you, your friends, neighbor or elderly friends or relatives. There are so many ways that we can help.[5]

A similar message was issued by the Rabbinic Council of California and was republished in synagogue e-newsletters, and kosher food businesses needing patronage were highlighted. By the end of the next week, no schools remained open, and the streets were empty except for people entering and exiting grocery stores and pharmacies. Retail stores, salons, and nonessential businesses closed. Home hospitality came to a halt.

The practice of feeding the poor changed. The usual population of needy who appeared at daily prayer services or stood outside food businesses or along the sidewalks asking for cash, grocery gift cards, and gifts of food were without these resources. Rabbis and laypeople spread the word to each other about how to supply ready-made food or funds to needy congregational members. During the weeks before *Pesaḥ* (Passover), rabbis and Tomchei Shabbos, the city-wide Orthodox food charity, reminded the community to contribute *maʾot ḥittim*, literally, "wheat money"—that is, donations made according to the command-ment to provide funds so that needy Jews would have the essential provisions for the holiday. Tomchei Shabbos announced that the num-ber of food recipients had grown and that its administrators—not the public—would henceforth be assembling household food packages.

In 2021, Pico-Robertson street life gradually revived. Retail stores selling nonessential goods and nonkosher food businesses were the most common of the permanent casualties of the pandemic. Yet virtually all the kosher restaurants and fast-food eateries remained in business. Side-walk, back lot, and parking lot "patio dining" structures remained in place but improved in appearance after the worst of the pandemic was over. While some kosher eateries survived because they expanded their food delivery to parts of Los Angeles without local kosher options, others stayed in business because of loans or outright gifts. The Pico-Robertson Orthodox groups had come together as a unified community and suc-ceeded in protecting their kosher resources and institutions that sustain the Orthodox neighborhood.

ORTHODOXY AND FOOD ETHICS

Attitudes among the Orthodox toward food ethics are markedly different from those of Reform, Conservative, and secular food activists. Ortho-dox rabbis struggling to deal with the claims of evolutionary theory argue that morality is dependent upon the belief that humans are supe-rior to animals. In response to the increased popularity of animal welfare advocacy and state regulation of meat production, they have had to con-tinually defend and protect the legality of kosher animal slaughter. Some go so far as to argue that humane animal welfare activism and ethical vegetarianism lead to immorality and antisemitism. The Modern Orthodox Jews most favorable to secular culture distinguish themselves from all the others by their favorable attitude toward ethical vegetarianism.

What most surprised me during my research was the lack of response to the internal critique by some in the community of the disregard for ethics in the practice of *kashrut*. It is likely that this disregard stood out for me because I am a vegetarian. One of the initial questions I asked in interviews dealt with the role of ethics in the community's foodways: "Do ethics and morality figure in your understanding of why the dietary laws look the way they do?" This is a crucial question. The Orthodox themselves would say no; the rationale is not ethical; rather, it is a *ḥok*, a law that is followed and not questioned.[6]

The use of ethical reasoning to explain and defend *halakhah* is compelling to non-Jews and to liberal Jews. The moral elements of religion matter far more to them than the ritual elements. As discussed in chapter 4, this difference between the non-Orthodox and the Orthodox Jews explains why Orthodox rabbis and teachers do not reference the word *ethics* even while discussing matters of good and evil; it is a term from the vocabulary of Conservative and Reform Judaism. Orthodox "Torah ethics" lead to far different conclusions from secular ethics and those of liberal Jews, as shown by the Orthodox moral arguments in favor of a carnivorous versus a vegetarian diet. Orthodox rabbis and teachers have marshaled many arguments in favor of a type of religious faith that is not based on ethics or reason. This disparagement of an appeal to reason renders young adherents to Orthodoxy unable to discuss their religious practice using contemporary American society's mode of discourse. From what I observed and heard, the curriculum they are taught does not include anything to do with *ta'amei hamitzvot*, the reasons given to do the *mitzvot*. A rabbi in the Mishnah advises, "Know how to respond to a heretic," and consequently one might think that a responsible parent would want his or her more mature children to learn how to explain matters that society regards as ethically charged. Instead, specialists take on that task. Criticism from within and from outsiders is countered by the charge that the accuser is a rebel or an anti-Semite.

With increased attention to the ethics of how food is sourced wide-spread today in secular society and among Conservative, Reform, and Reconstructionist Jews, Orthodox society may be handicapped by its exclusive appeal to tradition and religious authority. It might cut itself off from potential defenders. I wonder what impact not identifying ethical concerns in response to questions about them might have on the growth of the Orthodox community. This problem is evident in the adults who go "off the *derekh*" (leave the path) because they witness ethical lapses within the community that are excused and swept over. That ethics was such a sensitive topic suggested to me that there was an awareness of the problem. On the other hand, perhaps it is the inscrutability of the commandments related to *kashrut* that enables the following of these commandments to weather cultural changes over time in ways that culturally influenced ethical concerns could not.

ORTHODOX FOODWAYS AND INSIGHTS FROM THE FIELD OF BIOLOGY

One way I came to understand Orthodox foodways during the course of my research was through insights from the field of biology, especially what it teaches about "growth from within" and species preservation. My approach of "thinking with" biology is perhaps unique for illustrating Orthodox foodways. Biology, with its focus on food and the theme of adaptation and evolution, provides a helpful way of understanding how religious Jews, with their distinctive foodways, have adapted together under changing conditions for so many years. In biology, an animal species is defined as a group that can interbreed and produce fertile offspring. For example, horses and donkeys are separate species, and when they breed within their groups, they produce fertile offspring identical to themselves. However, when they interbreed, their offspring, a mule, is sterile. Every animal species has adapted to its physical environment to find ways of obtaining food so that its young grow to maturity and reproduce the original species. Animals do not consciously decide to follow these methods; they are merely following their impulses and learned behaviors.

The human species is exceptional because humans may augment their natural strategies of reproduction with conscious decision-making and strategic alterations in behavior. Furthermore, unlike nonhumans, one reason that human groups desire to bear offspring is to perpetuate their culture, that is, to ensure that their religious teachings, ideals, and artistic expressions are carried on by the next generation. Jews have regarded themselves as "a nation apart," a separate nation devoted to God and His Torah. They believe that marrying within and not outside their group ensures that their offspring will be wholehearted devotees who, in turn, will produce the next generation of wholehearted devotees. Orthodox Jews who marry outsiders are likely to raise offspring who are not Orthodox, that is, children who are "sterile" in a cultural sense. Orthodox foodways promote the social insularity essential to the survival of the group. The dietary and commensal rules help them grow, protect, and perpetuate their culture while permitting a degree of individuation within the bounds of the larger collective.

Devoutly religious people may take umbrage at explanations such as this, which highlight the ways that religions preserve and strengthen the collective. After all, Orthodox Jews typically regard their religion as divinely revealed and true in and of itself, irrespective of its ability to sustain and reproduce the group over time. Yet, Orthodox Jews have no difficulty admitting that the dietary rules are designed to keep them distinct from others, to strengthen their community, and to ensure that their children marry other Orthodox Jews. Orthodox Jews today feel privileged to be singled out to fulfill God's commandments. They believe the laws of the Torah—which require them to adhere to numerous, detailed rules for preparing and eating food, to recite food blessings, to experience the pleasures of eating and of eating together, to invite selected guests to their tables, and to provide food for the poor—make them into moral, contented, and loving human beings. They appreciate that God had the wisdom to mandate foodways that would ensure the survival of a separate *am kadosh*, a holy nation.

Glossary

Unless otherwise noted, italicized terms are in Hebrew. An asterisk signifies an Ashkenazic pronunciation of the Hebrew.

ahavat Hashem (*ahavas Hashem**)	Love of God.
Ashkenazi (*Ashkenazim*, pl.)	A person who is of Ashkenazic background.
Ashkenazic	Signifying the German or Eastern European (although not Spanish or Italian) background of a person or religious or cultural practice.
ba'al teshuvah (*ba'alei teshuvah*, pl.)	Literally, "master of repentance"; newly religious; a Jew who was raised in a non-Orthodox family and adopts Orthodoxy as a teenager or adult.
berakhah (*berakhot* or *berakhos**, pl.)	The formulaic blessing recited prior to eating a food, said before performing a ritual act, or mandated for other experiences.
bishul akum	The cooking by non-Jews.
bishul yisra'el	The cooking by Jews.
Centrist Orthodox	American Orthodox Jews who espouse a faithful adherence to strict *halakhah* while selectively and cautiously participating in secular academic learning, entertainment, and the arts.

Chabad or Lubavitch	A Hasidic group that originated in Belarus and eventually associated with the town of Lyubavichi. Chabad is an acronym for the group's ideals of (in Hebrew) wisdom, understanding, and knowledge. Chabad was led by rebbes until the death of the last, seventh Chabad rebbe, Menachem Mendel Schneerson, in 1994, whom Chabad Jews refer to as "the Rebbe."
Chassid (see Hasid)	
Chassidus* (see Hasidus)	
cholent	Stew made from beef and beans and often potatoes.
commensal laws, commensality	Commensal laws dictate with whom one may eat; typically, they restrict eating partners to other members of one's community. Commensality refers to the act of eating together at the same table.
Conservative Judaism	A modern denomination of Judaism that affirms the authority of *halakhah* as defined by Conservative rabbis.
ever min haḥai	Literally, "a limb from a living animal"; refers to the prohibition against eating an animal's flesh or body part while the animal is still alive.
emunah	Belief; faith.
frum (Yiddish)	Orthodox; religious.
gemilut ḥasadim	Acts of lovingkindness, such as helping the poor and showing hospitality; such acts may be obligatory commandments.
glatt (Yiddish)	A standard of kosher meat in which the mammal's lungs have been found to be smooth; colloquially, strictly kosher.
hakhnasat orḥim	Bringing guests into the household; hospitality.
halakhah (halakhic, adj.)	Practical religious law.

ḥalav yisraʾel	Milk that is assured through kosher super-vision to be entirely the product of a kosher mammal that was milked under Jewish supervision.
Hashem	Literally, "the name"; a respectful way of referring to God.
hashgaḥah	Kosher supervision; the symbol on a food label or certificate on a food establishment testifying that the food has been inspected and certified as kosher.
hashkafah	Religious outlook.
Hasidism, Hasid (Hasidim, pl.)	A form of modern Judaism, originating in the late eighteenth century in Eastern Europe, originally organized under the leadership of a rebbe (rabbi) associated with an Eastern European town and later under his dynastic successors. The religious style is emotional and ecstatic, and the theology is heavily dependent upon the mystical Jewish teachings known as Kabbalah.
Ḥasidus* (*Ḥasidut*)	Religious teachings, including stories written by and about past rebbes, associated with Hasidism.
hekhsher	Kosher certification.
ḥilul	Desecration.
ḥok (*ḥukim*, pl.)	Decree; a divine law of unfathomable meaning.
ḥumrah (*ḥumrot*, pl.)	A practice that goes beyond the require-ments of the law.
Kabbalah	Received tradition; more often a collective term for Judaism's mystical teachings. These have been incorporated into present-day legal traditions of Hasidim and non-Hasidic *Ashkenazim* (e.g., those of the school of the Vilna Gaon).
kadosh	Holy.

kashrut (kashrus*)	Literally, "fit" or "proper"; the collective term for the laws designating which animal species are permissible for eating, how foods should be prepared, and how they may be combined in accordance with Jewish law.
kelim	Dishware and utensils.
kiddush	Literally, "sanctification"; the blessing over wine; also, the repast after worship.
kiruv	Literally, "bringing near"; the effort to bring non-Orthodox Jews into a life of Orthodoxy or, minimally, to the practice of Jewish ritual.
kollel	A small group of married men, advanced in Talmudic knowledge, subsidized by the community to engage in full-time Talmud study.
korban pesaḥ	Passover sacrifice.
kosher	Proper; fit to eat according to the laws of *kashrut*.
Litvish (Yiddish)	Literally, "Lithuanian"; used to describe a style of Orthodoxy, non-Hasidic, associated with the Lithuanian-style yeshiva.
maʿaser	Tenth; referring to the proportion donated to the priest and the poor.
mashgiaḥ	Inspector of kosher food.
meḥitzah	Room divider between the men's and women's sections in a synagogue or makeshift prayer area.
mesirat nefesh, mesiras nefesh*	Self-sacrifice.
mesorah	In Jewish law, an ancestral tradition that is obligatory for Jews who stemmed from that region or are longtime residents in that region; a tradition passed down by a particular rabbi that is honored by his followers.
mevushal	Literally, "cooked"; referring to wine that is boiled as part of its production process.

mikvah (also: *mikveh*)	Pool of pure water (as defined by Jewish law) for immersion of women seven days after the end of their menstrual period or for immersion of newly purchased kitchenware made by non-Jews. Men may immerse for spiritual reasons, and immersion is mandatory during conversion to Judaism.
minhag	Custom; some customs are given the status of law; that is, they are obligatory.
minyan (*minyanim*, pl.)	Prayer group, or quorum, of ten men.
Mishnah	The first code of Jewish law, completed circa 200 CE and included in the Jerusalem Talmud and Babylonian Talmud, which purports to be a written recording of the laws received orally at the revelation at Mount Sinai and the authorities of later generations of prophets, sages, and rabbis.
mitzvah (*mitzvot* or *mitzvos**, pl.)	A single religious law or mandated religious deed.
Modern Orthodox	A designation for American Orthodox Jews who espouse a faithful adherence to pluralism, while participating in secular academic learning, entertainment, and the arts. More so than Centrist Orthodox, they believe that a balance between American and Torah values is possible.
nikkur	The act of removing the sciatic nerve of an animal to make it kosher.
off the *derekh*	Rejecting the Orthodox way of life.
pareve	Neutral, that is, a food that is not meat, fowl, or containing milk.
pat yisra'el (*pas yisra'el**)	Bread made by Jews.
posek (*poskim*, pl.)	A rabbi who specializes in making decisions about practical law.
pushke (Yiddish)	Collection box for coin donations.
Rashi	The most widely accepted medieval Bible and Talmud commentator.

rebbe (Yiddish)	Hasidic rabbinic leader.
rebbetzin (Yiddish)	Wife of a rabbi, who may have the role of a teacher or counselor.
Reform Judaism	A modern denomination of Judaism that affirms as obligatory only ethical components of *halakhah*.
Sephardic	Adjective signifying the Iberian origin of a religious or cultural practice or a person with ancestral background in medieval Iberia or (less literally) in the Middle East.
sheḥitah, shoḥet	The term for kosher animal slaughter, conducted by a licensed *shoḥet*.
shul (Yiddish)	Synagogue.
Shulḥan arukh	The code of Jewish law first published in 1563 and currently considered authoritative by all Orthodox Jews.
simḥah	Joyous occasion.
taʾamei hamitzvot	Suggested underlying reasons for or explanations of the commandments.
Talmud	The central text of rabbinic Judaism completed in Palestine circa 400 CE (the Jerusalem Talmud) and a variant version known as the Babylonian Talmud completed in Mesopotamia circa 600 CE. The Babylonian Talmud is the preferred of the two for Torah study and for legal rulings. The Talmud is not a law code but a discussion of laws, legal theory, stories, prayers, and theological speculation. The Talmud consists of the earlier (ca. 200 CE) Hebrew law code called Mishnah and an Aramaic rabbinic commentary.
tikkun	Repair.
tikkun olam	Repair of the world.
timtum halev	Obstructed heart or soul.

Torah	The Pentateuch or the entire Hebrew Bible and its rabbinic interpretations; in its widest denotation, any form of Orthodox learning.
treif (Yiddish)	Not kosher, not proper.
tza'ar ba'alei ḥayyim	The principle that one should not needlessly harm or cause suffering to animals.
tzedakah	Literally, "righteousness"; charity.
tzitzit	The corner fringes on a four-squared under-garment or prayer shawl (*tallit*) mandated by Jewish law for males ages thirteen and older.
yashan	Literally, "old"; refers to wheat and other grains grown in the winter season and har-vested in the spring but not consumed until months later when the spring barley harvest offering would no longer be obligatory.
yashar	Upright, good.
yeshiva	A school at the high school or post–high school level focusing on the study of the Talmud, Jewish law, and Torah commentar-ies, for men only.
Yeshivish	American Orthodox Jews who define them-selves by adherence to the rulings of promi-nent yeshiva-associated rabbinic authorities.
Yiddishkeit	Jewishness.
yir'at shamayim, yir'as shamayim	Fear of God; reverence for God.
zekhus	Merit.
zemirot	Sabbath and festival table songs.

Notes

PREFACE

1 Pew Research Center, "Jewish Americans in 2020," May 11, 2021, https://www.pewforum.org/2021/05/11/jewish-americans-in-2020/.

2 Jody Myers, *Kabbalah and the Spiritual Quest: The Kabbalah Centre in America* (Westport, CT: Praeger, 2007).

3 Aaron S. Gross, Jody Myers, and Jordan D. Rosenblum, eds., *Feasting and Fasting: The History and Ethics of Jewish Food* (New York: New York University Press, 2019).

4 OU Kosher Staff, "Playing with Fire," May 4, 2004, Orthodox Union Kosher, https://oukosher.org/blog/consumer-kosher/playing-with-fire.

5 David Hall, ed., *Lived Religion in America: Toward a History of Practice* (Princeton: Princeton University Press, 1997). In addition to Hall's introduction, vii–xiii, in the same volume see Robert Orsi's article, "Everyday Miracles: The Study of Lived Religion," 3–21, which illuminates the methodology with examples and reflections from his own experiences in the field. See also Kim Knibbe and Helena Kupari, "Theorizing Lived Religion: Introduction," *Journal of Contemporary Religion* 35.2 (2020): 157–76, for an overview of the emergence of the field since 1997 and the various approaches that scholars have taken for conceptualizing and studying lived religion. That the *Journal of Contemporary Religion* would devote an entire issue to this field signifies its importance among scholars of religion as well as sociology.

6 Hall, *Lived Religion in America*, ix, viii.

7 Nancy Tatom Ammerman, *Studying Lived Religion: Contexts and Practices* (New York: New York University Press, 2021), 8, 5, 211. The multidimensionality of lived religion—involving embodiment, materiality, emotion, aesthetics, moral judgment, and narrative—requires that

researchers employ a variety of methods for studying it. Ammerman also emphasizes the importance of looking at the historical contexts that shape religious practice.

8 Ammerman, *Studying Lived Religion*, 113, 81, 21.

CHAPTER 1

1 See also Scott Garner, "Neighborhood Spotlight: Pico-Robertson an Evolving Hub of Jewish Culture," *Los Angeles Times*, February 3, 2017, https://www.latimes.com/business/realestate/hot-property/la-fi-hp -neighborhood-spotlight-pico-robertson-20170204-story.html.

2 Rabbi Aryeh Markman, quoted in Shraga Simmons, "Pico-Robertson: Story of a Torah Boomtown," *Ami Magazine*, February 6, 2019.

3 *Halakhah*, Jewish rabbinic law, mandates that married women cover their hair, with either a cloth wrapping like a scarf or snood, hat, or wig. Married women who follow different rabbinic authorities permit some of their hair to show, and some women—like Ruth—will cover their hair only while engaging in worship or other ritual activities.

4 On Elat Market, see Karmel Melamed, "Elat Market . . . Shoppers' Para- dise or Chaotic Madhouse?" *Jewish Journal*, December 14, 2007, https:// jewishjournal.com/uncategorized/16871/elat-market-shoppers-paradise -or-chaotic-madhouse/. See also Jasmine Hanasab and Rebecca Heikaly, "Elat Market," a report within the website created by Saba Soomekh, Ira- nian Jewish Life in Los Angeles: Past and Present, a project of the UCLA Center for Jewish Studies, accessed February 14, 2021, https://scalar.usc .edu/hc/iranian-jews-in-los-angeles/elat-market.

5 Jonah Lowenfeld, "Who Owns Young Israel of Beverly Hills?," *Jewish Journal*, July 7, 2010, https://jewishjournal.com/community/ 81042/.

6 The LINK Kollel website, accessed December 26, 2022, is https://linkla .org/. This community *kollel* also offers courses tailored to women.

7 For the most detailed history of the community kollel in Los Angeles, Kollel Los Angeles Bais Avrohom, see Iddo Tavory, *Summoned: Identifi- cation and Religious Life in a Jewish Neighborhood* (Chicago: University of Chicago Press, 2016), 34–35. Gaby Wenig, "The Kollel Community," *Jewish Journal*, March 7, 2002, https://jewishjournal.com/community/ 5630/, includes comments from the founder of the Los Angeles commu- nity kollel.

8 The fedora, on top of a yarmulke, is the hat of choice for weekday wear among Orthodox men who identify with the strict Orthodoxy of yeshiva rabbinic authorities.

9 The scandal, described in chapter 2, involved a butcher selling kosher meat that was not *glatt* kosher, as he claimed.

10 Since the writing of this book, this branch of Ralphs closed on May 15, 2022. A new wholesale discount grocery superstore, Koshco, opened in fall 2022 at the corner of Pico and Robertson.

11 See Saba Soomekh, *From the Shahs to Los Angeles: Three Generations of Iranian Jewish Women between Religion and Culture* (Albany: State University of New York Press, 2012), 109–11.

12 Soomekh, *From the Shahs*, 2. According to Soomekh, in 2007 there were 30,000–40,000 Iranian Jews in Los Angeles.

13 For the Baltimore initiative, see Ebony Brown, "Hanging on to Heritage," *Baltimore Jewish Times*, May 7, 2015, https://www.jewishtimes.com/hanging-on-to-heritage/. For the Chabad initiative, see Dovid Margolin, "Operation Exodus: The Chabad Effort That Saved 1,800 Iranian Jewish Children," Chabad.org, accessed January 6, 2023, https://www.chabad.org/library/article_cdo/aid/4299265/jewish/Operation-Exodus-The-Chabad-Effort-That-Saved-1800-Iranian-Jewish-Children.htm.

14 See OU Kosher Staff, "Tevilat Keilim: A Primer," Orthodox Union Kosher, April 24, 2007, https://oukosher.org/blog/consumer-kosher/tevilas-keilim-a-primer/; and Aryeh Citron, "Immersion of Vessels (Tevilat Keilim)," Chabad.org, accessed December 24, 2020, https://www.chabad.org/library/article_cdo/aid/1230791/jewish/Immersion-of-Vessels-Tevilat-Keilim.htm. The source is the Babylonian Talmud (hereafter cited as BT) *Avodah zarah* 75b. Conservative movement rabbis do not regard the biblical command as binding.

15 The main *mikvah* in the area is the Los Angeles Mikvah, and it does not permit immersion of dishes.

16 In 2004, the restaurant owner, a Chinese non-Jewish man born in Hong Kong who purchased the business in 1995, sold it to two Persian Jewish businessmen and stayed on as manager. He worked with the Kehilla Kosher certification agency to entirely overhaul the restaurant to be approved for kosher certification. See David Pierson, "Two Worlds at One Table," *Los Angeles Times*, December 24, 2005, https://www.latimes.com/archives/la-xpm-2005-dec-24-me-kosherxmas24-story.html.

17 Deborah Dash Moore's book *To the Golden Cities: Pursuing the American Jewish Dream in Miami and L.A.* (Cambridge, MA: Harvard University Press, 1996) does not deal with the development of this part of Los Angeles and its Orthodox enclave. She focuses on the establishment of Los Angeles Jewish liberal institutions, such as the University of Judaism and the Brandeis-Bardin Institute, and also on Jewish involvement in citywide liberal political activism.

18 These figures are based on the US Decennial Census and are found in "Demographics of Los Angeles County," Wikipedia, accessed February 19, 2021, https://en.wikipedia.org/wiki/Demographics_of_Los _Angeles_County.

19 This figure is based on Bruce Phillips's analysis (unpublished) of the data in the Los Angeles Jewish population survey (Pini Herman, *Los Angeles Jewish Population Survey, 1997*, sponsored by the Jewish Federation of Greater Los Angeles, https://www.jewishdatabank.org/api/download/ ?studyId=345&mediaId=C-CA-Los_Angeles-1997-Report.pdf) and the household data from the 2000 US Census data for zip code 90035 (which covers an area slightly larger than Pico-Robertson, to the northeast). Household density means that for every 1,000 households, 480 are Jewish. According to Phillips, "The 2022 LA Jewish population survey does not include zip codes but does show that the Jewish population of LA increased. Comparing the 1997 LA Jewish population survey figures for the 90035 zip code with the data in the 2019 Jewish Voter Poll (conducted by the Pat Brown Institute for Public Affairs at California State University, Los Angeles) on the heavily Jewish areas of Pico-Robertson, Fairfax Beverlywood, and West Hollywood, combined, shows no changes in the share of Jewish households in these areas. Since the share of Jewish households in the cluster that includes Pico-Robertson remained the same, and the overall Jewish population of LA increased, it is safe to assume that the Jewish population of Pico-Robertson remained stable or possibly even grew between 1997 and 2019. It is important to note that the clientele of the Jewish markets and restaurants in Pico-Robertson comes from the heavily Jewish neighborhoods in the combined clusters represented in the above surveys, not just from Pico-Robertson itself" (email correspondence with Jane Myers, February 3, 2023).

Jane Myers would like to thank Jody Myers's friend and colleague Professor Bruce Phillips for access to his unpublished findings. See also Bruce A. Phillips, "Faultlines: The Seven Socio-Ecologies of Jewish Los Angeles," in Bruce Zuckerman and Jeremy Schoenberg, eds., *The Jewish*

Role in American Life: An Annual Review (West Lafayette, IN: Purdue University Press, 2007), 5:87–88.

20 "California Agricultural Production Statistics," California Department of Agriculture, https://www.cdfa.ca.gov/Statistics/.

21 "Pico-Robertson," "Mapping L.A." project, *Los Angeles Times*, 2009, http://maps.latimes.com/neighborhoods/neighborhood/pico-robertson/.

22 "Stadium Theatre," Los Angeles Theatres blog, accessed February 16, 2021, https://losangelestheatres.blogspot.com/2017/03/stadium-theatre .html. The theater shut down in 1961 and shortly afterward was purchased and refurbished as B'nai David Synagogue, which had been located across the street. A later synagogue merger resulted in the name change to B'nai David-Judea. In its mission statement it designates itself Modern Orthodox; see "Mission," B'nai David-Judea, accessed February 16, 2021, https://www.bnaidavid.com/mission.

23 This is Temple Beth Am. Its founding group first met in an empty market, and in 1937 the first structure was built on La Cienega Boulevard between Pico and Olympic Boulevards. For its history, see "Our History," Temple Beth Am, https://www.tbala.org/about/our-history.

24 A large proportion of Jews departing Los Angeles's urban core settled in the Fairfax district and the area next to it, which today is known as Beverly–La Brea.

25 Rabbi Abraham Maron founded Mogen David in the late 1920s at the western edge of the current Pico-Robertson boundary, near the recently opened Fox Studios; see Julie Gruenbaum-Fax, "Youth Appeal," *Jewish Journal*, December 28, 2000, https://jewishjournal.com/community/ 3720/. On Robertson Boulevard just south of Pico Boulevard, Anshe Emes opened in 1948. On the synagogue's history, see Aaron Gross, "Building Program – Brochure and Dedication Opportunities," Anshe Emes, December 19, 2008, https://anshe.org/building-program-brochure -and-dedication-opportunities/.

26 A description of Jewish residential choices may be found in Bruce A. Phillips, "Not Quite White: The Emergence of Jewish 'Ethnoburbs' in Los Angeles 1920–2010," *American Jewish History* 100.1 (January 2016): 73–104; discussion of the research committee is on pp. 96–98. In the same source (p. 87), the author brings data from a 1959 Los Angeles Jewish Community Council report showing that a Jewish population concentration to the north of Pico-Robertson in Beverly Hills was 53 percent and to the south of Pico-Robertson in Beverlywood–Cheviot Hills–Mar Vista was 27 percent. Marc Lee Raphael, *Diary of a Los*

Angeles Jew, 1947–1973: Autobiography as Autofiction (Williamsburg, VA: Department of Religious Studies, College of William and Mary, 2008), 20–21, vividly describes how the Jewish real estate brokers "relentlessly" pressured his parents to sell their home before, as they claimed, the incoming African Americans made their property worthless.

27 Bruce Phillips, "Los Angeles Jewry: A Demographic Profile," in *American Jewish Yearbook*, vol. 86 (New York: American Jewish Committee, 1986), 136–37.

28 The Beverly–La Brea Orthodox communities are the focus of the socio-logical study by Tavory, *Summoned*.

29 Raphael, *Diary of a Los Angeles Jew*, 22.

30 On the larger revitalization of this area, see Jonathan D. Sarna, *American Judaism: A History* (New Haven: Yale University Press, 2004), 323–24.

31 On the increased adoption of the yarmulke, see Zev Eleff, *Authentically Orthodox: A Tradition-Bound Faith in American Life* (Detroit: Wayne State University Press, 2020), 64–67. The Israeli Ortho-dox who opposed Zionism and were politically opposed to the existence of a secular Jewish state wear black hats and black velvet yarmulkes; American Hasidic and Haredi Jewish men do the same.

32 Alan Cooperman, Gregory Smith, and Becka Alper, "A Portrait of American Orthodox Jews: A Further Analysis of the 2013 Survey of U.S. Jews," Pew Research Center, August 26, 2015, https://www.pewforum .org/2015/08/26/a-portrait-of-american-orthodox-jews/. The family origins data is at https://www.pewforum.org/2015/08/26/a-portrait-of -american-orthodox-jews/#how-were-todays-orthodox-jewish-adults -raised. According to this data, 4 percent of all Orthodox Jews in 2013 were raised not Jewish; that is, they went through conversion to Judaism.

33 According to historian Jeffrey Gurock, Orthodox Judaism "was now pitching a narrower but stronger religious tent. For the first time in American Orthodoxy's history, the pious and punctilious were beginning to outnumber those who were not." See Jeffrey S. Gurock, *Orthodox Jews in America* (Bloomington: Indiana University Press, 2009), 209. This change occurred in major cities throughout the United States.

34 Samuel C. Heilman, *Sliding to the Right: The Contest for the Future of American Jewish Orthodoxy* (Berkeley: University of California Press, 2006), 67–69, cites data from the 2000 National Jewish Population Study showing a 38 percent retention rate in the 2002 data. Bruce Phillips, "American Judaism in the Twenty-First Century," in Dana Evan Kaplan, ed., *The Cambridge Companion to American Judaism* (Cambridge:

Cambridge University Press, 2005), 409, shows that the retention rate for respondents who report being raised in an Orthodox home increases with the age of the respondents' cohort.

35 Rabbi Eli Hecht, "Kiddush Hashem in California," Chabad of South Bay, accessed February 18, 2021, https://www.chabadsb.org/templates/articlecco_cdo/aid/59872/jewish/Kiddish-Hashem-in-California.htm. Tavory, *Summoned*, 30–31, describes a slightly different formation narrative for the Beverly–La Brea Orthodox enclave.

36 One native-born Orthodox Jew points out that many who tell that story were not living in the neighborhood at the time, so their perspective is simply inaccurate. According to him, "There was robust Jewish life in the 1960s. Beth Jacob was a flourishing center. Kids went to Orthodox summer camps and a thriving number of summer programs. B'nai Akiba [an Orthodox youth movement] held group meetings. Hillel Academy [an Orthodox day school] was dedicated in 1964. While it might be true that the proliferation of kosher restaurants dates to the mid-1970s and 80s, the vitality of [Orthodox] Jewish life was obvious."

37 Hecht, "Kiddush Hashem in California."

38 Julie Gruenbaum-Fax, "B'nai David-Judea's Renaissance," *Jewish Journal*, June 11, 1998, accessed September 1, 2020, https://jewishjournal.com/old_stories/944/. See also Gruenbaum-Fax, "Youth Appeal," on the new stricter standards for Mogen David synagogue in the year 2000, where she pithily states, "Mogen David, one of the last Traditional synagogues left in Los Angeles, installed a *meḥitzah* and took out its microphones this month, choosing to become Orthodox rather than defunct."

39 This data is from the "Mapping L.A." project, accessed February 25, 2021, http://maps.latimes.com/neighborhoods/neighborhood/pico-robertson/#housing.

40 Ann Forsyth, "What Is a Walkable Place? The Walkability Debate in Urban Design," *Urban Design International* 20.4 (2015): 274–92.

41 Interview, date not found.

42 For a general overview of the eruv and its maintenance, see Avishai Artsay, "West LA's Eruv, the Hidden Wall Built and Maintained by Orthodox Jews," *KCRW*, March 13, 2018, https://www.kcrw.com/culture/shows/design-and-architecture/west-las-eruv-the-hidden-wall-built-and-maintained-by-orthodox-jews. See also "100 Square Miles of Los Angeles Are Surrounded by a Hidden Religious Wall," *Los Angeles* magazine, March 21, 2017, https://www.lamag.com/citythinkblog/100-square-miles-los-angeles-surrounded-hidden-religious-wall/.

43 Also see "Shabbat Tetzaveh – 5783 – Shabbat Zachor," Los Angeles Community Eruv, which updates the community on whether the integrity of the continuous border is sound, https://www.laeruv.com.

44 Here I am paraphrasing the words of James Borchert, quoted in Grady Clay, *Being a Disquisition Upon the Origins, Natural Disposition, and Occurrences in the American Scene of Alleys, Together with Special Attention Being Given to Some Small Scale and Easily Completed Proposals for Their Improvement in Louisville, Jefferson County, Kentucky, Where They Do Constitute a Hidden Resource* (Louisville: Grady Clay, 1978), 6.

45 This is Livonia Glatt Market. An online video shows its Sunday barbecue: "Livonia Glatt Kosher Market Sunday Kabob Grill Cookout BBQ Los Angeles," YouTube video, June 3, 2012, accessed September 25, 2020, https://www.youtube.com/watch?v=7lLSAQ0TgUk&ab_channel=LivoniaGlattMarket.

46 The *mikvah* may also be used for religious purposes not requiring such privacy, for example, as a spiritual experience for men prior to Sabbaths and holidays, for women about to wed, and during the conversion rite. A woman dealing with infertility, for whom menstruation indicates another month's failure and for whom the *mikvah* visit inaugurates another two weeks of trying to conceive, may not want to be the subject of other people's pity or concern.

47 It is probably not surprising that Orthodox women do not generally regard their separate seating areas and entrances as offensive. I was once present at a Shabbat service when the rabbi announced that the front of the building would soon be rebuilt with a separate women's entrance directly into their prayer section, so they would no longer need to walk past the men. Laughter filled the room when a man called out, "Do we get to vote on this?" The rabbi faced the women and asked if they wanted it. They all called out, "Yes!" He assured them that it would be a double door (an outside door, a space, then an inner door) so that the kids—presumably, their responsibility more than their husbands'—wouldn't run out onto the street.

48 "Mapping L.A." project, accessed February 23, 2021, http://maps.latimes.com/neighborhoods/neighborhood/pico-robertson/.

49 Census data does not provide religious data, so the estimate of Jews is based on the study by Herman, *Los Angeles Jewish Population Survey, 1997.*

50 In 2021, about 20 percent of the units on the streets between Pico and Airdrome and between La Cienega and Robertson were decorated; the percentage was lower on other streets.

51 Bruce Phillips suggests this; see note 19 above.

52 Although the Kabbalah Centre does not designate itself as Jewish, its liturgy and behavioral rules are taken from Jewish tradition and its top leaders are rabbis ordained in Orthodox rabbinic seminaries. The Pico-Robertson Kabbalah Centre has been the headquarters of the movement for decades. See Jody Myers, *Kabbalah and the Spiritual Quest: The Kabbalah Centre in America* (Westport, CT: Praeger, 2007).

53 Interview, August 12, 2010.

54 OU Kosher Staff, "Playing with Fire," May 4, 2004, Orthodox Union Kosher, accessed March 1, 2020, https://oukosher.org/blog/consumer-kosher/playing-with-fire/.

55 Sylvia Barack Fishman, *The Way into the Varieties of Jewishness* (Woodstock, VT: Jewish Lights, 2008), chap. 5, 127–52. The author thanks Zev Eleff for providing this source.

56 David Biale et al., *Hasidism: A New History* (Princeton: Princeton University Press, 2017); Rachel Elior, *The Mystical Origins of Hasidism* (Liverpool: Littman Library, 2008); Moshe Idel, *Hasidism: Between Ecstasy and Magic* (Binghamton: SUNY Press, 1995).

57 Hasidic men's outer clothing is modeled after Eastern European aristocratic styles; see Olga Goldberg-Mulkiewicz, "Dress," *The Yivo Encyclopedia of Jews in Eastern Europe*, trans. from Polish by Christina Manetti, accessed March 4, 2021, https://yivoencyclopedia.org/article.aspx/Dress. It is difficult to identify Chabad women by their dress, since it is virtually the same as that of other Hasidic and Haredi women: high neckline, long sleeves, long skirts, stockinged legs, and covered hair for married women.

58 Jody Myers, "Kabbalah as a Tool of Orthodox Outreach," in Brian Ogren, ed., *Kabbalah in America: Ancient Lore in the New World* (Leiden: Brill, 2020), 343–57.

59 On Hasidism, see most recently, Biale et al., *Hasidism*. On Mitnagdim, see Allan Nadler, *The Faith of the Mithnagdim: Rabbinic Responses to Hasidic Rapture* (Baltimore: Johns Hopkins University Press, 1999).

60 These yeshivas differentiated themselves from the rabbinical seminary associated with Yeshiva University in New York City, which requires completion of a bachelor's degree and previous position in Modern Orthodox congregations. The Lithuanian-style yeshivas do not require college degrees.

61 Yeshivat Maharat is a post-baccalaureate women's academy in New York whose mission is "to educate, ordain and invest in passionate and

committed Orthodox women who model a dynamic Judaism to inspire and support individuals and communities." See Yeshivat Maharat website, accessed March 8, 2021, https://www.yeshivatmaharat.org/mission -and-history. The Rabbinical Council of America, which is the overarching organization of US and Canadian Modern Orthodox rabbis, has declared rabbinic ordination of women to be illegitimate; see Jewish Telegraphic Agency, "Rabbinical Council of America Officially Bans Ordination and Hiring of Women Rabbis," press release, November 1, 2015, https://www.jta.org/2015/11/01/united-states/rabbinical-council-of -america-officially-bans-ordination-and-hiring-of-women-rabbis.

62 Jews as a whole—and this includes Orthodox Jews—are at a higher economic level than the US general public. See Cooperman, Smith, and Alper, "A Portrait of American Orthodox Jews." Fifty-six percent of households earn less than $50,000 per year, and 8 percent earn $150,000 and higher. The 30 percent of Modern Orthodox Jews earning a household income of less than $50,000 is virtually the same as the 31 percent of "other Jews," that is, Conservative, Reform, no denomination, Jews of no religion and Jews who declare themselves "Jews by religion." In the Pew survey, Orthodox Jews self-identified either as Modern Orthodox or Haredi—which would include Hasidic, Yeshivish, and others who rejected the Modern Orthodox designations.

63 A survey of the halakhic sources for this may be found in Aaron Potek, "The Case for Limiting Meat Consumption to Shabbat, Holidays, and Celebrations," in Shmuly Yanklowitz, ed., *Kashrut and Jewish Food Ethics* (Boston: Academic Studies Press, 2019).

64 The pros and cons and halakhic issues connected to home *minyanim* are discussed in the biannual Torah journal published by Adas Torah, *Nitzachon* 6.1 (Fall–Winter 5779): 99–130.

65 Menachem Keren-Kratz, "The Contemporary Study of Orthodoxy: Challenging the One-Dimensional Paradigm," *Tradition* 49.4 (2016): 38, https://www.jstor.org/stable/44737112.

CHAPTER 2

1 As a guide for people who wish to avoid the new grain, Rabbi Yosef Herman (who died in 2019) published a website and periodic, updated bulletins informing people of the current status of grain products and providing an extensive list of permitted grain products based on information he culled from a variety of company reports, government

records, and kosher supervisors. The website is still active and extensive. See http://yoshon.com/, accessed April 30, 2017. See also David Gorelik, "Yoshon," Orthodox Union Kosher consumer blog, October 8, 2015, https://oukosher.org/blog/consumer-kosher/yoshon/.

2 *Kashrus* is the Ashkenazic pronunciation now being used by Orthodox Jews who define themselves as Centrist Orthodox, Haredi, and Hasidic, and Modern Orthodox rabbis are increasingly adopting it. *Kashrut* is the pronunciation used among Jews from Muslim countries and Sephardic Jews, and it was adopted as the standard pronunciation in Modern Hebrew. I will use the latter usage except for actual quotations from interviews and written literature.

3 Before the Common Era, when many of the patriarchal narratives and the legal corpus of the Pentateuch were recorded, the Israelites formed the majority of the population and were politically dominant. Key figures such as Joseph and Moses married non-Israelites. In the later centuries of the biblical period, when political dominance was weakening and violations of religious traditions appeared to stem from encroaching outsiders, commensal rules appeared. Exodus 34:12–17: "Beware of making a covenant with the inhabitants of the land against which you are advancing, lest they be a snare in your midst. . . . You must not make a covenant with the inhabitants of the land, for they will lust after their gods and sacrifice to their gods and invite you, and you will eat of their sacrifices. . . . And when you take wives from among their daughters for your sons, their daughters will lust after their gods and will cause your sons to lust after their gods."

4 BT *Avodah zarah* 31b: "It was stated: For what reason did the Sages prohibit the beer of gentiles? Rami bar Hama says that Rabbi Yitzhak says: It is due to the concern that Jews will befriend gentiles while drinking with them, which might lead to marriage with gentiles." In subsequent passages the marriage concern is also expressed as "because of their daughters." See Jordan D. Rosenblum, *Food and Identity in Early Rabbinic Judaism* (New York: Cambridge University Press, 2010), 92–96, 188.

5 Pew Research Center, "A Portrait of Jewish Americans," October 1, 2013, http://www.pewforum.org/2013/10/01/jewish-american-beliefs-attitudes -culture-survey/. According to the 2013 Pew Research data, 90 percent of all self-declared Orthodox respondents who are married have a Jewish spouse. Among the non-Orthodox the percentage is far less: 73 percent among Conservative Jews, 50 percent among Reform Jews, and 31 percent among the unaffiliated. See "Chapter 2: Intermarriage and Other

Demographics," October 1, 2013, http://www.pewforum.org/2013/10/01/chapter-2-intermarriage-and-other-demographics/.

6 See David Hall, *Lived Religion in America: Toward a History of Practice* (Princeton: Princeton University Press, 1997); Robert Orsi, "Everyday Miracles: The Study of Lived Religion," in Hall, ed., *Lived Religion in America*; and Nancy Tatom Ammerman, *Studying Lived Religion: Contexts and Practices* (New York: New York University Press, 2021).

7 David C. Kraemer, *Jewish Eating and Identity through the Ages* (New York: Routledge, 2009), 45–46, describes a Talmudic discussion between Rabbis Asi, Yohanan, and Hisda in which the conversation about variant opinions results in a more nuanced, common rule that explains the disagreement. In other cases, the rabbis do not arrive at a common rule.

8 The Jerusalem Talmud, completed at the start of the fifth century CE, is less authoritative for subsequent *halakhah*.

9 There are specific Hebrew and Aramaic terms for different kinds of rabbinic rules, such as *gezerah* (decree) or *takanah* (directive). The mere existence of *halakhah*, religious Jewish law, does not mean that it was widely obeyed. At times, rabbinic authors make clear that Jews are not following their guidance. There is still much debate among historians about the extent of actual rabbinic authority, although the consensus now is that rabbinic authority cannot be assumed prior to the seventh century CE, and thereafter widespread compliance varied considerably depending on time and region. See David C. Kraemer, "Food in the Rabbinic Era," in Aaron S. Gross, Jody Myers, and Jordan D. Rosenblum, eds., *Feasting and Fasting: The History and Ethics of Jewish Food* (New York: New York University Press, 2019), 59–61. Orthodox Jews today assume that from the time of the Mishnah until the modern rebellion against tradition in the nineteenth century, Jews respected the rabbis and obeyed *halakhah*.

10 Other regional or ancestral traditions were considered exceptions to these two norms. See the entry "Shulhan Arukh," by Louis I. Rabinowitz, in *Encyclopaedia Judaica* (Jerusalem: Keter, 1971–72), 14:1475–76.

11 The formal determination of *halakhah* is in rabbinic hands, and rabbis are to make decisions in consultation with other rabbis according to majority opinion. The tension between community practice and rabbinic authority is one of the themes developed in Kraemer, *Jewish Eating and Identity*. For his description of how this played out in the medieval era, see 117–20.

12   The most often cited proofs are "the *minhag* of our fathers is [equivalent to] Torah" (BT *Menakhot* 20b) and "*minhag* overrules law" Mishnah (hereafter m. for a particular mishnah) (*Bava metzia* 7:1). The relationship between custom and law has been discussed in rabbinic scholarship over centuries.

13   Karen Barrow, "More People Choosing Kosher for Health," Well blog, *New York Times*, April 13, 2010, https://archive.nytimes.com/well.blogs .nytimes.com/2010/04/13/more-people-choosing-kosher-for-health/.

14   Some of the more persuasive arguments are summarized by Chaim I. Waxman, *Social Change and Halakhic Evolution in American Orthodoxy* (Liverpool: Littman Library of Jewish Civilization, 2017), 89–104.

15   Elaine Adler Goodfriend, "Food in the Biblical Era," in Gross, Myers, and Rosenblum, eds., *Feasting and Fasting*, 40–45, summarizes some theories explaining the ancient preferences.

16   Daniel M. T. Fessler and Carlos David Navarrete, "Meat Is Good to Taboo: Dietary Proscriptions as a Product of the Interaction of Psychological Mechanisms and Social Processes," in *Journal of Cognition and Culture* 3.1 (2003): 1–40. The authors include a summary of other explanations they do not find convincing.

17   The lists of species are found in Leviticus 11 and Deuteronomy 14. Rabbinic lists included more species, derived by inference from the principle that permitted mammals are cloven-hoofed ruminants. For a full discussion of this developmental process, see Jordan R. Rosenblum, *The Jewish Dietary Laws in the Ancient World* (Cambridge: Cambridge University Press, 2016), especially 9–12, 116–33.

18   Birds are discussed in m. Ḥullin 3:6 and in BT Ḥullin 59a and following. The rabbis attempted to eliminate guesswork by listing four characteristics of permitted birds: they may not be predators, they have an extra talon, and their innards include a crop and a gizzard that (after slaughter) can be peeled off. However, they did not agree about what makes a bird a predator, hence the reversion to a *mesorah* (regional tradition): BT Ḥullin 63b, "A [kosher] bird may be eaten based on a *mesorah*."

19   For a variety of opinions on the turkey, see Rabbi Ari Z. Zivotovsky, "Is Turkey Kosher?," Kashrut.com, accessed March 5, 2017, http://www .kashrut.com/articles/turk_part5/. For a video lecture on this subject from the perspective of the avian specialist of the Orthodox Union, see "Megillat Esther in Depth," Orthodox Union, accessed February 23, 2018, https://www.ou.org/torah/kashrut/halakhah/the_turkey_kashrus

_with_all_the_stuffings_-_video/. See also Rosenblum, *Jewish Dietary Laws in the Ancient World*, 13, 16n.

20 This restaurant, Mexikosher, closed in 2018. Mexican-style foods, such as tacos, can be found on the menu of Los Angeles kosher restaurants, fast-food eateries, and kosher food trucks.

21 Significantly, an article on this appears on the Chabad website, which engages extensively in outreach to the non-Orthodox; see Yehuda Shurpin, "Are Imitation Crab, Pork, and Cheeseburgers Kosher?," Chabad .org, accessed February 1, 2018, http://www.chabad.org/library/article _cdo/aid/3907949/jewish/Are-Imitation-Crab-Pork-and-Cheeseburgers -Kosher.htm.

22 The rabbis of the Talmud lived after the destruction of the Jerusalem Temple and the cessation of its priest-administered sacrificial rites, although they expected these both would be restored one day.

23 There are many biblical references to different types of tithes; for example, see Exodus 25 and Numbers 18. Leviticus 23:14 is a source for the prohibition related to the *omer* offering.

24 The law against eating newly harvested grains until the offering of the *omer* sacrifice was transformed into the requirement to eat only old, *yashan*, grains for certain months of the year.

25 Each certifying agency has a rabbi or committee of rabbis who determines the policy for that agency, for example, regarding whether it will confirm as kosher produce from Israel during a sabbatical year. See the various approaches described in the website of the largest US kosher-certifying agency, Orthodox Union Kosher: Rabbi David Bistricer, "Practical Shemittah," accessed April 2, 2017, https://oukosher.org/ publications/practical-shemittah/.

26 For the formula, see "Separating Terumah and Maaser," Orthodox Union Kosher, accessed September 3, 2020, https://oukosher.org/blog/consumer -kosher/separating-terumah-and-maaser/.

27 This exhortation to transcend one's animal nature is a common religious theme seen in many religious systems and is part of what Aaron Gross calls the animal/human binary; see Aaron S. Gross, "Introduction and Overview," in Aaron Gross and Anne Vallely, eds., *Animals and the Human Imagination: A Companion to Animal Studies* (New York: Columbia University Press, 2015), 13–15. The term "animal/human binary" recurs throughout the book as a central underlying concept.

28 Contemporary Jews inclined toward an ethical approach to the dietary laws interpret this requirement as a deliberate strategy to promote animal

welfare, but concern for the animal is not stated explicitly in the sacrificial laws or in the rules for nonsacrificial eating.

29 The Chabad.org translation of Deuteronomy 14:21 is "You shall not eat any carcass. You may give it to the stranger who is in your cities, that he may eat it, or you may sell it to a foreigner; for you are a holy people to the Lord, your God."

30 The prohibition in Genesis 9:6 that is attributed to God at the restart of human history after the great flood appears to apply to all descendants of Noah: "Every creature that lives shall be yours to live. . . . You shall not, however, eat flesh with its life-blood in it." According to Leviticus 17:3–4 and 17:10–14, the person who violates this taboo assumes "blood-guilt" and will be cut off from his kin. See also Leviticus 7:26–27. See Jacob Milgrom, *Leviticus 1–16*, Anchor Yale Bible Commentaries (New Haven: Yale University Press, 1998), 1470. While one can certainly interpret the blood prohibition as teaching reverence for life and as a symbolic statement of other ethical principles, it can also be understood as an inexplicable decree or an ethically neutral ritual principle. Biblical texts permit hunting, a mode of killing that certainly does not always offer the opportunity for halakhically mandated slaughtering (e.g., Leviticus 17:33). When hunting for food, the animal's blood must be poured into the ground. In the postbiblical era, rabbis nearly abolished the permissibility of hunting through additional regulations.

31 On the connection between the blood prohibition and *sheḥitah*, see Milgrom, *Leviticus 1–16*, 716. The mode of slaughter for sacrificial offerings described uses the verb *shaḥat*, a word that implies slitting the throat. Because the Bible's discussion of nonsacrificial meat slaughtering likewise requires draining the blood, it has been presumed that the latter was modeled on the former.

32 The most cited medieval sources for the rationale are the commentary of Nahmanides (Moses ben Nahman, 1194–1270) on Genesis 1:29 and the anonymous author of the thirteenth-century book *Sefer haḥinukh* on commandment number 451. See chapter 3.

33 This debate is presented in chapter 4.

34 See David M. Freidenreich, *Foreigners and Their Food: Constructing Otherness in Jewish, Christian, and Islamic Law* (Berkeley: University of California Press, 2011), chaps. 2 and 3. He points out that the exclusion is not specified in the Hebrew Bible and that Leviticus 17:3–9 permits "strangers" within the land to slaughter animals and contribute a portion to the priests. The exclusionary principle is first expressed in rabbinic

legal texts composed around the time of the Mishnah (ca. 200 CE) and continues to be a key element of rabbinic law thereafter.

35 On women as slaughterers in Italy, see Robert Bonfil, *Jewish Life in Renaissance Italy*, trans. Anthony Oldcorn (Berkeley: University of California Press, 1994), 132–33. On more recent Italian history, see Kate Cohen, *The Neppi Modona Diaries: Reading Jewish Survival through My Italian Family* (Hanover, NH: University Press of New England, 1997), 90.

36 Deeming animals slaughtered by non-Jews as carrion, even if the other rules for *shehitah* are followed, appears in the Tosefta tractate *Shehitat hullin* 1:1 and following. See Freidenreich, *Foreigners and Their Food*, 49–51; see also Jordan D. Rosenblum, *Food and Identity*, 77–79. The best overview of modern kosher meat production is Roger Horowitz, *Kosher USA: How Coke Became Kosher and Other Tales of Modern Food* (New York: Columbia University Press, 2016), chaps. 7 and 8.

37 See Jessica Harlan, "What Are the Differences Between a Forged and Stamped Knife?" The Spruce Eats, accessed March 16, 2017, https://www .thespruce.com/what-is-a-forged-knife-what-is-a-stamped-knife-908924. On the purpose of this innovation as a vehicle for social separatism, see Chone Szmeruk, "The Social Implications of Hasidic Slaughter" [in Hebrew], *Zion* 20 (1955): 47–72. His findings are summarized in Jacob Katz, *Tradition and Crisis: Jewish Society at the End of the Middle Ages*, rev. ed. (Syracuse, NY: Syracuse University Press, 2000), 208 and n15.

38 Interview, May 23, 2017.

39 Sue Fishkoff, *Kosher Nation: Why More and More of America's Food Answers to a Higher Authority* (New York: Schocken Books, 2010), 165–66, discusses the marketing issue today.

40 The Hebrew term for such adhesions is *sirhot* (*sirhah*, singular). Adhesions on the lungs are scar tissue, perhaps indicating past disease or healing of lung puncture wounds likely caused by the animal swallowing objects such as stones and sticks. The leniency was applied to cattle and buffalo but not to lambs, goats, and deer, which are required to have smooth lungs.

41 Today's American Ashkenazic *glatt* rules permit a few adhesions on the lungs as long as they are soft and can be easily removed without perforating the lung. See Horowitz, *Kosher USA*, 167–68, 182–91, 198–99, for a more detailed version of the *glatt* distinction and its application in American kosher meat production. One major non-*glatt* kosher company is Hebrew National, which produces hot dogs. On its kosher policies, see

Kenneth Lasson, "Holy Wars and Hot Dogs," *Jerusalem Post*, April 20, 2016, http://www.jpost.com/Opinion/Holy-wars-and-hot-dogs-451871. Many Orthodox sources point to Hebrew National's unreliability in obeying kosher regulations as the reason for its lack of acceptance among Orthodox Jews. On the difficulty of purchasing non-*glatt* meat, see Nathaniel Popper, "Lack of Meat Choices Not Kosher, Say Conservative Shuls in St. Paul," *Forward*, July 21, 2006, http://forward.com/news/478/lack-of-meat-choices-not-kosher-say-conservative/. In Israel, non-*glatt* beef is readily available and is not regarded negatively.

42 The high rate of cattle found to have adhesions is stated in Y. H. Hui, ed., *Handbook of Meat and Meat Processing*, 2nd ed. (Boca Raton, FL: CRC Press, 2012), 425. The business owner purchases the animals and pays the expenses for the *sheḥitah*, but the disqualified beef must be sold at a loss to the nonkosher market. People knowledgeable about the meat business say that cattle raised in feed lots—which became the norm in the United States with industrialized agriculture—have a greater number of blemishes than ones fully grass-fed. This is one reason why many kosher meat companies import meat from South America, where the free-range and grass-fed cattle are more likely to meet the *glatt* standard. Roger Horowitz, email correspondence with author, December 11, 2018.

43 Jonah Lowenfeld, "Kosher Consumers Reeling after Doheny Scandal," *Jewish Journal*, March 28, 2013, https://jewishjournal.com/mobile_20111212/114764/. A person who unintentionally eats *treif* food is advised to repent in various ways; see the post addressing this by Aron Moss, "I Ate Non-Kosher Food—Now What?" Chabad.org, accessed October 26, 2020, https://www.chabad.org/library/article_cdo/aid/1614932/jewish/I-Ate-Non-Kosher-Food-Now-What.htm.

44 See Dovid Cohen, "Doing Business Involving Non-Kosher Food," Chicago Rabbinical Council, January 2008, accessed April 4, 2017, http://www.crcweb.org/kosher_articles/business_involving_non_kosher.php.

45 In Poland during the late 1920s, when antisemitic legislation forbade the selling of meat produced by kosher slaughterers to non-Jews, the rabbinic leaders in the city of Lodz began once again training kosher slaughterers in the removal of the thigh nerve, so as not to waste the meat. See Antony Polonsky, *The Jews in Poland and Russia: 1914–2008* (Oxford: Littman Library of Jewish Civilization, 2012), 3:131. For an Orthodox Union history of this matter, see OU Kosher Staff, "What's the Truth About . . . Nikkur Achoraim," Orthodox Union Kosher, accessed April 2, 2017, https://oukosher.org/blog/consumer-kosher/whats-the-truth-about

-nikkur-achoraim/. According to this source, Ashkenazic Jews are pro-hibited from eating the hindquarter cuts, even if *nikkur* was performed, because of the Ashkenazic *mesorah* (tradition). Horowitz, *Kosher USA*, 169–71, describes how collaboration shaped US meat production in the New York area during the interwar era.

46 Interview, August 6, 2018.

47 At a local kosher butcher shop I was advised to find hindquarter meat at Bakar, whose commercial website, Bakarmeats.com, offers such meat at tremendous cost. Bakar's slaughterers are trained in Israel by experts in the Sephardic *sheḥitah* methods, and the rabbinic supervision is likewise Sephardic. The hindquarter cuts are more readily available in Israel.

48 Aaron Gross, *The Question of the Animal and Religion: Theoretical Stakes, Practical Implications* (New York: Columbia University Press, 2015), 176–78. Gross presents much additional information and discussion throughout the book about industrialized slaughterhouses and the especially cruel practices of AgriProcessors, the kosher slaughterhouse and meat processing plant in Postville, Iowa, that was raided on May 12, 2008, by US Immigration and Customs Enforcement.

49 See Horowitz, *Kosher USA*, chap. 7.

50 Personal communication, medium and date unknown.

51 M. *Avodah zarah* 2:6. See Ethan Tucker, "Maintaining Jewish Dis-tinctiveness: The Case of Gentile Foods," Hadar Institute, print and audio file, https://www.hadar.org/torah-resource/maintaining-jewish -distinctiveness-case-gentile-foods.

52 Tucker, "Maintaining Jewish Distinctiveness," 5ff. Tucker relies on the research of Zvi Arie Steinfeld to argue that these two approaches vied for supremacy through the Talmudic period, but by the medieval era the rationale favoring the social approach dominated. Rashi, the medieval Ashkenazic commentator on the Bible and Babylonian Talmud, wrote the following in reference to the expression of this in BT *Avodah zarah* 35b: "[Prohibited is] everything that idol worshipers cook, even if all the vessels are pure. It is all because of marriage."

53 OU Kosher Staff, "Playing with Fire," Orthodox Union Kosher, May 4, 2004, https://oukosher.org/blog/consumer-kosher/playing-with-fire/. See also the explanation from the Star-K kosher certification agency, which gives broader reasons: Rabbi Moshe Heinemann, "Food Fit for a King: Reviewing the Laws of Bishul Akum & Bishul Yisroel," Star-K, accessed December 18, 2018, https://www.star-k.org/articles/articles/1182/food-fit -for-a-king-reviewing-the-laws-of-bishul-akum-bishul-yisroel/.

54 Rabbi Yitzchak (Kenneth) Kaufman shared a different perspective on this issue, introduced to him by Rabbi Yitzchok Adlerstein, of eating food prepared by non-Jews and eating with them: "I do not see the rabbinic restrictions regarding consumption of some foods made or handled by non-Jews that would otherwise be kosher as a tool to *prevent* fraternization between Jews and non-Jews, but as a tool to remind Jews, when they do socialize with non-Jews, to avoid assimilation and intermarriage to maintain their distinctiveness as a people in order to fulfill their G-d-assigned and nationally accepted responsibilities. I know of no halakhic source that prohibits Jews from eating together socially with non-Jews if the food meets Torah and rabbinic standards of kashrut." Rabbi Yitzchak Kaufman, email correspondence with author, April 6, 2022. The author thanks Rabbi Kaufman for providing this information and perspective.

55 M. *Avodah zarah* 35 declares that milk bought from a non-Jew is kosher only if a Jew watched him, but no explanation is provided. See Alfred S. Cohen, "Chalav Yisrael," *RJJ Journal of Halachah and Contemporary Society* 5 (1983): 92–102, 102–6. Cohen discusses the legal issues in cheese making. Contemporary opinions on this are summarized on the Orthodox Union Kosher website: Rabbi Avrohom Gordimer, "Kosher Cheese," June 13, 2013, accessed January 24, 2018, https://oukosher.org/blog/consumer-kosher/kosher-cheese/. Some hard cheese requires rennet, an enzyme from an animal, and so kosher hard cheese would require rennet from a kosher species. Some rabbis insisted that a Jew merely has to supervise the cheese-making process, whereas some insisted that the Jew would actually need to add the rennet. For soft cheese, some did not require Jewish involvement, while others did.

56 Feinstein, *Igrot Moshe* (New York: M. Feinstein, 1959), *Yoreh de'ah* I:47, II:31.

57 Rosenblum, *Food and Identity*, 75–89, calls the rabbinic requirement that Jews hold top authority the "chef/sous-chef" principle, meaning that the primary authority in the kitchen must be a Jew, whereas the non-Jew is subservient.

58 Interview, January 24, 2013.

59 Interview, August 13, 2012.

60 The requirement applies only when a substantial amount, nearly five pounds, of flour is used.

61 Freidenreich, *Foreigners and Their Food*, 17–26, describes what he calls "the Hebrew Bible's nonchalant attitude toward the food of foreigners." He examines the rabbinic hardening of a Jewish aversion to consuming

gentile foods, already apparent in Hellenistic Jewish literature, on p. 47 and following, and especially with regard to wine, pp. 57–60. On rabbinic rules about wine and other alcoholic and nonalcoholic beverages, see Jordan D. Rosenblum, *Rabbinic Drinking: What Beverages Teach Us about Rabbinic Literature* (Oakland: University of California Press, 2020). For medieval rabbinic rulings on wine, see Kraemer, *Jewish Eating and Identity*, 129–35. See also Haym Soloveitchik, *Jews and the Wine Trade in Medieval Europe: Principles and Pressures* (Liverpool: Littman Library, 2023; Hebrew original: Yaynam [Tel-Aviv: Maggid, 2017]).

62 On the production of kosher wine, see Horowitz, *Kosher USA*, 129–30 and following. See also Sue Fishkoff, *Kosher Nation*, 116–21.

63 During the Talmudic era rabbis permitted the use of the same cooking pot after being cleaned and remaining unused for a time, but during the Middle Ages the preference for entirely different cooking pots and utensils became more pronounced, and this is the current practice. It is still regarded as permissible to use a single oven for cooking meat and milk separately, although careful cleaning between use is considered necessary to avoid contamination from food residue. Orthodox Jews who can afford to have separate ovens are advised to do so. Binyomin Forst, *The Laws of Kashrus*, 2nd ed. (New York: Mesorah Publications, 2010), 356–57, has much to say on the matter.

64 See Exodus 23:19; Exodus 34:26; and Deuteronomy 14:21.

65 Jordan D. Rosenblum, "Why Chicken and Cheese Became Prohibited but Chicken and Egg Remained Permitted," Torah.com, accessed October 26, 2020, https://www.thetorah.com/article/why-chicken-and-cheese -became-prohibited.

66 See m. *Ḥullin* 8:1 and following. Kraemer, *Jewish Eating and Identity*, chap. 4, deals with the history of rabbinic law regarding the no-meat-with-milk rule. Jonathan Brumberg-Kraus points out that the exclusion of fowl is evident in the writings of the Spanish Rabbi Bahye ben Asher (1255–1340), referencing the Italian and his own practice, but in the late sixteenth century *Shulḥan arukh* fowl was included in the prohibition. See Jonathan Brumberg-Kraus, "Food in the Medieval Era," in Gross, Myers, and Rosenblum, eds., *Feasting and Fasting*, 93–95. According to Forst, *The Laws of Kashrus*, 43, the inclusion of fowl is a rabbinic injunction.

67 The meat-fish prohibition is mentioned in BT *Pesaḥim* 76b and in the *Shulḥan arukh, Oraḥ ḥayyim* 173:2. There are ways to honor this

separation, such as using separate pots or dish plates for meat and fish. A Sephardic halakhic tradition to avoid combining fish with milk or milk products was first mentioned in writing in Joseph Caro's law code *Beit Yosef* (1550–59), *Yoreh de'ah* 87. Ashkenazic rabbis have suggested that this was an error and Caro meant to refer to the unhealthy combination of fish and meat.

68 Today most American Orthodox Jews apply the temporal pause after eating dairy only if one has eaten hard cheese.

69 Kraemer, *Jewish Eating and Identity*, 119–21.

70 See chapter 1 for a description of the Keylim Mikvah in Pico-Robertson.

71 Interview, July 8, 2010.

72 Wikipedia, "Milk and Meat in Jewish Law," accessed December 22, 2022, https://en.wikipedia.org/wiki/Milk_and_meat_in_Jewish_law. "The prohibition against deriving benefit, on the other hand, was seen as being more nuanced, with several writers of the late Middle Ages, such as Moses Isserles, Rema 87:1[45], and David ha-Levi Segal (Taz), Yoreh De'ah 87:1, arguing that this restriction only applied to the milk and meat of *g'di* (kid), not to the much wider range of milks and meats prohibited by the rabbis. Other prominent medieval rabbis, like Solomon Luria, Dagul Mervava 87:1, disagreed, believing that the prohibition of deriving benefit referred to mixtures of all meats and milks."

73 Iddo Tavory, *Summoned: Identification and Religious Life in a Jewish Neighborhood* (Chicago: University of Chicago Press, 2016), 89.

74 Horowitz, *Kosher USA*, is the most lucid and evenhanded presentation of the development of kosher certification.

75 See Megan Poinski, "The 'Silent Salesman': How Kosher Certification Went Mainstream," Food Dive, April 13, 2022, Fooddive.com/news/kosher-food-certification-popularity/621865. See also Yuki Takunaga, "The Potential of the Jewish Kosher Certification Market—Synergies Expected to Expand Japanese Product Sales," *Mitsui & Co. Global Strategic Studies Institute Monthly Report*, July 2022, https://www.mitsui.com/mgssi/en/report/detail/__icsFiles/afieldfile/2022/08/15/2207e_tokunaga_e.pdf.

76 Fishkoff, *Kosher Nation*, 47. Although not citing her source, Fishkoff explains that this is due to ingredient-based concerns. Fishkoff's description of what is required by Jewish law is based on the strictest community practices.

77 This is a changing market. During a three-month observation of the Pico-Robertson retail food stores, one of the major certifiers was purchased by a national company and another national company was offering its services to restaurants.

78 See, for example, a forum claiming there is a real difference: "Heimishe Brands vs. Regular," Imamother.com, accessed February 7, 2018, http://www.imamother.com/forum/viewtopic.php?t=25230. For another in the same blog with voices coming to another conclusion, see "High Cost of Chalav Yisrael/Pas Yisrael/Heimish Hechsher," Imamother.com, http://www.imamother.com/forum/viewtopic.php?t=191927. A blog titled "Mi Yodea," which appears to have many male writers, addresses this topic: "Which Kosher Certifications Are Trusted by All?" Stack Exchange, accessed June 17, 2021, https://judaism.stackexchange.com/questions/10807/which-kosher-certifications-are-trusted-by-all.

79 I explore some effects of this loss on Jewish women in Jody Myers, "The Altared Table: Women's Piety and Food in Judaism," in Debra Orenstein and Jane Rachel Litman, eds., *Lifecycles: Jewish Women on Biblical Themes in Contemporary Life* (Woodstock, VT: Festival Lights Press, 1997).

80 Observation chart, "Mapping the Street," prepared by author, January 2018.

81 Kraemer, *Jewish Eating and Identity*, chap. 10, deals with this subject at length. The phrase "the Torah was not given to angels," first articulated in BT *Berakhot* 25b, was meant to remind rabbinic authorities not to establish standards impossible for ordinary human beings to follow. This principle was applied in the nineteenth century in order to reject the suggestion that food should be examined with microscopes to find insects. See the summary of *halakhah, Yoreh de'ah* 84:36, composed by Rabbi Yechiel Michel Epstein (1829–1908), known as *Arukh hashulḥan*, that appears on the Orthodox Union Kosher website: OU Kosher Staff, "Bedikas Tolaim (Checking for Insect Infestation)," January 26, 2005, https://oukosher.org/blog/consumer-kosher/bedikas-tolaim-checking-for-insects.

82 Frimet Blum, "Case Studies: Bodek Kosher Produce—First in the Kosher Vegetable Revolution," Bodek.com, accessed February 11, 2018, http://www.bodek.com/history.htm.

83 See chapter 1 on the grocery stores. The sign in the produce section of Glatt Mart was not present in Elat Market, even though both stores were under RCC certification.

84 Interview, August 13, 2010.

85 Interview, January 28, 2011.

86 Interview, 2017 (specific date not found).

87 M. *Makot* 3:16. This passage is recited at the end of reading a chapter of M. *Avot*, a Sabbath afternoon practice, or at the conclusion of other learning in the synagogue.

88 See note 14 above. For a recent summary of rabbinic views on religious stringency, see Sara Epstein Weinstein, *Piety and Fanaticism: Rabbinic Criticism of Religious Stringency* (Northvale, NJ: Jason Aronson, 1997). Rather than repeat the compelling explanations for the increase in strictness and in standards made by historians and sociologists, my focus here is on the social manifestations of the stricter and diverse *kashrut* practices in the Pico-Robertson neighborhood.

89 Interview, March 20, 2017.

90 Interview, date not found.

91 Interview, July 8, 2010.

92 Interview, date not found.

93 Rabbi Yitzchok Adlerstein, a former local rabbi and teacher, "Chumrah Done Wrong," Cross-Currents, March 20, 2012, https://cross-currents .com/2012/03/20/chumrah-done-wrong/.

94 Maoz Kahana and Ariel Evan Mayse, "Hasidic Halakhah: Reappraising the Interface of Spirit and Law," *AJS Review* 41.2 (November 2017): 384ff., describes how the early Hasidic masters justified the adoption of stringencies for the "common" Hasid, to the chagrin of non-Hasidic rabbis.

95 *Mesirat nefesh* is of central importance to Chabad piety, and women are quite aware of their special ways of actualizing it; see Jody Myers and Jane Rachel Litman, "The Secret of Jewish Femininity: Hiddenness, Power, and Physicality in the Theology of Orthodox Women in the Contemporary World," in T. M. Rudavsky, ed., *Gender and Judaism: The Transformation of Tradition* (New York: New York University Press, 1995), 60–61. On the conflict between Chabad and other Orthodox Jews about Chabad community-held stringencies, see the online essay by Elad Nehorai, "Why I Stopped Calling Myself Chabad," Hevria blog, September 20, 2016, http://hevria.com/elad/stopped-calling-myself -chabad/.

96 Interview, date not found.

97 For a study of the influence of Hungarian Jewish traditions in Passover *kashrut* in America, see Zev Eleff, "The Search for Authenticity and the

Case of Passover Peanut Oil," in Gross, Myers, and Rosenblum, eds., *Feasting and Fasting.*

98 Waxman, *Social Change*, 98, quoting Haym Soloveitchik, points out that what is being labeled a *ḥumrah* may be merely a stricter demand than what had been the norm or simply "more than what one had been accustomed to."

99 See his responsum in *Igrot Moshe Yoreh de'ah* 1:47, dated Sivan [June] 1954.

100 Rabbi Avi Billet, "New York—What Rav Moshe Feinstein Said about Kosher Milk in the U.S.," *Vos Iz Neias*, September 9, 2009, https://www.vosizneias.com/38090/2009/09/09/new-york-what-rav-moshe-feinstein-said-about-kosher-milk-in-the-us/.

101 Interview, May 23, 2017. Some who refuse to drink regular milk give credibility to the idea that non-Jews might surreptitiously mix unkosher ingredients into cow's milk, but the explanation I heard most often is that Chabad simply is following the rule as written in the Mishnah. I suspect that the Chabad movement's insistence that *ḥalav yisra'el*, milk extracted from an animal by a Jew or under Jewish watch, is spiritually different from other milk is likely connected to their kabbalistic principles that associate non-Jews with negativity.

102 Interview, June 25, 2012.

103 For a Chabad explanation for *yashan* and its stance on it, see Menachem Posner, "What Is 'Yashan'?," Chabad.org, accessed April 26, 2017, http://www.chabad.org/library/article_cdo/aid/584873/jewish/What-is-Yashan.htm#footnote2a584873.

104 Class observation, June 2018 (specific date unknown).

105 Interview, June 17, 2010.

106 Interview, June 18, 2018.

107 Interview, December 30, 2009.

108 Interview, July 8, 2010.

109 The RCC is "the largest body of Orthodox rabbis in the Western United States," according to its website: see "About the RCC," accessed February 25, 2018, http://rccvaad.org/about/.

110 The shameful character of this challenge has kept it out of public view, even though it is widely known among Los Angeles Orthodox rabbis, and it is no accident that I have found written evidence of it only on a discontinued blog of Luke Ford, a pornography gossip columnist who became an Orthodox Jew. He posted an interview with one of the opponents of the RCC action along with a copy of the petition complete

with 147 names of Los Angeles rabbis and laypeople. See Luke Ford, "The RCC Vs. Rabbi Bukspan," August 8, 2010, http://lukeford.net/blog/?p= 22250.

111 A disparaging attitude toward the lax religious standards of the Pico-Robertson Orthodox Jews is common among the Orthodox Jews of the La Brea–Beverly neighborhood, and Pico-Robertson Jews are well aware of this. See Tavory, *Summoned*, 79–80.

112 I thank Jonah Lowenfeld, the *Los Angeles Jewish Journal* journalist who covered the event, for some of these observations; see Jonah Lowenfeld, "New Doheny Meats Owner Explains His Purchase of Scandal-Ridden Store," *Jewish Journal*, April 13, 2013, https://jewishjournal.com/news/los _angeles/115060/. He also gave me access to other related articles and to *Jewish Journal* blog posts that have since been removed by the publisher.

113 Class observation, June 2017.

114 Interview, date not found.

115 Interview, July 8, 2010.

116 Interview, date not found.

117 The Hebrew term for trustworthiness is *ne'emanut*, and the Talmud describes ways of establishing it for witnesses and agents in financial matters and for *kashrut*, among other things; see BT *Gittin* 2b–3a and especially *Ḥullin* 10b. Kraemer, *Jewish Eating and Identity*, 166–68, describing how contemporary Orthodox Jews exclude Conservative rabbis and even other Orthodox rabbis from meaningful authority over *kashrut* and other religious functions, seems to imply that this is illegitimate. The RCC disparagement of a local rabbinic kosher certifier (see note 99 above) was partly made on the basis that the rabbis gave approval to eateries that were open on the Sabbath, which, according to the rabbinic defenders of the rabbi, was in accordance with *halakhah*.

118 Fishkoff, *Kosher Nation*, shows how kosher certifiers have marketed this concern.

119 Horowitz's description of the activities of Abraham Goldstein, a chemist and non-rabbi who worked for the Orthodox Union *kashrut* division and butted heads with the rabbis, illustrates this problem; see Horowitz, *Kosher USA*, 19–45.

120 I found a great deal about *kashrut* issues on an website forum for Orthodox women called Imamother: Connecting Frum Women. These include such issues as the problems with keeping a sink kosher and family members' refusal to eat at each other's homes when only one kitchen sink is used. See "Living with 1 Sink in Your Kitchen," http://www.imamother

.com/forum/viewtopic.php?t=331020, December 19, 2017. The laundry detergent opinion came after several posters pointed out that a *hekhsher* was not required by *halakhah*—one women cited as proof what her husband learned at an Orthodox Union *kashrut* seminar—and that these items are given kosher certification because businesses believe it increases sales. See "Laundry Detergent Need a Hechsher?" June 20, 2014, http://www.imamother.com/forum/viewtopic.php?t =246495.

121　Interview, August 3, 2010.

CHAPTER 3

1　Interview, August 28, 2012.

2　Interview, July 3, 2018.

3　Jonathan Haidt, "The Moral Emotions," in R. J. Davidson, K. R. Scher, and H. H. Goldsmith, eds., *Handbook of Affective Sciences* (Oxford: Oxford University Press, 2003), 852–70.

4　Moral foundations theory is summarized in Jesse Graham, Jonathan Haidt, Sena Koleva, Matt Motyl, Ravi Iyer, Sean P. Wojcik, and Peter H. Ditto, "Moral Foundations Theory: The Pragmatic Validity of Moral Pluralism," *Advances in Experimental Social Psychology* 47 (2013): 55–130. For a discussion of the five moral foundations, see 67–71.

5　Jonathan Haidt, *The Righteous Mind: Why Good People Are Divided by Politics and Religion* (New York: Vintage Books), 2012.

6　There are some dietary rules that differ: for example, the prohibition against eating the part of an animal containing the sciatic nerve, found in Genesis 32:25–33. It is described there as an acknowledgment that an angel wrenched the patriarch Jacob's hip at that place. Some rabbis insist that this is not the foundational reason for the prohibition but an after-the-fact reminder. Abraham ibn Ezra, a medieval commentator, explained the source of the law as an injunction that the Israelites not eat with—and thus not socialize with—their Canaanite neighbors.

7　Genesis 3. Another example is Saul's reasoned disobedience of God's decree to utterly destroy the Amalekite king and the war booty in I Samuel 15.

8　Christine Hayes, *What's Divine about Divine Law: Early Perspectives* (Princeton: Princeton University Press, 2015), 2–3; Jordan D. Rosenblum, *The Jewish Dietary Laws in the Ancient World* (New York: Cambridge University Press, 2016), 1–3.

9 Roy Rappaport, "The Sacred in Human Evolution," *Annual Review of Ecology and Systematics* 2 (1971): 29–37; Haidt, *The Righteous Mind*, 299.

10 Rabbi Yitzchok Adlerstein (YULA educator, retired) translated and paraphrased selections from the writings by Rabbi Sholom Noach Berezovsky (1911–2000, known as "the Slonimer Rebbe" or by "Nesivos Sholom," the name of his book series) in *Essays on the Weekly Parsha Based on Nesivos Shalom* (self-pub., 2012), 71, 74.

11 See Sifra, explaining Leviticus 18:4, Sefaria, accessed March 1, 2018, https://www.sefaria.org/Sifra,_Acharei_Mot,_Chapter_13.9?lang=bi& with=all&lang2=en.

12 The secrecy of the reasons is found in BT *Pesaḥim* 119a. For another discussion of Talmudic attitudes, as well as laws for which the rabbis supplied reasons, see Isaac Heinemann, *The Reasons for the Commandments in Jewish Thought: From the Bible to the Renaissance*, trans. Leonard Levin (Boston: Academic Studies Press, 2008), 25–33.

13 Deuteronomy 22:6–7; m. *Berakhot* 5:3; BT *Berakhot* 33b. Others objected to this stance, which is why the debate continued. A recent book on this commandment, written for an Orthodox audience, is Naftali Weinberger, *A Practical Guide to the Mitzvah of Shiluach Hakan* (Nanuet, NY: Feldheim, 2006), which addresses on 37–47 the many rabbinic opinions on this question, including the opinion of Rabbi Judah Loew ben Bezalel (Maharal) that the act is cruel. See also Hayes, *What's Divine about Divine Law*, 260.

14 There is no established creed, but philosophical summaries of the articles of faith include belief in God's providence. God's grace (*ḥesed*) and love for the Jewish people are fundamental in Jewish liturgy. See Hayes, *What's Divine about Divine Law*, 258.

15 M. *Makot* 3.16; see chapter 2, note 87.

16 *Bereishit rabbah* 44:1 (Midrash); author's translation.

17 The Hebrew word *tzaref* (*letzaref* in its more familiar infinitive form) is commonly used for the act of refining silver by removing impurities from it, a process involving fire and filtering. It also refers to purging evil from a person. It does not refer to *ritual* purity; for that, the Hebrew word *taher* (*letaher* in its more familiar infinitive form) would be used.

18 M. *Avot* 1:3; author's translation.

19 Rabbi Daniel Cavalier, "Rabbi's Message," Young Sefardic Community Center weekly email, Shabbat Nachamu—Parashat Vaetchanan, July 28, 2018.

20 BT *Berakhot* 33b, *Megillah* 25a, and *Nidah* 16b.

21 The rabbis defined these as two distinct commandments in Deuteron-
    omy 10:20 and Deuteronomy 6:5, respectively. The *Sh'ma* prayer starts
    with Deuteronomy 6:4–9.

22 They give the example of the taboo against eating pork: the person who
    desires to eat it but refrains from doing so to comply with God's law is at
    a higher level than the person who regards eating pork as disgusting or
    unappealing. These perspectives are examined in Heinemann, *The Rea-
    sons for the Commandments*, 15–20; see also Hayes, *What's Divine about
    Divine Law*, 248–57.

23 The first is *The Letter of Aristeas*, which scholars date to the second
    century BCE. Philo of Alexandria (20 BCE–50 CE) composed a number
    of such works; see especially *On the Jews* and *On the Contemplative Life*.
    Another work from this era is by Flavius Josephus (37–100 CE), *Antiqui-
    ties of the Jews*.

24 Heinemann, *The Reasons for the Commandments*, 53–54.

25 Ara Norenzayan, "Does Religion Make People Moral?," *Behaviour*
    151.2–3 (2014): 372. The principle of collective punishment applies over
    the generations, according to Exodus 20:7 in the Ten Commandments:
    "For I the LORD your God am an impassioned God, visiting the guilt of
    the parents upon the children, upon the third and upon the fourth gener-
    ations of those who reject Me, but showing kindness to the thousandth
    generation of those who love Me and keep My commandments." This was
    refuted later by the prophet Jeremiah 31:29–30 (also by Ezekiel 18:2–3),
    who denied the truth of the conventional belief that "the fathers eat sour
    grapes and the children's teeth are set on edge."

26 Iddo Tavory, *Summoned: Identification and Religious Life in a Jewish
    Neighborhood* (Chicago: University of Chicago Press, 2016), 7.

27 Ayala Fader, *Mitzvah Girls: Bringing Up the Next Generation of Hasidic
    Jews in Brooklyn* (Princeton: Princeton University Press, 2009), 35.

28 Interview, 2010 (specific date unknown).

29 Interview, August 6, 2018.

30 Interview, July 24, 2012.

31 Interview, August 18, 2010.

32 Interview, July 24, 2012.

33 Interview, July 5, 2011.

34 This is the focus of Richard Sosis and Eric R. Bressler, "Cooperation
    and Commune Longevity: A Test of the Costly Signaling Theory of
    Religion," *Cross-Cultural Research* 37 (2003): 211–39; see also Rappaport,
    "The Sacred in Human Evolution."

35 Interview, date not found. There is an extensive literature in anthropology and psychology on disgust as a result of cultural (not merely biological) conditioning; see Paul Rozin, Jonathan Haidt, Clark McCauley, and Sumio Imada, "Disgust: Preadaptation and the Cultural Evolution of a Food-Based Emotion," in Helen Macbeth, ed., *Food Preferences and Taste: Continuity and Change* (Providence: Berghahn Books, 1997), 65–82. In Carol Nemeroff and Paul Rozin, "Sympathetic Magical Beliefs and Kosher Dietary Practice: The Interaction of Rules and Feelings," *Ethos* 20.1 (March 1992): 96–115, the authors examine the effect of Jews' learned disgust and its effect on their distaste for food that only appears to be nonkosher. The teaching of disgust is also a strategy used in scholarly texts, such as Jewish (and Muslim) explanations for why pigs are prohibited; Marvin Harris, "The Abominable Pig," reprinted in Carole Counihan and Penny Van Esterik, eds., *Food and Culture: A Reader*, 2nd ed. (New York: Routledge, 2008), 54–55.

36 Personal communication, medium and date unknown.

37 Roger Horowitz, *Kosher USA: How Coke Became Kosher and Other Tales of Modern Food* (New York: Columbia University Press, 2016), 105–6, 123–25. Of course, this is a gross exaggeration. Even in the Pico-Robertson neighborhood, half of the eateries lining the streets are not kosher. Well-known American fast-food restaurants like McDonalds, In-N-Out Burger, and Chipotle's are still a temptation, and the local big-chain grocery store was filled with prohibited foods.

38 Haidt, *The Righteous Mind*, 298, citing Richard Sosis, "Religion and Intragroup Cooperation: Preliminary Results of a Comparative Analysis of Utopian Communities," *Cross-Cultural Research* 34 (2000): 70–87.

39 Interview, date not found.

40 Interview, December 31, 2012. I have heard fear-based Chabad rationales for *mitzvot*, some connected to the dangers of eating *treif* food or milk that is not *ḥalav yisraʾel*. For more such explanations, see also Sue Fishkoff, *The Rebbe's Army: Inside the World of Chabad-Lubavitch* (New York: Schocken Books, 2003), 126.

41 Interview, August 1, 2011.

42 Chabad volunteers may do this, and there are also nonprofit agencies that offer this service. Their work is considered a mitzvah, but they may request a donation. See "What We Do," GoKosher.org, accessed May 9, 2018, http://www.gokosher.org/What-we-do.

43 Interview, June 17, 2010.

44 A list of the various types of schools appears in chapter 1.

45 A description of the religious history of the Los Angeles Iranian Jewish immigrant community, with a focus on those on the Orthodox side of the spectrum, is included in chapter 1. See also Barbara Bensoussan, "Iranian Revolution," *Mishpacha*, June 6, 2018, 46–55.

46 Personal communication, medium and date unknown.

47 Personal communication, medium and date unknown.

48 Faranak Margolese, *Off the Derech: Why Observant Jews Leave Judaism* (Jerusalem: Devora, 2005), 23, citing the 1994 study conducted by Yeshiva University. According to the 2013 Pew Research Forum data, 92 percent of Orthodox Jews report compliance with *kashrut* in their homes. See "A Portrait of American Orthodox Jews: A Further Analysis of the 2013 Survey of U.S. Jews," Pew Research Center, August 26, 2015, https://www.pewresearch.org/religion/2013/10/01/jewish-american -beliefs-attitudes-culture-survey/.

49 Margolese, *Off the Derech*, 11.

50 In Margolese's interviews with ex-Orthodox, 44 percent identified observant people as one factor in their defection (p. 42), 7 percent of her online survey respondents reported that "negative behaviors in their observant communities" were a contributing factor (p. 274), and 51 percent reported that they had been physically or verbally abused by someone who was observant (99, 384). See also her summary of this data (p. 392). Once the *ba'alei teshuvah* are ensconced within the Orthodox community, Margolese reports, their consequent dissatisfaction with the community may also incline them to leave for the same reasons given by the ex-Orthodox raised from birth in Orthodox homes. Margolese, *Off the Derech*.

51 This was the career trajectory of Rabbi Daniel Mechanic, as reported by Malki Lowinger, "Taking the Aspirin before the Headache: Project Chazon," *Mishpocha* (Chanuka 5766), reprinted on the Project Chazon website, accessed March 20, 2018, http://www.projectchazon.com/ images/Article_Mishpacha.pdf.

52 Margolese, *Off the Derech*, 216–17, quoting Rabbi Mendel Weinbach, a cofounder and leader of Aish HaTorah and Ohr Somayach yeshivas and their affiliated outreach organizations.

53 Lowinger, "Taking the Aspirin."

54 https://www.yulagirls.org/apps/pages/index.jsp?uREC_ID=124364& type=d&pREC_ID=1039748, accessed March 12, 2018 (yulagirls.org site discontinued).

55 Class observations and interviews, June 25, 2012; October 30, 2012; November 6, 2012; June 25, 2020.

56 The principals of these boys' and girls' schools and the principal of the Chabad boys' high school observed that boys not only have less opportunity to explore questions of meaning, but they simply care less about them. They said that boys' questions pertain to why they are restricted from doing what non-Jews do. This conclusion about gender differences was not supported by the teachers in the coed Modern Orthodox school: "Boys talk plenty about reasons and meanings—I cannot support that generalization," I was told.

57 Interview, June 25, 2012.

58 For example, there are texts teaching about the transfer of meat into milk through heat and steam, rules about using dishwashers for meat and milk, and a chart showing vegetables and fruits prone to infestation by insects. There is nothing about salting and washing meat—a task essential for making meat kosher, which was formerly performed by women at home but is now undertaken by kosher meat-packing companies.

59 Class observation, October 2012.

60 Binyomin Forst, *The Laws of Kashrus*, 2nd ed. (New York: Mesorah Publications, 2010), 24.

61 From the commentary of Moses ibn Ezra on Exodus 23:19; author's translation. The medieval commentator David Kimchi made a similar observation; see John Cooper, *Eat and Be Satisfied: A Social History of Jewish Food* (Northvale, NJ: Jason Aronson, 1993), 35–36. Cooper implies, without evidence, that Jews universally accepted the view that boiling a kid in its mother's milk is inhumane.

62 Rav Asher Meir, "The Kitzur: Meaning in Mitzvot—by Parasha," a lecture that included the views of Rabbi Abraham ibn Ezra and appeared in the online Israel Koschitzky Virtual Beit Midrash of Yeshivat Har Etzion, accessed October 4, 2012, but no longer available. See also numerous essays by Modern Orthodox rabbis in Shmuly Yanklowitz, ed., *Kashrut and Jewish Food Ethics* (Boston: Academic Studies Press, 2019).

63 Interview, date not found.

64 Interview, September 4, 2012.

65 Interview, August 28, 2012.

66 The teacher called this "the AJS [Association for Jewish Studies, the academic Jewish studies organization] perspective, which allows academic studies to affect your perspective on Judaism."

67　Interview, August 28, 2012 (same teacher as in note 63 above). This teacher's source for this Modern Orthodox *hashkafah* is Rabbi Aharon Lichtenstein, who expressed it in his talk "'The Woods Are Lovely, Dark and Deep'—Reading a Poem by Robert Frost," Israel Koschitzky Torat Har Etzion, accessed March 12, 2018, but no longer available, http://etzion.org.il/en/woods-are-lovely-dark-and-deep-reading-poem-robert-frost.

68　Interview, June 25, 2012.

69　Interview, June 25, 2012.

70　They point to the teachings of Rabbi Aharon Lichtenstein, whose article "Does Jewish Tradition Recognize an Ethic Independent of Halakha?" in Marvin Fox, ed., *Modern Jewish Ethics: Theory and Practice* (Columbus: The Ohio State University Press, 1975), 62–88, was published in several books and journals. According to David Shatz, "Ethical Theories in the Orthodox Movement," in Elliot N. Dorff and Jonathan K. Crane, eds., *The Oxford Handbook of Jewish Ethics and Morality* (New York: Oxford University Press, 2013), 254n11, Lichtenstein's article is "the single most cited article in Modern Orthodox writings about how *halakhah* relates to ethics."

71　Interview, June 25, 2012. Rabbi Shmuly Yanklowitz, a Modern Orthodox rabbi who used to reside in the Pico-Robertson neighborhood and who publicly advocates reforming current practices to be more ethical, promotes veganism and better treatment of workers in Jewish-owned food businesses. His article "How Kosher Is Your Milk?" was scorned by several rabbis I interviewed; see *Jewish Journal*, June 7, 2012, https://jewishjournal.com/culture/food/104874/how-kosher-is-your-milk/.

72　This narrowness does not extend to pedagogical and psychological works, which Chabad women read with great eagerness. Adoption of American values occurs despite the insularity. See Zev Eleff, *Authentically Orthodox: A Tradition-Bound Faith in American Life* (Detroit: Wayne State University Press, 2020), especially chap. 5, "Mitzvah Merchants and the Creation of an Orthodox Children's Culture."

73　The outreach mission appeared on the local girls' school website, chabadeducation.com: http://www.chabadeducation.com/templates/articlecco_cdo/aid/453474, accessed March 8, 2018 (site discontinued).

74　Fishkoff, *The Rebbe's Army*, 244. Ideally, they continue their education at a Chabad women's seminary to train as teachers in a Chabad school or with their husbands as emissaries to unaffiliated Jews.

75　Interview, December 31, 2012.

76 For a full description of the investigation and the aftermath of the
    investigation of the kosher slaughtering house, see Aaron S. Gross,
    *The Question of the Animal and Religion: Theoretical Stakes, Practical
    Implications* (New York: Columbia University Press, 2015), chap. 2.
77 Interview, December 31, 2012.
78 Interview, December 31, 2012.
79 Far fewer of the boys' class hours consist of secular studies compared to
    those of the girls. The Los Angeles Chabad boys' high school meets seven
    days a week. The principal explained that these hours enable the school
    to meet secular accreditation standards and to devote the boys' twelfth
    grade entirely to Talmud study. Friday is a short learning day, and in the
    afternoon prior to the start of the Sabbath, the boys are sent, with super-
    vision, to places around town to approach Jewish men to put on *tefillin*
    (phylacteries). This is their introduction to outreach work. Boys return
    to the school on Saturday for Sabbath-appropriate activities and Torah
    learning.
80 Interview, August 28, 2012.
81 This opinion may be found in the writings of Maimonides (Moses ben
    Maimon [Rambam], 1138–1204), *Guide of the Perplexed* III:48, although
    Hannah Kasher, "Well-Being of the Body or Welfare of the Soul: The
    Maimonidean Explanation of the Dietary Laws," in Fred Rosner and
    Samuel S. Kottek, eds., *Moses Maimonides: Physician, Scientist, and
    Philosopher* (Northvale, NJ: Jason Aronson, 1993) argues that this is a
    misreading of the original Arabic. Nahmanides (Moses ben Nahman
    [Ramban] ca. 1194–1270), in his commentary on Leviticus 11:13, points
    out the health problems of eating birds of prey (bad for the heart) but
    also implies that their prohibition is based on these animals as bad mod-
    els for human behavior. *Sefer haḥinukh*, vol. 1, attributed to Rabbi Aaron
    haLevi of Barcelona (ca. 1235–1300), commandment 73, presents this
    view, although some read this as referring to spiritual and not physical
    health.
82 Marketing data shows that kosher-certified food is preferred by non-
    Jewish consumers for just this reason; see Sue Fishkoff, *Kosher Nation:
    Why More and More of America's Food Answers to a Higher Authority*
    (New York: Schocken Books, 2010), 150–51.
83 Tzvi Freeman, "Why Do We Keep Kosher," Chabad.org, accessed
    April 19, 2018, https://www.chabad.org/library/article_cdo/aid/82894/
    jewish/Why-Do-We-Keep-Kosher.htm. Pinchas Taylor, "Not Based
    on Physical Health," Chabad.org, accessed April 20, 2018, https://www

.chabad.org/library/article_cdo/aid/2837509/jewish/Not-Based-on
-Physical-Health.htm, argues the primary reason is *not* health but cites
testimony from several doctors who claim that kosher meat is the safest
and the kosher diet is the best. Yet, Velvel Green, "Spiritual Molecules,"
Chabad.org, accessed April 20, 2018, https://www.chabad.org/library/
article_cdo/aid/82889/jewish/Spiritual-Molecules.htm, adamantly
disagrees. The non-Hasidic Aish HaTorah outreach organization is
also likely to offer these claims; see Rabbi Packouz, "Why Kosher?
Keeping Kosher Offers a Variety of Spiritual and Practical Benefits,"
Aish HaTorah, February 2, 2002, accessed May 8, 2018, http://www
.aish.com/jl/m/mm/48945306.html?s=srcon; and course resource material entitled "Why Keep Kosher?" Olami Resources, accessed May 8,
2018, http://nleresources.com/wp-content/uploads/2012/07/
kashrut.pdf.

84 This particular quotation is from Forst, *The Laws of Kashrus*, but it is
excerpted and included in an online essay for Aish HaTorah, "Philosophy
of Food: Medicine for the Body or Salve for the Soul?" accessed May 11,
2018, http://www.aish.com/jl/m/mm/48958906.html. See Jody Myers,
Kabbalah and the Spiritual Quest: The Kabbalah Centre in America (Westport, CT: Praeger, 2007), 150–54, for how the Kabbalah Centre uses this
strategy.

85 Rabbi Moshe Hayyim Luzzatto (Ramhal) (1707–46), *Mesillat yesharim*,
chap. 11, verse 61, Sefaria, accessed May 3, 2018, https://www.sefaria.org/
Messilat_Yesharim.11.62?lang=bi&with=all&lang2=en.

86 Some argued that because nowhere in the Pentateuch is there a single
interdiction against cruelty to animals, the prohibition is a rabbinic enac-
tion and therefore of lesser importance than a Torah law, but the consensus is not with them.

87 The Hebrew word for slaughter, *shaḥat*, refers to killing by slicing at the
neck. The procedures for slaughter for animal sacrifice may be presumed
by the near-slaughter of Isaac as described in Genesis 22.

88 The most authoritative code for present Orthodox practice is *arukh*,
and these laws appear in the section called *Yoreh de'ah*.

89 *Séfer haḤinnuch: The Book of [Mitzvah] Education*, translated and notes
by Charles Wengrov (Jerusalem: Feldheim, 1988), 399.

90 Rabbi Moshe Feinstein, *Igrot Moshe, Even Ha-ezer* (June 1982), 4:92. The
translation from the Hebrew and Aramaic is by the author.

91 A rabbi who is disturbed by the suffering of animals under modern
modes of animal husbandry can only argue against such practices on

the basis of the disqualifying blemishes that such treatment is likely
to produce in the properly slaughtered animal. Indeed, this is what
Feinstein did: he required that the calf's innards be checked far more
scrupulously than normal, a procedure that would likely result in the
pronouncement that the meat is *treif*. This is not the same as declaring
that such meat is *treif* by virtue of *tza'ar ba'alei ḥayyim*.

92 *Séfer haḤinnuch*, 399.

93 I thank Martin Lockshin for clarifying this principle (*lo darshinan taama
diqera*) and referencing a number of Talmudic passages that cite it, for
example, BT *Bava metzia* 115a.

94 Non-Orthodox rabbis also do not give precedence to more recent
halakhic decisions or privilege the rulings in the *Shulḥan arukh* as the
Orthodox do. The distinction between Orthodox and non-Orthodox
halakhic decision-making procedures is not well known outside the
Orthodox community.

95 Interview, June 25, 2012.

96 Joseph B. Soloveitchik, "On Humane Methods of Handling Meat for
Slaughter," in Nathaniel Helfgot, ed., *Community, Covenant and Commit-
ment: Selected Letters and Communications of Joseph B. Soloveitchik* (New
York: KTAV Publishing House, 2021).

97 Horowitz, *Kosher USA*, chap. 8.

98 Dr. Yvette Alt Miller, "Banning Shechitah in Europe," Aish, accessed
February 19, 2019, https://aish.com/banning-shechita-in-europe
.html.

99 "What Is Shechitah?," Chabad.org, accessed February 19, 2019, https://
www.chabad.org/library/article_cdo/aid/222240/jewish/What-Is
-Shechitah.htm. For a contrasting point of view on the Chabad website, see Rabbi Tzvi Freeman, "Why Do We Keep Kosher?," accessed
June 21, 2021, https://www.chabad.org/library/article_cdo/aid/82894/
jewish/Why-Do-We-Keep-Kosher.htm: "Nevertheless, the prohibition
of cruelty towards animals and the laws of kosher slaughter are two
separate realms. Just because the slaughter of the animal was deemed
kosher doesn't mean it was not raised or slaughtered in a cruel way. A
proper, kosher slaughter should be done with minimal suffering to the
animal—indeed the laws of sheḥitah and the traditional methods greatly
facilitate this. In some cases, however, there is a need today for correction
of this issue, as many have already realized."

100 OU Kosher Staff, "Setting the Record Straight on Kosher Slaughter,"
Orthodox Union Kosher, December 29, 2004, accessed February 19,

2019, https://oukosher.org/blog/news/setting-the-record-straight-on
-kosher-slaughter/.

101 Interview, July 11, 2011.

102 The Shalom Pizza website makes this claim on its page titled "What Is
Kosher?," http://www.shalompizza.com/kosher.php. Its website encourages viewers to access Shalom Grill, accessed January 31, 2021, http://
shalomgrill.com/shalom-grill-buys-elat-burger.php, which has a link to
the "What Is Kosher" page. Shalom Grill's marketing to non-Jews and
non-Orthodox Jews is obvious in the photograph of male customers not
wearing yarmulkes, as well in as the stated aspiration of the restaurant to
attract a "hip" crowd on the page describing the new ownership.

103 Rabbi Moshe T. Schuchman, "A Cut Above: Shechitah in the Crosshairs, Again," Star-K, accessed February 19, 2019, https://www.star-k.org/
articles/kashrus-kurrents/548/a-cut-above-shechita-in-the-crosshairs
-again/.

104 This is well known in the Orthodox world. See Samantha M. Shapiro,
"Kosher Wars," *New York Times*, October 9, 2008, quoting Rabbi Avi
Safran, https://www.nytimes.com/2008/10/12/magazine/12kosher-t.html.

105 Interview, September 4, 2012.

106 The Talmudic rabbis did not differentiate between Jewish and non-Jewish
souls, and from their perspective all human beings needed refinement.
Kabbalistic writings, which appeared in the twelfth century, were the first
to claim that non-Jews had structures that were different from those of
Jews. They were perhaps preceded by Rabbi Judah ha-Levi in his book
Kuzari. See Jochanan H. A. Wijnhoven, "The Zohar and the Proselyte,"
in Michael Fishbane, ed., *Texts and Responses: Studies Presented to
N. Glatzer* (Leiden: Brill, 1957), 123–25.

107 Because these were given to Noah and all his descendants, they are called
the seven Noahide laws. First enumerated in BT *Sanhedrin* 59a, they represent the rabbis' full version of God's words to Noah in Genesis 9:1–9.

108 After all, the Talmudic statement references kosher slaughter: "Were not
the commandments given so that man might be refined by them? Do
you really think that The Holy One Blessed Be He cares if an animal is
slaughtered by the throat or the nape of the neck?"

109 Fader, *Mitzvah Girls*, 36–41, describes how this process works within the
Hasidic family.

110 Orthodox communities that have far greater familiarity with scientific
disciplines than Chabad regard such arguments as bad science and therefore counterproductive. See Abarbanel, commentary on Leviticus 11,

translation by Rabbi Michael Hattin, on the website Sefaria, accessed April 19, 2018, https://www.sefaria.org/sheets/64402.

111 BT *Yoma* 39a.

112 Joel Hecker, *Mystical Bodies, Mystical Meals: Eating and Embodiment in Medieval Kabbalah* (Detroit: Wayne State University Press, 2005), 111.

113 Isaac Abravanel's opinion, originally cited in his commentary on Leviticus 11, was included in the Yeshiva University of Los Angeles High School "10th Grade Dinnim (practical laws) Kashrut Curriculum" booklet. It appears there within an excerpt from Forst, *The Laws of Kashrus.*

114 This interpretation of *Mesillat yesharim*, chap. 11, appears in the booklet within an interpretation of BT *Yoma* 39a. A portion from *Mesillat yesharim*, which teaches that a person who eats forbidden foods "remains bestial and corporeal, immersed in the coarseness of this world," appears in the booklet elsewhere.

115 Class observation, June 25, 2012. In Israel, hotels are mandated by law to serve kosher foods, and many eateries purchase kosher meat. The teacher described himself as closer to Haredi—more culturally insular—than Modern Orthodox.

116 Class observation and interview with principal, June 25, 2012.

117 Interview, December 6, 2018.

118 Forst, *The Laws of Kashrus*, 26–27.

119 A thorough study of this method was written by a cofounder of the local coed Modern Orthodox high. See Stephen Bailey, *Kashrut, Tefillin, Tzitzit: Studies in the Purpose and Meaning of Symbolic Mitzvot Inspired by the Commentaries of Rabbi Samson Raphael Hirsch* (Northvale, NJ: Jason Aronson, 2000).

120 Samson Raphael Hirsch, *Horeb: A Philosophy of Jewish Laws and Observances*, trans. Dr. I. Grunfeld (New York: Soncino Press, 1962), chap. 57 ("Regarding the Species as Divine Order"), 282–89; chap. 77 ("Marriage with Non-Jews and Imitation of Strange Customs and Usages"), 378–81.

121 Hirsch, *Horeb*, chap. 68 ("Food"), 328–29.

122 This is a paraphrase of Hirsch's commentary on Exodus 23:19 by Rabbi Yitzchok Adlerstein, "Parshas Mishpatim—Cheeseburgers for Dummies," in his blog Torah.org, accessed April 23, 2018, https://torah.org/torah-portion/ravhirsch-5771-mishpatim/. According to Bailey, *Kashrut, Tefillin, Tzitzit*, 74 (no source reference), Hirsch teaches that the combination of the vegetative (nourishing) and animal (pursuit of need and avoidance of pain) that occurs is the same as "primal, instinctual animal motivation," which Jews are enjoined to transcend.

123 Interview, September 4, 2012.

124 Interview, September 4, 2012.

125 The Chabad.org articles, classes, and other posts in the areas of Jewish practice are designed for outreach purposes. I have not found references to Hirsch in my perusal of the website material on *kashrut* or in my interviews with Chabad rabbis, teachers, or laypeople.

126 "The Chassidic Masters on Food and Eating," based on *Tanya*, chap. 7, 8, Chabad.org, accessed May 3, 2018, https://www.chabad.org/library/article_cdo/aid/133912/jewish/The-Chassidic-Masters-on-Food.htm. See also Hecker, *Mystical Bodies, Mystical Meals*.

127 "The Human Biosphere," a summary of some of the writings of the seventh Lubavitcher rebbe, Chabad.org, accessed May 3, 2018, https://www.chabad.org/library/article_cdo/aid/82892/jewish/The-Human-Biosphere.htm.

128 Pinchas Taylor, "Kabbalistic Eating," Chabad.org, accessed May 3, 2018, https://www.chabad.org/library/article_cdo/aid/2837524/jewish/Kabbalistic-Eating.htm.

129 Tali Loewenthal, "Why Shechitah Is Important," Chabad.org, accessed May 3, 2018, https://www.chabad.org/library/article_cdo/aid/412206/jewish/Why-Shechitah-Is-Important.htm.

130 Class observation, date not found.

131 Interview of rabbi, who explained how *kiruv* is understood within Chabad today. See the video of the Rebbe, "Every Jew Is Close," Chabad.org, accessed January 25, 2021, https://www.chabad.org/therebbe/livingtorah/player_cdo/aid/319001/jewish/Every-Jew-is-Close.htm.

132 See Rabbi Kalman Packouz, "Why Kosher?," Aish, accessed December 28, 2022, http://www.aish.com/jl/m/mm/48945306.html?s=srcon.

133 Interview, October 4, 2018. Much has been written about this. See Hecker, *Mystical Bodies, Mystical Meals*.

134 Jody Myers, "Kabbalah for the Gentiles: Diverse Souls and Universalism in Contemporary Kabbalah," in Boaz Huss, ed., *Kabbalah and the Contemporary Spiritual Revival* (Beer-Sheva, Israel: Ben Gurion University Press, 2011), 198–99.

135 See "The Chassidic Masters on Food and Eating," Chabad.org, accessed December 29, 2022, https://www.chabad.org/library/article_cdo/aid/133912/jewish/The-Chassidic-Masters-on-Food.htm

136 See chapter 2, note 4.

137 Interview, March 2017.

138 Interview, May 23, 2017.

139 Margolese, *Off the Derech*, 198.
140 Fader, *Mitzvah Girls*, 35.

CHAPTER 4

1 See, for example, Robin E. Judd, *Contested Rituals: Circumcision, Kosher Butchering, and Jewish Political Life in Germany, 1843–1933* (Ithaca, NY: Cornell University Press, 2007).
2 Jewish tradition divides the entire Pentateuch into portions, each of which is assigned for weekly chanting in the synagogue.
3 Genesis 1:28–30, Chabad.org translation.
4 Jeremy Cohen, *"Be Fertile and Increase, Fill the Earth and Master It": The Ancient and Medieval Career of a Biblical Text* (Ithaca, NY: Cornell University Press, 1989), 23–24, mentions varied opinions by modern academics, including some who argue that the language does not preclude eating meat.
5 "Permission to Eat Meat: Exegetical Approaches," Alhatorah.org, accessed June 23, 2021, http://alhatorah.org/Permission_to_Eat_Meat/2; Yael Shemesh, "Vegetarian Ideology in Talmudic Literature and Traditional Biblical Exegesis," *Review of Rabbinic Judaism* 9 (2006): 141–46.
6 Rashi, on Genesis 1:30, emphasizes the similarity between the first humans and animals, even though humans are given dominion. Rabbinic commentators agree that Cain's sacrifice is rejected because of his grudging attitude, but the biblical text alone gives no reason for God's rejection; see Genesis 4:2–7.
7 The last Lubavitcher rebbe based this view on Rashi's statement, "He did not permit Adam and his wife to kill a creature and to eat its flesh," along with BT *Sanhedrin* 59b, where a rabbi suggests that Adam ate meat killed by heavenly angels, and other commentators. *Chumash*, Gutnick Edition, ed. Chaim Miller (Brooklyn: Kol Menachem, 2009), 13; *Chumash*, Michaan Edition (Brooklyn: Kehot, 2016), 11 (interpretive translation of Genesis 1:29). Also, Saul Wolf, "Are You Sure Meat Was Forbidden Until After the Flood?" Chabad.org, accessed June 4, 2021, https://www.chabad.org/parshah/article_cdo/aid/3087361/jewish/Are-You-Sure-Meat-Was-Forbidden-Until-After-the-Flood.htm.
8 *Chumash*, Gutnick Edition, 57. Citing the Rebbe's published lectures, the commentary on this passage states that God prohibited meat because of the moral and spiritual weakness in the first ten generations, noting that "meat is an extremely coarse food that can lead a person to excessive

physicality." Only when people are at a higher level can they withstand this effect.

9 Genesis 8:21 and Genesis 9:1–4, Chabad.org translation.

10 Writings and anthologies by Jewish vegetarians give a different impression of the relative weight of rabbinic opinions and actual practices. See, for example, Louis A. Berman, *Vegetarianism and the Jewish Tradition* (New York: KTAV Publishing House, 1982); David Sears, *The Vision of Eden: Animal Welfare and Vegetarianism in Jewish Law and Mysticism* (Spring Valley, NY: Orot, 2003); Jacob Ari Labendz and Shmuly Yanklowitz. *Jewish Veganism and Vegetarianism: Studies and New Directions* (New York: SUNY Press, 2020).

11 The rabbis do not interpret this passage as God prohibiting the consumption of animal blood, although it could be read this way and is regarded as such by Jacob Milgrom, *Leviticus 1–16*, Anchor Yale Bible Commentaries (New Haven: Yale University Press, 1998), 705.

12 Genesis 9:6, Chabad.org translation.

13 The Noahide laws are first enumerated in the BT *Sanhedrin* 59a.

14 See Diane L. Beers, *For the Prevention of Cruelty: The History and Legacy of Animal Rights Activism in the United States* (New York: Swallow Press, 2007); Judd, *Contested Rituals*.

15 According to Rod Preece, *Sins of the Flesh: A History of Ethical Vegetarian Thought* (Vancouver: University of British Columbia Press, 2008), 267–90, Joseph Brotherton was not a member of a mainstream Christian church, and his message was given little attention.

16 Jeffrey C. Blutinger, "Creatures from Before the Flood: Reconciling Science and Genesis in the Pages of a Nineteenth-Century Hebrew Newspaper," *Jewish Social Studies* 16.2 (Winter 2010): 74, points out that Darwin's claim about human evolution was barely given credibility until the twentieth century. See also Geoffrey Cantor and Marc Swetlitz, eds., *Jewish Tradition and the Challenge of Darwinism* (Chicago: University of Chicago Press, 2006).

17 Samson Raphael Hirsch, "Religion Allied to Progress" [in German] (1854), ed. and trans. Isidor Grunfeld, excerpted in Paul Mendes-Flohr and Jehuda Reinharz, eds., *The Jew in the Modern World*, 3rd ed. (New York: Oxford University Press, 2011), 220–23.

18 This was likely in German lands and in England. His reception was much slower in the United States, according to Zev Eleff, "American Orthodoxy's Lukewarm Embrace of the Hirschian Legacy, 1850–1939," *Tradition* 45 (Fall 2012): 35–53.

19 Alan T. Levenson, *The Making of the Modern Hebrew Bible: How Scholars in Germany, Israel, and America Transformed an Ancient Text* (Lanham, MD: Rowman & Littlefield, 2011), 48–63, describes Hirsch's approach and explains his continuing popularity.

20 Ephraim Oratz, ed., *Trumath Tzvi: The Pentateuch with a Translation by Samson Raphael Hirsch and Excerpts from The Hirsch Commentary*, 7 vols. (New York: Judaica Press, 1986), 12–13 (in reference to Genesis 2:7) and 16 (in the introductory comments to Genesis, chap. 3). The *Trumath Tzvi* commentary includes excerpts from several Hirsch works.

21 *Trumath Tzvi*, comment on Genesis 9:6, 47.

22 This translation of Genesis 9:4 is found in Samson Raphael Hirsch, *Der Pentateuch*, 5 volumes (Hebrew with Hirsch's German translation in parallel columns and his commentary in German) (Frankfurt am Main: J. Kauffman, 1867–78).

23 *Trumath Tzvi*, comment on Genesis 9:6, 46.

24 *Trumath Tzvi*, comment on Genesis 9:4.

25 Hirsch's comment on Genesis 9:3, based on Rabbi Mordechai Breuer's Hebrew translation from the original German, found in David Sears, *The Vision of Eden*, 241–42. Hirsch's reference to vegetarianism is not included in the *Trumath Tzvi* volume used in local synagogues.

26 *Trumath Tzvi*, comment on Genesis 4:3–6, 23, and on Genesis 9:20, 43.

27 See Judd, *Contested Rituals*. Hirsch insists that the Torah requires humans to act compassionately toward animals and to restrain themselves in making use of the earth and its plant and animal life. Excerpts of these points are included in Jewish vegetarian anthologies such as Sears, *Vision*, 69n27, 235.

28 Judd, *Contested Rituals*.

29 Isaac Lewin, Michael I. Munk, and Jeremiah J. Berman, *Religious Freedom: The Right to Practice Shehitah (Kosher Slaughtering)* (New York: Research Institute for Post-War Problems of Religion, 1946), 48, sums up the new legislation from 1864–1926.

30 There were various methods used, but the most common was to fracture the animal's skull with a hammer blow, manually or mechanically performed; see Lewin, Munk, and Berman, *Religious Freedom*, 278.

31 Boria Sax, *Animals in the Third Reich: Pets, Scapegoats, and the Holocaust* (New York: Continuum International Publishing Group, 2000), shows the complexity of Nazi-era attitudes and legislation regarding the humane treatment of animals. On the closure of the German

organization Deutscher Vegetarier-Bund (German Vegetarian Federation), see "History of the German Vegetarian Society," International Vegetarian Union, accessed June 22, 2021, https://ivu.org/history/societies/vbd.html.

32 The American Jewish Committee, a secular Jewish organization devoted to global Jewish advocacy, teamed with the Agudath Israel World Organization (Orthodox Jewish) to publish Lewin, Munk, and Berman, *Religious Freedom*. In 1967, an American Orthodox rabbi reassured his colleagues in Israel that antisemitism was not a factor in the kosher meat business in America, as they would expect; Rabbi Eliezer (Louis) Bernstein, "Problems of Kosher Slaughter in the United States" [in Hebrew], *Shana Bashana* (1967), 366–67.

33 Roger Horowitz, *Kosher USA: How Coke Became Kosher and Other Tales of Modern Food* (New York: Columbia University Press, 2016), 215–17, provides a history of the legislation and the erroneous idea, frequently repeated in many accounts of kosher slaughter in America, that shackle-and-hoist became the norm because US law mandated raising the animal off the ground. According to Aaron Gross, *The Question of the Animal and Religion: Theoretical Stakes, Practical Implications* (New York: Columbia University Press, 2015), 254n23, the Orthodox Union does not consider animals slaughtered in the US this way to be kosher, but it does accept the meat as kosher when *sheḥitah* includes this practice in other countries, like South America.

34 "On the Matter of Danger to *Sheḥitah*, Heaven Forbid" [in Hebrew], *Hamaor* 8.5 (May 1958): 48. This is a rabbinic monthly journal.

35 Berman, *Vegetarianism and the Jewish Tradition*, 61–62, mentions publications (the earliest in 1896) by Jewish immigrants who wrote in English and Yiddish.

36 Samuel H. Dresner, Seymour Siegel, and David M. Pollock, *The Jewish Dietary Laws: Their Meaning for Our Time*, rev. and exp. ed. (New York: Rabbinical Assembly and United Synagogue Commission on Jewish Education, 1966), 22. The themes in this little volume are like those in an essay by Conservative rabbi and Bible scholar Jacob Milgrom, "The Biblical Diet Laws as an Ethical System: Food and Faith," *Interpretation* 7.3 (July 1963), and they were incorporated into Milgrom's later published scholarship on Leviticus.

37 Dresner, Siegel, and Pollock, *The Jewish Dietary Laws*, 23–24. Italics in the original.

38 Dresner, Siegel, and Pollock, *The Jewish Dietary Laws*, 26–27. The original essay was published by Samuel H. Dresner in 1966. All three authors were Conservative rabbis, and the second publishers were the central rabbinic and synagogue organizations of the Conservative denomination.

39 Richard Siegel, Michael Strassfeld, and Sharon Strassfeld, eds., *The Jewish Catalog: A Do-It-Yourself Kit* (Philadelphia: Jewish Publication Society, 1973), 18–19. Karen Iacobbo and Michael Iacobbo, *Vegetarian America: A History* (Westport, CT: Greenwood Publishing Group, 2004), 183–84, quoting founding director Jonathan Wolf.

40 Richard Schwartz, *Judaism and Vegetarianism* (Smithtown, NY: Exposition Press, 1982). This volume was expanded and republished in 1988 and 2001. The other anthology was Berman, *Vegetarianism*.

41 Alfred S. Cohen, "Vegetarianism from a Jewish Perspective," *Journal of Halacha and Contemporary Society* 1.2 (1981): 39.

42 Cohen, "Vegetarianism"; J. David Bleich, "Vegetarianism and Judaism," *Tradition* 23.1 (1987): 82–90.

43 Louis Jacobs, *What Does Judaism Say About . . . ?* (New York: Quadrangle, 1973), quoted in Berman, *Vegetarianism*, 65. Jacobs did not identify as an Orthodox Jew, yet many of his writings were defenses of what would today be considered Orthodox Jewish doctrines.

44 Cohen, "Vegetarianism," 44.

45 David Shatz, "Ethical Theories in the Orthodox Movement," in Elliot N. Dorff and Jonathan Crane, eds., *The Oxford Handbook of Jewish Ethics and Morality* (New York: Oxford University Press, 2013), 241–58.

46 Bleich, "Vegetarianism," 82.

47 Interview, following class observation, November 6, 2012.

48 See Arthur O. Lovejoy, *The Great Chain of Being: A Study of the History of an Idea* (Cambridge, MA: Harvard University Press, 1976).

49 Class observation, July 24, 2019.

50 Cohen, "Vegetarianism," 52.

51 Aaron Gross, *The Question*, 30–31.

52 That is, his physical enjoyment of meat eating would not be a legitimate reason; Cohen, "Vegetarianism," 50.

53 Bleich, "Vegetarianism," 84. Bleich mentions by name only Rabbi Isaac Abarbanel and Rabbi Joseph Albo.

54 Bleich, "Vegetarianism," 84.

55 Hirsch, "Religion Allied to Progress," quoted in synagogue edition of *Trumath Tzvi* Pentateuch, xvi.

56 Bleich, "Vegetarianism," 84. For an analysis of Albo in the context of the formation of "the humane subject," see Gross, *The Question*, 162–65.

57 Bleich, "Vegetarianism," 85, based on a statement in BT *Sanhedrin* 108a: "Animals [during the Flood] could be destroyed by a righteous God only because the sole purpose of those creatures was to serve man. Hence, if man is to be destroyed, the continued existence of animal species is purposeless."

58 Berman, *Vegetarianism*, 63, 69; Schwartz, *Vegetarianism*, 122. Ari Z. Zivotofsky, "Butchering of Sources in a Failed Attempt to Demonstrate That Judaism Demands Vegetarianism: An Analysis of Asa Keiser's Booklet *Velifnei Iver*," *Times of Israel*, November 14, 2014, http:// blogs.timesofisrael.com/butchering-of-sources-in-a-failed-attempt-to -demonstrate-that-judaism-demands-vegetarianism-an-analysis-of-asa -keisers-booklet-velifnei-iver/, refutes the vegetarians' claim that Kook favored vegetarianism.

59 Bleich, "Vegetarianism," 86.

60 Bleich, "Vegetarianism and Judaism," 86.

61 "The Letter Writer," in Isaac Bashevis Singer, *The Seance and Other Stories* (New York: Farrar, Straus & Giroux, 1968), 270.

62 Charles Patterson, *Eternal Treblinka: Our Treatment of Animals and the Holocaust* (New York: Lantern Books, 2002).

63 For just two responses to this exhibit, see Jill Hamilton, "Using the 'Holocaust' Metaphor," Ethical Case Studies, Society of Professional Journalists, accessed March 20, 2023, https://www.spj.org/ecs14.asp; and Betsy Reed, "'Holocaust on a Plate' angers US Jews," *The Guardian*, March 3, 2003.

64 For details, see Horowitz, *Kosher USA*, 234–43; Gross, *The Question*, 27–34. Horowitz and Gross speculate that the second cut sped up the slaughtering line and reduced blood splashing on the rest of the animal. The online report, "PETA Reveals Extreme Cruelty at Kosher Slaughterhouses," and video are on the PETA website, accessed June 8, 2021, https://www.peta.org/features/agriprocessors/.

65 Forty-six articles or editorials about the AgriProcessors were published in the *New York Times* between December 2004 and May 2013.

66 Avi Shafran, "The Shechita Controversy," December 25, 2004, Aish, https://www.aish.com/jw/s/48894162.html. Mike Godwin, who coined the term "Godwin's Law" to describe the glib comparisons of Hitler and the Nazis in modern contentious debates, explains the phenomenon

in "Voices on Antisemitism," September 1, 2011, United States Holocaust Memorial Museum website, https://www.ushmm.org/antisemitism/podcast/voices-on-antisemitism/mike-godwin.

67   Horowitz, *Kosher USA*, 241. Horowitz believes that Dr. Temple Grandin, a non-Jewish scientist who insisted that AgriProcessor was unique among kosher meat producers for its cruel methods, should be credited for averting challenges to *sheḥitah* in the United States.

68   Interview, November 6, 2012.

69   Shmuly Yanklowitz founded Uri L'Tzedek as a social justice organization. Tav haYosher is an ethical seal certifying that the business promises to strictly follow labor laws and provide an abuse-free work environment for employees; see Uri L'Tzedek website, accessed June 7, 2021, http://utzedek.org/. The response of Pico-Robertson businesses was based partly on an interview with a local rabbi, December 30, 2009, and May 22, 2018.

70   Interview, December 31, 2012. Tali Lowenthal, "Why Shechitah Is Important," Chabad.org, accessed December 1, 2017, http://www.chabad.org/library/article_cdo/aid/412206/jewish/Why-Shechitah-Is-Important.htm, includes the observation that in the modern era, "attacks on *sheḥitah* are often a disguised form of antisemitism."

71   Interview, November 6, 2012.

72   Reform movement prayer books omit these prayers entirely, whereas Conservative movement prayer books include an alternative prayer alongside a traditional one.

73   The matter is summed up by Cohen, "Vegetarianism," 41: "Thus, there seems to be little halachic controversy concerning vegetarianism and the Sabbath. If a person is more comfortable not eating meat, there would be no obligation for him to do so on the Sabbath."

74   These rabbinic opinions are summarized in the article by Cohen, "Vegetarianism," 40–43; and in Bleich, "Vegetarianism," 87–89. See also Sears, *Vision*, 162–75, on Sabbath and holiday meat eating.

75   Interview, August 7, 2011.

76   The first two pages of the synagogue handout for January 12, 2013, were copies of "Lma'an Yishme'u Shabbos Table Companion," edited by Rabbi Shimon Hellinger, and the last two pages included teachings from the last Chabad rebbe on dietary matters. The source for the quotation is *Heichal Menachem* 1, 225, from the teachings of the seventh Chabad rebbe Menachem Mendel Schneerson.

77 Baruch S. Davidson, "Judaism and Vegetarianism," Chabad.org, July 30, 2017, accessed June 18, 2021, https://www.chabad.org/library/article _cdo/aid/858870/jewish/Judaism-and-Vegetarianism.htm.

78 Interview, August 7, 2011.

CHAPTER 5

1 Interview, May 20, 2019.

2 See Rabbi Daniel Feldman, "My House Is Your House: The Mitzvah of Hakhnassat Orchim," YUTorahOnline, accessed March 24, 2023, https:// www.yutorah.org/togo/5769/pesach/articles/Pesach_To-Go_-_5769 _Rabbi_Feldman.pdf.

3 See Walter Jacob and Walter Homolka, eds., *Hesed and Tzedakah: From Bible to Modernity* (Berlin: Frank and Timme, 2006), for sources. For sources and an Orthodox perspective on these laws, see Shimon Taub, *Laws of Tzedakah and Maaser* (New York: Mesorah, 2001).

4 Genesis 18:1–3.

5 Rashi on Genesis 17:3, summarizing BT *Shabbat* 127a.

6 BT *Shabbat* 127a.

7 *Tanhuma*, 1:7 (Midrash); *Zohar* III 198b. Rabbinic midrash in the Talmud and in other sources adds details demonstrating Abraham's determination to show hospitality. These made their way into Rashi and other sources familiar to educated Orthodox Jews.

8 Interview, date not found.

9 BT *Avot* 1:5.

10 Noam Zion, *For the Love of God: Comparative Religious Motivations for Giving: Christian Charity, Maimonidean Tzedakah and Lovingkindness (Hesed)* (Cleveland: Zion Holiday Publications, 2013), 73. He documents the approaches of various Talmudic rabbis, some of whom insisted only on hosting guests who are Torah scholars or distinguished in some way.

11 Rashi on Genesis 12:5 (Abram left Haran with "all the people he had acquired"), summarizing *Bereishit rabbah* 39:14.

12 Yet Jewish proselytizing persisted into the medieval era even after Christian and Muslim rulers outlawed it as a crime punishable by death. See L. H. Feldman, "Proselytism by Jews in the Third, Fourth, and Fifth Centuries," *Journal for the Study of Judaism in the Persian, Hellenistic, and Roman Period* 24.1 (June 1993): 1–58; and Yosi Yisraeli and Yaniv Fox,

eds., *Contesting Inter-Religious Conversion in the Medieval World* (London and New York: Routledge, 2017).

13 For Talmudic attitudes toward proselytes and proselytization, see BT *Yevamot* 46a–47b, 109b; *Pesaḥim* 87b. Proselytes can also be a tremendous benefit to the Jewish people. The rabbinic sources are ambivalent, and I heard both perspectives while attending lectures in Pico-Robertson Orthodox synagogues. American Orthodox Jews' rejection of interfaith dialogue on theological matters became a public matter when Rabbi Joseph Soloveitchik objected to interfaith dialogue on intellectual and halakhic grounds. See Joseph B. Soloveitchik, "Confrontation," *Tradition: A Journal of Orthodox Thought* 6.2 (1964). The Rabbinic Council of America, the organization dominated then by the Modern Orthodox, affirmed his position as praxis in 1966, and I have seen no evidence that this stance has changed even within the most liberal wing.

14 Maimonides, *Mishneh Torah*, "Laws of Mourning," chapter 14:1 on "You shall love your neighbor as yourself" (Leviticus 19:18), defines "neighbor" as "your brothers in Torah and precepts."

15 Meir Tamari, *"With All Your Possessions": Jewish Ethics and Economic Life* (New York: Free Press, 1987), 262–63.

16 See the comments by Rabbi Moses Isserles, *Shulḥan arukh, Oraḥ ḥayyim*, 333.

17 Tamari, *Ethics*, 242–60.

18 BT *Avot* 1:5. Maimonides on *Avot* 1:5. Jews regularly hired non-Jews as household servants, a practice that did not please rabbis.

19 Tamari, *Ethics*, 242.

20 Zion, *Love of God*, 72, 179–84, 228–33, highlights opinions of rabbis who disagreed with these priorities, for example, noting that Maimonides (in Mishneh Torah, Gifts to the Poor 7:13) insists that one's own needs and those of one's relatives have greater priority than the poor of his town and his land.

21 Tamari, *Ethics*, 251; Fishbane, "*Mipnei Darkei Shalom*: The Promotion of Harmonious Relationships in the Mishnah's Social Order," *Studies in Judaism, Humanities, and the Social Sciences* 1.1 (2017): 73–84.

22 Maimonides, *Mishneh Torah, Matanot le'evyonim* 9:7–14.

23 Joel Hecker, *Mystical Bodies, Mystical Meals: Eating and Embodiment in Medieval Kabbalah* (Detroit: Wayne State University Press, 2005), 145, 174–75.

24 BT *Shabbat* 68b.

25 Interview, July 9, 2019. This is Chabad's reputation.

26 Chabad understands this mitzvah to pertain to Jews hosting other Jews. See Yehudah Leib Schapiro, "The Mitzvah of Inviting Guests" (audio lecture), Chabad.org, accessed March 12, 2020, https://www.chabad.org/multimedia/audio_cdo/aid/612952/jewish/The-Mitzvah-of-Inviting-Guests.htm.

27 Philip Wexler, with Eli Rubin and Michael Wexler, *Social Vision: The Lubavitcher Rebbe's Transformative Paradigm for the World* (New York: Crossroad, 2019), 83–91, 223–226.

28 "The Rebbe's 10-Point Mitzvah Campaign for Jewish Awareness and Observance," accessed June 16, 2021, Chabad.org, https://www.chabad.org/therebbe/article_cdo/aid/62228/jewish/10-Point-Mitzvah-Campaign.htm; David Biale et al., *Hasidism: A New History* (Princeton: Princeton University Press, 2018), 696–98.

29 Shloma Majeski, "The Chassidic Approach To Joy," Chabad.org, accessed June 18, 2020, https://www.chabad.org/library/article_cdo/aid/88574/jewish/The-Chassidic-Approach-To-Joy.htm.

30 Moshe Yaakov Wisnefsky, "Abraham's Hospitality," Chabad.org, accessed June 9, 2020, https://www.chabad.org/kabbalah/article_cdo/aid/379749/jewish/Abrahams-Hospitality.htm.

31 Phone interview, July 9, 2019.

32 "Hachnasat Orchim: Hospitality," Chabad.org, accessed June 19, 2019, https://www.chabad.org/library/article_cdo/aid/691769/jewish/Hakhnasat-Orhim-Hospitality.htm.

33 Menahem Mendel Schneersohn, "Every Jew Is Close" (video), Chabad.org, March 18, 1990, https://www.chabad.org/therebbe/livingtorah/player_cdo/aid/319001/jewish/Every-Jew-is-Close.htm.

34 Notes documenting email correspondence with Rabbi Tzvi Freeman and his colleagues, October 4, 2018.

35 Interview, date not found.

36 BT *Pesaḥim* 22b; *Bava metzia* 75b; *Mo'ed katan* 17a.

37 Interview, date not found.

38 Interview, date not found.

39 Yanki Tauber, "Love According to the Rebbe," Chabad.org, accessed August 24, 2019, https://www.chabad.org/therebbe/article_cdo/aid/2756/jewish/Love-According-to-the-Rebbe.htm. This all-important message is based on chapter 32 of *Tanya*.

40 The essay winners were posted on the website of Bais Bezalel, the largest Chabad synagogue in the Pico-Robertson neighborhood, baisbezalel.org, accessed May 8, 2018 (now unavailable).

41 Interview, May 20, 2019.

42 Interview, July 3, 2019.

43 Interview, May 20, 2019.

44 B'nai David-Judea website, accessed January 13, 2023, https://www .bnaidavid.com/mission.

45 Interview, December 30, 2009. Two versions of this expression from BT *Shevu'ot* 39a, permit it to be translated also as "All Israel is mixed up with one another."

46 Interview, date not found. The blessing "for not making me a woman" is recited by males; females are to praise God "for making me according to His will." She called the congregation "Open Orthodox," a term coined by a New York rabbi espousing increased intellectual openness, more flexible *halakhah*, and greater roles for women in Orthodox Judaism—behaviors that she finds scandalous. In fact, the congregational prayers do retain that traditional prayer, and the senior rabbi refuses to use the "Open Orthodox" label.

47 Interview, date not found.

48 Interview, date not found.

49 Interview, June 21, 2019.

50 Interview, June 21, 2019.

51 Interview, May 22, 2018.

52 Interview, May 22, 2018.

53 Interview, June 21, 2019.

54 Interview, June 21, 2019.

55 Interview, December 6, 2018.

56 Interview, December 6, 2018.

57 Interview, December 6, 2018.

58 Author's notes about experience with The Giving Spirit in the synagogue, church, and on the street, August 18, 2019.

59 Interview, May 22, 2018.

60 Interview, May 22, 2018.

61 SOVA Community Food and Resource Program has a website: https:// www.jfsla.org/SOVA.

62 Interview, July 9, 2013.

63 Maimonides seems to imply that a Jew is obligated to give to a non-Jew only if asked and then to behave toward the poor non-Jew just as one

would with a Jew. See Maimonides, Hilkhot Matanot L'Evyonim, chapter 7:7. An article on the Chabad.org website attributes to the founder of Hasidism, the Baal Shem Tov, the practice of unsolicited giving because "when you give unsolicited gifts, you receive unsolicited blessings from above, far more than you could have asked for"; see Aron Moss, "Why Give Tzedaka Before Being Asked?" Chabad.org, June 15, 2020, https:// www.chabad.org/library/article_cdo/aid/4463918/jewish/Why-Give -Tzedakah-Before-Being-Asked.htm.

64 Wexler, *Social Vision*, chaps. 5 and 6, describes his efforts on behalf of improving public education and incarceration policies.

65 Broadcast around the United States, the telethon features celebrities' enthusiastic endorsements and their singing, dancing, and joking with Chabad rabbis and male students, along with clips of their own and Chabad's activities; Chabad Telethon 2020, Chabad.com, accessed June 25, 2021, http://www.chabad.com/telethon/about.html.

66 To view all the programs and services offered through the Chabad Treatment center, see https://chabadrehab.com.

67 Interview, June 21, 2019.

68 "Charity Basics," Chabad.org, accessed June 15, 2020, https://www .chabad.org/library/article_cdo/aid/2719201/jewish/Charity-Basics.htm.

69 Rabbi Baruch S. Davidson, "What If a Charity Turns Out to Be Fake?" Chabad.org, accessed June 25, 2021, https://www.chabad.org/library/ article_cdo/aid/845611/jewish/What-If-a-Charity-Turns-Out-to-Be-Fake .htm.

70 Rabbi Yitzchak Etshalom, "The Greatest Good," *Jewish Journal*, June 19, 2003, https://jewishjournal.com/judaism/torah/8045/.

71 Written reply to interview questions, June 5, 2020.

72 Interview, June 3, 2020.

73 David Suissa, "Rabbi Pinto's Miracles," *Jewish Journal*, November 30, 2006, https://jewishjournal.com/news/united-states/14096/.

74 Phone conversation, June 3, 2020.

75 Interview, June 3, 2020.

76 Interview, August 6, 2018.

77 Interview, July 18, 2018.

78 Interview, December 6, 2018.

79 Interview, August 6, 2018.

80 Interview, July 3, 2018.

81 Interview, date not found. For the dilemma faced by such women, as well as those who have been abandoned, are childless, or are parents of gay

children, see Anne Gordon, "The Second-Best Time to Plant a Tree Is Right Now (or: When Life Doesn't Go According to Plan and the Jewish Community Is Slow to Catch On)," *JOFA Journal* 15.1 (Fall 2017).

82 Interview, July 24, 2019.

83 Interview, May 22, 2018.

84 Interview, date not found.

85 Interview, July 24, 2019.

86 Interview, July 24, 2019.

87 Interview, July 18, 2018.

88 Interview, date not found.

89 Interview, May 22, 2018.

90 Bat Sheva Marcus, "A Bigger Tent," *JOFA Journal* 15.1 (Fall 2017): 3.

91 Phone interview, July 9, 2019.

92 Interview, July 8, 2010.

93 Interview, August 14, 2019.

94 Interview, August 14, 2019.

95 Interview, date not found.

96 Interview, August 11, 2010.

97 Interview, July 3, 2018.

98 Interview, July 8, 2010.

99 Interview, July 18, 2018.

100 Interview, June 3, 2020.

101 Interview, July 8, 2010.

102 The rest of Hillel's aphorism follows: "And if I am only for myself, what am I? And if not now, when?"

CONCLUSION

1 Menachem Keren-Kratz, "The Contemporary Study of Orthodoxy: Challenging the One-Dimensional Paradigm," 49.4 *Tradition* (2016): 24–52, https://www.jstor.org/stable/44737112.

2 Interview, June 3, 2020.

3 The letter was published March 12 and signed and circulated by a few rabbis, and over the next week more added their signatures and disseminated it among their congregants. The Rabbinical Council of California posted its own letter on a local Los Angeles online Jewish newsletter, *Hillygram*.

4 Susan Josephs, "On Pico-Robertson, Kosher Restaurants Adjust, and Struggle," *Forward*, May 14, 2020, https://forward.com/news/446523/

letter-from-los-angeles-on-pico-robertson-kosher-restaurants-adjust
-and/.

5 "People Supporting Kosher Restaurants, Caterers + Event Planners in
   Crisis," Facebook, accessed June 24, 2020, https://www.facebook.com/
   groups/605852150257186/.

6 Interview, June 18, 2018, for example.

Bibliography

BOOKS AND CHAPTERS IN BOOKS

Abusch-Magder, Ruth Ann. "Kashrut: The Possibility and Limits of Women's Domestic Power." In *Food and Judaism*, edited by Leonard J. Greenspoon, Ronald Simkins, and Gerald Shapiro. Omaha: Creighton University Press, 2004.

Adlerstein, Yitzchok. *Essays on the Weekly Parsha Based on Nesivos Shalom*. Self-Published, 2012.

Allen, James P., and Eugene Turner. *The Ethnic Quilt: Population Diversity in Southern California*. Northridge: Center for Geographical Studies, California State University, Northridge, 1997.

Ammerman, Nancy Tatom. *Studying Lived Religion: Contexts and Practices*. New York: New York University Press, 2021.

Bailey, Stephen. *Kashrut, Tefillin, Tzitzit: Studies in the Purpose and Meaning of Symbolic Mitzvot Inspired by the Commentaries of Rabbi Samson Raphael Hirsch*. Northvale, NJ: Jason Aronson, 2000.

Berman, Louis A. *Vegetarianism and the Jewish Tradition*. New York: KTAV Publishing House, 1982.

Biale, David, David Assaf, Benjamin Brown, Uriel Gellman, Samuel C. Heilman, Moshe Rosman, Gadi Sagiv, and Marcin Wodzinski. *Hasidism: A New History*. Princeton: Princeton University Press, 2018.

Bomzer, Herbert W. *The Kolel in America*. New York: Sheingold, 1985.

Bonfil, Robert. *Jewish Life in Renaissance Italy*. Translated by Anthony Oldcorn. Berkeley: University of California Press, 1994.

Brumberg-Kraus, Jonathan. "Food in the Medieval Period." In *Feasting and Fasting: The History and Ethics of Jewish Food*, edited by Aaron S. Gross, Jody Myers, and Jordan D. Rosenblum, 83–109. New York: New York University Press, 2019.

Chumash. Michaan Edition. Brooklyn: Kehot, 2016.

Clay, Grady. *Being a Disquisition Upon the Origins, Natural Disposition, and Occurrences in the American Scene of Alleys, Together with Special Attention Being Given to Some Small Scale and Easily Completed Proposals for Their Improvement in Louisville, Jefferson County, Kentucky, Where They Do Constitute a Hidden Resource.* Louisville: Grady Clay, 1978.

Cohen, Jeremy. *"Be Fertile and Increase, Fill the Earth and Master It": The Ancient and Medieval Career of a Biblical Text.* Ithaca: Cornell University Press, 1989.

Cohen, Kate. *The Neppi Modona Diaries: Reading Jewish Survival through My Italian Family.* Hanover, NH: University Press of New England, 1997.

Cooper, John. *Eat and Be Satisfied: A Social History of Jewish Food.* Northvale, NJ: Jason Aronson, 1993.

Dresner, Samuel H., Seymour Siegel, and David M. Pollock. *The Jewish Dietary Laws: Their Meaning for Our Time.* Rev. and exp. ed. New York: Rabbinical Assembly and United Synagogue Commission on Jewish Education, 1966.

Eleff, Zev. *Authentically Orthodox: A Tradition-Bound Faith in American Life.* Detroit: Wayne State University Press, 2020.

Eleff, Zev. "The Search for Authenticity and the Case of Passover Peanut Oil." In *Feasting and Fasting: The History and Ethics of Jewish Food,* edited by Aaron S. Gross, Jody Myers, and Jordan D. Rosenblum, 212–34. New York: New York University Press, 2019.

Fader, Ayala. *Mitzvah Girls: Bringing Up the Next Generation of Hasidic Jews in Brooklyn.* Princeton: Princeton University Press, 2009.

Fine, Lawrence. *Physician of the Soul, Healer of the Cosmos: Isaac Luria and His Kabbalistic Fellowship.* Stanford: Stanford University Press, 2003.

Fishkoff, Sue. *Kosher Nation: Why More and More of America's Food Answers to a Higher Authority.* New York: Schocken Books, 2010.

Fishkoff, Sue. *The Rebbe's Army: Inside the World of Chabad-Lubavitch.* New York: Schocken Books, 2003.

Forst, Binyomin. *The Laws of Kashrus.* 2nd ed. New York: Mesorah Publications, 2010.

Freidenreich, David M. *Foreigners and Their Food: Constructing Otherness in Jewish, Christian, and Islamic Law.* Berkeley: University of California Press, 2011.

Goodfriend, Elaine Adler. "Food in the Biblical Era." In *Feasting and Fasting: The History and Ethics of Jewish Food,* edited by Aaron S. Gross, Jody

Myers, and Jordan D. Rosenblum, 32–58. New York: New York University Press, 2019.

Gross, Aaron S. "Introduction and Overview." In *Animals and the Human Imagination: A Companion to Animal Studies*, edited by Aaron Gross and Anne Vallely, 1–23. New York: Columbia University Press, 2015.

Gross, Aaron S. *The Question of the Animal and Religion: Theoretical Stakes, Practical Implications*. New York: Columbia University Press, 2015.

Gurock, Jeffrey. *Orthodox Jews in America*. Bloomington: Indiana University Press, 2009.

Haidt, Jonathan. "The Moral Emotions." In *Handbook of Affective Sciences*, edited by R. J. Davidson, K. R. Scher, and H. H. Goldsmith, 852–70. Oxford: Oxford University Press, 2003.

Haidt, Jonathan. *The Righteous Mind: Why Good People Are Divided by Politics and Religion*. New York: Vintage Books, 2012.

Hall, David. "Introduction." In *Lived Religion in America: Toward a History of Practice*, edited by David Hall, vii–xiii. Princeton: Princton University Press, 1997.

Harris, Marvin. "The Abominable Pig." Reprinted in *Food and Culture: A Reader*, 2nd ed., edited by Carole Counihan and Penny Van Esterik. New York: Routledge, 2008.

Hayes, Christine. *What's Divine about Divine Law: Early Perspectives*. Princeton: Princeton University Press, 2015.

Hecker, Joel. *Mystical Bodies, Mystical Meals: Eating and Embodiment in Medieval Kabbalah*. Detroit: Wayne State University Press, 2005.

Heilman, Samuel C. *Sliding to the Right: The Contest for the Future of American Jewish Orthodoxy*. Berkeley: University of California Press, 2006.

Heinemann, Isaac. *The Reasons for the Commandments in Jewish Thought: From the Bible to the Renaissance*. Translated by Leonard Levin. Boston: Academic Studies Press, 2008.

Herman, Pini. *Los Angeles Jewish Population Survey, 1997*. Los Angeles: Jewish Federation of Greater Los Angeles, 1998.

Hirsch, Samson Raphael. *Horeb: A Philosophy of Jewish Laws and Observances*. Translated by Isador Grunfeld. New York: Soncino Press, 1962.

Hirsch, Samson Raphael. "Religion Allied to Progress." Translated by Isador Grunfeld. In *The Jew in the Modern World*, edited by Paul Mendes-Flohr and Jehuda Reinharz, 220–23. New York: Oxford University Press, 2011.

Horowitz, Roger. *Kosher USA: How Coke Became Kosher and Other Tales of Modern Food*. New York: Columbia University Press, 2016.

Hui, Y. H., ed. *Handbook of Meat and Meat Processing*. 2nd ed. New York: Routledge and CRC Press, 2012.

Iacobbo, Karen, and Michael Iacobbo. *Vegetarian America: A History*. Westport: Greenwood Publishing Group, 2004.

Jacob, Walter, and Walter Homolka, eds. *Hesed and Tzedakah: From Bible to Modernity*. Berlin: Frank and Timme, 2006.

Jacobs, Louis. *What Does Judaism Say About . . . ?* New York: Quadrangle, 1973.

Joselit, Jenna Weissman. *New York's Jewish Jews: The Orthodox Community in the Interwar Years*. Bloomington: Indiana University Press, 1990.

Judd, Robin. *Contested Rituals: Circumcision, Kosher Butchering, and Jewish Political Life in Germany, 1843–1933*. Ithaca: Cornell University Press, 2007.

Kasher, Hannah. "Well-Being of the Body or Welfare of the Soul: The Maimonidean Explanation of the Dietary Laws." In *Moses Maimonides: Physician, Scientist, and Philosopher*, edited by Fred Rosner and Samuel S. Kottek. Northvale, NJ: Jason Aronson, 1993.

Katz, Jacob. *Tradition and Crisis: Jewish Society at the End of the Middle Ages*. Rev. ed. Syracuse: Syracuse University Press, 2000.

Kraemer, David C. "Food in the Rabbinic Era." In *Feasting and Fasting: The History and Ethics of Jewish Food*, edited by Aaron S. Gross, Jody Myers, and Jordan D. Rosenblum, 59–82. New York: New York University Press, 2019.

Kraemer, David C. *Jewish Eating and Identity through the Ages*. New York: Routledge, 2009.

Krinsky, Alan D. "Relevant and Irrelevant Distinctions: Speciesism, Judaism, and Veganism." In *Jewish Veganism and Vegetarianism: Studies and New Directions*, edited by Jacob Ari Labendz and Shmuly Yanklowitz, 233–49. Albany: State University of New York Press, 2019.

Levenson, Alan T. *The Making of the Modern Hebrew Bible: How Scholars in Germany, Israel, and America Transformed an Ancient Text*. Lanham: Rowman & Littlefield, 2011.

Lewin, Isaac, Michael I. Munk, and Jeremiah Berman. *Religious Freedom: The Right to Practice Shehitah (Kosher Slaughtering)*. New York: Research Institute for Post-War Problems of Religion, 1946.

Lichtenstein, Aaron. "Does Jewish Tradition Recognize an Ethic Independent of Halakha?" In *Modern Jewish Ethics: Theory and Practice*, edited by Marvin Fox, 62–88. Columbus: The Ohio State University Press, 1975.

Margolese, Faranak. *Off the Derech: Why Observant Jews Leave Judaism*. Jerusalem: Devora, 2005.

Milgrom, Jacob. *Leviticus 1–16*. Anchor Yale Bible Commentaries. New Haven: Yale University Press, 1998.

Miller, Chaim, ed. *Chumash*. Gutnick Edition. Brooklyn: Kol Menachem, 2009.

Myers, Jody. "The Altared Table: Women and Food in Judaism." In *Lifecycles: Jewish Women on Biblical Themes in Contemporary Life*, edited by Debra Orenstein and Jane Rachel Litman, 158–65. Woodstock, VT: Festival Lights Press, 1997.

Myers, Jody. "Food in the Modern Era." In *Feasting and Fasting: The History and Ethics of Jewish Food*, edited by Aaron S. Gross, Jody Myers, and Jordan D. Rosenblum, 110–39. New York: New York University Press, 2019.

Myers, Jody. *Kabbalah and the Spiritual Quest: The Kabbalah Centre in America*. Westport, CT: Praeger, 2007.

Myers, Jody. "Kabbalah as a Tool of Orthodox Outreach." In *Kabbalah in America: Ancient Lore in the New World*, edited by Brian Ogren, 343–57. Leiden: Brill, 2020.

Myers, Jody. "Kabbalah for the Gentiles: Diverse Souls and Universalism in Contemporary Kabbalah." In *Kabbalah and the Contemporary Spiritual Revival*, edited by Boaz Huss, 181–211. Beer-Sheva, Israel: Ben Gurion University Press, 2011.

Myers, Jody, and Jane Rachel Litman. "The Secret of Jewish Femininity: Hiddenness, Power, and Physicality in the Theology of Orthodox Women in the Contemporary World." In *Gender and Judaism: The Transformation of Tradition*, edited by T. M. Rudavsky, 51–80. New York: New York University Press, 1995.

Newfeld, Schneur Zalman. *Degrees of Separation: Identity Formation while Leaving Ultra-Orthodox Judaism*. Philadelphia: Temple University Press, 2020.

Oratz, Ephraim, ed. *Trumath Tzvi: The Pentateuch with a Translation by Samson Raphael Hirsch and Excerpts from The Hirsch Commentary*. 7 volumes. New York: Judaica Press, 1986.

Orsi, Robert. "Everyday Miracles: The Study of Lived Religion." In *Lived Religion in America: Toward a History of Practice*, edited by David Hall, 3–21. Princeton: Princeton University Press, 1997.

Patterson, Charles. *Eternal Treblinka: Our Treatment of Animals and the Holocaust*. New York: Lantern Books, 2002.

Phillips, Bruce A. "American Judaism in the Twenty-First Century." In *The Cambridge Companion to American Judaism*, edited by Dana Evan Kaplan, 397–415. Cambridge: Cambridge University Press, 2005.

Phillips, Bruce A. "Faultlines: The Seven Socio-Ecologies of Jewish Los Angeles." In *The Jewish Role in American Life: An Annual Review*, edited by Bruce Zuckerman and Jeremy Schoenberg, 5:109–37. West Lafayette, IN: Purdue University Press, 2007.

Phillips, Bruce A. "Los Angeles Jewry: A Demographic Profile." In *American Jewish Yearbook*, vol. 86, 136–37. New York: American Jewish Committee, 1986.

Polonsky, Antony. *The Jews in Poland and Russia: 1914–2008*. Oxford: Littman Library of Jewish Civilization, 2012.

Potek, Aaron. "The Case for Limiting Meat Consumption to Shabbat, Holidays, and Celebrations." In *Kashrut and Jewish Food Ethics*, edited by Shmuly Yanklowitz, 218–34. Boston: Academic Studies Press, 2019.

Preece, Rod. *Sins of the Flesh: A History of Ethical Vegetarian Thought*. Vancouver: University of British Columbia Press, 2008.

Raphael, Marc Lee. *Diary of a Los Angeles Jew, 1947–1973: Autobiography as Autofiction*. Williamsburg, VA: Department of Religious Studies, College of William and Mary, 2008.

Rosenblum, Jordan D. *Food and Identity in Early Rabbinic Judaism*. New York: Cambridge University Press, 2010.

Rosenblum, Jordan D. *The Jewish Dietary Laws in the Ancient World*. Cambridge: Cambridge University Press, 2016.

Rosenblum, Jordan D. *Rabbinic Drinking: What Beverages Teach Us about Rabbinic Literature*. Berkeley: University of California Press, 2020.

Rozin, Paul, Jonathan Haidt, Clark McCauley, and Sumio Imada. "Disgust: Preadaptation and the Cultural Evolution of a Food-Based Emotion." In *Food Preferences and Taste: Continuity and Change*, edited by Helen Macbeth, 65–82. Providence: Berghahn Books, 1997.

Sarna, Jonathan D. *American Judaism: A History*. New Haven: Yale University Press, 2004.

Sax, Boria. *Animals in the Third Reich: Pets, Scapegoats, and the Holocaust*. New York: Continuum International Publishing Group, 2000.

Schwartz, Richard. *Judaism and Vegetarianism*. Smithtown, NY: Exposition Press, 1982.

Sears, David. *The Vision of Eden: Animal Welfare and Vegetarianism in Jewish Law and Mysticism*. Spring Valley, NY: Orot, 2003.

Séfer haḤinnuch: The Book of [Mitzvah] Education. Translated and notes by Charles Wengrov. Jerusalem: Feldheim, 1988.

Shatz, David. "Ethical Theories in the Orthodox Movement." In *The Oxford Handbook of Jewish Ethics and Morality*, edited by Elliot N. Dorff and Jonathan K. Crane, 241–58. New York: Oxford University Press, 2012.

Siegel, Richard, Michael Strassfeld, and Sharon Strassfeld, eds. *The Jewish Catalog: A Do-It-Yourself Kit*. Philadelphia: Jewish Publication Society, 1973.

Singer, Isaac Bashevis. *The Seance and Other Stories*. New York: Farrar, Straus & Giroux, 1968.

Soloveitchik, Joseph B. "On Humane Methods of Handling Meat for Slaughter." In *Community, Covenant and Commitment: Selected Letters and Communications of Joseph B. Soloveitchik*, edited by Nathaniel Helfgot. Jersey City: KTAV Publishing House, 2005.

Soomekh, Saba. *From the Shahs to Los Angeles: Three Generations of Iranian Jewish Women between Religion and Culture*. Albany: State University of New York Press, 2012.

Stampfer, Shaul. *Families, Rabbis and Education: Traditional Jewish Society in Nineteenth-Century Eastern Europe*. Oxford: Littman Library of Jewish Civilization, 2019.

Tamari, Meir. *"With All Your Possessions": Jewish Ethics and Economic Life*. New York: Free Press, 1987.

Taub, Shimon. *Laws of Tzedakah and Maaser*. New York: Mesorah, 2001.

Tavory, Iddo. *Summoned: Identification and Religious Life in a Jewish Neighborhood*. Chicago: University of Chicago Press, 2016.

Waxman, Chaim I. *Social Change and Halakhic Evolution in American Orthodoxy*. Liverpool: Littman Library of Jewish Civilization, 2017.

Weinberger, Naftali. *A Practical Guide to the Mitzvah of Shiluach Hakan*. New York: Feldheim, 2006.

Weinstein, Sara Epstein. *Piety and Fanaticism: Rabbinic Criticism of Religious Stringency*. Northvale, NJ: Jason Aronson, 1997.

Wexler, Philip, Eli Rubin, and Michael Wexler. *Social Vision: The Lubavitcher Rebbe's Transformative Paradigm for the World*. New York: Crossroad, 2019.

Wijnhoven, Jochanan H. A. "The Zohar and the Proselyte." In *Texts and Responses: Studies Presented to N. Glatzer*, edited by Michael Fishbane, 120–40. Leiden: Brill, 1957.

Yanklowitz, Shmuly, ed. *Kashrut and Jewish Food Ethics*. Boston: Academic Studies Press, 2019.

Yisraeli, Yosi, and Yaniv Fox, eds. *Contesting Inter-Religious Conversion in the Medieval World*. London: Routledge, 2017.

Zion, Noam. *For the Love of God: Comparative Religious Motivations for Giving: Christian Charity, Maimonidean Tzedakah and Lovingkindness (Hesed)*.
Cleveland: Zion Holiday Publications, 2013.

JOURNALS

Bernstein, Eliezer (Louis). "Problems of Kosher Slaughter in the United
States." [In Hebrew.] *Shana Bashana* (1967): 366–67.

Bleich, J. David. "Vegetarianism and Judaism." *Tradition* 23.1 (1987): 82–90.

Blutinger, Jeffrey C. "Creatures from Before the Flood: Reconciling Science
and Genesis in the Pages of a Nineteenth-Century Hebrew Newspaper."
Jewish Social Studies 16.2 (Winter 2010): 67–92.

Cohen, Alfred S. "Vegetarianism from a Jewish Perspective." *Journal of
Halacha and Contemporary Society* 1.2 (1981): 38–63.

Eleff, Zev. "American Orthodoxy's Lukewarm Embrace of the Hirschian
Legacy, 1850–1939." *Tradition* 45 (Fall 2012): 35–53.

Feldman, L. H. "Proselytism by Jews in the Third, Fourth, and Fifth Centuries." *Journal for the Study of Judaism in the Persian, Hellenistic, and Roman
Period* 24.1 (June 1993): 1–58.

Fessler, Daniel M. T., and Carlos David Navarrete. "Meat Is Good to Taboo:
Dietary Proscriptions as a Product of the Interaction of Psychological
Mechanisms and Social Processes." *Journal of Cognition and Culture* 3.1
(2003): 1–40.

Fishbane, Simcha. "*Mipnei Darkei Shalom*: The Promotion of Harmonious
Relationships in the Mishnah's Social Order." *Studies in Judaism, Humanities, and the Social Sciences* 1.1 (2017): 73–84.

Forsyth, Ann. "What Is a Walkable Place? The Walkability Debate in Urban
Design." *Urban Design International* 20.4 (2015): 274–92.

Gordon, Anne. "The Second-Best Time to Plant a Tree Is Right Now (or:
When Life Doesn't Go According to Plan and the Jewish Community Is
Slow to Catch On)." *JOFA Journal* 15.1 (Fall 2017): 12–16.

Graham, Jesse, Jonathan Haidt, Sena Koleva, Matt Motyl, Ravi Iyer, Sean P.
Wojcik, and Peter H. "Moral Foundations Theory: The Pragmatic Validity
of Moral Pluralism." *Advances in Experimental Social Psychology* 47 (2013):
55–130.

Keren-Kratz, Menachem. "The Contemporary Study of Orthodoxy:
Challenging the One-Dimensional Paradigm." *Tradition* 49.4 (2016):
24–52.

Marcus, Bat Sheva. "A Bigger Tent." *JOFA Journal* 15.1 (Fall 2017): 1–3.

Milgrom, Jacob. "The Biblical Diet Laws as an Ethical System: Food and Faith." *Interpretation* 7.3 (July 1963): 288–301.

Nemeroff, Carol, and Paul Rozin. "Sympathetic Magical Beliefs and Kosher Dietary Practice: The Interaction of Rules and Feelings." *Ethos* 20.1 (1992): 96–115.

Nitzachon 6.1 (Fall–Winter 5779): 99–130.

Norenzayan, Ara. "Does Religion Make People Moral?" *Behaviour* 151.2–3 (2014): 372.

"On the Matter of Danger to *Sheḥitah*, Heaven Forbid." [In Hebrew.] *Hamaor* 8.5 (May 1958): 48.

Phillips, Bruce A. "Not Quite White: The Emergence of Jewish 'Ethnoburbs' in Los Angeles 1920–2010." *American Jewish History* 100.1 (January 2016): 73–104.

Rappaport, Roy. "The Sacred in Human Evolution." *Annual Review of Ecology and Systematics* 2 (1971): 29–37.

Shemesh, Yael. "Vegetarian Ideology in Talmudic Literature and Traditional Biblical Exegesis." *Review of Rabbinic Judaism* 9 (2006): 141–66.

Soloveitchik, Joseph B. "Confrontation." *Tradition: A Journal of Orthodox Thought* 6.2 (1964): 5–29.

Sosis, Richard. "Religion and Intragroup Cooperation: Preliminary Results of a Comparative Analysis of Utopian Communities." *Cross-Cultural Research* 34 (2000): 70–87.

Sosis, Richard, and Eric R. Bressler. "Cooperation and Commune Longevity: A Test of the Costly Signaling Theory of Religion." *Cross-Cultural Research* 37 (2003): 211–39.

NEWSPAPERS AND MAGAZINES

Brown, Ebony. "Hanging on to Heritage." *Baltimore Jewish Times*, May 7, 2015. https://www.jewishtimes.com/36708/hanging-on-to-heritage/.

Clare, Erin. "The 21st-Century Iranian Jew." *Baltimore Jewish Times*, January 11, 2013. https://www.jewishtimes.com/the-21st-century-iranian-jew/.

Etshalom, Yitzchak. "The Greatest Good." *Jewish Journal*, June 19, 2003. https://jewishjournal.com/judaism/torah/8045/.

Gruenbaum-Fax, Julie. "B'nai David-Judea's Renaissance." *Jewish Journal*, June 11, 1998. Accessed September 1, 2020. https://jewishjournal.com/old_stories/944/.

Gruenbaum-Fax, Julie. "Overnight Fire Destroys Glatt Mart." *Jewish Journal*, December 30, 2004. https://jewishjournal.com/community/10756/.

Gruenbaum-Fax, Julie. "Youth Appeal." *Jewish Journal*, December 28, 2000. https://jewishjournal.com/community/3720/.

Hussain, Suhauna, and Dakota Smith. "Ralphs and Food 4 Less locations to Close in Los Angeles Over Hazard Pay Rules." *Los Angeles Times*, March 10, 2021. https://www.latimes.com/business/story/2021-03-10/ralphs-food-4-less-locations-close-los-angeles-hazard-pay.

Jewish Telegraphic Agency. "Rabbinical Council of America Officially Bans Ordination and Hiring of Women Rabbis." Press Release, November 1, 2015. www.jta.org/2015/11/01/united-states/rabbinical-council-of-america-officially-bans-ordination-and-hiring-of-women-rabbis.

Josephs, Susan. "On Pico-Robertson, Kosher Restaurants Adjust, and Struggle." *Forward*, May 14, 2020. https://forward.com/news/446523/letter-from-los-angeles-on-pico-robertson-kosher-restaurants-adjust-and/.

Lasson, Kenneth. "Holy Wars and Hot Dogs." *Jerusalem Post*, April 20, 2016. www.jpost.com/Opinion/Holy-wars-and-hot-dogs-451871.

Los Angeles Times. "Neighborhoods." Mapping L.A. Accessed June 1, 2021. http://maps.latimes.com/neighborhoods/.

Los Angeles Times. "Pico-Robertson." Mapping L.A. Accessed June 1, 2021. http://maps.latimes.com/neighborhoods/neighborhood/pico-robertson/.

Lowenfeld, Jonah. "Kosher Consumers Reeling after Doheny Scandal." *Jewish Journal*, March 28, 2013. www.jewishjournal.com/mobile_20111212/114764/.

Lowenfeld, Jonah. "Who Owns Young Israel of Beverly Hills?" *Jewish Journal*, July 7, 2010. https://jewishjournal.com/community/81042/.

Manetti, Christina. "Dress." Translated by Olga Goldberg-Mulkiewicz. *The Yivo Encyclopedia of Jews in Eastern Europe*. Accessed June 10, 2021. www.yivoencyclopedia.org/article.aspx/Dress.

Melamed, Karmel. "Elat Market . . . Shoppers' Paradise or Chaotic Madhouse?" *Jewish Journal*, December 14, 2007. https://jewishjournal.com/uncategorized/16871/elat-market-shoppers-paradise-or-chaotic-madhouse/.

Olson, Carly. "There's No Labor Shortage—Just Not Enough Good Jobs." *Los Angeles Times*, July 2, 2021. https://www.latimes.com/business/story/2021-07-02/labor-shortage-is-workers-crisis-as-covid-economy-recovers.

Pierson, David. "Two Worlds at One Table." *Los Angeles Times*, December 24, 2005. https://www.latimes.com/archives/la-xpm-2005-dec-24-me-kosherxmas24-story.html.

Popper, Nathaniel. "Lack of Meat Choices Not Kosher, Say Conservative Shuls in St. Paul." *Forward*, July 21, 2006. www.forward.com/news/478/lack-of-meat-choices-not-kosher-say-conservative/.

Shapiro, Samantha M. "Kosher Wars." *New York Times*, October 9, 2008. www.nytimes.com/2008/10/12/magazine/12kosher-t.html.

Shulman, Eliezer. "The Horn of the Dilemma." *Mishpacha*, January 15, 2020. https://mishpacha.com/irans-jews-on-the-horns-of-dilemma/.

Simmons, Shraga. "Pico-Robertson: Story of a Torah Boomtown." *Ami Magazine*, February 6, 2019.

Suissa, David. "Rabbi Pinto's Miracles." *Jewish Journal*, November 30, 2006. https://jewishjournal.com/news/united-states/14096/.

Wenig, Gaby. "The Kolel Community." *Jewish Journal*, March 7, 2002. https://jewishjournal.com/community/5630/.

Yanklowitz, Shmuly. "How Kosher Is Your Milk?" *Jewish Journal*, June 7, 2012. https://jewishjournal.com/culture/food/104874/how-kosher-is-your-milk/.

WEBSITES

Adlerstein, Yitzchok. "Parshas Mishpatim—Cheeseburgers for Dummies." Torah.org. Accessed June 15, 2021. www.torah.org/torah-portion/ravhirsch-5771-mishpatim/.

Alhatorah. "Permission to Eat Meat: Exegetical Approaches." Accessed June 23, 2021. http://alhatorah.org/Permission_to_Eat_Meat/2.

Alt Miller, Yvette. "Banning Shechitah in Europe." Aish, January 6, 2018. https://aish.com/banning-shechita-in-europe.html.

Anshe Emes. Accessed February 26, 2021. https://anshe.org/.

Bais Bezalel. "11 Nissan Essay Contest Winners." Children's Programs. Accessed May 8, 2018. http://www.baisbezalel.org/templates/articlecco_cdo/aid/3424677/jewish/11-Nissan-Essay-Contest-Winners.htm (now unavailable).

Bakar Kosher Meats. Accessed June 18, 2021. www.bakarmeats.com/.

Beth Jacob Congregation. "Mission—Beth Jacob Congregation." Accessed February 16, 2021. www.bethjacob.org/mission.html (now unavailable).

Bistricer, Dovid. "Practical Shemittah." Orthodox Union Kosher. Accessed April 2, 2017. www.oukosher.org/publications/practical-shemittah/.

B'nai David-Judea. "Mission." Accessed February 16, 2021. www.bnaidavid.com/mission.

Chabad. "Charity Basics." Accessed June 15, 2020. https://www.chabad.org/library/article_cdo/aid/2719201/jewish/Charity-Basics.htm.

Chabad. "The Chassidic Masters on Food and Eating." Accessed May 3, 2018. www.chabad.org/library/article_cdo/aid/133912/jewish/The-Chassidic-Masters-on-Food.htm.

Chabad. "Hachnasat Orhim: Hospitality." Accessed June 19, 2019. https://www.chabad.org/library/article_cdo/aid/691769/jewish/Hakhnasat-Orhim-Hospitality.htm.

Chabad. "The Human Biosphere." Accessed June 22, 2021. www.chabad.org/library/article_cdo/aid/82892/jewish/The-Human-Biosphere.htm.

Chabad. "The Rebbe's 10-Point Mitzvah Campaign for Jewish Awareness and Observance." Accessed June 16, 2021. https://www.chabad.org/therebbe/article_cdo/aid/62228/jewish/10-Point-Mitzvah-Campaign.htm.

Chabad. "What Is Shehitah?" Accessed February 19, 2019. https://www.chabad.org/library/article_cdo/aid/222240/jewish/What-Is-Shehitah.htm.

Chabad Telethon. "About the Telethon." Accessed June 25, 2021. http://www.chabad.com/telethon/about.html.

Chabad Treatment Center. Accessed March 22, 2023. https://chabadrehab.com.

Citron, Aryeh. "Immersion of Vessels (Tevilat Keilim)." Chabad.org. Accessed December 24, 2020. https://www.chabad.org/library/article_cdo/aid/1230791/jewish/Immersion-of-Vessels-Tevilat-Keilim.htm.

Cohen, Dovid. "Doing Business Involving Non-Kosher Food." Chicago Rabbinical Council, January 2008. Accessed April 4, 2017. www.crcweb.org/kosher_articles/business_involving_non_kosher.php.

Cooperman, Alan, Gregory Smith, and Becka Alper. "A Portrait of American Orthodox Jews: A Further Analysis of the 2013 Survey of U.S. Jews." Pew Research Center, August 26, 2015. www.pewforum.org/2015/08/26/a-portrait-of-american-orthodox-jews/.

Davidson, Baruch S. "Judaism and Vegetarianism." Chabad.org, July 30, 2017. Accessed June 18, 2021. www.chabad.org/library/article_cdo/aid/858870/jewish/Judaism-and-Vegetarianism.htm.

Davidson, Baruch S. "What If a Charity Turns Out to Be Fake?" Chabad.org. Accessed June 25, 2021. https://www.chabad.org/library/article_cdo/aid/845611/jewish/What-If-a-Charity-Turns-Out-to-Be-Fake.htm.

Facebook. "People Supporting Kosher Restaurants, Caterers + Event Planners in Crisis." Accessed June 24, 2020. https://www.facebook.com/groups/605852150257186/.

Farm Forward. Accessed July 5, 2021. www.farmforward.com.

Feldman, Rabbi Daniel. "My House Is Your House: The Mitzvah of Hakhnassat Orchim." YUTorahOnline. Accessed March 24, 2023. https://www

.yutorah.org/togo/5769/pesach/articles/Pesach_To-Go_-_5769_Rabbi
_Feldman.pdf.

Ferziger, Adam F. "The Emergence of the Community Kolel: A New
Model for Addressing Assimilation." Rappaport Center for Assimilation
Research and Strengthening Jewish Vitality. Bar Ilan University, 2006.
https://www.rappaportcenter.biu.ac.il/Research/PDF/Hoveret%2013_01-64
.pdf.

Forst, Binyomin. "Philosophy of Food: Medicine for the Body or Salve for
the Soul?" Aish. Accessed May 11, 2018. https://www.aish.com/sp/ph/
Philosophy_of_Food.html.

Freeman, Tzvi. "What Gives Us the Right to Kill Animals?" Chabad.org.
Accessed July 27, 2017. www.chabad.org/library/article_cdo/aid/77318/
jewish/What-Gives-Us-the-Right-to-Kill-Animals.htm.

Freeman, Tzvi. "Why Do We Keep Kosher?" Chabad.org. Accessed June 21,
2021. www.chabad.org/library/article_cdo/aid/82894/jewish/Why-Do-We
-Keep-Kosher.htm.

The Giving Spirit. Accessed July 12, 2021. https://www.thegivingspirit.org/.

Gordimer, Avrohom. "Milk from Non-Kosher Species and Its Relationship
with the US Kosher Dairy Industry." Orthodox Union Kosher. Accessed
June 20, 2021. www.oukosher.org/publications/milk-from-non-kosher
-species-and-its-relationship-with-the-us-kosher-dairy-industry/.

Gorelik, David. "Yoshon." Orthodox Union Kosher, October 8, 2015. www
.oukosher.org/blog/consumer-kosher/yoshon/.

Green, Velvel. "Spiritual Molecules." Chabad.org. Accessed April 20, 2018.
www.chabad.org/library/article_cdo/aid/82889/jewish/Spiritual-Molecules
.htm.

Gross, Aaron. "Building Program—Brochure and Dedication Opportunities." Anshe Emes, December 19, 2008. www.anshe.org/building-program
-brochure-and-dedication-opportunities/.

Hanasab, Jasmine, and Rebecca Heikaly. "Elat Market." Iranian Jewish Life in
Los Angeles: Past and Present. Accessed February 14, 2021. https://scalar
.usc.edu/hc/iranian-jews-in-los-angeles/elat-market.

Hecht, Eli. "Kiddush Hashem in California." Chabad of South Bay. Accessed
February 18, 2021. www.chabadsb.org/templates/articlecco_cdo/aid/
59872/jewish/Kiddish-Hashem-in-California.htm.

Heinemann, Moshe. "Food Fit for a King: Reviewing the Laws of Bishul
Akum & Bishul Yisroel." Star-K. Accessed December 18, 2018. www.star-k
.org/articles/articles/1182/food-fit-for-a-king-reviewing-the-laws-of-bishul
-akum-bishul-yisroel/.

Imamother: Connecting Frum Women. Accessed June 20, 2021. https://www
.imamother.com/forum/.

International Vegetarian Union. "History of the German Vegetarian Society."
Accessed June 22, 2021. https://ivu.org/history/societies/vbd.html.

Leib Schapiro, Yehuda. "The Mitzvah of Inviting Guests." Audio lecture. Chabad.org. Accessed March 12, 2020. https://www.chabad.org/
multimedia/audio_cdo/aid/612952/jewish/The-Mitzvah-of-Inviting-Guests
.htm.

LINK Kollel. Accessed February 14, 2021. https://linkla.org/.

Living Torah. "Every Jew Is Close." Video. Chabad.org, March 18, 1990. www
.chabad.org/therebbe/livingtorah/player_cdo/aid/319001/jewish/Every-Jew
-is-Close.htm.

Livonia Glatt Market. "Livonia Glatt Kosher Market Sunday Kabob Grill
Cookout BBQ Los Angeles." YouTube video, June 3, 2012. Accessed September 25, 2020. www.youtube.com/watch?v=7lLSAQ0TgUk.

Loewenthal, Tali. "Why Shechitah Is Important." Chabad.org. Accessed May 3,
2018. https://www.chabad.org/library/article_cdo/aid/412206/jewish/Why
-Shechitah-Is-Important.htm.

Los Angeles Theaters. "Stadium Theater." Accessed February 16, 2021. www
.losangelestheatres.blogspot.com/2017/03/stadium-theatre.html.

Lowinger, Malki. "Taking the Aspirin before the Headache: Project Chazon."
Mishpocha, Chanuka 5766 (2005). Reprinted, Project Chazon website.
Accessed March 20, 2018, http://www.projectchazon.com/images/Article
_Mishpacha.pdf.

Majeski, Shloma. "The Chassidic Approach to Joy." Chabad.org. Accessed
June 18, 2020. https://www.chabad.org/library/article_cdo/aid/88574/jewish/
The-Chassidic-Approach-To-Joy.htm.

Margolin, Dovid. "Operation Exodus: The Chabad Effort That Saved 1,800 Iranian Jewish Children." Chabad. Accessed November 1, 2020. https://www
.chabad.org/library/article_cdo/aid/4299265/jewish/Operation-Exodus
-The-Chabad-Effort-That-Saved-1800-Iranian-Jewish-Children.htm.

Meir, Asher. "Mishpatim: Cooking Meat and Milk." Orthodox Union, January 25, 2011. www.ou.org/life/torah/mm_cooking_meat_and_milk/.

Moss, Aron. "I Ate Non-Kosher Food—Now What?" Chabad.org. Accessed
October 26, 2020. www.chabad.org/library/article_cdo/aid/1614932/
jewish/I-Ate-Non-Kosher-Food-Now-What.htm.

Moss, Aron. "Why Aren't We Vegetarians?" Chabad.org. Accessed July 27,
2017. www.chabad.org/library/article_cdo/aid/160995/jewish/Why-Arent
-We-Vegetarians.htm.

Moss, Aron. "Why Give Tzedaka before Being Asked?" Chabad.org, June 15, 2020. https://www.chabad.org/library/article_cdo/aid/4463918/jewish/Why-Give-Tzedakah-Before-Being-Asked.htm.

Olami Resources. "Why Keep Kosher?" Accessed May 8, 2018. http://nleresources.com/wp-content/uploads/2012/07/kashrut.pdf.

Orthodox Union Kosher. "Playing with Fire." May 4, 2004. www.oukosher.org/blog/consumer-kosher/playing-with-fire/.

Orthodox Union Kosher. "Tevilat Keilim: A Primer." April 24, 2007. www.oukosher.org/blog/consumer-kosher/tevilas-keilim-a-primer/.

Orthodox Union Staff. "Separating Terumah and Maaser." May 4, 2004. www.oukosher.org/blog/consumer-kosher/separating-terumah-and-maaser/.

Orthodox Union Staff. "Setting the Record Straight on Kosher Slaughter." December 29, 2004. https://oukosher.org/blog/news/setting-the-record-straight-on-kosher-slaughter/.

Orthodox Union Staff. "What's The Truth About . . . Nikkur Achoraim?" September 13, 2006. www.oukosher.org/blog/consumer-kosher/whats-the-truth-about-nikkur-achoraim/.

Packouz, Kalman. "Why Kosher? Keeping Kosher Offers a Variety of Spiritual and Practical Benefits." Aish, February 2, 2002. Accessed May 8, 2018. www.aish.com/jl/m/mm/48945306.html?s=srcon.

People for the Ethical Treatment of Animals. "PETA Reveals Extreme Cruelty at Kosher Slaughterhouses." Accessed June 8, 2021. https://www.peta.org/features/agriprocessors/.

Pew Research Center. "Chapter 2: Intermarriage and Other Demographics." October 1, 2013. http://www.pewforum.org/2013/10/01/chapter-2-intermarriage-and-other-demographics/.

Pew Research Center. "A Portrait of Jewish Americans." October 1, 2013. www.pewforum.org/2013/10/01/jewish-american-beliefs-attitudes-culture-survey/.

Rabbinical Council of California. Accessed November 10, 2020. https://rccvaad.org/.

Schuchman, Moshe T. "A Cut Above: Shehitah in the Crosshairs, Again." Star-K, Fall 2012. Accessed February 19, 2019. https://www.star-k.org/articles/kashrus-kurrents/548/a-cut-above-shehitah-in-the-crosshairs-again/#_ftn44.

Schuchman, Moshe T. "Sharp Awareness in the Kitchen." Star-K, Spring 2011. www.star-k.org/articles/kashrus-kurrents/597/sharp-awareness-in-the-kitchen/.

Shafran, Avi. "The Shechita Controversy." Aish, December 25, 2004. https://www.aish.com/jw/s/48894162.html.

Shalom Grill. "Shalom Kosher Grill Buys Elat Burger." Accessed June 22, 2021. http://shalomgrill.com/shalom-grill-buys-elat-burger.php.

Shalom Pizza. "What Is Kosher?" Accessed January 31, 2021. www .shalompizza.com/kosher.php.

Shurpin, Yehudah. "Are Imitation Crab, Pork and Cheeseburgers Kosher?" Chabad.org. Accessed February 1, 2018. www.chabad.org/library/article _cdo/aid/3907949/jewish/Are-Imitation-Crab-Pork-and-Cheeseburgers -Kosher.htm.

Slonim, Rivkah. "The Rebbe on the Jewish Woman's Hair Covering: Blessings from Above and Blessings from Below." Chabad.org. Accessed March 1, 2012. https://www.chabad.org/theJewishWoman/article_cdo/aid/840202/ jewish/The-Rebbe-on-the-Jewish-Womans-Hair-Covering.htm.

SOVA Community Food and Resource Program. Jewish Family Service LA. Accessed July 12, 2021. https://www.jfsla.org/SOVA.

Stack Exchange. "Mi Yodea." Accessed June 17, 2021. www.judaism .stackexchange.com/.

Tauber, Yanki. "Love According to the Rebbe." Chabad.org. Accessed August 24, 2019. https://www.chabad.org/therebbe/article_cdo/aid/2756/ jewish/Love-According-to-the-Rebbe.htm.

Taylor, Pinchas. "Kabbalistic Eating." Chabad.org. Accessed June 20, 2021. www.chabad.org/library/article_cdo/aid/2837524/jewish/Kabbalistic -Eating.htm.

Taylor, Pinchas. "Not Based on Physical Health." Chabad.org. Accessed June 21, 2021. www.chabad.org/library/article_cdo/aid/2837509/jewish/ Not-Based-on-Physical-Health.htm.

Temple Beth Am. "Our History." Accessed February 14, 2021. www.tbala.org/ about/our-history.

Tomchei Shabbos of Los Angeles. Accessed June 25, 2021. https:// tomcheishabbos.org/.

Tucker, Ethan. "Maintaining Jewish Distinctiveness: The Case of Gentile Foods." Hadar. Accessed June 20, 2019. www.hadar.org/torah-resource/ maintaining-jewish-distinctiveness-case-gentile-foods.

Uri L'Tzedek. Accessed June 7, 2021. http://utzedek.org/.

Wikipedia. "Beverly Hills Oil Field." Last modified May 28, 2021. https://en .wikipedia.org/wiki/Beverly_Hills_Oil_Field.

Wikipedia. "Los Angeles County Demographics." Last modified May 28, 2021. https://en.wikipedia.org/wiki/Los_Angeles_County,_California #History.

Wisnefsky, Moshe Yaakov. "Abraham's Hospitality." Chabad.org. Accessed June 9, 2020. https://www.chabad.org/kabbalah/article_cdo/aid/379749/jewish/Abrahams-Hospitality.htm.

Wolf, Saul. "Are You Sure Meat Was Forbidden Until After the Flood?" Chabad.org. Accessed June 4, 2021. https://www.chabad.org/parshah/article_cdo/aid/3087361/jewish/Are-You-Sure-Meat-Was-Forbidden-Until-After-the-Flood.htm.

Yachad Kollel. "Class Schedule." Accessed June 14, 2021. https://www.yachadkollel.com/class-schedule/.

Yachad Kollel. "Team." Accessed June 14, 2021. www.yachadkollel.com/team/.

Yachad Kollel. "Yachad Kollel." Accessed December 17, 2020. www.yachadkollel.com/.

Yeshivat Maharat. "Mission and History." Accessed March 8, 2020. www.yeshivatmaharat.org/.

Yoshon Network Inc. Accessed April 30, 2017. www.yoshon.com/.

YULA Boys High School. "Academics." Accessed May 27, 2021. https://www.yulaboys.org/apps/pages/index.jsp?uREC_ID=124435&type=d&pREC_ID=1717466.

YULA Girls High School. "Academics." Accessed May 27, 2021. https://yulagirls.org/academics/.

Zivotovsky, Ari Z. "Is Turkey Kosher?" Accessed March 5, 2017. www.kashrut.com/articles/turk_part5/.

RABBINIC WRITINGS

Babylonian Talmud.

Caro, Yosef. Shulḥan arukh.

Feinstein, Moshe. Igrot (Igros) Moshe. New York: M. Feinstein, 1959.

Frank, Rabbi Tzvi Pesach. Teshuvot (Teshuvos) Har Zvi.

Luzzato, Moshe Hayyim. Mesillat yesharim.

Maimonides. Guide of the Perplexed.

Maimonides. Mishneh Torah.

Midrash.

Mishnah.

Rashi (Rabbi Solomon ben Isaac). Commentary on Torah and Talmud.

Index

Note: Page numbers appearing in *italics* indicate figures.

About the Author

JODY MYERS (1954–2022) was a professor at California State University, Northridge, for 35 years and served as director of its Jewish Studies Program. She also served on the executive board of the Western Jewish Studies Association. Widely known in the Los Angeles Jewish community, she taught in synagogues and other community forums. She authored two previous books, *Seeking Zion: Modernity and Messianic Activity in the Writings of Tsevi Hirsch Kalischer* and *Kabbalah and the Spiritual Quest: The Kabbalah Centre in America*, and coedited *Feasting and Fasting: The History and Ethics of Jewish Food*. She also published numerous articles on these and other topics, including contemporary women's rituals and education. A native of St. Louis Park, Minnesota, she lived in West Los Angeles near the Pico-Robertson neighborhood from the time she began graduate school at UCLA in 1975.

Milton Keynes UK
Ingram Content Group UK Ltd.
UKHW011820141223
434384UK00004B/339